The Myth of German Villainy

Benton L. Bradberry

authorHOUSE®

AuthorHouse™
1663 Liberty Drive
Bloomington, IN 47403
www.authorhouse.com
Phone: 1-800-839-8640

Published by AuthorHouse 6/29/2012

ISBN: 978-1-4772-3181-4 (e)
ISBN: 978-1-4772-3182-1 (hc)
ISBN: 978-1-4772-3183-8 (sc)

Library of Congress Control Number: 2012911498

Index

Preface

I served in the United States Navy from 1955 until 1977, mostly as a Navy pilot, and saw a lot of the world as a result. Aircraft carriers on which I served regularly visited European ports, as well as other ports around the world. I have also traveled extensively in the years since leaving the Navy.

After traveling around most of Europe, Germany emerges as my favorite country. During our visits there we found the German people to be pleasant, industrious, disciplined and civilized with many similarities to traditional Americans. They in no way resemble the stereotypes depicted in all the anti-Nazi movies, books and articles we have been subjected to over the years.

I am 74 as I write these words. My generation grew up virtually inundated with anti-German propaganda. We were taught, quite literally, to hate the Germans as a people. Yet, Germans I have met or befriended through the years seem no different from other Europeans, or even Americans, and they seem no more inclined to violence and militarism than anyone else; if anything, less. I have never detected anything that might be considered intrinsically "wrong" with the German character. They are a highly cultured, highly civilized people in every respect. When studied objectively, even Germany's leaders of the 1930s and 40s were not very different from other European leaders. They were only made out to be different by the relentless hate propaganda directed against them.

Germany suffered more than any other country by far as a result of World War II. Some 160 of her largest cities and towns were completely destroyed by the Allied bombing campaign and perhaps as many as 20 million Germans lost their lives as a result of the war. Yet, no one wants to hear their tales of suffering, and no sympathy has been allowed the defeated and disgraced Germans. The anti-German propaganda has cultivated the general feeling that they got what they deserved.

The entire responsibility for starting both wars and for all the death and destruction resulting from them has been assigned to the Germans (though the facts don't bear that out). Because they were the losers of both World Wars, they were never permitted to present their case before the world court, nor to tell their side of the story through any medium. The winners of wars, after all, write the history books. Neither did the true story of what happened during the war come out in the Nuremberg Trials. The Nuremberg Trials were nothing more than Soviet style show trials which violated every standard of traditional British and American justice. Their purpose was not to discover guilt or innocence, but to spread a legal gloss over a decision which had already been made to execute Germany's leaders. The entire Nuremberg circus was a sham and a travesty.

The anti-German propaganda, used to create the climate of hatred that made the massive destruction and the mass slaughter of German civilians possible, continued relentlessly long after the war was over when it would seem natural for sober minded historians to begin to moderate their extreme views about Germany. The fantastic atrocity stories continue even today. One needs only to tune in to the History Channel to see them repeated again and again. In contrast, World War I was not long over before the atrocity stories attributed to the Germans during that war were exposed as the deliberate lies they were. Responsible men conducted thorough investigations and found that none of it was true. All the lurid stories were deliberately fabricated to win British public support for the war against Germany and also to bring America into the war.

But a different factor was in play after World War II to keep the phony horror stories alive which did not exist after World War I. After WWII, the Jews exploited the anti-German world sentiment, which they themselves had largely created with their propaganda, to justify the creation of their long sought after state of Israel as a homeland for the Jewish people. Through manipulation of the international information media, the Jews won worldwide sympathy for themselves with their sensational stories of unique Jewish suffering at the hands of the cruel Germans. They claimed that Germany had followed a systematic plan to exterminate all of Europe's Jews and that by war's end had managed to kill 6 million of them. The alleged method was to round the Jews up from all over Europe, haul them in trains to so-called "death camps" where they were herded into gas chambers and killed, and their bodies then burned in giant crematoria, with, conveniently, no forensic evidence of what had happened left behind. In the absence of forensic evidence, eye witness testimony, no matter how bazaar, sufficed to convict Germany and to make her the pariah of civilized nations.

The judges at the Nuremberg Trials were themselves not immune to the torrents of anti-German hate propaganda, and were already predisposed before the trials ever began to believe any horror story, no matter how fantastic, about the Germans. Another factor which preordained the outcome of the trials was that the accusers also served as investigators, prosecutors and final judges. The trials were also permeated throughout with an atmosphere of Jewish vengeance seeking. Just behind the Gentile front men, most of the lawyers, prosecutors, and investigators were Jews. Hundreds of Jews who could barely speak English disported themselves in American Army officer uniforms. Two of the eight Nuremberg judges were Jews, Robert Falco of France, and Lt. Col. A.F. Volchkov (real name Berkman) of the Soviet Union. The General Prosecutor for the "High Court" was Dr. Jakob Meistner, a Jew. Their dominance and control of the trials was blatant. Even the hangman for the 10 Nazi leaders sentenced to death, Master Sergeant John C. Woods, was a Jew, and the hangings took place on October 16, 1946, the Jewish holiday of "Purim." In the Book of Esther, the 10 sons of Haman, an enemy of the Jews, were hanged on Purim day. According to Louis Marschalko, a wartime Hungarian journalist who wrote about the trials: "Out of 3,000 people employed on the staff at the Nuremberg Courts, 2,400 were Jews." The Holocaust story that we all know so well today was developed during the Nuremberg Trials.

By skillfully cultivating and propagating this Holocaust story, the Jews have been able to extort hundreds of billions of dollars out of Germany and the United States, much of which was used to fund the new state of Israel. The claim that the Jews in Israel "made the desert bloom" was true. They did it with German and American money. They are now hard at work extorting more billions out of other European countries in what has been contemptuously but correctly called "the Holocaust industry." Even now, more than half a million so-called "Holocaust survivors" living mainly in Israel and the United States receive lifetime pensions from the German government. And what is a "Holocaust survivor?" Any Jew who lived anywhere in German controlled territory at any time during the war, whether living in a concentration camp or in the lap of luxury, is a Holocaust survivor and therefore eligible for a German pension. Moreover, any Jew who was forced to leave Europe during the Nazi era is a Holocaust survivor. Christian survivors of the war, no matter how horrific their experience are not eligible for pensions. "Shoah" is the Hebrew word for Holocaust. It has been joked around that "there's no business like shoah business." The entire Holocaust racket has become nothing so much as a vast shakedown of European countries, especially Germany. The Holocaust story has other uses as well. It is routinely invoked to disarm the general public from defending itself against Jewish predations. Prime Minister Netanyahu regularly invokes the Holocaust to justify Israeli attacks upon its neighbors.

Keeping this gravy train moving requires the continued legitimization of Jews as history's ultimate victim group, which, in turn, requires an ultimate victimizer of the Jews, and Germany has been designated to fill that role in perpetuity. The Jewish controlled History Channel, or the "Hitler Channel," as it is sometimes derisively called, owes its success to endlessly repeating these anti-German propaganda programs. Any modification or revision of this carefully cultivated image of Germany as the evil monster of history, and particularly as the evil victimizer of the Jews, would threaten the entire Holocaust story. Therefore this image is jealously and carefully guarded by the Jewish controlled press and information media, and woe upon anyone who dares to question it. Anyone who does so is immediately attacked and smeared as a deranged anti-Semite.

The Jews are also unwilling to relinquish or even to moderate their quest for revenge. Old men who have suffered all their lives as fugitives, are still being tracked down as "war criminals," and either "brought to justice," or summarily murdered on the spot (they call it vengeance). The only crime these old men may be guilty of was being an officer or soldier in the German army during the war.

But, why, one might ask, amidst all the carnage, death and destruction that occurred during World War II, has the so-called Holocaust emerged as the central atrocity story? Approximately 55 million people died during the war, only a tiny percentage of them Jews -- surely only a fraction of the 6 million claimed. All other combatant nationalities have long since put the war behind them and have tried to make peace with their former enemies, but not the Jews! Two thirds of a century has gone by, but the Jews are still nourishing their grievances, still building Holocaust museums and memorials (at various governments' expense, incidentally), and still investigating new ways to extort money out of various countries as "compensation." But why should only the Jews be compensated? Scores of millions of other people across Europe lost everything in the war.

The "Holocaust" has evolved over the years to become the national myth of the Jewish people with all the characteristics of a religion, complete with its very own Satan -- Hitler. The Holocaust myth is the glue that holds the Jewish people together as a distinct nationality, and because of that they carefully guard and protect it. As a consequence, the poor Germans are consigned in perpetuity to the role of history's evil monster, regardless of what the actual facts may be.

But even if all the stories of German atrocities during WWII were true in every detail, they would still not compare in their inhumanity to the atrocities committed against the Germans. The indiscriminate saturation bombing of German cities, the brutal expulsion of entire German populations after the war, the Allied imposed postwar deprivations, the Soviet massacres and political liquidations, simply dwarf the Holocaust in their destruction of human life and their destruction of the accumulated works of human civilization. Any final accounting and balancing of the conduct of *all* combatants during WWII could only result in the exculpation of Germany as "uniquely" barbarous in her methods of waging war, or in her treatment of subject populations.

The German people were devastated by the war, to a greater extent than any other participant, including the Jews, while at the same time they have been stigmatized as the evil, predatory perpetrators of the war. They have been made to pay a terrible price for atrocities during World War II which may never have occurred, or at least, never occurred to the extent alleged. It is becoming clearer as time goes by that the Germans were the real victims of both World Wars I and II, and continue to be.

Chapter 1

The Myth of Germany as an Evil Nation

As the result of losing two apocalyptic world wars, Germany has acquired a reputation as the evil nation of Europe, and, perhaps the evil nation of all time. Just mentioning the word "German" still brings forth an image in the mind's eye of robotic, goose-stepping storm troopers, under the command of stiff-necked Prussian officers, ready to march off to inflict gratuitous murder and destruction upon their peace loving

neighbors. We have been brainwashed by relentless propaganda to regard the Germans as intrinsically militaristic, aggressive, brutish, racist and anti-Semitic, with a predilection for blind obedience to authority figures. Hundreds of Hollywood movies, relentless Holocaust propaganda, and countless books and magazine articles have permanently reinforced this negative image of Germany in the popular mind. Rational motives for the inexplicable horrors Germans are accused of having routinely committed are not required. It is axiomatic that their evil nature explains it all.

Consider the movie, "Schindler's List," by the Jewish director, Stephen Spielberg, for example. The Nazi commandant of the concentration camp (supposedly the Plaszow camp outside of Krakow, not far from Auschwitz), is standing shirtless on the balcony of his house with a hunting rifle over his bare shoulders. The rifle is equipped with a telescopic sight. In the movie, the house is located on a hill above the camp so that he can look down on the throngs of prisoners milling around in the compound below. He lifts the rifle to his shoulder and through the telescope begins casually scanning from one prisoner to another. The image through the telescope now fills the movie screen. The crosshairs of the scope stop on a randomly selected prisoner. He pulls the trigger and the prisoner drops to the ground, dead. The screen then cuts back to the Nazi commandant to show bored insouciance as he actuates the bolt of his rifle and casually raises it back to his shoulder. He fires again, and again a prisoner drops to the ground, dead. Bored with his "target practice," he turns his attention to the beautiful, sexy, naked woman lying on a bed just inside the house from the balcony. The woman is purportedly one of his Jewish housemaids selected from the camp, who also apparently serves as his sex slave. His face expresses disdainful, though lackadaisical, cynicism.

The point of the shootings, as well as bringing in the naked, Jewish housemaid, is to show the Nazi officer as totally depraved, without conscience, morality, or empathy for other humans; in short, a psychopath. It is presumed, of course, that the murdered prisoners were all Jews. Two popular Jewish themes are combined here: Nazi evil and Jewish persecution.

This episode is entirely fictional, based on a novel by Thomas Keneally, an Australian, who only visited the concentration camps once in 1980. No such actual event as described above has ever been recorded, yet the vast majority of movie goers swallow it whole and accept it as actual history.

The real Plaszow camp was located on the other side of a hill from the commandant's house, and completely out of sight from the commandant's balcony. It would have been impossible for him to shoot down into the compound as shown in the movie even if he had been inclined to do so, which is highly unlikely. The actual commandant of Plaszow, Amon Goeth, on which the character in the movie was based, lived in the house with his fiancé Ruth Kalder, with whom he had a child. Ruth said that they intended to marry but were unable to do so due to the chaos at the end of the war. She had her name and the child's name changed to Goeth after the war with the help of Amon Goeth's father. Amon Goeth was hanged after the war by the Polish government primarily for being a member of the Nazi party and a member of the Waffen-SS, not for shooting prisoners. Ruth described Amon Goeth as a cultured man who had a beautiful singing voice. Goeth did, indeed, have two Jewish housemaids, selected from the camp while he was commandant, but there is no information that he had untoward relations with them. That story was only included to add spice to the movie.

Another example is the movie, "Sophie's Choice," by another Jewish director, Alan J. Pakula, in which "Sophie" and her two small children are sent to Auschwitz (Auschwitz is the holy temple of Holocaust lore). During the "selection" process (the "selection" is now one of the "stations of the cross" of the Holocaust religion) immediately after their arrival, Sophie is told by a stereotypically evil Nazi officer (supposedly Dr. Joseph Mengele of Auschwitz notoriety) that she can only keep one of her children and that the other must go to the gas chamber. She is forced to choose which one to keep and which one to be sent to the gas chamber, hence, "Sophie's choice." The evil Nazi officer provides no reason or explanation for requiring one child to die or for forcing her to make this heart rending choice. That he is an "evil" Nazi is presumed to be explanation enough. This preposterous movie was based on a novel by the American Southern writer William Styron, who had no firsthand knowledge of the camps. Auschwitz was simply used as the setting for a tale which came out of his imagination. Nothing of the sort ever happened in real life. Yet, evil Nazi stories such as these have long been a staple in Hollywood. The movie-going public has been so conditioned by this poppycock that fiction has become fact in the public mind. We have all been brainwashed to accept such absurdities without skepticism. Germans are "evil," so they do "evil" things. No further explanation needed.

Yet, Germany was not always seen in this light. The image of Germany as a sinister, predatory, warlike nation only took root in the twentieth century. Nineteenth century Germany, by contrast, was seen as a place of peace and enlightenment. The English historian, Frederic William Maitland, described the way the English people saw the Germans during the nineteenth century: "*...it was usual and plausible to paint the German as an unpractical, dreamy, sentimental being, looking out with mild blue eyes into a cloud of music and metaphysics and tobacco smoke.*"

The highly influential French writer and Salon matron, Madame de Stael, portrayed the Germans during the period of the Napoleonic Wars as a nation of *"poets and thinkers, a race of kindly, impractical, other-worldly dreamers without national prejudices and disinclined to war."*

The Americans also held a benign opinion of the Germans prior to the twentieth century. The American historian, Henry Cord Meyer, wrote, "*...whether seen in their newly united nation [Germany was united into one nation in 1871] or in this country [German immigrants in the United States], the Germans were generally regarded as methodical and energetic people who were models of progress, while in their devotion to music, education, science, and technology they aroused the admiration and emulation of Americans.*"

In 1905 Andrew Dickson White, a noted American historian, educator, and United States Ambassador to Germany, wrote just nine years before the outbreak of World War I: "*Germany, from a great confused mass of warriors and thinkers and workers, militant at cross-purposes, wearing themselves out in vain struggles, and preyed upon by malevolent neighbors, has become [after consolidation] a great power in arms, in art, in science, in literature; a fortress of high thought; a guardian of civilization; the natural ally of every nation which seeks the better development of humanity."*

The German people have historically made great contributions in every sphere of cultural, intellectual, and scientific achievement. In the field of music, there were such eighteenth century geniuses as Bach, Hayden, Mozart, Beethoven, Shubert and Schuman, to name a few. This musical genius continued in the nineteenth century with the Strausses, Mahler and Richard Wagner. There were the literary contributions of Goethe and Schiller; the historical works of Ranke and Niebuhr; the philosophical studies of Kant and Hegel; and the great scientific contributions of Alexander von Humboldt and William Conrad Roentgen. These are only a few examples of a very long list. The Prussian system of higher education and the cultural flowering which characterized Prussia during the years following the Napoleonic wars greatly influenced both Europe and America. The American public school system as well as our university system was deliberately modeled after the Prussian public school system and university system. Germany was admired by the world as a center of learning, for its high culture and for its achievements in every field; but also for its culture of honesty, hard work, orderliness and thrift, which existed even at the lowest level of society.

British scholars and journalists had been very favorably disposed toward all things German, including their history, culture, and institutions throughout the nineteenth century. The highly respected Cambridge historian Herbert Butterfield commented extensively on Britain's high regard for Germany.

"In England the view once prevailed that German history was particularly the history of freedom, for it was a story that comprised federation, parliament, autonomous cities, Protestantism, and a law of liberty carried by German colonies to the Slavonic east. In those days it was the Latin States which were considered to be congenial to authoritarianism, clinging to the Papacy in Italy, the Inquisition in Spain and the Bonapartist dictatorships in militaristic France. The reversal of this view in the twentieth century, and its replacement by a common opinion that Germany had been the aggressor and enemy of

freedom throughout all the ages, will no doubt be the subject of historical research itself someday, especially as it seems to have coincided so closely with a change in British foreign policy ... Up to the early 1900's when historical scholarship in England came to its peak in men like Acton and Maitland, words can hardly describe the admiration for Germany -- and the confessed discipleship -- which existed amongst English historians."

And then British author Thomas Arnold (June 13, 1795 - June 12, 1842) saw Germany not as a nation with a unique predisposition toward authoritarianism and regimentation, but rather as a *"cradle of law, virtue, and freedom,"* and considered it a *"distinction of the first rank"* that the English belonged to the Germanic family of peoples.

The following photos and drawings represent the way in which the world saw Germany during the eighteenth and nineteenth centuries, right up to the beginning of World War I. Pre-WWI Germany was seen as a peaceful land of fairy tales and dreamy castles, and of industrious, law abiding, disciplined people.

A nineteenth century festival in a German town.

Mayday in Germany

German farm girls headed for the fields

Germany's positive image changes over night

This view of Germany was to change almost overnight with the outbreak of World War I. After the war began in 1914 a grotesque image of a rapacious, bloodthirsty and uniquely aggressive Germany quickly took form and became the stereotypical image of Germany in Europe and America. This new image of Germany was the direct result of a virulent anti-German propaganda campaign conducted by the British government and later joined by the United States government in which deliberate and systematic lies, distortions and false atrocity stories were disseminated to the British and American publics. The emotions of both the British and American publics were deliberately whipped up to a fever pitch of hatred for the "Hun." A pathological hostility towards all things German, which later became such a familiar and integral part of Western thinking about Germany, had its birth in this skillful propaganda campaign.

After World War Two, Historian Harry Paxton Howard examined this transformation of Germany's reputation which began immediately after the start of WWI. It was made out, he said, that Germany was not only evil but had always been that way, and that Germany, contrary to the facts, had always been the historical enemy of Europe and America. He wrote: *"Actually, in the literal sense of the word, the biggest job of revising history was done during the First World War when our 'histories' were completely revised to show that Germany had always been our enemy, that Germany had started the war in 1914, that Germany had even started the Franco-Prussian War in 1870, and that in the Revolutionary War we had not been fighting the British but the Hessians -- not to mention such things as the Germans cutting the hands off Belgian babies, instead of the Belgians cutting off the hands of Congolese. This was a real revision of our histories which has distorted the American mind for more than forty years."* Harry Paxton Howard.

All belligerents, of course, including Germany, used propaganda against their enemies, as all belligerents have done in all wars throughout history, but the propaganda efforts of Germany and the Central Powers were amateurish and ineffectual compared to the British. In their propaganda efforts, the Germans tended to appeal to reason instead of to the emotions. They never portrayed their enemies as bloodthirsty, inhuman beasts. The Allies, Great Britain in particular, by contrast, proved themselves masters at adroitly manipulating world opinion by widespread propagation of fantastic tales of German villainy. From the beginning of the war, stories of German atrocities filled British and American newspapers. (American newspapers depended at that time on British news services for most of their news stories about Europe, which came across undersea cables controlled by Britain. The Germans had no access to the American media. Great Britain made sure of that by cutting Germany's six trans-Atlantic cables to America.)

The first atrocity stories came out of the German march through Belgium at the beginning of the war. Germany's purpose was not to attack Belgium, per se, but to pass through Belgium in order to outflank French defenses and then make a drive toward Paris. This strategy was known as the Schlieffen Plan, which the Germans believed was the only way to achieve a quick victory over France. Germany's "violation" of neutral Belgium served as Britain's pretext for going to war against Germany, though the decision to go to war for other reasons (mainly economic) had already been made. Belgium was only a pretext. To enter the war, it was necessary to win public support, and the propaganda opportunities resulting from Germany's invasion of Belgium, as well as the fabricated stories of German atrocities in Belgium served that purpose. "Eyewitnesses" were found who described hairy knuckled Huns in *Pickelhaube* helmets tossing Belgian babies in the air and catching them on their bayonets as they marched along, singing war songs. Stories of German soldiers amputating the hands of Belgian boys were widely reported (reputedly to prevent them from firing rifles). Tales of women with their breasts cut off multiplied even faster. There were also tales of crucifixions of Allied soldiers. Europeans and Americans were more religious then than they are today and the crucifixion stories aroused outrage. (It should be mentioned that of all forms of evidence accepted in modern courts of law, eyewitness testimony is considered the least reliable.)

But rape stories were the favorite of all atrocity tales. One "eyewitness" described how the Germans dragged twenty young women out of their houses in a captured Belgian town and stretched them on tables in the village square, where each was raped by at least twelve "Huns" while the rest of the soldiers watched and cheered. After being fed a steady diet of this kind of propaganda, the British public veritably demanded revenge against the loathsome Hun. A group of Belgians toured the United States (at British government expense) telling these stories to Americans. (Britain wanted to draw the United States into the war.) President Woodrow Wilson solemnly received the group in the White House.

The propaganda portrayed Britain as "a knight on a white horse" coming to the defense of violated, neutral Belgium. This was cynical manipulation of public opinion, of course, because if Germany had not violated Belgian neutrality, Britain would have done so without a second thought.

Germany angrily denied all of these stories. So did American reporters who were with the German army and knew that they were lies. But these denials did not find their way into American newspapers. The British controlled what went into American papers and it was the British who were generating the atrocity stories. To enhance the credibility of these fantastic atrocity stories, the British government asked Viscount Bryce early in 1915 to head a royal commission to conduct an investigation. The British government, of course, intended that Bryce would support this false propaganda, which he obediently did. Bryce was a well known historian with a good reputation in America. He not only had served as the British ambassador in Washington, but had written several complimentary books about the American government. The British knew that he was highly respected and admired in America, and that he had a reputation for rectitude and honesty. America would believe whatever he said. Bryce was also intensely loyal to his own country and therefore perfect for the job.

False anti-German propaganda poster of World War I

The propaganda poster shown at left and in the following pages are examples of the way in which the British portrayed their German foes - always as brutish, barbaric murderers of women and children. Following these British propaganda posters are German propaganda posters against the British, French and Russians. Note the different styles. The Germans do not portray their foes as barbaric murders.

ONLY THE NAVY CAN STOP THIS

Stop him!

The Germans are portrayed as inhuman beasts.

A German soldier cuts the hands off a Belgian child.

An innocent Belgian girl about to be raped by a Hun.

Following are German propaganda posters directed against the British, French and Russians. Note that the Germans use ridicule against their enemies but do not portray them as inhuman beast.

3um Donnerwetter noch mal! Euch werde ich mal den Marsch blasen!

The cartoon characters represent (L to R): Great Britain, France and Russia, and far right, Germany.

Die verknüppelte Allianz.

Ein 42er Gruß!

ALLES GEHT WIE AM SCHNÜRCHEN!

Bryce and his six fellow commissioners, all lawyers, historians and legal scholars, "analyzed," if you can call it that, 1,200 depositions of "eyewitnesses" who claimed to have seen these German atrocities first hand. Almost all of the eyewitness accounts came from Belgians who had left Belgium for England as refugees, though some accounts also came from British soldiers in France. The commission never interrogated a single one of these eyewitnesses, but relied on their written statements instead (Shades of the Nuremberg Trials after the next war). Since there was a war on, there were no "on site" investigations of any reported atrocity. Not a single witness was identified by name, including the soldiers who had provided written accounts. Yet, the commission officially confirmed that all the atrocity stories, no matter how fantastic, were true. This bogus investigation was just another part of Britain's anti-German propaganda campaign.

The "Bryce Report" was released on May 13, 1915, and the British government made sure it went to every newspaper in America. The impact was phenomenal, especially coming just after the torpedoing of the British liner Lusitania which caused the deaths of 135 Americans. Americans from coast to coast were outraged. A wave of revulsion for all things German swept the country. Hatred of Germans reached fever pitch. Suddenly the American public was clamoring for war. (There is well founded suspicion that the Lusitania was set up as a decoy by the First Lord of the Admiralty, Winston Churchill, deliberately exposing it to a German submarine attack for the purpose of bringing America into the war).

But there were skeptics of the Bryce report. In England, Sir Roger Casement called the report a lie, and wrote a report of his own refuting it, though no one paid much attention to it. The American lawyer, Clearance Darrow, was so skeptical that he travelled to France in 1915 and searched in vain for a single eyewitness who could confirm even one of the Bryce stories. Increasingly dubious, Darrow announced that he would pay $1,000, equivalent to around $25,000 today, to anyone who could produce a Belgian boy whose hands had been amputated by a German soldier, or any other Belgian or French victim who had been mutilated by German troops. None were found.

The "proofs" provided by the Bryce Committee in its investigation, as well as the methods employed in gathering them, violated every elementary rule of evidence. Careful scholars have long since demonstrated that the entire report was made up of nothing more than distortions and outright falsehoods. But Britain was determined to pull the United States into the war and Bryce and his colleagues were willing accomplices in that effort. They justified their lies and exaggerations because it served the higher cause of Mother England. After the war most historians dismissed 99 percent of Bryce's atrocities as fabrications. One called the report "in itself one of the worst atrocities of the war." "After the war," recounts Thomas Fleming in his book *Illusion of Victory*, "historians who sought to examine the documentation for Bryce's stories were told that the files had mysteriously disappeared."

As the war drew on, another fabricated story was widely circulated. It was reported that the Germans were operating a "corpse factory" where the bodies of both German and Allied soldiers killed in battle were supposedly melted down for fats and other products useful to the German war effort. The Germans were accused of making soap out of human fat. Human skins were used to make fine leather goods such as lampshades, driving gloves and riding breeches. The bones of these corpses were said to have been ground up and used as fertilizer on German farms.

A detailed account of this so-called "corpse factory" appeared in the highly respected British newspaper, *The Times*, on April 17, 1917. According to the story, trains full of corpses arrived at a large factory. The bodies were attached to hooks connected to an endless chain. The article carefully described the process inside the corpse factory. *"The bodies are transported on this endless chain into a long, narrow compartment, where they pass through a bath which disinfects them. They then go through a drying chamber, and finally are automatically carried into a digester or great cauldron, in which they are dropped by an apparatus which detaches from the chain. In the digester they remain from six to eight hours, and are treated by steam, which breaks them up while they are slowly stirred by the machinery. From this treatment result several products. The fats are broken up into stearin, a form of tallow, and oils, which require to be redistilled before they can be used. The process of distillation is carried out by boiling the oil with carbonate of soda, and some of the by-products resulting from this are used by German soap makers. The oil distillery and refinery lie in the south-eastern corner of the works. The refined oil is sent out in small casks like those used for petroleum, and is of a yellowish brown color."* Note the meticulous detail.

The story was a total fabrication, but it was a "plausible" story, especially with all the detail, and it was not possible for the Germans to completely refute it while the war was still going on. After the war, of course, the story was exposed as the lie it was. No such corpse factory existed. It is interesting that the story of making soap out of bodies emerged again during World War II when the Germans supposedly made soap out of Jewish corpses. That lie is still widely believed and remains a staple of Jewish Holocaust propaganda. The "lampshades out of human skin" story also had its origin in World War I and emerged again during World War II when Germans were supposedly making lampshades out of Jewish skin. There was nothing to it, yet it also remains a staple of Jewish Holocaust propaganda.

"The purpose of war propaganda," Historian Thomas Fleming, in his book "The Illusion of Victory," observes, *"as peddled by both the Anglo and American elite, was to create a widespread public image of Germans*

as 'monsters capable of appalling sadism' -- thereby coating an appeal to murderous collective hatred with a lacquer of sanctimony." "The trick," said Fleming, "is to leave the target audience at once shivering in horror at a spectacle of sub-human depravity, panting with a visceral desire for vengeance, and rapturously self-righteous about the purity of its humane motives. People who succumb to it are easily subsumed into a hive mind of officially sanctioned hatred, and prepared to perpetrate crimes even more hideous than those that they believe typify the enemy."

The Bryce Report as well as all the other anti-German propaganda unquestionably helped England win the war. It convinced millions of Americans and other neutrals that the Germans were beasts in human form, and this, as much as anything else, helped bring America into the war. But there were adverse consequences to this lurid atrocity propaganda campaign. It poisoned public opinion against the Germans to such an extent that it could not be undone. It was an obvious factor, for example, in the British decision to maintain the total blockade of Germany for seven months after the war was over, which, incidentally, was a violation of international law. The blockade caused a million German civilians to starve to death, and unbearable suffering of millions more. The blockade itself was far and away the greatest atrocity of World War I, though it receives very little publicity, and it was done, not by the evil Germans, but by the saintly British.

By creating blind hatred of Germany, the anti-German propaganda campaign also contributed to the harsh peace terms imposed on Germany at the end of the war, which then sowed the seeds of World War II. Though historians and other scholars have exposed these German atrocity stories as nonsense, the image of German villainy has remained fixed. The benign world opinion of Germany which existed right up to 1914 was replaced overnight by the myth of unique German savagery which left a permanent residue of Germanophobia deep in Western minds. This explains why "our boys" were so willing to obliterate whole German cities and kill hundreds of thousands of German civilians with air bombardments during the Second World War. This hate propaganda, as false as it was, also had the effect of totally demoralizing the German people.

Chapter 2

Aftermath of the War in Germany

The long stalemate which World War I became would most likely have ended in a negotiated peace with no winner and no loser if the United States had stayed out of it. But the combined weight of British, French and American armies in October, 1918 was more than the Central Powers could withstand, and one after another began to seek a way to pull out of the war. Bulgaria signed an armistice on September 29, Turkey at the end of October, and Austria/Hungary signed on November 3.

Stalemate -- 1918

The British starvation blockade of Germany was taking a terrible toll, which eventually caused Germany to begin to crumble from within. Faced with the prospect of putting to sea to fight the British blockade, the sailors of the German High Seas Fleet stationed at Kiel mutinied on October 29. They had been persuaded by agitators that such an attack would be a suicide mission. Within a few days the entire city of Kiel was under their control and the revolution then spread throughout the country. On November 9 the Kaiser abdicated and slipped across the border into exile in the Netherlands. A German "republic" was declared to replace the monarchy and peace feelers were then extended to the Allies. At 5 A.M. on the morning of November 11, 1918 an armistice between Germany and the Allies was signed in a railway car parked in a French forest near the front lines. At 11 A.M. that same day, the armistice became effective. After more than four years of bloody fighting, the Great War had come to an end.

Peace comes at last with the Armistice of 11/11/1918

But what had it all been for? No combatant nation gained from it, at least nothing remotely worth the sacrifices made. The accumulated wealth of Europe, the result of decades of peace, was completely dissipated and replaced by crushing national debt. The war had been a horrific experience unlike anything Europeans had ever experienced before, leaving them psychologically, economically and politically devastated. Before the war, all of Europe had come to believe that a steady, continuing improvement in the conditions of life was the inexorable trend of history. That generalized belief was replaced by a feeling of pessimism and cynicism. There was the feeling that Europe had been profoundly and permanently damaged, a feeling that turned out to be highly prescient, in retrospect. Ancient empires -- the Austro/Hungarian Empire, the Ottoman Empire, the Russian Empire, the German Empire -- crumbled as a result of the war. These empires had been the source of political and social stability, and now chaos reigned throughout Europe. The Paris Peace Conference after the war did a very imperfect job of putting it all back together again. It is clear from the perspective of today that World War I precipitated an irreversible decline in Western Civilization.

In addition to these adverse psychological and political consequences, there was also a considerable amount of physical destruction. Vast areas of northeastern France had been reduced to rubble. Flanders in Belgium had been all but destroyed, and the ancient city of Ypres was completely devastated. The homes of 750,000 French people had been destroyed and the infrastructure of the entire region had been severely damaged. Roads, coal mines and telegraph poles had been destroyed, greatly hindering the area's ability to recover and begin to function normally again.

But all of that was insignificant compared to the massive, industrialized slaughter of human beings. Nearly every family in Europe had lost a family member, if not a father, son, brother or husband, then a cousin of one degree or another. All combatant countries suffered casualties never experienced before in all of history. The British, for example, suffered 50,000 casualties in a single afternoon at the Battle of Passchendaele, and 350,000 casualties before the battle finally ended. The battle ended with no ground gained and no ground lost. The entire trench war was characterized by mass suicidal attacks against entrenched machine guns, and by massive artillery barrages which blew their targets to smithereens. This was mechanized, industrial death. Nothing on this scale had ever happened before. The scale of the slaughter can be appreciated by the lists presented below.

Allied Casualties:
Britain: 885,000 soldiers killed; 1,663,000 wounded
France: 1,400,000 soldiers killed; 2,500,000 wounded
Belgium: 50,000 soldiers killed; 45,000 wounded
Italy: 651,000 soldiers killed; 954,000 wounded
Russia: 1,811,000 soldiers killed; 5,000,000 wounded
America: 117,000 soldiers killed; 206,000 wounded

Central Powers Casualties:
Germany: 2,037,000 soldiers killed; 4,250,000 wounded
Austria/Hungary: 1,200,000 soldiers killed; 3,600,000 wounded
Turkey: 800,000 soldiers killed; 400,000 wounded
Bulgaria: 100,000 soldiers killed; 152,000 wounded

The number of soldier killed on all sides totaled 9.7 million with 21 million wounded. Of the wounded, millions were maimed for life and unable to work. Nearly 7 million civilians on all sides lost their lives.

The Versailles Treaty

The lurid anti-German propaganda campaign conducted by Britain and America throughout the war had created such hatred for the Germans that a harsh peace was virtually inevitable. Germany, rightly or wrongly, was to be held accountable for the war, including all the death and destruction resulting from it, and Germany would be required to pay for all of it. As if the war itself were not enough, during mid-1918, Europe was hit by Spanish flu, causing the deaths of an estimated 25 million more Europeans. That comes to some 41 million Europeans who died from all causes during the war - a sizable percentage of the European population. Death on this scale had not occurred in Europe since the "black plague" of the Middle Ages. This added to the feeling of bitterness and gloom that ran through Europe and this anger was primarily directed at the hated and despised Germans -- hated and despised as the result of the anti-German propaganda. Europe wanted to punish Germany and would do so with the Versailles Treaty.

The terms of the treaty, as finally hammered out by the victors of the war -- Britain, France and the United States -- were harsh by any standard. The idealistic President Woodrow Wilson had presented his "Fourteen Points" as the basis for a fair and just peace settlement but they were mostly ignored after the armistice was signed, especially by the French. The French had no interest in a "just" peace. What the French wanted was revenge!...that, and their two provinces back. The provinces of Alsace and Lorraine had been taken from France by the Victorious Prussians after the Franco/Prussian War of 1871. French Prime Minister Georges Clemenceau considered Wilson sanctimonious and naïve, and privately ridiculed his Fourteen Points. He sneered that "God almighty only had ten."

Basically the terms of the Versailles Treaty were as follows: 28,000 Sq. miles of Germany's territory and 6.5 million of her people were handed over to other countries. Alsace-Lorraine went to France; Eupen and Malmedy were given to Belgium; Northern Schleswig went to Denmark; Hultschin to Czechoslovakia; West Prussia, Posen, Upper Silesia and Danzig went to Poland (Danzig was placed under Polish management but was designated a "free city" under League of Nations supervision); Memel to Lithuania; and the Saar, Germany's industrial heartland, was put under the control of the League of Nations. All of Germany's overseas colonies were taken away.

Severe military Limitations were imposed. Germany's army was reduced to 100,000 men, and was not allowed to have tanks or armored cars. Germany was not allowed an air force, and was allowed to have only 6 capital naval ships and no submarines. The west of the Rhineland and 50 kilometers (31 miles) east of the Rhine River was made into a demilitarized zone. No German soldier or weapon was allowed into this zone. The Allies (meaning Britain and France) were to keep an army of occupation on the west bank of the Rhine for 15 years.

Financial penalties were equally severe. The loss of vital industrial territory would impede all attempts by Germany to rebuild her economy.

Coal from the Saar and Upper Silesia in particular was a vital economic loss. The coal went to France and England. Germany's richest farmland was given to Poland. Reparations were to be paid to the Allies in an amount to be decided by the Allies at a later time. It seemed clear to Germany that the Allies intended to bankrupt the country.

Germany was also forbidden to unite with Austria to form one large German state (even though both Germany and Austria wanted it), in an attempt to keep her economic potential to a minimum.

General terms of the treaty included three vital clauses:

1. Germany had to admit full responsibility for starting the war (The War Guilt clause - Clause 231).

2. Germany was thereby responsible for all the damage caused by the war, and was therefore required to pay reparations, the bulk of which was to go to France and Belgium. The amount of reparations was not set at Versailles, but was to be determined later. In other words, Germany was to sign a blank check which the Allies would cash when it suited them in whatever amount they decided. The amount was eventually put at $33 billion (in 1919 dollars).

3. A League of Nations was set up to keep world peace, though Germany was not allowed in as a member.

After agreeing to the Armistice in November, 1918, the Germans believed that the peace treaty to follow would be based on President Wilson's "Fourteen Points" which would have ensured a fair and just peace, and that they would participate in drawing up the peace treaty. They had, in fact, signed the Armistice and laid down their arms with that understanding. Instead, the treaty was drawn up without German participation and then handed to them as a *diktat*, which the Germans were required to sign without discussion. The term "armistice" is generally understood to mean, "a cessation of hostilities while a peace treaty is worked out." That is what Germany signed onto, but the Allies treated Germany as a defeated foe instead. According to the accepted meaning of an armistice, Germany should have had full participation in the peace conference.

**The German delegation at Versailles. They
were forced to sign the Treaty.**

The German delegation was astonished at the harshness of the treaty. They were particularly offended by the charge that Germany had started the war. In the minds of Germans, Germany had been fighting a defensive war imposed upon her by Russia and France, and soon afterwards by Britain. The way Germany saw it, France and Russia started the war. The officer sent to sign the Versailles Treaty refused to do so. "To say such a thing would be a lie," he said. The German Chancellor Phillip Scheidemann resigned rather than accept the treaty, saying, "May the hand wither that signs this treaty." He characterized the terms of the treaty as "unbearable, unrealizable and unacceptable," and proclaimed that the treaty would make the German people "slaves and helots."

The German people were both shocked and outraged over the terms of the treaty. As a symbolic protest against it, all forms of public entertainment throughout Germany were suspended for a week. Flags across the country were lowered to half mast. Some wanted to start the war again, but Germany's leaders knew that that was impossible. There was nothing they could do. The German army had disintegrated and gone home after the Armistice was signed and Britain was maintaining a starvation blockade around Germany, letting nothing in and nothing out, causing the deaths of thousands of German civilians every day. Britain declared that the blockade would be maintained until the German representatives signed the treaty. Finally, Britain and France gave the Germans an ultimatum. Sign the treaty within four days or be invaded. The British and French armies were still intact. A German representative finally signed the treaty in the Hall of Mirrors at the Palace of Versailles on June 28, 1919. (He was later assassinated under mysterious circumstances; no doubt the result of having signed the treaty.)

The Treaty was signed, but only reluctantly, and without the slightest intention of actually cooperating in its imposition. In the words of the British historian, AJP Taylor, in his book, The History of the First World War (1963), *"Though the Germans accepted the treaty in the formal sense of agreeing to sign it, none took the signature seriously. The treaty seemed to them to be wicked, unfair, dictation, a slave treaty. All Germans intended to repudiate it at some time in the future, if it did not fall to pieces of its own absurdity."* In one last gesture of defiance, after the treaty was signed, the captured German naval ships held at Scapa Flow were scuttled by their crews.

Effect of the Treaty on the German Economy

The German economy was the most powerful in Europe going into the war, but like all the other combatant countries (except the United States), Germany was bankrupt by the end of it. Reconstructing her ruined economy after the war would have been a daunting task under the best of circumstances, but it was made doubly hard by the crushing impact of the Versailles treaty. Under the treaty Germany was forced to pay exorbitant reparations payments to the victorious powers at the same time that her ability to do so was drastically reduced by other terms of the treaty. Under the treaty, Germany lost 13 percent of her territory, 10 percent of her population, 25 percent of her potato and wheat production, 80 percent of iron ore, 68 percent of zinc ore, 33 percent of coal production, the entire Alsatian potash and textile industries, and the communications system built around Alsace-Lorraine and Upper Silesia. Her entire merchant fleet was confiscated along with numerous

**Map showing German territory taken by the Versailles Treaty.
The dark or shaded areas were taken from Germany.**

shipping facilities. Moreover, for 5 years, Germany's shipyards were required to produce ships to be given to the victorious powers. She was also required to surrender 5,000 locomotives, 150,000 railway cars and 10,000 trucks. All German property abroad was confiscated.

Because of Germany's weakened state the reparations payments demanded by the victorious powers were completely beyond her ability to pay. The confiscation of Germany's coal mines was particularly devastating because the resultant coal shortage severely limited industrial production. Her agricultural production was also drastically reduced because she had no merchant fleet with which to import the phosphates necessary to produce fertilizers. She could not import other necessary raw materials because her colonies had been taken away as well as her merchant fleet. This caused factories to shut down resulting in increased unemployment. All those who had previously worked in shipping and trade were also now unemployed.

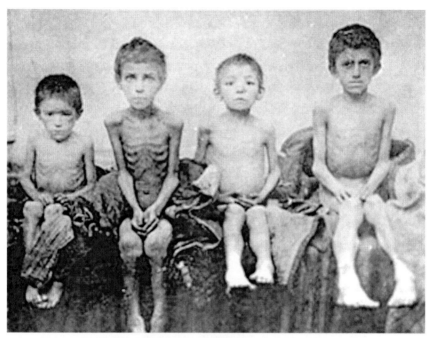

A million German civilians, mainly women, children and old people, starved to death as the a result of the British naval blockade.

A million Germans, mainly women, children and old people, starved to death as the result of the Royal Navy's food blockade, but millions of others were reduced to a weakened state from lack of food. A plague of malnutrition caused diseases affected Germany's children; many with permanently stunted growth, and disfiguring bone development. The war was over, but the starvation blockade continued to be imposed on an entirely helpless civilian population for seven more months, to force the unwilling Germans to sign the peace treaty. It was cruel beyond belief, yet it was imposed by the saintly British against the savage Hun. In fact, the main force behind the blockade was the much admired Winston Churchill.

The confiscation of Germany's merchant fleet exacerbated an already disastrous situation. Germany was an industrial nation with a very dense population, closely integrated into the economic system of the world. She was therefore required to import enormous quantities of food and raw materials. The loss of her merchant fleet and the restrictions on trade imposed by the Versailles Treaty produced chaos in Germany, and served to extend the famine which existed as a result of the blockade.

Adolf Hitler wrote in *Mein Kampf*: *"Germany suffered most as a consequence of this Peace Treaty and the general insecurity which was bound to arise from it. The unemployment figures rose to a third of the number usually employed in the nation, which means, however, that by counting the families of the unemployed as well there were 26 million people in Germany out of a population of 65 million faced by an absolutely hopeless future."*

Was the War Guilt Clause Fair? Did Germany Really Start the War?

The chain of cause and effect in international relations is interminable, but if one is to make a point, one must begin somewhere. To a considerable extent, WWI had its genesis in the Franco-Prussian War of 1870/71. But the Franco-Prussian War itself was the culmination of years of tension between the two states, which finally came to a head over the issue of a Hohenzollern candidate for the vacant Spanish throne. France believed it was being surrounded by Prussian Hohenzollerns, and declared war on Prussia to prevent it. Prussia, under Chancellor Otto von Bismarck won the war, and without going into detail here, that victory made it possible for Bismarck to unite all the various German states, principalities, and estates into one unified German confederation. Included in this new German confederation were the two provinces, Alsace and Lorraine, taken from France as war booty and annexed to Germany. There was, of course, historical justification for Germany's annexation of the two provinces, as France had previously taken them from Germany during the reign of Louis IV. Moreover, the populations of Alsace and Lorraine were still majority German speaking, ethnic Germans. As mentioned above, the chain of cause and effect is interminable.

The German annexation of Alsace-Lorraine, whether justified or not, left France humiliated and seething with anger over their loss. France had grown accustomed during her 400 years of war making and aggression to humiliating others -- Germany in particular -- and this role reversal was hard for France to swallow. *Revanche* (policy to regain lost territory) became a major French goal, and revenge against Germany became a French national obsession, particularly among the political and military elite. France's determination to have a war of revenge against Germany was a factor in all of the diplomatic maneuvers that ultimately led to war in 1914. According to J.S. Ewart, in his book, "The Roots and Causes of War," 1925.

"The Alsace-Lorraine annexation by Prussia in 1871 was the principle factor in the counter-alliances, ententes, and antagonisms which perturbed continental Europe for forty-three years.... Not France only, but all Europe, kept in mind, between 1871 and 1914, with varying intensity, the prospect -- one might say the assumed certainty -- of the recurrence of the Franco-Prussian war."

After unification into a single state in 1871, Germany experienced an extraordinary period of economic growth and development. Industrialization progressed rapidly and German manufacturers began to take markets away from Britain. Germany produced more and more of her own consumer products, and imported less and less of British made products. But Germany also began to compete with British commerce abroad, particularly in the United States. German textile production and steel production quickly surpassed those of Britain. Germany invested heavily in research and development, to a far greater extent than Britain, which produced impressive technological advances, especially in chemistry, electricity and electric motors, and in devices driven by electric motors. Germany was dominant in physics and chemistry to the extent that one-third of all Nobel Prizes went to German inventors and researchers. By 1913 Germany produced 90% of the world's dyestuffs and began to excel in other areas of chemistry such as pharmaceuticals, photographic film, agricultural chemicals and electro-chemicals. With a population of 65 million, Germany became the dominant economic power on the continent and was the world's second largest exporting nation after Britain. (The populations of Britain and France were 45 million and 40 million respectively.)

No one had worried much about Germany prior to its unification in 1871. Up to then "Germany" was only a geographic expression, referring to the multiplicity of German speaking kingdoms, principalities, city states and sovereign estates located in Central Europe. But Germany's rapid rise in power after unification created anxiety amongst her neighbors. The old balance of power system, worked out by Prince Metternich at the Congress of Vienna in 1815 at the end of the Napoleonic Wars, had served as the basis for European relations until thrown off kilter by Germany's growing power after unification.

Germany quickly displaced France as the dominant power on the European continent, causing consternation among the British elite. Britain had always seen France as her traditional enemy and rival on the continent, but British power had already long eclipsed that of France, and France was no longer in a position to challenge British dominance. The extraordinary growth of Germany as an industrial power, however, was beginning to challenge that of Britain. As a result, Britain began making efforts to develop friendly relations with France as leverage against Germany. It appeared to Britain that the entire continent was about to become organized as a single economic union under an all powerful Germany, which threatened to sideline Britain into insignificance. The more powerful Germany became, the more apprehensive British leaders became, to the point that they began to speculate on how to cut the "upstart" Germany down to size. An eventual war with Germany began to seem inevitable.

On April 8, 1904 Britain entered an "Entente Cordiale" with France, followed by an "Anglo-Russian Entente." France and Russia then forged the "Franco-Russian Alliance." Thus the "Triple Entente" of Britain, France and Russia was formed for the purpose of containing the growing power of Germany.

To ameliorate this developing hostility against her, Germany made vigorous efforts in the years before World War One to arrive at an understanding with Russia and France, and particularly with Britain, but got nowhere because the real problem was Germany's very existence as a growing super power. Each had interests of their own which put them in conflict with Germany. First, Russia wanted control of the

Bosporus Straights leading out of the Black Sea, as a warm water outlet for her Navy and merchant fleet, and was willing to go to war to get it. The Bosporus Straights were at the time controlled by Germany through her alliance with the Ottoman Empire. Next, Britain saw Germany as a threat to her economic dominance and wanted only to reduce Germany's power. Then, France wanted revenge for the loss of the Franco/Prussian War in 1871, and also wanted her two provinces, Alsace and Lorraine, back. All three powers wanted to reduce Germany's economic power, and the only way they saw to achieve that was by military force. All of Germany's diplomatic efforts were frustrated by these factors. Germany's very existence as a unified nation state was the problem, and it seemed that nothing short of dissolving itself would satisfy these rival nations. France and Russia together began to scheme against Germany and to develop plans for an eventual war. Britain was also looking for a pretext for war against Germany. Yet, Germany was guilty of nothing except becoming too successful.

(Left, a cartoon in 1904 from the German perspective. John Bull, as the symbol of Britain, is walking off with the harlot, Arianne, symbol of France, in what is supposed to be a tri-colored dress, turning their backs on the Kaiser.)

Britain and Germany have often been called the "identical twins" of Europe. They were the same race, with similar, highly organized, high achieving cultures, both Protestant (in the main), both aggressive in pursuing their aims, and both with a history of constitutional monarchies. Britain had no quarrel with Germany, nor Germany with Britain, except that Britain became obsessed with Germany's growing economic power. Britain, though smaller than Germany in size and population, headed the largest empire in the world; in fact, the largest empire in history.

Yet, Germany was eclipsing Britain as an industrial power. Moreover, Germany was building a navy which threatened to rival that of Britain. Britain was also painfully aware of the comparative trajectories of the economic power of Britain and Germany. Britain's was trending downward, while Germany's was trending upwards; and this did not bode well for Britain's future. The British believed that they needed to act against Germany while they were still powerful enough to do so.

Between 1912 and 1914, the Russian Ambassador in Paris, Alexander Izvolsky and President Raymond Poincare of France entered into an agreement to go to war against Germany, "in event of any diplomatic crisis that would bring Britain in on their side." Such a crisis soon erupted with the Serbian assassination of the Austrian Archduke Franz Ferdinand in June, 1914. Austria-Hungary declared war on Serbia after obtaining Germany's unqualified backing (the blank check). The "blank check" was given because Germany's governing elite believed that by doing so, Russia would be discouraged from intervening against Austria-Hungary on behalf of Serbia. Germany reasoned that If Austria-Hungary were to be defeated by Serbia and Russia, then Germany would be left completely surrounded by enemies. Propping up Austria-Hungary was crucial to Germany's security. But Russia, who considered herself Serbia's mentor and protector (Serbia was Russia's "little Slavic brother"), ignored Germany's "blank check" and threatened war against Austria-Hungary anyway. Germany tried mediating with Russia to prevent war, but Russia and her ally France, seeing this as the opportunity they had been waiting for, refused to be conciliatory. Instead, Russia abruptly ordered a general mobilization. Such a mobilization had long been recognized in European capitals as tantamount to a declaration of war. After urgent demands for Russia to cancel her mobilization, to no avail, Germany declared war on Russia on August 1, and immediately began her own mobilization. France began mobilizing three days later, but, in fact, had already informed the Russians that she had decided on war a day before Germany declared war on Russia and three days before Germany declared war on France. France's mobilization was not, therefore, the result of Germany's declaration of war on Russia. The mobilization had already been decided on. Germany, instead of being the aggressor in this case, was reacting to Russian and French initiatives.

Germany is located on a flat plain in the heart of Europe without natural defenses, completely surrounded by potential enemies, and therefore uniquely vulnerable to invasion from two or more sides. She was in no position, therefore, to wait and see before mobilizing her own armed forces. Germany was well aware of the plotting and scheming between France and Russia to create a pretext for war against her, and was, therefore, on continuous alert. The worst nightmare for Germany's military leaders was a two front war with France on one side and Russia on the other. To counter that likelihood, Germany had worked out a military strategy called the "Schlieffen Plan." The plan called for rapid mobilization, concentration of Germany's armed forces, and a lightening attack through Belgium to first knock France out of the war, after which the German army would wheel around and take on Russia, thus avoiding a two-front war. Even though the Schlieffen Plan called for a pre-emptive attack, first on France and then Russia, the plan was, at bottom, a defensive strategy and not an aggressive one. To wait to be attacked first, from two sides, would be suicidal. On August, 3, 1914, when war seemed unavoidable, Germany swept through Belgium and into France, but was unable to deal France the quick, knock-out blow strategized in the Schlieffen plan.

Britain then declared war on Germany on August 4, on the pretext that Germany had violated Belgian neutrality, though Britain's actual reason for war against Germany was to destroy Germany as an economic rival. On that basis alone, Britain's leaders decided to join France and Russia in a war against Germany. In reality, Belgium had not figured into the British cabinet's discussion at all when war with Germany was decided upon. Belgium was used only as a pretext for war. Moreover, had Germany not invaded Belgium, Britain would have done so without a second thought.

Soon after pouring into France through Belgium, Germany became bogged down in the Battle of the Marne, just short of her goal of reaching Paris, which quickly brought an end to the "war of movement." Stalemate and trench warfare followed in which neither side could predominate. This condition remained until the American forces came in to break the deadlock.

Germany eventually lost the war, and for that reason alone, was blamed for starting it. Article 231 of the Versailles Treaty formally blamed Germany for starting the war, which then served as the basis for all of the punitive measures taken against Germany. After the war was over and passions began to cool, a number of historians -- known as "revisionists" -- began to look through the intemperate propaganda to uncover the real facts. Scholars like Harry Elmer Barnes, Charles Beard, et al, began to tell a different story. Barnes argued in his book, *The Genesis of the World War*, 1926, that , on the record, Serbia, Russia and France bore a greater responsibility for starting the war than did Austria and Germany, and Germany's responsibility was less than Austria-Hungary's. In Barnes view, German "war guilt" was about equal to that of Britain. The most pro-German view was that Germany was forced into a war she did not want and was required to defend herself against rapacious foes out to destroy Germany as an economic power. President Wilson had sent his personal representative, Colonel Edward Mandel House, to Europe to study the situation three months before the war began. The view that Germany was being threatened by military aggression from Russia, France and Britain was supported by Colonel House's report. He wrote in his report that, "when England consents, France and Russia will close in on Germany," which is precisely what eventually happened. Germany was, in fact, the "defender" against Allied aggression.

Germany did not want war, had nothing to gain from war, and everything to lose from it. After all, Germany was obtaining everything she wanted without war, that is, economic expansion and the acquisition of colonies from which to obtain raw materials and to which to sell industrial products. But France *did* want war, as revenge against Germany for the Franco-Prussian War of 1870/71 and to regain her lost provinces of Alsace and Lorraine. Russia also *did* want war with Germany in order to obtain the warm water Bosporus Straits which Germany controlled, and Britain *did* want war in order to crush a commercial competitor. All three of these Allied powers believed that Germany was becoming too big and too powerful. The Versailles Treaty itself proves that, in that its main effect was to reduce the physical size of Germany and to reduce her economic and military power. The treaty took away large portions of German territory and gave it to other countries, along with 6.5 million German people,. A separate clause barred Austria form combining with Germany. During the peace deliberations, Georges Clemenceau, President of France, is supposed to have said, "Germany has 20 million too many people."

Germany not only did not want war in the beginning, but put out peace feelers as early as 1916 to try to bring the war to an end, even though Germany appeared at that time to be about to win the war, but the Allies had no interest in bringing the war to an end. What the Allies wanted was to destroy Germany, as they had set out to do from the beginning, and so, Germany's peace feelers were ignored. Clearly Germany was the victim and not the perpetrator of aggression.

The United States had no reason whatever to enter the war against Germany. Germany had done nothing to the United States and was not a threat to the United States in any way. Moreover, German-Americans along with British-Americans constituted the very core of the American culture. The United States had had only good relations with Germany, and American citizens had always looked upon Germany with warmth and admiration. Though the British anti-German propaganda campaign conducted in the United States had influenced public opinion, the vast majority of Americans were still opposed to entering the war. That could not be said, however, of America's ruling elite. America's ruling elite was strongly Anglophilic, with an attitude towards Great Britain not unlike that of Canada and Australia, innately predisposed to go to the aid of the "mother country." America was virtually a vassal state to Great Britain in those days.

These were all factors, but the deciding influence in taking America into the war was the pressure on President Wilson by American Jewish financiers. It was these powerful Jews who had financed Wilson's political career. Without their financial and media support, he probably would never have become president. These Jews exerted extreme pressure on Wilson to take the United States into the war on the side of Britain to ensure an Allied victory, in exchange for the Balfour Declaration which promised the Jews a homeland in Palestine after the war (of which more in the following chapter). Jews controlled most of the large newspapers and they controlled Hollywood, so they had all the means necessary to control American public opinion. The sinking of the Lusitania, the Zimmerman telegram, etc. were not reasons to go to war, only fabricated pretexts.

The German people had every reason to be outraged over the shameful peace treaty imposed upon them by the victorious powers. The Versailles Treaty was unfair and immoral, and had been imposed by force by the victors upon the vanquished. Germany was forced into signing the hated treaty by a "food" blockade imposed by the British navy, which caused a million Germans to starve to death, and by a threat of military invasion of Germany. Therefore, the imposed treaty had no moral or legal force and Germany was in no way obligated to adhere to the treaty and had every moral right to abandon it as soon as she was militarily able to do so.

Though America's entry brought a quick end to the carnage, entering the war was actually disastrous in its long term consequences for Western, Christian Civilization. Had America stayed out of it, it is almost certain that the war would have ended in a negotiated peace with neither side achieving a victory. There would therefore have been no Versailles Treaty. Germany would not have been dismembered. Germany would have maintained her army intact and would have maintained her peace agreement with Russia (Treaty of Brest-Litovsk). The Czar would likely not have abdicated and the German Empire would have remained intact. Bolshevism would most likely have been nipped in the bud instead of taking control of Russia. The Austro-Hungarian Empire would have remained intact. So, also, would the Ottoman Empire, which would have precluded the creation of the state of Israel and all of the negative consequences resulting from that. There would have been no Communist revolution in Germany, Hungary or Italy. The Spanish Civil War would not have occurred. There would have been no World War II, no Cold War, and Communism would not have taken control of Central and Eastern Europe. A unified Europe, not unlike the European Union of today, except much larger and much more prosperous, would almost certainly have formed with Germany as its dominant member. In short, Europe would have stabilized and become a dynamic economic power in the world. America's entry into the war was perhaps the greatest disaster in European history in its unintended consequences.

Chapter 3

The Jewish Factor in the War

On December 12, 1916, two and a half years into the war, Germany made a peace offer to the Allies to end the war on a *status quo ante* basis. That is, no one wins and no one loses, and no one pays reparations; everyone just stops fighting and goes back home. Germany had never wanted the war in the first place. By that time in the course of the war, Germany seemed on the verge of victory. Germany's submarine force had effectively stopped the supply convoys coming from America to Britain, creating critical shortages of all war materiel in Britain. France had already lost 600,000 men in the battles of Verdun and the Somme, and French soldiers were beginning to mutiny. The Italian army had collapsed completely and Russian soldiers were deserting in droves and returning home. Germany appeared to be winning on both fronts. But the slaughter had been too great and the British and the French were unwilling to stop fighting short of a victory. The only way to justify the carnage and the horrific loss of life was to fight on until victory could be obtained. Moreover, as explained in the previous chapter, Britain had entered the war to destroy Germany as an industrial and commercial rival, and that remained her goal. British leaders were determined to find a way to break the stalemate and win the war, and they knew that the one sure way of doing so was to bring America in on their side. A relentless effort was already under way to bring that about, but so far, without success.

Zionist Jews and the British government had already been finagling behind the scenes over a Jewish homeland in Palestine. In October, 1916, two months prior to the German peace offer, a group of Zionist Jews led by Chaim Weitzman (later the first president of Israel) had met with British leaders with a proposition. If Britain would guarantee the creation of a Jewish state in Palestine after the war, the Jews would use their influence through powerful Jews in America to bring America into the war on the side of Britain and the Allies, which would assure an Allied victory. These Jews were so confident of their power and influence that they virtually guaranteed that they would be able to achieve this.

Sir Arthur Balfour   **Chaim Weizman**

At that time, Palestine was under the control of the Ottoman Empire, which was allied to Germany. If Germany were to win the war, the Ottoman Empire would have remained intact with no possibility of a Jewish homeland there, but if the Allies were to win the war, then Britain would control Palestine and be in position to hand it over to the Jews. (Whether or not Britain had the right to give other people's land to the Jews is another issue.)

With the offer of the Zionists Jews to bring America into the war in hand, Britain rejected Germany's peace offer and decided to take the Zionists up on their proposition. The British promised the Jews that if they could, indeed, bring America into the war, that Palestine would be theirs. The Zionist Jews went to work immediately.

The tiny group of elites who ran the United States, including President Wilson and his administration, all resided on the East Coast, and all were enthusiastic Anglophiles and already predisposed to enter the war on the side of mother England. They only needed a push and a pretext, which could easily be manufactured. But the great heartland of America, which included millions of ethnic Germans, wanted nothing to do with the war. The job at hand, then, was to bring public opinion around from opposing entry into the war to supporting it. That would be achieved through propaganda. The British had already been waging a very sophisticated anti-German propaganda campaign of their own in America since the war first began, and had had considerable success in turning American public opinion against Germany, but they by no means yet had a majority.

The Jews were very powerful in America. In addition to owning most of the big banking firms, they also owned most of the newspapers, and they owned Hollywood. They controlled all the means of running an effective propaganda campaign. Because of their wealth and their willingness to support the campaigns of politicians, they also had enormous political influence and would have little trouble in persuading politicians to see things their way.

Jewish motivations in international affairs were complicated at the time, which requires a bit of explaining. Jews, then as now, lived as minorities in numerous other "host" countries, without a state of their own, but all considered themselves to be a part of the "International Nation of Israel," a single nation, encompassing all Jews everywhere. What happens to Jews in one corner of the world is a concern of Jews worldwide. As a nation of its own, International Jewry has "national interests," and one of their national interests at that time was the eventual destruction of the Czarist regime in Russia. Jews in Russia had long been restricted and suppressed by one Czarist regime after another, to the extent that millions of Jews had left Russian controlled areas for other European countries, but mainly to America. Czarist Russia was the avowed enemy of the International Jewish nation, and since Germany was at war with Russia, International Jewry tended to support Germany in the war on the principle that "the enemy of my enemy is my friend." At the same time, they restricted their support of all kinds to Britain and France because Britain and France were allied with Russia. Jacob Schiff, the German Born head of the Kuhn, Loeb bank in New York, and the most influential figure of his day in American Jewish life, wrote in "The Menorah Journal" of April, 1915: *It is well known that I am a German sympathizer...England has been contaminated by her alliance with Russia...am quite convinced that in Germany anti-Semitism is a thing of the past.* Schiff's pro-Germany sympathies were shared by Jews everywhere, particularly by Zionist Jews.

Nevertheless, after the Zionists saw their chance of obtaining Palestine as a Jewish homeland by switching their support to Britain, International Jewry switched sides overnight, and Germany then became their avowed enemy. They not only withdrew their financial support, they also began a vicious propaganda attack against Germany. American and British Jews joined the British government's already intense anti-German propaganda campaign. All the Jewish owned newspapers and other publications, as well as Jewish owned Hollywood, joined in the attack. The Germans who had so recently been the Jews favored nationality, suddenly became brutal, knuckle dragging, baby killing "Huns" in the International Jewish press. International Jewish bankers cut off financial support to Germany and began to pour their money into France and Britain instead. Even Jewish banks in Germany refused further financing of the German war effort.

Prior to the war, Germany had been a hospitable country for Jews. Due to the absence of any kind of restrictions on them, Jews became very powerful in Germany, and through their dominance of banking and finance, they were able to control much of Germany's industrial power. Once Palestine had been promised to the Jews by Britain, even German Jews were no longer willing to support the German war effort. Instead, they became something of an Allied "fifth column" inside

Germany, betraying the country they lived in. Jewish newspapers in Germany began to criticize and condemn the war. Jewish labor leaders in Germany began to agitate for strikes and work stoppages, and Jewish Communist leaders began to agitate for revolution. This combined effort of Jewish groups in undermining war production and in creating unrest among the German people proved very detrimental to Germany's war effort. The Jews had taken the British bribe, and proved once again that their primary interest in all events is, "what is good for Jews," and that their loyalty is first and foremost to the international Nation of Israel.

Immediately after the British promise of a Jewish homeland in Palestine, American Jews began pressuring the Wilson administration to enter the war against Germany. President Woodrow Wilson was highly malleable in the hands of the Jews, as his political career had been a product of Jewish financial and media support and he remained closely associated with Jews throughout his political career. Even his non-Jewish right hand man, "Colonel" Edward Mandell House, had been closely associated with Jews prior to his association with Wilson. House had been employed as an agent for the Jewish House of Rothschild, negotiating U.S. cotton purchases for them before he linked up with Wilson. Wilson's campaign for governor of New Jersey was financed by a group of Jewish bankers and financiers, including Jacob Schiff, president of the Kuhn, Loeb Bank, Paul Warburg, brother-in-law to Schiff and Wilson appointee to the Federal Reserve Board; and by Henry Morgenthau, Sr., a financier and Wilson appointee as ambassador to the Ottoman Empire. These same Jews, as well as others, financed his run for the presidency. Other Jews who influenced Wilson included the first Jewish Supreme Court Justice, Louis Brandies, whom Wilson had appointed; Barnard Baruch, the wealthy and powerful financier; Rabbi Stephen Wise, founder of the Federation of American Zionists in 1897, who later became Wilson's most trusted advisor; and Felix Frankfurter, a crypto communist, who was later appointed to the Supreme Court by FDR. These Jews virtually controlled Wilson because they had been responsible for his career. All of them applied relentless pressure on Wilson to enter the war against Germany, which, as previously mentioned, he was already predisposed to do. Meanwhile,

Jacob Schiff

Paul Warburg

Henry Morgenthau, Sr.

Louis Brandeis

Bernard Baruch

Rabbi Stephen Wise

These powerful American Jews financed, and therefore controlled President Woodrow Wilson's political career. They used that influence to pressure Wilson into entering the war against Germany.

Felix Frankfurter (L)

the Jewish information and entertainment media had completely converted American public opinion from opposition to the war to virtually demanding it. Wilson, himself, made the decision that America would enter the war and he then went before Congress and persuaded Congress to declare war on Germany.

On April 6, 1917, less than six months after the meeting between Weitzman and the British leaders during which these Zionist Jews promised to bring America into the war, the United States Congress declared war on Germany.

On November 2, 1917, as a *quid pro quo,* the British government issued the Balfour Declaration in the form of a letter from the British government to Zionist, Baron Walter Rothschild, promising Palestine to the Jews as a national homeland.

The war ended on November 11, 1918 after an armistice was signed, based on President Wilson's "Fourteen Points." If the Peace Conference which met in Paris to work out the peace treaty after the war had kept its word and used Wilson's Fourteen Points as the basis for the treaty, all would have been different, but as outlined in the previous chapter, that is not what happened. The Peace Conference ignored Wilson's Fourteen Points – which would have guaranteed a just peace for all sides. Germany was blamed for the war and a harsh, punitive treaty was drawn up which turned out to be anything but a just peace. It was destructive and demoralizing for the German people. The treaty was presented to Germany as a *dicktat* which Germany was forced to sign under duress. The German people were astounded when they learned of the contents of the treaty. They were outraged and wanted someone to blame for it. Their wrath became focused on the Jews.

Thus, the "stab-in-the-back" theory was established blaming communists and Jews for the loss of the war, as well as for the harsh peace treaty. There was enough truth in these allegations for it to be widely believed. International Jewry *did*, in fact, take sides against Germany in exchange for the promise of a Jewish homeland in Palestine, which only the British were in position to grant. Jews also poured money into the British and French war effort and used their international banking influence to cut off financing to Germany. Moreover, many of these Jews were German Jews who wound up undermining their own country.

Jews at the Paris Peace Conference

The extent of Jewish influence at the Paris Peace Conference after the war is not very well known today, but, the fact is that Jews flocked there from all over the globe. They came from Russia, Eastern Europe, France, and particularly from the United States and Britain. From Britain came Lord Walter Rothschild, Lionel de Rothschilld, Chaim Weizmann, Lucien Wolfe, Moses Montefiore, Nachum Sokolove, Julius Kahn, Professor Sylvain Levi, and M. Bigar, among others.

From the United States came Rabbi Stephen Wise, Felix Frankfurter, Oscar Strauss, Supreme Court Justice Louis Brandeis, Walter Lippman, the historian Simon Dubnow, Harry Friedenwald, Jacob de Haas, Mary Fels, Louis Robison, Bernard Flexner, and Judge Julian Mack of Philadelphia, among others. Ten additional Jews came as members of the American Jewish Congress, formed in 1918 specifically for the Paris Peace Conference.

From France came a group of Jews representing the *Alliance Israelite Universelle,* a Paris based international Jewish organization founded in 1860 to safeguard the human rights of Jews around the world.

Representing the American banking interests was the Jewish banker Paul Warburg, Chairman of the Federal Reserve. His brother Max Warburg, head of the German banking firm of Warburg and Company, was there, along with other German Jews, as a representative of German banking interests (but not representing Germany, per se, only Germany's Jewish banking interests). These groups were joined by large numbers of Jews from Bolshevik Russia, Poland and Ukraine. Though they ostensibly represented several different countries, all the Jewish delegates congregated together as one group, first and foremost to secure the interests of International Jewry. The interests of the various countries they represented were only secondary, and of a much lower priority, if considered at all.

Astonishingly, each of the Allied leaders at the peace talks had a Jew as his primary advisor. President Wilson had Bernard Baruch. France's Clemenceau' had Jeroboam Rothschild, aka Georges Mandel. Britain's David Lloyd George had Sir Phillip Sassoon. Italy's representative at the talks, Prime Minister Vittorio Emanuele Orlando, was himself half Jewish, and self identified as a Jew.

All of these Jews were comprehensively involved at every level in the numerous decisions which had to be made by the Conference, particularly those pertaining to their own interests. Jewish interests were given an inexplicably high priority in the final drafting of the peace settlement known as the Versailles Treaty. The Jews had a number of interests which they vigorously pursued, but they were especially determined to have the following three requirements included in the final treaty: (1) A League of Nations as the first step toward world government; (2) the recognition of Jewish "minority rights" in Eastern Europe and; (3) the creation of a British Mandate in Arab Palestine as the necessary first step toward an eventual Jewish state there. They accomplished all three.

It seems remarkable that Jewish interests could have so predominated at the conclusion of a war in which Jews had not participated as a separate corporate entity. And yet, there they were, at war's end, having come from countries on both sides of the conflict, fully participating in the Peace Conference, and securing for themselves a major share of the spoils. Jewish power has never been more overtly demonstrated. They achieved everything they had set out to obtain.

Jews in Britain

The Jews have long been powerful in Britain. So powerful that the British social critic Hilaire Belloc, in his book, *The Jews*, 1922, described the British Empire as a partnership between Jewish finance and the British aristocracy. Britain was the financial capital of the world, and the Rothschilds dominated British finance. Belloc goes on to say that *"...the Jews, in spite of their small numbers, color every English institution, especially the Universities and the House of Commons...through their control of the politicians by Jewish finance..."* (The same can be said of the United States today.)

In his book, *Tales of the British Aristocracy*, 1956, L. G. Pine claims that the British Aristocracy is thoroughly mixed with Jewish blood. In fact, Pine says, the British aristocracy is about half Jewish. Ancient estates fell on hard times after the Industrial Revolution as the shift of financial power slipped away from agriculture and the great landed estates and went over to manufacturing. Jews controlled the money in Britain and even financed the British government through the Rothschild controlled Bank of England, and they financed British industry. Down-and-out gentry with ancient titles and large estates, but no money, began marrying the daughters of rich Jews, so the marriage of Jewish finance and British aristocracy took place literally. Pine gives as an example the marriage of the 5th Earl of Roseberry who married the only daughter and heiress of Baron Mayer de Rothschild, head of the Bank of England. Roseberry went on to become Prime Minister in 1894. Roseberry's Rothschild wife *"...stayed in the Jewish religion but her children were educated as Christians...The alliances between Jewish ladies and British lords are mostly of this type, the wife providing large sums...while the aristocrat has the title and ancient estate. The children are able to look back upon a varied bag of ancestors."*

Other wealthy and powerful Jewish families who penetrated into British aristocracy included the Sassoons, the Cassels, the Montefories, the Montagues, and the Goldsmids, among others. These Jews were the money men behind important politicians and political leaders on the make, especially so in the case of Winston Churchill. Churchill had no money, yet, he lived like an oriental pasha, thanks to a group of wealthy Jewish backers known among themselves as "The Focus." This group backed Churchill throughout his entire career, and were particularly instrumental in making him Prime Minister. All of these wealthy Jews were socially intertwined with the most powerful men of Britain, including the King, himself. Cassel's daughter married Lord Louis Mountbatten, a member of the Royal family. Cassel was related to the Rothschilds, the preeminent Jewish family in Europe. Thus, the marriage of a Cassel to a Mountbatten tied the Rothschilds to the Royal family by marriage.

Before the First World War, much of the British aristocracy was

Jewish, and the rest was thoroughly mixed with Jewish blood. Britain even had a Jewish Prime Minister, Benjamin Disraeli; who wrote: *"the Jews have made themselves so closely connected with the British peerage that the two classes are unlikely to suffer loss which is not mutual."* Thus, the Jews had a powerful influence upon every aspect of British policy, including entry into World War One against Germany.

Chapter 4

The Russian Revolution of 1917

Germany actually won World War I on the Eastern Front, though that aspect of the war is less well known than the war on the Western Front, which Germany lost. The war on the Eastern Front began on August 17, 1914 when Russia invaded East Prussia with a full scale offensive. The Russian attack was launched a little more than two weeks after Germany had crossed into Belgium in its drive on France, which marked the beginning of the war. To meet the Russian invasion of East Prussia, Germany immediately diverted large numbers of soldiers from the Western Front. The massive German troop transfer from the Western Front to the Eastern Front is one of the reasons the Western Front bogged down in stalemate so soon after the war began. Germany's Schlieffen Plan called for a lightening attack through Belgium, into France, to knock France out of the war, whereupon the German army would wheel around and take on the Russians on the Eastern Front. A two front war was to be avoided at all cost. When Germany's attack on France did not produce the expected quick victory, the German Army dug trenches and assumed a defensive position until the war on the Eastern Front could be resolved. Germany fought a defensive war on the Western Front with reduced forces through most of the war while aggressively engaging the Russians on the Eastern Front. Germany was now fighting the two front war the Schlieffen Plan had been designed to avoid.

Russia and Germany clashed in a series of bloody battles on the Eastern Front, in which Russia came out second best in all of them. In East Prussia the Russian armies were crushed by German forces at both the Battle of Tannenberg and the Battle of Masurian Lakes. In the disastrous Battle of Tannenberg, only 10,000 of General Samsonov's Russian Second Army managed to escape. The remainder of his 150,000 troops were either killed or captured. General Samsonov then shot himself rather than face the humiliation of his disastrous defeat. The Russians were then pushed completely out of East Prussia by the victorious Germans.

Russian forces fared better in their invasion of the Austro-Hungarian province of Galicia by winning an important victory at the Battle of Lemberg (now Lvov), but the German army came quickly to the rescue and drove the Russians back into Russia. In just six months time, the Russian Army had gained nothing, yet lost over 2 million men, either killed or captured. German troops then seized the initiative by advancing into Russian held territory, seizing Warsaw in early August, 1915, Brest Litovsk on August 25, and Vilna, Lithuania on September 19. These battles resulted in the loss of another million Russian soldiers.

The heavy losses sustained in these battles literally wiped out the old Russian officer corps and nearly destroyed the entire pre-war Russian army. Military commanders were thereafter forced to rely on inexperienced and reluctant conscripts, most of whom were simple peasants. The situation deteriorated to the point that Czar Nicholas II felt it necessary to take personal command of the Army, effective on August 22, 1915. Because of his lack of experience in military matters, the Czar was indecisive and vacillating, and managed only to exacerbate an already deteriorating situation.

German troops in East Prussia

Morale in the Russian army deteriorated rapidly. Soldiers began deserting the front and returning home in droves. These conscripted peasant soldiers refused to accept orders from their officers, and even shot their officers in many cases. They were not professional soldiers and had no feeling of commitment to either the army or to the war.

The German Army crosses into Russia, September, 1917

Russian soldiers flee advancing Germans

By January 1917, it was clear that Czar Nicholas had lost control of the situation in the field and that Russia was losing the war. Back home, food supplies were low throughout Russia, unemployment was high, and inflation was spiraling out of control, all a result of the war. Widespread strikes had shut down factories, throwing even more people out of work. Leftist revolutionaries took full advantage of the chaos to incite the people to revolt. Street demonstrations were organized in which workers, peasants and soldiers demanded bread, redistribution of land, and an end to the war. "Workers Soviets (counsels)" were organized by the revolutionaries. The situation became so explosive that the Czar abdicated and a "Provisional Government" was put in his place, headed by Alexander Kerensky. Significantly, as a sign of things to come, Kerensky was a Jew. In March 1917 one of the first measures of the Provisional Government under Kerensky was to abolish all restrictions on Jews throughout Russia. This was to prove disastrous for traditional Russia, for it had the effect of opening any and all public offices to revolutionary Jews, which they quickly flooded into.

Alexander Kerensky, head of the new Provisional Government.

When the Provisional Government took power, the Workers "Soviets" (councils) remained in existence, so for a time there was a sort of duality of power. "Workers Soviets" were a Marxist Jewish creation, and their principle accomplishment was to immediately free all political prisoners and to lift the ban on political exiles to permit them to return to Russia. This brought some of the most radical, revolutionary minded leaders back into the capital city of Petrograd from Russian prisons, the great majority of whom were Jews. This was a momentous event for old Russia, the significance of which was not immediately recognized. By this invasion of revolutionary Jews, the Russian body politic was fatally infected, and old Russia was doomed. Altogether, some 90,000 exiles returned from all over Europe and America, and from as far away as Argentina. These 90,000 exiles constituted the heart of the approaching Bolshevik revolution. They were almost to the last man professional revolutionaries, and with few exceptions they were Jews. Stalin, Sverdlov, and Zinoviev were among the exiles who returned from Siberia. Lenin, Martov, Radek, and Kamenev returned from Switzerland. Trotzky returned with hundreds of his Yiddish brethren from New York's Lower East Side. Until their return the revolution had been under the leadership of second string Bolsheviks who happened to be on hand. Now the elite with international reputations had returned and began to take charge.

Bolsheviks Take Control

This group, the "Bolsheviks," overthrew the Provisional Government in October1917, in what amounted to a Jewish *coup d'état* of the Russian government. Kerensky had wanted to gradually implement a mild form of socialism within a structure of democracy, but this was much too mild and much too slow for the Bolsheviks' taste. Lenin and Trotsky wanted to completely remake Russian society, and they knew that that could only be done through violence. These men were Jacobins, and what they wanted was a French Revolutionary style "reign of terror." One of the first acts of these Jewish Bolsheviks after seizing control of the government was to enact a law forbidding anti-Semitism, violation of which carried the death penalty.

Lenin addresses a crowd on a street in Petrograd (St. Petersburg). Leon Trotsky stands just to the right of the podium.

Jews and the Russian Revolution

The fact that Jews constituted the majority of the Bolshevik leadership in the Russian Revolution of 1917, as well as in the numerous Bolshevik revolutions that erupted throughout Europe afterwards, is carefully suppressed today. As a result, Jewish involvement has largely been erased from modern academic historiography. Contemporary historians today are virtually compelled, on pain of professional ruin, to support the view that not only did the Jews play no special role in Bolshevism, but that they were actually victimized by it.

This, of course, is a cover-up and a contradiction of the actual facts. Statesmen and journalists of that time were well aware of the Jewish nature of the Russian Revolution, and that the revolution amounted to a Jewish coup d'état of the Russian state. It was also well known that the Bolshevik regime that came into power as a result of the revolution was made up mostly of Jews. Moreover, the Communist revolutions throughout Europe that soon followed the Russian Revolution were orchestrated by Jews whose goal was to do the same in other European countries that they had done in Russia -- that is, to overthrow existing regimes and replace them with Soviet Socialist Republics controlled by Jews. It is significant that in every single case where Communists managed to take control of a European country, however temporary, one of their first acts was to outlaw anti-Semitism and to lift all restrictions on Jews. To obtain the real facts of the matter, one only needs to read the newspapers, magazine articles, and books written at that time, all of which are now available on the Internet.

Two attempts were made by international Jewry to take control of the Russian government; the first in 1905, which did not succeed, and the second in 1917, which did. Both coup attempts were planned and organized by revolutionary Jews, both inside and outside Russia, and both attempts were financed by outside Jewish banking houses. To associate Jews with the Russian Revolution in any way is strictly taboo today, but to understand what actually happened in Russia during and after the revolution, and also to understand the impact of the revolution on other nations at the time, it is essential to understand the role Jews played, both in the revolution and in the Russian government thereafter, as well as in the Bolshevik revolutions throughout Europe which followed the Russian Revolution. It is also necessary to understand the nature of the mutual hostility which had long existed between the Czarist government in Russia and its Jewish subjects. It is necessary, as well, to understand the nature of the mutual animosity that Jews and the ordinary Russian people felt for each other. And finally, it is necessary to understand the vengeful enmity held by Jews throughout the world for the Czarist regime in Russia, and their relentless determination to one day bring it down.

Origin of East European Jews

At the end of the nineteenth century, the majority of the world's Jews lived in Eastern Europe in a region designated by the Russian government as the "Pale of Settlement;" a region made up of Poland, Belarus, Ukraine and Lithuania, all a part of the Russian Empire, but not of Russia itself. Just how these Jews got there is an interesting question all its own. The answer is that they were always there. They did not immigrate in from someplace else, this was their native land.

These Jews were not the same as the Biblical Jews of the Holy Land. They were, rather, the descendents of the Khazar people who had lived since ancient times in the region between the Black Sea and the Caspian Sea which is today predominantly occupied by the country of Georgia. The Khazars converted *en masse* to Judaism during the late eighth century. There is no biological connection between these Yiddish speaking Khazar Jews and the ancient Semitic Jews of the Holy Land. The descendents of the Khazars are the *Ashkenazi* Jews of today. 85% of the world's Jews today, and 90% of Jews who live in the United States are Ashkenazi Jews. Yiddish was a sort of Creole language which the Khazar's developed and used in their trade and business dealings with Central Europe. Some say that Yiddish is a German dialect, but not quite. The grammatical structure is different from German, though about half of the words of Yiddish are German words. Numerous words in Yiddish are Kazarian in origin. Kagan, for example, a common Jewish last name is a Khazar word for "king." The Jewish last name, "Kazan," as in Elia Kazan, is a Khazar name.

Khazaria, home of the Khazars who are the ancestors of today's Ashkenazi Jews. 85% of the world's Jews today are Ashkenazis.

The Khazar people ranged widely over the steppes between the Black Sea and the Caspian Sea, north to the Ukrainian city of Kiev, and were a mixture of two ethnic types. According to Arthur Koestler, in his book, *The Thirteenth Tribe*, the southern Khazars tended to be a swarthy, Turkish-Mongol type, while the northern Khazars nearer to Kiev, tended to be blonde and blue eyed, or more European in appearance. Those two strains can be seen in the Ashkenazi Jews of today.

The Khazars adopted Judaism as their national religion at about the same time the Russians adopted the Greek Orthodox religion as their national religion. Both peoples went about their mass conversions in approximately the same way. The Russians brought in numerous Orthodox priests from Constantinople to help build churches and to teach the new religion to the Russian people. The Khazars, likewise, brought in numerous rabbis to teach Judaism to the Khazar people and to help them build synagogues. The Khazar Jews adopted the Talmud, the central text of mainstream Judaism, which incorporates Jewish law, ethics, philosophy, customs and Jewish history, and took the whole package as their own. They also adopted all Jewish holy days, as well as all the traditional Jewish rituals and ceremonies. In other words, they adopted Judaism in its entirety, including the Jewish custom of race purity, and forbidding marriage outside of Judaism.

These warlike people once ruled the entire region but eventually lost power and then settled in as a religious and ethnic minority amongst the Viking Russ and the Slavic people of Eastern Europe. The Jews of nineteenth and twentieth century Eastern and Central Europe were all descendants of the Khazars. These Khazar Jews, or Ashkenazi Jews, formed the largest ethnic minority in the Russian Empire, totaling 5.2 million according to the 1897 census. Almost all of the Jews of Europe, contrary to popular opinion, migrated into Europe from Khazaria in the East, not from Palestine or the Mediterranean.

Though concentrated in Eastern Europe, they also spread throughout Europe and formed small minority populations within the cities and towns of host countries, and formed a sort of "parasite/host" relationship with the majority Christian populations. They tended to establish themselves in "parasitic" occupations such as merchant, middleman, trader, and money lender, and avoided agriculture and labor intensive occupations. They also tended isolate themselves in closed communities which became know as "ghettos," and they did not marry outside their race. These Ashkenazi Jews were characterized by high intelligence and highly cohesive social organizations with close cooperation and mutual support between themselves, usually at the expense of their non-Jewish "host" populations.

The Jews also had their own laws and code of ethics to govern their lives. The Talmud permits Jews to treat non-Jews differently than they treat fellow Jews. They are instructed to be fair and honest with each other, but are not required to be so with Gentiles. Consequently, they developed a reputation for sharp practice and for taking advantage of well meaning, unassuming Gentiles. Wherever Jews lived, they were invariably accused of being a "parasitic" people who created nothing of their own, but lived off the industry of their host populations.

Reason for the Russian Pogroms Against the Jews

At the turn of the twentieth century, most of the world's Jews lived within the territory controlled by the Russian Empire. At that time, there existed some 650 anti-Jewish statutes as official law in Imperial Russia; deemed necessary to protect the Russian people from Jewish rapaciousness. In no other country in the world was anti-Semitism so deeply ingrained, from the lowest level bureaucrats and ordinary Russian soldiers who formed the Imperial Army, to the Russian Orthodox Church, the Government, and the Czar himself. Those who filled these organizations, and who therefore regulated and controlled the lives of the millions who fell under their authority, were nearly unanimous in their suspicion, fear, and outright hatred of Russia's Jews. The Jews had a reputation for being mutinous troublemakers, as well as avaricious, aggressive exploiters of their Christian, Gentile host populations.

Because they perceived themselves as defenders of the Christian faith and protectors of the Russian people, the Czars had kept the Jews out of Russia since the Middle Ages. But after the partition of Poland in 1772, at which time the eastern part of Poland was ceded to Russia, most East

European Jews became incorporated into the Russian Empire. Even more Jewish subjects were added when Catherine the Great annexed the Ukraine and Crimea. In order to deal with this new "Jewish problem," the infamous "Pale of Settlement" was established in 1791. The Pale of Settlement was a region which began at the western edge of Russia, and included Poland, Lithuania, Ukraine, Belorussia and Bessarabia. This is where the "undesirables" of the Russian Empire, which included the Jews, were required to live. The Russian government regarded the Jews as "a perpetual menace to the continued well-being of the Russian State." This view of the Jews as perpetual troublemakers grew even stronger after the French Revolution of 1789 when the large Jewish role in bringing about that revolution became known. (The Jacobins who instigated the French Revolution were predominantly, if not entirely, Jewish. It was also the Jews who financed the French Revolution; men such as Benjamin Goldsmid and his brother Abraham Goldsmid, their partner Moses Mocatta and his nephew Moses Montifiore, all of London, along with Daniel Itsig and his son-in-law David Friedlander of Berlin, and Herz Cerfbeer of Alsace, among others.) The Czars were worried about the stability of the Russian Empire and worried about this Jewish tendency to foment revolution. The draconian restrictions on Jews were imposed in defense of Russia, not just to make life difficult for Jews.

Alexander II, a kindly and compassionate man by all accounts, came to the Russian thrown in 1855 and began to implement fundamental changes in Russia, notably the emancipation of the serfs in 1861, but with the best of intentions he also lifted many of the restrictions on Jews. Jews considered "useful," like merchants, doctors and some artisans were permitted to settle in Russia on a limited basis. Opening Russia's borders to Jewish immigration, even on a limited basis, proved difficult to control, however, and Jews flooded into Russia in large numbers. The Jewish communities in St. Petersburg, Moscow and Odessa especially grew rapidly. Through their close, in-group cooperation, their emphasis on acquiring higher educations, and their pattern of working together to advance themselves and their fellow Jews at the exclusion of Gentiles, they soon began to dominate certain professions such as medicine, journalism, the law, finance and entrepreneurship. Jews also gradually achieved monopolies over the liquor, tobacco and retail industries, as the Gentiles were elbowed out. This pattern of behavior created hostility among the Russian people, and a predictable wave of anti-Semitism then ensued. Jews were accused of creating a "state within a state" for the purpose of dominating and exploiting Russia.

A Jewish shtetl (town) in the Pale of Settlement.

**Ashkenazi Jews in a shtetl in the "Pale of Settlement,"
a large region which included Poland, Ukraine,
Belorussia and Lithuania and Bessarabia. Ashkenazi
Jews were the descendants of the Khazarians.**

Konstantin Petrovich Pobedonostsev, who was a political advisor to both Alexander III and Nicholas II, wrote in a letter to the openly anti-Semitic writer Feodor Dostoyevsky, *"What you write about the Yids is completely just. They have engrossed everything, they have undermined everything, but the spirit of the century supports them. They are at the root of the revolutionary socialist movement and of regicide, they own the periodical press, they have in their hands the financial markets, the people as a whole fall into financial slavery to them; they even control the principles of contemporary science and strive to place it outside of Christianity."*

Despite the prosperity they were able to achieve in Russia, and the fair treatment accorded them by Russian Czars, the Jews began fomenting unrest, particularly labor unrest, and they involved themselves in revolutionary activities. The Jews formed the "Social Revolutionary Party," for example, for the specific purpose of overthrowing the Czar.

Both Anarchism and Nihilism were Jewish movements. In 1881 Czar Alexander II was assassinated by a group of Jewish revolutionaries. Soon thereafter, this same group began a series of assassinations of other government or public officials. In 1901 they murdered the Czar's Minister of Education; in 1902 they killed the Minister of the Interior; in 1903 the Governor of Ufa was assassinated; in 1904 the Premier of Russia was killed; in 1905 Grand Duke Sergei, the Czar's uncle was killed. Then, in 1905 the Jews attempted a revolution to overthrow the Czarist government, though it did not succeed. In 1906 the Jews assassinated General Dubrassov. In 1911, the Jewish terrorist Mordecai Bogrov assassinated Prime Minister Peter Stolypin. He shot him in the back of the head during a gala in Kiev, which was also attended by the Czar. (Assassination of those who stand in the way of Jewish interests has a long tradition amongst the Jews. The Israeli MOSSAD carries out routine assassinations today. Five Iranian nuclear scientists have most recently been assassinated by the MOSSAD. See also, the movie"Munich," in which MOSSAD assassinations are carried out.)

These Jewish assassinations, as well as other Jewish revolutionary activities, so infuriated the New Czar, Alexander III, especially the assassination of his own father, that he issued the following statement: *"For some time the government has given its attention to the Jews and to their relations with the rest of the inhabitants of the empire, with a view of ascertaining the sad condition of the Christian inhabitants brought about by the conduct of the Jews in business matters. During the last 20 years, the Jews have gradually possessed themselves of not only every trade and business in all its branches, but also of a great part of the land by buying or farming it. With few exceptions, they have as a body devoted their attention, not to enriching or benefiting the country, but to defrauding, by their wiles, its inhabitants, and particularly its poor inhabitants. This conduct of theirs has called forth protests on the part of the people, as manifested in acts of violence. The government, while on the one hand doing its best to put down the disturbances and to deliver the Jews from oppression and slaughter, has also on the other hand, thought it a matter of urgency and justice to adopt stringent measures in order to put an end to the oppression practiced by the Jews on the inhabitants, and to free the country from their malpractices, which were, as is known, the cause of the agitation."*

The Czarist government ordered a crackdown, and one by one, most of these Jews were rounded up and brought to trial. Though more than justified, the Czar's retaliation against these Jewish assassins produced the usual outcries of "anti-Semitism" and "persecution," as well as predictions of "extermination," which were then trumpeted throughout the International Jewish press. The Russian people eventually became fed up with the Jews, and a wave of pogroms spread throughout the Southwestern regions of Russia where Jews were most populous. More than 250 pogroms, varying in length and severity, occurred in 1881 alone. These were for the most part, spontaneous attacks on Jews by ethnic Christian Russians, and not the work of the Czarist government.

These pogroms received extensive coverage in international Jewish magazines and newspapers at the time, with the usual sensational exaggerations and dire predictions of planned genocide. International Jewry's desire to retaliate against Russia was extremely intensified by these breathless exaggerations and by the malicious propaganda attacks on the Czar. The truth is that it was the Russian people, themselves, who were behind the pogroms, not the Czarist government. The Czarist government even conducted an investigation to find out who was behind them, and did all it could to prevent them. The investigation concluded that the pogroms were the result of Jewish financial exploitation of the peasants and the accumulated resentment among the peasants as a result of it.

The Jews constantly fomented trouble of one kind or another throughout Russia. As already described, they assassinated Russian officials; they incited labor unrest by pitting workers against their employers; they organized demonstrations; and they made continuous attempts to stir up revolution. To contain this revolutionary activity the government began a policy of repression of the Jews in 1882 which continued right up to the Russian Revolution in 1917. In 1888, Alexander III began to push the Jews out of Russia, back into the Pale of Settlement. Jews were forbidden to buy or rent property in Russia. They were denied jobs in the civil service, and they were forbidden to trade on Sundays and Christian holidays. Nicholas II succeeded his father Alexander III in 1894, and he continued his father's strict rules against the Jews. He felt the repressive rules were necessary to protect the Russian people against the schemes and intrigues of the Jews, and also to prevent public disorder. But he was unable to stop the pogroms against the Jews which were being carried out by ordinary Russian people. These seemed to erupt spontaneously on a regular basis out of hostility and hatred of the Jews, and could not be contained.

Jews leave Russia for America

The Jews accepted no responsibility for any of this, but saw it instead as just more of the usual unjustified "persecution" of guiltless Jews by hostile Gentiles. As a result of this hostility and hatred, Jews saw the Russian Empire as an inhospitable and dangerous land for Jews. Their plight was made worse by an explosive population growth rate, the highest of any ethnic group in Europe, which further limited economic possibilities for them. There were too many Jews and too few opportunities for them in Russia. At the end of the nineteenth century they decided to leave Russia, en masse, for the "new world," that is, the Unites States of America. Between 1881 and 1924, more than 2 million Russian and East European Jews immigrated to the United States -- the largest mass migration of Jews in history. A great number also spread out over Western Europe. The two great Jewish movements of Zionism and Communism had been developed and nurtured within the Pale of Settlement, and when they migrated to America, they took these two movements with them. Communism was introduced to America for the first time by these new immigrant Jews.

The United States turned out to be everything they had hoped for. It proved to be the land of opportunity for Jews, with no constraints or restrictions on them of any kind. The American people had no experience with Jews, and therefore had formed no negative attitudes towards them. After becoming settled in the new world, mainly in New York City, they quickly began to fill up the universities; find positions in banking and finance; start up newspapers; and they began to flood into the professions. The German Jewish immigrants who had preceded them were already powerful in all of these areas and they gave their fellow tribesmen from Russia a hand up. By employing their usual methods of intense networking, in-group cooperation and mutual support, these new Jewish immigrants began to rise to positions of dominance in America. Following their usual pattern, once ensconced in a position of power, a Jew will then invariably bring in only other Jews until all the non-Jews who preceded them are gradually displaced. By these methods, they soon came to dominate journalism, academia and particularly banking and finance.

But these *nouveau riche* "American" Jews still remained an integral part of the International Jewish Nation, and they were more than willing to use their new found wealth to support and defend the interests of international Jewry. Their visceral hatred of Russia remained a part of the Jewish psyche, which was only exacerbated by frantic stories of continued repression of their brethren who had remained in Russia. As their power and influence in America grew, they plotted and schemed about ways to use their power to undermine and destroy the Czarist government. Jewish bankers in both Europe and America were ready to provide any funding necessary to bring about the downfall of the Czar and his regime. Russian officials were well aware of this Jewish scheming against Russia, and frequently commented on the fact that Jewish power and influence in Western countries was directed at undermining Russia and the Czar.

The German born Jew, Jacob Schiff, one of the wealthiest bankers in the world, and head of the international bank, Kuhn Loeb & Co., based in New York, had a particularly virulent hatred for Russia and was determined to do all he could to bring down the Czar. In 1905, Russia and Japan went to war over control of Manchuria in Northern China. Schiff and his Kuhn, Loeb Bank floated a huge loan to finance Japan in the war, while at the same time, using his international banking influence to block funding of Russia. The result was a shocking Japanese victory. Japan defeated the Russian army at Port Arthur in Manchuria, and then sank the Russian fleet in the battle of Tsushima in the waters between Korea and Japan. This was to be the first defeat of a European power by a non-European power, but it could not have been achieved without the backing and support of International Jewry.

The attempted Russian Revolution of 1905 was planned by Jewish revolutionaries, financed by Jewish banks, and staged to coincide with Russia's war with Japan. The official *Jewish Communal Register* of New York City of 1917-1918 carried the following statement: *"The firm of Kuhn, Loeb and Company [Jacob Schiff's bank] floated the large Japanese war loans of 1904-5, thus making possible the Japanese victory over Russia...Mr. Schiff has always used his wealth and influence in the best interest of his people [Jews]. He financed the enemies of autocratic Russia and used his influence to keep Russia from the money market of the United States."*

Financing the 1917 Revolution

Two great blocks of Jewish bankers; the London and Paris based Rothschilds with their extensive network of banks, and the so-called German-American bankers, under the control of Jacob Schiff, cooperated together to finance the Russian Revolution. Schiff, a German born Jew, was an international banker of Wall Street, closely allied with other German and American Jewish bankers, including the (German born) Warburgs of New York and Hamburg, the Guggenheims, the Hanauers, the Kahns, and others. The Warburgs, both in Germany and in the U.S., were actually related to Jacob Schiff. One was his brother-in-law and the other a son-in-law. Other International Jewish financiers allied with Jacob Schiff and the Kuhn, Loeb Bank included, the Westphalian-Rheinland Syndicate in Germany; the Lazare brothers of Paris; the Ginzburgs of Petrograd (formerly St. Petersburg), Tokyo and Paris; Speyer and Company of London, New York and Frankfurt am Main; and, significantly, the Nya Banken of Stockholm, Sweden, under a Swedish Jew, Olof Aschberg. These banking blocks were "international" in the truest sense; owned and operated by international Jews who were loyal to no nation except International Jewry.

In their mission to bring down the Czar, the two banking groups jointly financed a propaganda campaign against Czarist Russia which had the effect - as intended - of creating world-wide hostility toward the

Russian Empire. This anti-Czarist propaganda campaign was propagated through and trumpeted by all the major newspapers throughout Europe and America, as well as through all other information media, almost all of which was under Jewish control. (They were to conduct this same kind of propaganda campaign, except on a much larger scale, against Germany after Adolf Hitler became Chancellor.)

As mentioned above, Jacob Schiff hated Czarist Russia and was especially active in attempts to undermine the Czarist government. But it was the Rothschilds who were behind the dethroning of Czar Nicholas II in 1917, after which a "Provisional Government" was established, with Prince Georgy Lvov as its Prime Minister, soon thereafter to be replaced by the Jew Alexander Kerensky (Mother's name - Nadezhda Adler). As mentioned previously, one of the first acts of the Provisional Government under Kerensky (March 16, 1917) was to abolish all restrictions on Jews throughout Russia.

Up to that time Jews had been barred from government jobs, but suddenly they were allowed to take positions in any available government office in Russia. With all restrictions against them removed, Jews quickly became active in every aspect of the Revolution, obtaining leadership positions in several political parties. Seeing opportunity for themselves, Jews in large numbers began to flood into St. Petersburg and Moscow from the shtetls in the Pale of Settlement, from Europe, and from America. (Shtetl is a Yiddish word meaning "town." Shtetl life was depicted in the movie, " Fidler on the Roof.") These rural Jewish towns -- shtetls -- were spread throughout the Pale of Settlement, that is, Poland, Ukraine, Belarus, Moldava, and Lithuania.

Now that the Czar was gone, Lenin and 32 other Bolsheviks, nearly all Jews, were brought into Petrograd by the German General Staff by train from Switzerland for the purpose of destabilizing the Russian government. The intent was to take Russia out of the war. Lenin had opposed Russia's entry into the war from the beginning, and even called for ordinary soldiers to turn their guns against the officers who had led them into the slaughter.

Lenin and his entourage arrived at "The Finland Station" in Leningrad on April 16, 1917. The Germans were well aware of the

Jewish character of this revolutionary movement and recruited a Jew, Alexander Helphand (who took the name of Parvus), to act as an intermediary between the German government and the Bolsheviks. Large sums of money were sent in to Lenin and the Bolsheviks by the German government through Helphand. Helphand was born in a shtetl in Belarus, got a PhD in economics, moved to Berlin and became an associate of the Jewish Communist revolutionary, Rosa Luxemburg. Lenin received funding from both the German government and International Jewish banks. With secret German funding, Lenin immediately went to work setting up some 41 newspapers and other periodicals in Russia, including the newspaper "Pravda," which was to eventually become the official mouthpiece of the Bolshevik government, through which to trumpet the Communist line to the Russian public. Germany's interest in funding Lenin, as stated above, was to take Russia out of the war. But the international Jewish bankers had another agenda. Their interest in funding Lenin was to bring down the Czarist government and replace it with a Jewish revolutionary government. Germany was later to learn that she had made a pact with the Devil. A member of the German General Staff later wrote: *"We neither knew nor foresaw the danger to humanity from the consequences of this journey of the Bolsheviks to Russia."*

It was Jacob Schiff and the Kuhn, Loeb Bank, together with the Warburg banks, both in America and in Germany, who engineered Trotsky's return to Russia. Trotsky's revolutionary activities were financed through the Nya Banken in Stockholm, Sweden, headed by the Jew, Olof Aschberg, who had close ties with Max Warburg and Jacob von Furstenberg, both Jewish bankers. A trust account was set up at Nya Banken into which millions of Kuhn, Loeb's dollars were deposited. Nya Banken became known as "the Bolshevik Bank." The Jewish ambassador from America to Sweden, Ira Nelson Morris, served as a virtual conduit between Kuhn Loeb in New York and Nya Banken in Stockholm. Ambassador Morris ostensibly represented American interests in Sweden, but as a Jew, he used his office to serve the interests of International Jewry.

Trotsky and 267 Russian, Yiddish speaking Jews from the Jewish immigrant community in New York City made their way to Petrograd with Schiff's help to join Lenin in the revolution. Numerous other New York Jews were to follow. Trotsky arrived on April 17, the day after Lenin's arrival. Though Trotsky and the other Jews who came with him were not American citizens, they had obtained American passports which facilitated their re-entry into Russia. This was done by the intervention of the Jewish U.S. Supreme Court Justice, Louis Brandeis. Brandeis was very close to President Wilson, and he persuaded Wilson to direct the State Department to issue the passports. After arriving in Petrograd, Lenin and Trotsky joined forces. With the money provided by Jacob Schiff, combined with the money from the German government, Trotsky and Lenin organized an armed Bolshevik uprising. The Provisional Government was overthrown and on November 7, 1917 (October 25, according to the Russian calendar) a Soviet Socialist

Lenin   **Trotsky**

Republic was established. Trotsky soon took control of the Russian army and set about to reorganize it into the "Red Army of the Proletariat." One of his first acts was to set up "soviets" (counsels) of soldiers for every detachment, battalion, regiment, and division in the army. The old Czarist officers were then purged out of the army. Eventually these "soviets" took the places of all the commanding officers and their staffs. This turned out to be unworkable and had a demoralizing effect on the army. To make matters worse, inexperienced Jewish officers filled the important vacancies left by the purged Czarist officers. Chaos reigned. This new Red Army was no match for the German Army and was unable to resist the German offensive of February, 1918, which finally took Russia out of the war.

Trotsky and the Red Army

To correct the problems he had created, Trotsky formed a military council of former Russian generals that would function as an advisory body. He was eventually forced to bring former Czarist officers back into the army, but this was fiercely resented by the new Bolshevik leaders of the army. They believed that the Red Army should consist only of dedicated revolutionaries. They viewed the former imperial officers and generals as potential traitors who should be kept out of the new military, much less put in charge of it. Trotsky solved this problem by creating a corps of "Political Commissars," one of which would be attached to each and every unit in the Red Army and who then reported directly to Trotsky. The Commissars were to be supreme in all matters, even superior to the commanding officers, but their main job was to keep an eye on the regular army officers and report back on their attitudes, utterances and activities to Trotsky himself. The Commissars set up a spy network which made it impossible for anyone to oppose Trotsky. Trotsky saw to it that any individual or group even suspected of disloyalty was ruthlessly exterminated. Nearly all of the Commissars were Jews. Of the few who were not, almost none were ethnic Russians. It was by this method that Trotsky and his fellow Jews gained complete control of every branch of the Army and Navy.

The Bolsheviks' hold on Russia was still tenuous at this point and opposition rose against them from every quarter. Civil war broke out when the "White Army," composed of Cossacks and former Czarist officers, rose up against the Bolsheviks and the new "Red Army" under Trotsky and his Jews. The White army was Christian and virulently anti-Semitic. Their slogan was "Strike the Jews and save Russia." Young Jewish men from all over Russia, as well as from surrounding countries, rushed into the ranks of the Red army, many of whom could not even speak Russian. Several hundred Jews even came from the United States to join the new Red Army, most from the lower east side of New York City.

The Christian "White Army" lost the civil war to the Jewish controlled "Red Army" for one reason and one reason only. Jewish Financiers controlled the money supply in Europe and the United States, as well as in much of the rest of the world, and they provided the Red Army with unlimited funding as well as unlimited supplies of arms and ammunition, while at the same time refusing funding to the White Army. They also used their influence to block funding to the White Army from any other sources.

Anthony C. Sutton wrote in his book, "Wall Street and the Bolshevik Revolution," New Rochelle, 1974: *"A number of very wealthy Jews in Wall Street firms contributed to the Communist regime during its early years when it was already soaked with the blood of innocent people who were being killed, exiled and expropriated simply because of their former class status. The largely Jewish government was taking a terrible vengeance against those who had prospered in the days of the Czars. The Wall Street capitalists were aiding the mostly Jewish rulers of Russia in a government dedicated to the overthrow of capitalism is vivid proof of the solidarity of a race with a long record of being perpetual aliens, no matter in what land they happened to be residing. Blood is thicker than water."*

Jews comprised less than 2 percent of the Russian population, yet they now had total control of every branch of the government as well as the armed forces.

Jews in the Government of Bolshevik Russia

According to British newspaperman Robert Wilton, in his book, "The Last Days of the Romanovs," 1920, the Bolshevik government in Russia was totally dominated by Jews. Wilton had been The Times of London's man-in-Moscow from 1902 through 1919 and was in position to witness everything that happened in the revolution and who was behind it, and he regularly reported back on it. Wilton was in Russia during her shocking defeat in the Russo-Japanese War of 1904-05, through all the stresses and strains of internal Russian politics, the violent Potemkin and Bloody Sunday events of 1905, and the ominous revolutionary activities, from exile, of Lenin and Trotsky. He was there through the Great War of 1914-1918 (WWI) and witnessed the chaotic conditions that followed. He witnessed and reported on the Russian Revolution. He knew the facts as few others did. He knew and reported the fact that it was the Jews who were behind the revolution and the Jews who had taken over the Russian state.

In 1919, the Soviet Press provided a list of 556 important figures of the Soviet Government, identifying their ethnicity. Wilton obtained this list and reported it back to London. He also included it as an "appendix' in his book, "The Last Days of the Romanovs," 1920, of which this author has a copy. The list included 17 Russians, 2 Ukrainians, 11 Armenians, 35 Letts, 15 Germans, 1 Hungarian, 10 Georgians, 3 Poles, 3 Finns, 1 Czech, 1 Karaim (Jewish sect) and **457 Jews.** This list is provided below, so there can be no refuting the fact that Jews dominated the Communist government of the Soviet Union.

Central Committee

62 Members	42 Jews	20 Gentiles

Name	Nationality
Sverdlov (president)	Jew
Avanessof (secretary)	Armenian
Bruno	Lett (Latvian)
Babtchinski	Jew
Bukharin	Russian
Gailiss	Jew
Ganzburg	Jew
Danichevski	Jew
Starck	German
Scheinmann	Jew
Erdling	Jew
Landauer	Jew
Linder	Czech (Probably Jew)
Dimanstein	Jew
Encukidze	Georgian
Ermann	Jew
Joffe	Jew
Karkline	Jew
Knigissen	Jew
Rosenfeldt (Kamenef)	Jew
Apfelbaum (Zinovief)	Jew
Krylenko	Russian
KrassikofSachs	Jew
Kaprik	Jew
Kaoul	Lett
Ulyanov (Lenin)	Russian (part Jew)
Latisis	Jew
Lander	Jew
Lounstcharski	Russian
Peterson	Lett

Peters	Lett
Roudzoutas	Jew
Rosine	Jew
Smidovitch	Jew
Stoutchka	Lett
Nakhamkes (Steklof)	Jew
Sosnovski	Jew
Skrytnik	Jew
Bronstein (Trotskyu)	Jew
Teodorovitch	Jew
Terian	Armenian
Ouritski	Jew
Telechkine	Russian
Feldmann	Jew
Froumkine	Jew
Souriupa	Ukranian
Tchavtchevadze	Georgian
Scheikmann	Jew
Rosental	Jew
Achkinazi	Imeretian (Jew)
Karakhane	Karaim (Jew)
Rose	Jew
Sobelson (Radek)	Jew
Schlichter	Jew
Schikolini	Jew
Chklianski	Jew
Levine (Prafdine)	Jew

Extraordinary Commission of Moscow

36 Members	24 Jews	12 Gentiles

Name	Nationality
Dzerjinski (president)	Pole (Jew)
Peters (vice-president)	Lett

Chklovski	Jew
Kheifiss	Jew
Zeistine	Jew
Razmirovitch	Jew
Kronberg	Jew
Khaikina	Jewess
Karlson	Lett
Schaumann	Jew
Leontovitch	Jew
Jacob Goldine	Jew
Glaperstein	Jew
Kniggisen	Jew
Latzis	Lett
Schillenkuss	Jew
Janson	Lett
Rivkine	Jew
Antonof	Russian
Delafabre	Jew
Tsitkine	Jew
Roskirovitch	Jew
G. Sverdlof	Jew
Beisenski	Jew
Blioumkine	Jew
Alexandrevitch	Russian
I. Model	Jew
Routenberg	Jew
Pines	Jew
Sachs	Jew
Daybol	Lett
Saissoune	Armenian
Daylkenen	Lett
Liebert	Jew
Bogel	German
Zakiss	Lett

The Council of the Peoples Commissars

22 Members	17 Jews	5 Gentiles
Ministry	Name	Nationality
President	Ulyanov (Lenin)	Russian (part Jew)
Foreign Affairs	Tchitcherine	Russian
Nationalities	Djugashvili (Stalin)	Georgian
Agriculture	Protian	Armenian
Economic Council	Lourie (Larine)	Jew
Food	Schlichter	Jew
Army & Navy	Bronstein (Trotsky)	Jew
State Control	Lander	Jew
State Lands	Kauffman	Jew
Works	V. Schmidt	Jew
Social Relief	E. Lelina (Knigissen)	Jewess
Public Instructions	Lounatcharsky	Russian
Religions	Spitzberg	Jew
Interior	Apfelbaum (Zinovief)	Jew
Hygiene	Anvelt	Jew
Finance	Isidore Goukovski	Jew
Press	Voldarski	Jew
Elections	Ouritski	Jew
Justice	I. Steinberg	Jew
Refugees	Fenigstein	Jew
Refugees (assist.)	Savitch	Jew
Refugees (assist.)	Zaslovski	Jew

Central Committee of the Bolshevik Party

12 Members	10 Jews	2 Gentiles

Name	Nationality
Bronstein (Trotsky)	Jew
Apfelbaum (Zinovief)	Jew

Lourie (larine)	Jew
Ouritski	Jew
Voldarski	Jew
Rosenfeldt (Kamanef)	Jew
Smidovitch	Jew
Sverdlof (Yankel)	Jew
Nakhamkes (Steklof)	Jew
Ulyanov (Lenin)	Russian (part Jew)
Krylenko	Russian
Lounatcharski	Russian

Central Committees

Mensheviks	11 members, all Jews
Communists of the People	6 members, 5 Jews
Socialist Rev. Party (Right Wing)	15 members, 13 Jews
Socialist Rev. Party (Left Wing)	12 members, 10 Jews
Committee of the Anarchists	5 members, 4 Jews
Polish Communist Party	12 members, all Jews

Ministry of the Commissariat

22 Members	17 Jews	5 Gentiles

Central Executive Committee

61 Members	41 Jews	20 Gentiles

It has often been noted that Jews are the only ethnic group who routinely change their names. One of their methods of gaining power and control is to insinuate themselves into high office "insidiously," while concealing the fact that they are Jewish. Adopting a Russian name in Russia or an English name in America is done for that purpose. That accounts for the adoption of different names by so many of the Jewish Bolsheviks involved in the Russian revolution.

According to Albert Lindemann, in his book "Esau's Tears, Modern Anti-Semitism and the Rise of the Jews," 1997, several of the leading non-Jews in the Bolshevik movement, including Lenin, might be termed

"Jewified non-Jews." For example, he writes, *"Lenin openly and repeatedly praised the role of Jews in the revolutionary movement."* He was married to a Jew, spoke Yiddish and his children spoke Yiddish. Lenin once said, *"An intelligent Russian is almost always a Jew or someone with Jewish blood in their veins."* Even if he was only one fourth Jew, Lenin lived as a Jew and surrounded himself with Jews.

A British Government White Paper, of April, 1919 stated: *"It was an open secret that the overthrow of the Russian Government and the seizure of power with incalculable consequences for the rest of the world was largely organized by international Jewish revolutionaries. The world's greatest land mass was being hi-jacked."*

Mr. M. Oudendyke, the Representative of the Netherlands Government in St. Petersburg, who was in charge of British interests after the liquidation of the British Embassy by the Bolsheviks, sent in a report to Foreign Secretary Sir Arthur Balfour.

"I consider that the immediate suppression of Bolshevism is the greatest issue now before the world, not even excluding the war which is still raging, and unless Bolshevism is nipped in the bud immediately it is bound to spread in one form or another over Europe, and the whole world, as it is organized and worked by Jews, who have no nationality, and whose one object is to destroy for their own ends the existing order of things."

Winston Churchill agreed with this view, in an article he wrote for the "Illustrated Sunday Herald," Feb. 8, 1920: *"It may well be that this same astounding race (Jews) may at the present time be in the actual process of providing another system of morals and philosophy, as malevolent as Christianity was benevolent, which if not arrested, would shatter irretrievably all that Christianity has rendered possible. This movement among the Jews is not new. It has been the mainspring of every subversive movement during the nineteenth century; and now at last this band of extraordinary personalities from the underworld of the great cities of Europe and America have gripped the Russian people by the hair of their heads and have become practically the undisputed masters of that enormous empire."*

Hilaire Belloc wrote in the "British G.K. Weekly," on February 4, 1937: *"As for anyone who does not know that the present revolutionary movement is Jewish in Russia, I can only say that he must be a man who is taken in by the suppression of our despicable Press.*"

Even the Jews did not deny it. An article in the "Jewish Chronicle" on April 4, 1919 stated: "*The conceptions of Bolshevism are in harmony in most points with the ideas of Judaism.*"

In his book, "The Jewish Century," Yuri Sliezkine describes the astonishing rise of Jews to elite status in all areas of Soviet society after the revolution -- in culture, the universities, professional occupations, the media, and government. Sliezkine, a Russian Jew himself, immigrated to America in 1983 and became a professor at U.C. Berkeley. "*After the revolution,*" he wrote, "*millions of Jews left the shtetl towns of Russia to move to Moscow and other Russian cities, to take up elite positions in the new Soviet state.*"

Claire Sheridan, the notorious cousin of Winston Churchill, and a well known sculptress, and friend of Leon Trotsky, travelled to Russia in the autumn of 1920 to create sculptures of prominent Bolsheviks, including Lenin, Trotsky, Dzerzhinsky and Kamenev. She said, "*The Communists are Jews, and Russia is being entirely administered by them. They are in every government office. They are driving out the Russians.*"

The Jewish Chronicle of January 6, 1933 stated: "*Over one-third of Jews in Russia have become officials.*"

M. Cohen wrote, in "The Communist," April 12, 1919: "*The great Russian revolution was indeed accomplished by the hands of the Jews. There are no Jews in the ranks of the Red Army as far as privates are concerned, but in the Committees, and in the Soviet organizations' Commissars, the Jews are gallantly leading the masses. The symbol of Jewry has become the symbol of the Russian proletariat, which can be seen in the fact of the adoption of the five-pointed star, which in former times was the symbol of Zionism and Jewry.*"

Adriana Tyrkova-Williams, in her book, "From Liberty to Brest-Litovsk," McMillan, 1919, wrote: "*There are few Russians among the Bolshevist wire-pullers, i.e. few men imbued with the all-Russian culture and interests of the Russian people. None of them have been in any way prominent in any stage of former Russian life...Besides obvious foreigners, Bolshevism recruited many adherents from among émigrés who had spent many years abroad. Some of them had never been to Russia before. They especially numbered a great many Jews. They spoke Russian badly. The nation over which they had seized power was a stranger to them, and besides, they behaved as invaders in a conquered country. Throughout the revolution generally and Bolshevism in particular, the Jews occupied a very influential position. This phenomenon is both curious and complex."*

An article in a widely known French journal, "L'Illustration," of September 14, 1918, carried this comment: *"When one lives in constant contact with the functionaries who are serving the Bolshevik Government, one feature strikes the attention, which is that almost all of them are Jews. I am not at all anti-Semitic; but I must state what strikes the eye: everywhere in Petrograd, in Moscow, in provincial districts, in commissariats, in district offices, in Smolny, in the Soviets, I have met nothing but Jews and again Jews."*

And this, in a speech by Adolf Hitler, September, 1937: *"In 1936 we proved by means of a whole series of astounding statistics that in Russia today more than 98% of the leading positions are occupied by Jews... Who were the leaders in our Bavarian Workers Republic? Who were the leaders of the Spartacist Movement? Who were the real leaders and financiers of the Communist Party? Jews, every one of them. The position was the same in Hungary and in the Red parts of Spain."*

And Churchill, again, in an article he wrote for the "Illustrated Sunday Herald," in London, on February 8, 1920: *"There is no need to exaggerate the part played in the creation of Bolshevism and in the actual bringing about of the Russian Revolution by these international, and for the most part, atheistical, Jews. It is certainly a very great one, it probably outweighs all others. With the notable exception of Lenin [Lenin was 1/4 Jew, spoke Yiddish and had a Jewish wife], the majority of the leading figures are Jews. Moreover, the principal inspiration and driving power comes from the Jewish leaders... In the Soviet institutions the predominance of Jews is even more astounding. And the principal part in the system of terrorism applied by the extraordinary Commissions for combating Counter-Revolution (Cheka) has been taken by Jews..."*

Proof of the Jewish nature of the Russian Revolution and of the preponderance of Jews in the Bolshevik government, as well as their role in the Communist revolutions which swept Europe afterwards, is irrefutable. Nevertheless, one will not find this information in modern text books in either American or European universities. No scholar may state these facts or write them in a book if he hopes to have his book published and promoted in the mainstream publishing industry, or if he hopes to have a career as a scholar. No politician dares utter these facts if he hopes to remain a politician. The only permissible story is that the Jews are now and always have been Western Christian Civilization's blameless victims. To say otherwise makes one an anti-Semite, worthy only to be cast out of civilized society. This is the nature of Jewish power.

Chapter 5

The Red Terror

The Jewish controlled media uses the word "Holocaust" (with a capital H) today in reference to what purportedly happened to Jews at the hands of Nazi Germany during World War II. But the real holocaust of the twentieth century was that which the Jews inflicted upon the Russian people during and after the Russian Revolution of 1917. This was one of the bloodiest episodes in history during which vast millions of Russian Christians were murdered. The aim of the new Jewish overlords was to completely eliminate the upper classes, or the possessing classes, collectively known as the bourgeoisie, including men, women and children. The most intelligent, most able, most high achieving segment of the population was wiped out, leaving a population of ignorant workers and peasants. Even the Czar and his family were murdered by the Jews. In order to bring about their new Marxist Utopia, the old Russian culture would have to be completely deracinated and replaced by the new Marxist culture. By the time the Bolshevik Jews completed the extermination of these classes, the "old" Russia portrayed in the novels of Tolstoy, Pushkin, Dostoyevsky, Chekov and Gorky simply did not exist anymore.

After gaining control of the state, the Jews began to extend their control to every corner of the Russian government and of Russian society. In order to overcome opposition and to subdue the Russian population, a secret police organization was established in December, 1917, called the "Extraordinary Commission for Combating Counter-Revolution and Sabotage," known by its acronym, "Cheka." At this time, a half dozen other political parties were in existence, in addition to the Bolshevik party, all of which were also controlled by Jews. One of them was the Socialist Revolutionary Party, or the Left S.R. party. When the Left S.R. party revolted against the Bolsheviks, the Cheka rounded 350 of them up and summarily shot them. Ironically, most of the members of the S.R. party were also Jews.

On August 17, 1918 a young military cadet assassinated the Jewish head of the Petrograd Cheka, Moisei Uritsky, in retaliation for the execution of his friend and fellow cadet. Soon afterwards, on August 28, 1918, the Jewess, Fanya Kaplan, a member of the Left S.R. Party, incensed over the execution of her fellow party members by the Cheka, nearly succeeded in assassinating Lenin. In reaction to these two events, the Bolsheviks began a bloody wave of persecutions which became known as the "Red Terror."

The Red Terror was set in motion within hours of the attempted assassination of Lenin by the Jewish Chairman of the Central Executive Committee, Yakov Sverdlov, in an official decree. The decree called for *"a merciless mass terror against all the enemies of the revolution."* All political parties were banned, and some 800 members of the Soviet Socialist Parties, both the Left S.R. and the Right S.R., were rounded up and shot. In addition, 6,300 other political enemies were also reported to have been shot within the first year, though this number is almost certainly greatly understated.

(Left - <u>Yakov Sverdlov</u>, the Jewish Chairman of the Central Executive Committee, initiated the "Red Terror." He also ordered the murder of the Czar and his family.)

An unrestrained orgy of rape, torture, summary executions and murder all over Russia on an unheard of scale then ensued, carried out by the Cheka. Whole populations were liquidated, including independent farmers known as Kulaks, ethnic minorities, the aristocracy, the bourgeoisie, the landed gentry, senior military officers, intellectuals, artists, clergy, opposition members and anyone who aroused the slightest suspicion. Bolshevik leaders openly proclaimed that the Red Terror was necessary for the extermination of entire social groups, especially the former "ruling classes," in order to make way for the "Dictatorship of the Proletariat." The Jew, Martin Latsis, chief of the Ukrainian Cheka, explained in the newspaper, "Red Terror": *"We are engaged in exterminating the bourgeoisie as a class. Do not look in the file of incriminating evidence to see whether or not the accused rose up against the Soviets with arms or words. Ask him instead to which class he belongs, what is his background, his education, his profession. These are the questions that will determine the fate of the accused. That is the meaning and essence of the Red Terror."*

The Cheka grew rapidly and became a very large, very cruel state security organization. It's organizational structure was changed several times over the following years, as was its name, from Cheka to GPU, to NKVD, and finally to KGB, but its mission remained essentially the same. Cheka offices were set up in every city and town. By 1921 a single branch of the Cheka called, "The troops for the internal Defense of the Republic," numbering 200,000, was given the responsibility of policing and actually running the massive Gulag system of labor camps.

There is no way to know the precise number of deaths the Cheka was responsible for, but it surely ran into the scores of millions. This would include victims of forced collectivization, the forced famine, of which more later, large purges, expulsions, banishments, executions, and mass death in the Gulag.

Harvard historian Richard Pipes (himself a Jew), in his book "The Russian Revolution" (1990), verifies that *"three quarters of the staff [of the Cheka] were Jews, many of them riff raff, incapable of any other work, cut off from the Jewish community, although careful to spare fellow Jews."*

Russian poet and writer, Vladimir Soloukhin, in "Bloodlust of Bolshevism" wrote that fifty percent of the Cheka were Jews with Jewish names, while twenty five percent were Jews who had taken Russian names. The remaining twenty five percent was made up of Letts (Latvians), Poles, Georgians, and other minorities, but very few members of the Cheka were ethnic Russians. Moreover, of the non-Jewish members,

(Left - Cheka head, Felix Dzerzhinski)

a significant number of them had Jewish wives. Conclusion? The Cheka was a Jewish organization, formed as the enforcement branch of the now Jewish controlled state. These Cheka members had no compunctions about killing Russians, as they were not ethnic Russians themselves. In fact, they harbored a deep, burning hatred for the Russians and eagerly looked forward to the opportunity for revenge.

Every single one of those in supervisory positions in the Cheka were Jews. The first head of the Cheka was Moses Uritsky, a Jew, who was soon assassinated. His successor was a Polish Communist revolutionary from a noble family named Felix Dzerzhinski. Dzerzhinski was a non-practicing Roman Catholic, but was what has been called a "Jewified non-Jew." Some sources say he was half Jew. He spoke Yiddish and his family spoke Yiddish, so he may well have been. Dzerzhinski's second in command was the Jew, I.S. Unschlicht. The torture branch of the Cheka was controlled over the years by Genrik Yagoda and Yuri Andropov, both Jews, and finally by Lavrenti Beria who was also not Russian, but Georgian, as was his boss Stalin.

About the Cheka, Felix Dzerzhinski was quoted as saying, *"The Cheka is not a court. We stand for organized terror. The Cheka is obligated to defend the revolution and conquer the enemy even if it's sword by chance sometimes falls upon the heads of the innocent."*

Creation of the Gulag

Matvei Berman and Natalfy Frenkel, both Jews and both members of the Cheka, created the infamous Gulag, which was the largest concentration camp system and the most horrendous slave labor system in history in which millions of Russian Christians were slaughtered. The Nazi system of concentration camps and slave labor camps which came later was miniscule by comparison, yet, the term "concentration camp" is universally associated, not with Communist Russia under the Jews,

Yuri Andropov   **Genrik Yagoda**   **Lavrenti Beria**

These three men in succession ran the torture branch of the Cheka over the years, and were responsible for the deaths of millions of Russians. Yagoda and Andropov were Jewish. Beria was a Georgian, as Stalin was, and one of the few top Cheka leaders who was not a Jew. Beria later became head of the NKVD.

but with Nazi Germany. Everybody knows about Auschwitz today, but who has ever heard of Kolyma, Magadan, the Solovetsky Islands, or the great centers of massive death in Siberia? Only those who have read the works of Alexander Solzhenitsyn. There is no mention of them in the mainstream media. Yet, exponentially more people died in those camps than died at Auschwitz, or all of the Nazi camps combined. Alexander Solzhenitsyn said that all the camps were commanded by Jews with names like, Rappoport, Soltz, and Spiegelglas.

But international Jewry has gone to great lengths to make sure that this kind of information does not become common knowledge. When Solzhenitsyn's books, the "Gulag Archipelago," and "One Day in the Life of Ivan Denisovich," among others, were published back during the Cold War, Solzhenitsyn not only received the Nobel Prize, but also world acclaim for exposing the brutality and inhumanity of the Soviet system, though the Jewish role in it was never emphasized. All of his books were published in several languages, including English, and were highly promoted both in Britain and the United States.

Not so, his latest book, "Two Hundred Years Together," first published in Russia in 2003, which is about the 200 years the Jews lived in Russia amongst the Russian people. In this book, Solzhenitsyn exposes the Jewish nature of the Russian Revolution and identifies the Jews as the perpetrators of the mass murder of scores of millions of Russian Christians during the revolution and afterwards. This book, unlike all his others, has yet to be published in English, and no interest has yet been shown by any publishing house in doing so. Jews control the publishing industry in the English speaking world and they have no intention of publishing this book in English. Moreover, they have exerted extreme pressure to prevent non-Jewish publishers from doing so. This kind of information is taboo today and its suppression is strictly enforced. Nevertheless, facts are facts, and sooner or later, someone will translate this book into English. Some parts of it have already been translated into English and posted on the Internet.

Bolsheviks kill the Czar

On July 17, 1918, the Czar and his family were murdered by a group of Jewish Bolsheviks. After the Czar's abdication, the Bolsheviks took him and his family to the Ural Mountain town of Ekaterinburg where they remained for several months as political prisoners, living in a house under guard by the Cheka. The Czar, his wife Alexandra, their 14 year old son Alexis, their four daughters, their doctor, their cook and two other attendants were finally taken to the cellar of the house and shot. The bodies were then wrapped in sheets and dumped into a remote mine shaft. They were later retrieved when word got out about their murders.

Czar Nicholas II and his family

**Yakov Sverdlov (real name Yankle Solomon) (L), Jewish
Chairman of the Central Executive Committee, ordered
the execution of the Czar and his family. Yakov Yurowsky
(real name Yankle) (R) Jewish head of the Cheka squad
which carried out the murders. All involved were Jews.**

The Czar's face was smashed in an effort to make it unrecognizable.
They tried burning the bodies but that took too long. They then
doused the bodies with sulfuric acid and buried them in a shallow
grave in a forest outside the city. The murderers were Yakov (Yankel)
Yurowsky, Alexander Belobarodov and Filip Goloschtschokin, all Jews.
The execution of the Czar and his family was ordered by the Jewish
Chairman of the Soviet Central Executive, Yakov Sverdlov (real name
Yankel Solomon). The Jews had finally achieved their aim. They brought
down the Czarist regime with their revolution, and now they had killed
the hated Czar, himself.

As discussed previously, long lists of groups were designated for
slaughter. Hundreds of thousands of Cossacks were rounded up and
killed. The order was to kill every single one of them, and those who

A group of Cheka agents standing by an armored car in St. Petersburg. Note the all-leather garb. The unofficial uniform of Cheka agents was all leather -- boots, pants, jackets, gloves and hats -- causing them, according to one observer, to resemble a fetish club. The style was called "glisten and squeak." Almost all were Jews; most nothing more than brutish thugs recruited from the shtetls, who enjoyed nothing more than torturing and killing Christian Russians.

Two typical Cheka agents, armed to the teeth.

Two more typical Cheka agents, these with obvious Jewish faces.

escaped initial roundups were tracked down and killed like animals. The same for the aristocracy. 200,000 members of the clergy -- priests, monks and nuns -- were systematically murdered in a horrific orgy of "bestial tortures." They were reportedly scalped, strangled, drowned, crucified, and subjected to any other horrific death their murderers could dream up. Czarist officers were forced aboard sealed barges by the hundreds, the barges were then towed out to sea and sunk with all aboard drowning. The Jews now controlled everything and were free to indulge their most cherished revenge fantasies against the hated, though now helpless Russians. Local branches of the Cheka, comprised mainly of Jews, many of the lowest kind, and many of them violent, sadistic psychopaths, had total autonomy and were not required to report to anyone in carrying out this nightmare of torture and slaughter. Any Cheka member was completely free, without fear of censure or punishment, to kill, rape or torture anyone he chose (outside the government, that is), and he could do it in the most sadistic manner imaginable. They not only were not required to justify it, they were encouraged by the highest leaders, including Lenin himself, to show no mercy and to kill as many as possible. The Cheka was an incredibly brutal organization, with standing orders to execute at will.

What distinguished killings by the Cheka, according to one observer, was that they were "rage-fueled." The Cheka agents didn't just kill "class enemies," they went at them in orgiastic frenzies, beating, stabbing, chopping and mutilated them -- including men, women and children. An article in "Defender Magazine," of October, 1933 describes their orgy of killing:

"Christians were dragged from their beds, tortured and killed. Some were sliced to pieces, bit by bit, while others were branded with hot irons, their eyes poked out to induce unbearable pain. Others were placed in boxes with only their heads, hands and legs sticking out. Then hungry rats were placed in the boxes to gnaw upon their bodies. Some were nailed to the ceiling by their hands or by their feet and left hanging until they died of exhaustion... Others had hot lead poured in their mouths. Many were tied to horses and dragged through the streets of the city, while Jewish mobs attacked them with rocks and kicked them to death... Pregnant women were chained to trees and their babies cut out of their bodies."

During the second half of 1919, the Red Army was driven out of the Ukraine by the White Army. A number of investigations of the mass murders were then carried out by special commissions under the White Army's occupation, one of which was the "Rohrbach Commission of Enquiry." There were numerous places of public execution during the Red Army occupation. After the city of Kiev was taken by the White Army in August, 1919, Paul Rohrbach was sent by the British government to conduct an investigation. When the members of the Rohrbach Commission entered the execution hall of the Cheka of Kiev, they found:

"The whole cement floor was flooded with blood; it formed a level of several inches and had stopped flowing [coagulated]. It was a horrible mixture of blood, brains and pieces of skull with tufts of hair and other human remains. All of the walls were riddled with thousands of bullets and bespattered with blood. Pieces of brains and of scalps were sticking to them. A gutter of 25 centimeters [10 inches] wide by 25 centimeters deep [10 inches] and about

10 meters [33 ft.] long was along its length full to the top with blood. Some bodies were disemboweled, others had limbs chopped off, some were literally hacked to pieces. Some had their eyes put out, the head, face and neck and trunk were covered with deep wounds. Further on, we found a corpse with a wedge driven into its chest. Some had no tongues. In a corner we discovered a quantity of dismembered arms and legs belonging to no bodies that we could locate."

In his book, "The Secret Powers Behind Revolution," French author Vicomte Leon de Poncins, published in the 1920s, wrote: *"The Red Terror became so wide-spread that it is impossible to give here all the details of the principal means employed by the Cheka to master resistance; one of the most important is that of hostages, taken among all social classes. These are held responsible for any anti-Bolshevist movements (revolts, the White Army, strikes, refusal of a village to give its harvest, etc.) and are immediately executed. Thus, for the assassination of the Jew Ouritzky, member of the Extraordinary Commission of Petrograd, several thousands of them were put to death, and many of these unfortunate men and women suffered before death various tortures inflicted by cold-blooded cruelty in the prisons of the Cheka."*

In his book, "The Blood-Lust of Bolshevism," Vladimir Soloukhin wrote that these Jewish Chekists *"were especially interested in handsome boys and pretty girls. These were the first to be killed. It was believed that there would be more intellectuals among attractive people."* He wrote that, *"The Semites, jealous of white beauty, massacred beautiful whites...The Jewish Chekists favored murder with various torture methods."*

In his documentary film, "The Russia We Lost," director Stanislav Govorukhin related how the priesthood in Kherson were crucified. The archbishop Andronnikov of Perm was tortured: *"his eyes were poked out, his ears and nose were cut off. In Kharkov the priest Dmitri was undressed. When he tried to make the sign of the cross, a Chekist cut off his right hand."*

"Several sources," Govorukhin said, *"tell how the Chekists in Kharkov placed victims in a row and nailed their hands to a table, cut around their wrists with a knife, pored boiling water over their hands and pulled the skin off. This was called pulling off the glove."* In other places, the victim's head

was placed on an anvil and slowly crushed with a steam hammer. Those due to undergo the same punishment the next day were forced to watch."

"The eyes of church dignitaries were poked out, their tongues were cut off and they were buried alive. There were Chekists who used to cut open the stomachs of their victims, following which they pulled out a length of the small intestine and nailed it to a telegraph pole and, with a whip, forced the unlucky victim to run around the pole until the whole intestine had been unraveled and the victim died. The bishop of Voronezh was boiled alive in a big pot, after which the monks, with revolvers aimed at their heads, were forced to drink the soup."

"Other Chekists crushed the heads of their victims with special head screws, or drilled them through with dental tools. The upper part of the skull was sawn off and the nearest in line was forced to eat the brains, following which the procedure would be repeated to the end of the line. The Chekists often arrested whole families and tortured the children before the eyes of their parents, and the wives before their husbands."

Mikhail Voslensky, a former Soviet functionary, described some of the cruel methods used by Chekists in his book, "Nomenclature" (Nomenklatura), Stockholm, 1982: *"In Kharkov, people were scalped. In Voronezh, the torture victims were placed in barrels into which nails were hammered so that they stuck out on the inside, upon which the barrels were set rolling. A pentacle (usually a five-pointed star formerly used in magic) was burned into the foreheads of the victims. In Tsaritsyn and Kamyshin, the hands of victims were amputated with a saw. In Poltava and Kremenchug, the victims were impaled. In Odessa, they were roasted alive... or ripped to pieces. In Kiev, the victims were placed in coffins with a decomposing body and buried alive, only to be dug up again after half an hour."*

These Chekist Jews took sadistic pleasure in torturing the hated Russians who were now helplessly under their control. Their methods of torture were limited only by their depraved imaginations.

******

The land owners and estate owners were one of the first targeted classes to be eliminated. In town after town, convoys of Chekist trucks left for the countryside as night began to fall, stopping at one estate or land owner's house after another to collect every member of each family – men, women, children and infants, including the servants. Any who resisted or tried to run away were shot. In those days of no telephones, there was no way to give forewarning to these families, so they were caught completely by surprise. They were brutally beaten with rifle butts and truncheons as they were herded onto the trucks, many of them injured and bleeding. These large trucks, a dozen or more at a time, then returned completely filled with their traumatized victims who had no idea what was in store for them. They were, in fact, being taken to clearings in the forest outside of town where bulldozers had already dug their mass graves. These frightened civilians, who were guilty of nothing except of being members of a condemned class, were forced to line up in front of the pits where they were machine gunned, after which the bulldozers covered them up. The following night, and every night thereafter, the trucks went out again, until all were captured and killed. Only those landowners lucky enough to make it out of the country escaped this fate. These victims were the people who had filled the pages as characters in stories by Pushkin, Tolstoy and Chekov and who embodied the culture of old Russia. Now they were being systematically wiped out by the alien Jews who had seized control of the country.

In 1926, a Russian émigré known as "Dr. Gregor" published a 12,000 word pamphlet in Munich, Germany in which he provided statistics on the numbers killed by the Cheka during the Red Terror. These statistics, he said, came from the Cheka's own published statistics. According to Dr. Gregor, by 1921 the Cheka reported that they had killed: 28 bishops, 1,215 priests and 6,000 monks. The Russian Orthodox Church was one of the first targets for destruction by the Jewish Bolsheviks. Next to be killed were all those Russian classes who had any kind of education or any kind of leadership role within the old Russian society. Of these groups and classes who were rounded up and killed, there were: 8,800 Russian doctors and medical assistants, 54,650 army and navy officers, 10,500 police officers (lieutenant and above), 48,500 lower ranking policemen, and 260,000 ordinary soldiers. 361,825 members of the "intelligentsia," including teachers, professors, engineers, building contractors, writers and judges were killed, and 12,950 large landowners were killed. In these cases of mass murder, there were no explanations or reasons given for their murder. The simple fact that they belonged to one of the above classes was the one and only reason.

The tragedy of all this cannot be measured by numbers alone; these people were the best people that Russia had. They were the leader class. They were the priests, and lawyers, and merchants, and army officers, and university professors. They were the cream of Russian civilization.

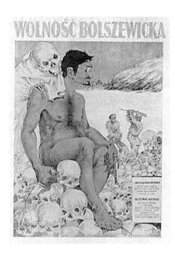

A poster of Leon Trotsky as director of the Red Terror.

The total effect was much the same as it would be in any country. With its small middle and upper class exterminated, Russia's peasant and worker population accepted Jewish Bolshevism without protest. The Russian masses, deprived of its spokesmen and leaders were simply incapable of counter-revolution. That was what the Red Terror had set out to accomplish.

After these elite groups were disposed of, the Cheka turned its attention to the workers and peasants, killing 192,350 workers and 815,000 peasants, according to their own records. These killings occurred between the years 1917 and 1921, and were only those "reported" killed by the Cheka, according to Dr. Gregor. Certainly there were vast numbers killed by the Cheka and not reported. Dr. Gegor's statistics are only for the Cheka and do not include the millions who died of disease and starvation, or those killed by forces other than the Cheka. In the years following 1921, such killings were to increase exponentially.

Jews as a Hostile Elite

After killing off the old Russian elite, the Jews simply took their places as the new ruling elite, albeit, without the elegance and grace of the old elite. Beyond the baggy suits, uncouth manners, and malevolent scowls, there was another important difference between the new Jewish ruling elite and the traditional Russian ruling elite. Professor Kevin McDonald of the University of California writes that because the Jews had traditionally been restricted and repressed in Czarist Russia, *"...the Jews had a long standing visceral antipathy, out of past historical grievances, both real and imagined, toward the people and culture they came to administer."*

Vladimir Purishkevich, the leader of Michael the "Archangel Russian People's Union" accused the Jews of *"irreconcilable hatred of Russia and everything Russian."* The Jews disliked Christians because of the traditional antagonistic relationship between Judaism and Christianity in Russia. According to Kevin McDonald, *"...when Jews achieved power in Russia, it was a hostile elite with a deep sense of historic grievance. As a result they became willing executioners of both the people and culture they came to rule..."*

The Jew, Anatoly Vasilyevich Lunacharsky, Lenin's Soviet People's Commissar of Enlightenment, wrote: *"We hate Christianity and Christians. Even the best of them must be regarded as our worst enemies. They preach love of one's neighbor and mercy which is contrary to our principles. Christian love is an obstacle to the development of the revolution. Down with love of one's neighbor. What we need is hatred; only thus shall we conquer the universe."*

Professor McDonald writes: *"After the Revolution...there was active suppression of any remnant of the older order and their descendants. Jews have always shown a tendency to rise because of their natural proclivities, e.g., high intelligence and powerful ethnic networking, but here they also benefited from "antibourgeois" quotas in educational institutions and other forms of discrimination against the middle class and aristocratic elements of the old regime that would have provided more competition with Jews.... The bourgeois elements from the previous regime... would have no future. Thus the mass murder of peasants and nationalists was combined with the systematic exclusion of the previously existing non-Jewish middle class."*

On October 9, 1920 while Trotsky was still head of the Red Army and laying waste to old Russia, an article in the *American Hebrew*, published in New York, stated, *"What Jewish idealism and discontent so powerfully contributed to accomplishing in Russia, the same historic qualities of the Jewish mind and heart are tending to promote in other countries."* In other words, what the Jewish Bolsheviks had done to Russia, they were working assiduously to do to Europe.

Vladimir Lenin said: *"We Bolsheviks are going to bring the Social Revolution as much to America as to Europe. It is coming systematically, step by step. The struggle will be long, cruel and sanguinary (bloody)... What matters the loss of 90% by executions if 10% of Communists remain to carry on the revolution? Bolshevism is not a seminary for young ladies. All children should be present at the executions and rejoice at the death of the enemies of the proletariat."*

The Ukrainian Famine (Holodomar)

In 1929, the Bolsheviks under Stalin announced their first five year plan for rapid industrialization of Russia and collectivization of agriculture throughout the Soviet Union. All the owners of vast estates across Russia had already been killed along with their families during the 1917 revolution, but now the Bolsheviks would turn their attention to gaining control over the millions of independent land owning peasant farmers. Their intent was to eliminate private farms altogether and create giant collective farms in their place. All the peasants were to become employees of the state, working on the collective farms.

The Ukraine was the most productive agricultural region of the Soviet Union, and was known as the "breadbasket of Europe." Ukraine's prosperous, self-reliant peasant farmers were accustomed to a high degree of independence, and had long harbored sentiments of Ukrainian nationalism. After the fall of the Czar, there was widespread support for revival of the Ukrainian culture and of the Ukrainian language, which was similar to Russian, but not the same. The aim of the Ukrainian people, most of whom were peasant farmers, was, if not outright independence, then a high degree of autonomy within the Soviet empire.

By this time, Lenin had died, Trotsky was in exile, and Stalin was in control of the Soviet Union. Stalin was not a Jew himself (he was also not a Russian, but a Georgian), but the vast majority of the positions within the Communist bureaucracy were filled by Jews, and most of those who surrounded Stalin were Jewish, including his main associate, Lazar Kaganovitch. Stalin and Kaganovitch were determined to crush this Ukrainian independence movement and collectivize Ukrainian agriculture with as much speed as possible. What Stalin and Kaganovitch intended was the complete destruction of the traditional way of life in the Soviet Union, particularly in the Ukraine, and replace it with Marxist collectivism.

The collectivization process was enormously disruptive for everyone, and extremely unpopular. Though the collectivization process proceeded more or less on schedule in Russia, the Ukrainians resisted it, to the point that the entire collectivization process in the Ukraine was brought to a standstill. The Ukrainian peasants refused to cooperate and even slaughtered their farm animals rather than hand them over to the state. Stalin and Kaganovitch would not stand for this. In 1932 they unleashed a terror campaign against the Ukrainians, the brutality of which was unprecedented. 25,000 fanatical young party militants were sent in to force the 10 million Ukrainian peasants onto the collective farms. When these 25,000 young militants proved insufficient for the job, a large Cheka force was ordered in to begin mass executions in order to intimidate the population. The resistance continued unabated, so an orgy of indiscriminate mass killing ensued. Quotas were even set for the numbers to be killed. When the Chekists failed to meet weekly execution quotas, Stalin

The Bolshevik Jew, Lazar Kaganovitch, headed up the project to starve the Ukrainians into submission to collectivization. 9 million Ukrainians starved to death in Kaganovitch's manufactured famine of 1932-33

sent in Lazar Kaganovitch, his Jewish assistant, along with a cadre of other Jews, to take charge of the situation. The

Jew Yakovlev-Epshtein was put in charge specifically of collectivization.

Kaganovitch set the shooting quota at 10,000 Ukrainians per week. But there were not enough Chekists to shoot that many people, so Kaganovitch and Stalin decided on a much cheaper and much more efficient method of mass murder -- starvation.

Troops were sent in, and all seed stocks, grain, silage, and farm animals were confiscated from Ukrainian farms. Chekist agents and Red Army troops sealed all roads and rail lines, letting nothing in and nothing out. Anyone trying to leave was shot. Farms were searched and all food and fuel was confiscated. There was nothing left to eat. Anyone caught stealing food, even a handful of grain, was shot. Ukrainians began to die of hunger, cold and sickness in large numbers.

The American journalist Eugene Lyons was sent to Russia in 1928 as chief correspondent for UPI. Arriving as an enthusiastic communist, he was able to experience the Soviet experiment at first hand, and became totally disillusioned by what he saw. He described the famine in his book "Assignment in Utopia" (published in 1937) as follows:

"Hell broke loose in seventy thousand Russian villages. A population as large as all of Switzerland's or Denmark's was stripped clean of all their belongings. They were herded with bayonets at railroad stations, packed indiscriminately into cattle cars and freight cars and dumped weeks later in the lumber regions of the frozen North, the deserts of central Asia, wherever labor was needed, there to live or die."

Lyons, himself Jewish, attributes the responsibility for this crime against humanity directly to Kaganovitch: *"Lazar Kaganovitch it was his mind that invented the Political Departments to lead collectivized agriculture, his iron hand that applied Bolshevik mercilessness."* Stalin merely enforced Kaganovitch's plan.

During the frigid winter of 1932-33, th mass starvation created by Kaganovitch took a drastic toll. Ukrainians ate anything they could find, including their pets, leather boots and belts, tree bark, grass and roots. Cannibalism became common. Parents even ate their children.

The precise number of Ukrainians who died in this deliberate famine, as well as by Cheka shootings, remains unknown, but the KGB's own archives which have recently been opened show that at least 7 million Ukrainians died. Ukrainian historians say it was worse than that, and put the figure at 9 million. Fully 25 percent of the Ukrainian population was wiped out by this deliberate, man-made extermination famine.

Starving Ukrainian peasants leave villages in search of food.

People were lying down and dying on the streets.

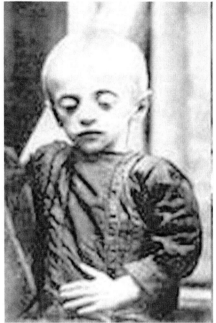
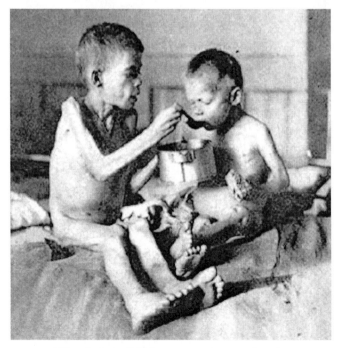

Ukrainian children starving to death.

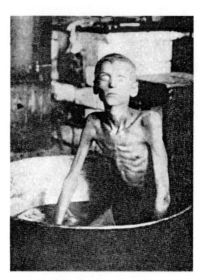

A starvation victim.

On top of this grim number in the Ukraine, millions of other peasant farmers across the rest of the Soviet Union were also starved to death or shot during this collectivization program. Stalin admitted to Churchill at one of their meetings during WWII that he had been forced to liquidate 10 million uncooperative peasants during the 1930s in order to achieve collectivization. When mass executions by the Cheka in Estonia, Latvia, and Lithuania are added in; the genocide of 3 million Muslims of the USSR; massacres of Cossacks and Volga Germans are added, the total comes to at least 40 million Christians murdered by the Bolshevik Jews during the time they controlled Russia.

This orgy of mass murder in Russia was well publicized throughout Germany as well as the rest of Europe while it was happening, and it was also well known that it was done largely by the hand of the Jews. Bolshevism, Communism and Judaism were correctly conflated in the German mind to mean one and the same thing. It is little wonder that the German people felt fear and hostility toward the Jews and saw them as a threat to their own existence.

Chapter 6

The Bolshevik Revolution Spreads throughout Europe

The Russian Revolution was seismic in its impact upon the world. Nothing had happened on this scale since the French Revolution, with which the Russian Revolution shared many characteristics. This revolutionary struggle was not confined to Russia, but soon began to explode all over Europe. With much of Europe on the verge of economic and political collapse in the aftermath of the war (WWI), revolutionary feelings began bubbling up from the lower classes in a hundred different places. The old order of monarchies and aristocracies was gone and something else would take its place; what, no one was precisely sure. The likely contenders were either some form of representative democracy, or some form of socialism, the extreme of which was Bolshevik Communism which had just taken control of Russia. The lower classes of Europe were enthralled by the idea of Communism, as it promised them unaccustomed power and control, but it struck fear in the hearts of the upper and middle classes who were determined to suppress it and prevent its spread into Europe.

Even though the Bolsheviks headed by Lenin and Trotsky were in complete control in Russia, they did not yet feel secure. They believed that unless socialist revolution swept over all of Europe, they could be rolled back and crushed by the military might of world capitalism. To this end, a "Communist International" or Comintern was organized which was funded by the Russian government and backed by Jewish banks in America and Europe. The purpose of the Comintern was to foment Communist revolution throughout Europe to bring down traditional regimes which would then be replaced by Soviet Socialist Republics.

The largest Communist party and the principal member of the Comintern outside of Russia was in Germany, the membership of which was, significantly, 78% Jewish. A network of Communist parties was established in every country in Europe, with its headquarters in Moscow, with the intention of seizing control of all of Europe and then the world. In each of these Communist parties, Jews dominated and made up a majority of its membership, and they reported back to the Jewish Bolsheviks who now ran Russia. It seemed clear that two cultures were now in a titanic struggle to determine the socio-economic and cultural future of Europe: one Jewish, under the flag of Communism, and the other, traditional Western Christian Civilization.

Jews in the Hungarian Revolution

The first country outside of Russia to fall to the Communists was Hungary. As a result of World War I, the ancient Austro/Hungarian Empire had dissolved into its constituent parts, leaving much of it in total disarray. Jewish Bolsheviks, funded and controlled by the Soviet Union based Comintern, took advantage of the chaos in Hungary. By enlisting the cooperation of the Jewish population in Hungary, almost all of whom were either Communists or sympathetic to Communism, they overthrew the government in March, 1919. They then imposed a reign of terror over Hungary which lasted until August 12 of that same year under the leadership of the Jew, Bela Kuhn (real name - Moritz Cohen), a native Hungarian, but an agent of Lenin. Kuhn had been a

Hungarian soldier during the war and taken prisoner by the Russians. After the Bolsheviks took over Russia, because he was a Jew, Kuhn was released from prison and became a member of the Cheka. He was then sent to the Ukraine where he participated in the murder of scores of thousands of Christian Ukrainians. Kuhn was then selected to undergo training to become a Bolshevik agent back in his home country of Hungary.

Left - Bela Kuhn (real name - Moritz Cohen)

The new Bolshevik regime now in control of Hungary under Kuhn's leadership was Jewish to a man; amounting to yet another Jewish *coup d'e etat* of a sovereign state. Among these new Jewish rulers of Hungary were, Otto Korvin (Kline), Bela Szanto, Tibor Szamuely, Jeno Varga, Jozseph Pogany (Joseph Swartz), Jeno Landler, Georg Lukacs, and Jeno Hamburger; as unsavory a lot as it was possible to find.

Hungary was then divided up into districts and Jews were appointed as Commissars of each district. Many of these Jews were crude thugs of the lowest type. One had been a janitor in a synagogue, and now a Commissar of a district (like a governor of a state in the U.S.). Terror squads were organized and a "Red Terror" began in full swing, mimicking that which was occurring in Russia at the same time. All private property was nationalized, all industry was nationalized, grain was expropriated from peasants by force, and the peasants were all herded onto collective farms. The army and the police force were eliminated and replaced by new Bolshevik terror squads. These Jewish Bolsheviks then began a reign of terror against the Christian clergy, burning churches and murdering priests and pastors all over Hungary. Landowners and their families, as well as other bourgeoisie were hauled away in trucks and murdered by the thousands. Rape became endemic. Red Army soldiers went around to the private homes of the upper class and forcefully took the most beautiful girls and young women, married or not, with them back to the barracks where they kept them for weeks at a time. Inside the barracks, all the soldiers took their turns with them until they grew tired of them, whereupon they were replaced by a new roundup of captive sex slaves. Any who resisted were killed. Many of the girls committed suicide rather than face their families again. The full scope of this Jewish Bolshevik terror in Hungary can be understood by the following order given by one of the commissars (All the commissars were Jews): *"Do not shrink from the shedding of blood, for nothing worthwhile can be obtained without it. Without blood there can be no terror, and without terror there can be no dictatorship of the proletariat."* This quote came from the book, "The Evolution of Hungary and its Place in European History," by Count Paul Teleki, former Prime Minister of Hungary. The Bolsheviks abolished the right of trial and the right of defense. The charge of "counter-revolutionary" resulted in immediate execution no matter how spurious the charge. Jewish tyranny was wreaking a terrible revenge upon Christian Hungary.

Kuhn resorted to the usual Jewish Bolshevik propaganda methods to break down the sanctity of religion, patriotism and morality in order to undermine the Hungarian culture. The conservative, Christian morals of the Hungarian people were ridiculed while debauchery and pornography were given full license.

Miklos Horthy saves Hungary

Hungarian Rear Admiral Miklos Horthy formed a National Army to fight the Bolsheviks who had taken over the country. In response to Bela Kuhn's "Red Terror," Horthy launched his "White Terror" campaign against the Bolsheviks. With the aid of the Romanian Army, Horthy managed to overthrow Kuhn and the Bolsheviks on August 1, 1919 and set up a new government under the Social Democratic Party, headed by Horthy. Kuhn managed to escape back to Russia. The "Red Terror" was over and the Christians took control of their country back from the Jewish Bolsheviks, but the Jews had taken a dreadful toll on the country during the brief period they were in power.

**Admiral Miklos Horthy takes Hungary
back from the Communists.**

The brutality of the Jews toward the Hungarian people set off a virulent wave of anti-Semitism and a wholesale massacre of Jews ensued across Hungary once they were removed from power. Jews numbered 5 percent of the population of Hungary, but held around half of the positions in trade, banking, and the professions. They completely dominated theater and film production and controlled most of the newspapers. In 1939 the Hungarian government enacted an anti-Jewish law that restricted Jewish participation in business and industry to 12 percent, and to only 6 percent within the professions. Jews were also banned from holding public office, and from holding leading positions in journalism, the theater or in film.

Jews in the German Revolution

As the social and economic order began to crumble in Germany near war's end in 1918, the working classes, including many soldiers and sailors in uniform, began to question their unthinking patriotism that had tied them to the war effort up until then. A sense of frustration and anger was rising in the armed forces, but also in the factories and the mills back home over the German government's refusal to end the war. This developing attitude of rebelliousness was encouraged and egged on by Communist revolutionary provocateurs, the majority of whom, as in all other cases, were Jews.

From the beginning of the war, the British navy had maintained a total naval blockade, preventing all food from entering Germany. By 1916 the German people began to starve. This "starvation" blockade eventually caused the deaths of a million German people, and the horrific suffering of millions more. On 30 October, 1918, the German High Command issued an order for a final, desperate naval assault to break this inhuman starvation blockade. This was an independent decision by the Navy and was not sanctioned by the government, but it was the spark that set off the revolution in Germany. The war weary German sailors in the northern port of Kiel were becoming rebellious as the result of Communist agitators. Such an attack against the much more powerful British navy, they believed, would have been suicidal. They were not willing to squander their lives in a pointless, futile *Gotterdammerung*, and rose in mutiny against their officers. Over 1,000 of the rebellious sailors were arrested, but four days later the workers of Kiel, led by Communist Jews, came to their rescue. A general strike was launched and a mass demonstration freed the sailors. Following this success 2,000 armed workers and sailors marched to the town hall, occupied it and established a "Workers' and Sailors Council" (or "Soviet") and took control of the city. The German Revolution had begun! From Kiel the "Workers' and Soldiers' Council" movement - inspired by the Russian revolution and instigated largely by Jews who were in close communication with their brethren in Russia -- spread rapidly throughout Germany.

In the Ruhr Valley, the industrial heartland of the country, factories, armed units of the army, and even whole towns, were brought under the control of "Councils," like the "Soviets" in Russia, an indication of Jewish influence. By November 7, the revolution had reached Berlin. Strikes and marches in the capital culminated in a massive demonstration outside the Reichstag on November 9. The old rulers were terrified by the scope and strength of the revolutionary movement, and began to panic. The Kaiser finally saw the hopelessness of the situation. Under pressure from leftist politicians, he abdicated and slipped across the border into forced exile in the Netherlands.

The old rulers turned to the Social Democratic Party (SPD) to save them from the insurgent masses. The SPD was Germany's largest political party which purported to represent the workers. Eager to placate the mass demonstration which was developing, SPD leader, Phillip Scheidemann, declared on November 9, 1918, the creation of a "German Republic" to replace the old monarchy. It was a calculated attempt to demobilize the mass movement by giving them what they wanted. On November 10, a "Provisional Government" of various socialist groups was established -- nominally answerable to the Workers' and Soldiers' "Councils." The Provisional Government included both the far left Independent Social Democratic Party (USPD), as well as the more centrist SPD. Combining these radically different groups within the same government, moreover, nominally subordinate to the Workers' and Soldier's Council, was inherently an unstable situation, and the struggle that followed was dominated by the conflict between these factions.

The USPD was led by two Jews, Hugo Hasse (real name Allenstein) and Karl Kautsky. The USPD was a coalition of leftist groups, which included the Communists. The USPD soon broke apart and disbanded, with the far left group known as the Sparticists leaving to form the Communist Party, while its more moderate members joined the SPD. The Spartacist group, the forerunner of the Communist Party, was led by the Jews, Rosa Luxemburg and Karl Liebknecht, who received their funding from the Communist International (Comintern) based in Moscow. The Spartacists represented the vanguard of the revolution, especially in Berlin. The Spartacists found their support amongst the urban working class, but the great majority of the Germany people, especially the middle and upper classes, as well as the rural farmers, were conservative and unsympathetic to Socialists of all stripes, and were totally against the Communists.

The political instability in Germany caused the old political structure to begin to fall apart all across the country. On November 7, 1918 the 700 year old Wittlesbach monarchy fell in Bavaria, after which Bavaria was declared a "Free State" by the Communist Jew, Kurt Eisner, of the USDP. Eisner then became Minister-President of Bavaria. But on 21 February, 1919, he was shot and killed by a German patriot, Count

Communist Jew Kurt Eisner (L), the new president of Bavaria, was assassinated by Count Anton von Arco auf Valley (R), a German patriot.

Anton von Arco auf Valley, who said of Eisner, *"Eisner is a Bolshevist, a Jew; he isn't German, he doesn't feel German, he subverts all patriotic thoughts and feelings. He is a traitor to this land."* The killing of Eisner made the count a hero to many Bavarians, though it did not stop the Communists. After Eisner's assassination, the Communists and Anarchists seized power in Bavaria.

(Left - Eugene Levine, a Jew, heads the Bavarian Soviet Republic after Eisner's assassination.)

A "Soviet Republic" was formally proclaimed on April 6, 1919, but collapsed within six days due to the ineptitude of its leaders. But another Communist Jew, **Eugene Levine**, was waiting in the wings and became the new head of the "Soviet" government. Levine took the usual Communist steps which included expropriating luxurious apartments and giving them to the homeless and placing factories under the ownership and control of the workers. Levine organized his own army, called the "Red Army" (what else?), similar to the Red Army in Russia. Hoards of unemployed workers swarmed into the new Red Army until its numbers swelled to 20,000. "Red Guards" then began arresting suspected "counter-revolutionaries," that is, those who opposed the Communist take-over of the government, and executing them. Among those executed were Prince Gustav von Thurn und Taxis and Countess Hella von Westarp. Bavaria's "Red Terror" was about to begin in imitation of those in Russia and Hungary.

But before their Russian-like "Red Terror" could get off the ground, they were brought down by right wing, patriotic forces. On May 3, 1919, a force of 9,000 German Army soldiers, operating independently of the government, combined with Freikorps units (volunteer para-military units made up of officers and soldiers who had returned home from the war) totaling 30,000, entered Munich and quickly put an end to the "Soviet Socialist Republic of Bavaria." Some 1,000 "Red Army" soldiers were killed, and around 700 of those associated with the Soviet Republic were executed by the Freikorps, including Levine himself. The Freikorps saved Bavaria.

**Units of the Army and the Freikorps enter
Munich to take on the "Reds."**

The Sparticist Uprising in Berlin

On January 5, 1919, the Communist "Sparticist Uprising" began in
Berlin, led by Rosa Luxemburg and Karl Liebknecht, both Jews. The

**Rosa Luxemburg and Karl Liebknecht, both Jews, headed
the Sparticists of Berlin, a Communist organization.**

Communists formed paramilitary units, which they called the "Red Army," modeled as usual after the Bolshevik Red Army in Russia. These units were made up mainly of armed revolutionary gangs of workers with no military experience. Bloody street fighting raged throughout the city between the Sparticists and the police.

The Government was moved to the city of Weimar because of the fighting in Berlin. "Freikorps" units were then brought in to put down the rebellion. The revolution quickly took on the character of a civil war, with the Communists and Bolsheviks on one side, and conservative, traditional, middle and upper class Germans on the other.

Bloody street battles also occurred in other German cities and towns between the Communist Red Army and the police and the Freikorps. The Communists, in typical fashion, began to assassinate political leaders and government officials, and to organize strikes designed to cause the maximum damage to the already struggling economy. Barracks and naval dockyards, as well as other state properties were seized and street barricades divided Germany's cities and towns into politico-criminal fiefdoms. Workers' and Soldiers' Councils were formed in all of these cities and officers and officials of the old regime were arrested and imprisoned. Kings and princes all over Germany abdicated and disappeared into exile.

The untrained Communist fighters were no match, however, for the disciplined, combat experienced Freikorps, so the rebellion was quickly brought down. No mercy was shown the Communist revolutionaries. Thousands were killed and both Luxemburg and Liebknecht were executed by the Freikorps. As a result of this defeat, the Communist movement temporarily collapsed, and the revolution ended in August, 1919 with the inauguration of the Weimar Republic headed by Friedrich Ebert of the Social Democratic Party (SDP).

These communist uprisings had been put down, not by the Weimar government, but by independently operating paramilitary groups of patriotic Germans, known as the Freikorps. Freikorps units had sprung up all over Germany in reaction to the Communist threat to the country, and, as stated above, were comprised mainly of soldiers who had returned from the war. They were led by ex-officers and tended to

Freikorps troops sent in to suppress the Sparticists were ex- soldiers from the German army. The Freikorps saves Germany from a Communist takeover.

be nationalistic, patriotic and ultra conservative in character. Unlike their Red Army opponents, the Freikorps were highly organized, and the officers who led them had the unswerving loyalty of the enlisted members. They were united in their hostility towards the Communists and were used unofficially by the Weimar government to put down left-wing revolts and uprisings in cities throughout Germany. Some of these units were eventually absorbed into the National Socialist movement.

Though the revolution was over, Germany was left in the grip of paranoia caused by the bitter reality of defeat in the World War, as well as the vindictive and punitive peace treaty which followed; but also by the frightening specter of a Bolshevik takeover of Germany like that which had occurred in Russia. The German people were well aware of the role played by Jews in the Bolshevik revolution in Russia, as well in Hungary, and they were well aware of the overrepresentation of Jews in the Communist revolution in Germany which had only just ended.

After the Bolsheviks had seized control in Russia, an opposing army was raised led by Czarist officers. They called themselves the "White Army," in opposition to the Bolshevik "Red Army." Their slogan became "kill the Jews and save Russia." Russia was now engaged in a civil war, the brutality of which knew no bounds, and the tentacles of the emerging internationalism of Communism were spreading out of Russia like a giant octopus into every corner of Europe. The revolution which had just been put down by the Freicorps could well have ended with a Bolshevik takeover of Germany. The German people were convinced of a Jewish-Bolshevik conspiracy against Western Christian civilization, and of its existential threat to Germany. A widespread surge of anti-Semitism developed among the German people as a result, combined with a distinct shift to the right in German public opinion.

On July 2, 1922, in an interview while in exile with a reporter from the *Chicago Tribune*, Kaiser Wilhelm II said: " *The Jews are responsible for Bolshevism in Russia, and Germany too. I was far too indulgent with them during my reign, and I bitterly regret the favors I showed to prominent Jewish bankers.*"

British intelligence had discerned a coordinated Jewish, Communist revolutionary effort even before the beginning of World War One. In the July 16, 1913 issue of the "Great Britain Directorate of Intelligence," a monthly review of the progress of revolutionary movements abroad, an article stated: *"There is now definite evidence that Bolshevism is an international movement controlled by Jews; communications are passing between the leaders in America, France, Russia, and England, with a view to concerted action."*

The Jews had traditionally maintained well established, highly efficient, international networks through which information of interest to Jews was quickly passed.

Adolf Hitler looked back on the period several years later and described the situation in Germany in this way: *"Germany, with more than 6 million communists was on the verge of a catastrophe which none but those wanting in common sense can possibly ignore. If red terrorism was to have swept over Germany the western countries of Europe would probably also have realized that it is not a matter of indifference to them whether the outposts of a destructive Asian world power stand guard on the Rhine and on the North Sea, or whether the land is populated by peaceful German peasants and working men whose only wish is to make an honest living and to be on friendly terms with other nations. By averting this disaster which was threatening to ruin Germany, the National Socialist movement saved not only the German people, but also rendered the rest of Europe a service of historical merit. The National Socialist revolution has but one aim: To restore order in our country, to provide work and bread for our starving masses and to lay down the ideas of honor, loyalty and decency as being the basis of our moral code, which far from doing harm to other nations, can be for the benefit of all."*

Jewish Bolsheviks Attempt to Take Italy

After the War (WWI), Bolshevism also threatened Italy. Jewish, Communist agitators, supported and paid for by Red Russia's Comintern, provoked conflicts and committed terrorist acts in an attempt to bring down the Italian government and establish a Bolshevik government in its place. Mussolini formed his Fascist party to oppose the Communists, and the struggle between the Communists and the Fascists cost thousands of lives in Italy. Jewish led Communists committed mass murders in Saraana, Modena, Bologna, Teatro, Diana, and Milan, but were eventually defeated by Mussolini's Fascist forces. The final defeat of the Bolshevks in Italy culminated in Mussolini's famous march on Rome.

Mussolini, like all other "fascists" have been defamed by war propaganda and by the Jewish controlled mainstream media, but he was well thought of and widely admired by world leaders prior to the war. Typically, in the Jewish propaganda, he was portrayed as a bombastic, barbaric buffoon.

One of fascism's bitterest enemies during World War Two, Winston Churchill, could not praise the Fascists enough before the war began. He was especially impressed with Mussolini. *"Of Italian Fascism, Italy has*

Mussolini saves Italy from the Communists

shown that there is a way of fighting the subversive forces which can rally the masses of the people, properly led, to value and wish to defend the honour and stability of civilised society. Hereafter no great nation will be unprovided with an ultimate means of protection against the cancerous growth of Bolshevism." (Winston Churchill, 11th, November 1938)

A group of British citizens living in Italy at the time of Mussolini's rise issued the following statement to contradict the false propaganda spewed out in the international Jewish press against Mussolini and the Fascists:

"We wish to state most clearly and emphatically that there exists here today nothing that can be justly termed either tyranny or suppression of personal freedom as guaranteed by constitutional law in any civilized land. We believe that Mussolini enjoys the enthusiastic support and admiration of the Italian people, who are contented, orderly and prosperous to a degree hitherto

unknown in Italy, and probably without parallel at the present time among other great European nations still suffering from the war." (Committee of British Residents, Florence. 'Financial Times', 1926)

Jewish Bolsheviks Attempt to Take Spain - The Spanish Civil War

Red Russia's Comintern began arming and funding Communism in Spain in 1936, which led to the bloody Spanish Civil War. Taking advantage of numerous national misfortunes they transformed what had been the most conservative, staunchly Catholic monarchy in Europe into a nightmarish, atheistic, Communist republic propped up by the Soviet Union. Communist activity in Spain, as in previous Communist revolutions in Europe, was organized and led by Jews. Volunteers from all over the world, including Poland, France, Britain, Germany, Canada, and Palestine joined the "International Brigade" to fight in Spain on the side of the Communists. An inordinately high percentage of these were Jews. Jewish women volunteered as nurses. Yiddish language publications such as *Der Fraihaits-Kempfer* and *Botwin* were published for all the Jewish volunteers in Spain. German volunteers formed the Thaelman Brigade; Italians, the Garibaldi Brigade; French, the "Commune de Paris;" Americans formed the Abraham Lincoln Brigade. A highly disproportionate percentage of all of these "brigades" were Jews. The Abraham Lincoln Brigade from America was led by the Jew, Milton Wolfe. Moe Fishman was the leader of the "Veterans of the Abraham Lincoln Brigade" for years after the war. 70% of medical personnel in the International Brigade were Jewish.

Milton Wolff, American Jewish leader of the Abraham Lincoln Brigade

Most of the Russian commanders were also Jews. Yaakov Shmushkevitsh organized the Spanish Republican Air Force. He was a Jew. Grigori Stern was the chief military advisor to the Spanish Republic, General Manfred Stern was the commander of the International Brigade, and Leiba Lazarevich Feldbin (Aleksandr Orlov) was Chief of Soviet Security. All were Jews. Feldbin (Orlov) supervised the massacres of Catholic priests and nuns in Spain. The Jew Mikhail Koltzov was correspondent in Spain for Pravda, and Moses Rosenberg was the Soviet ambassador to Spain.

Jewish led Communists "execute" Sacred Heart shrine in Spain during their assault on the Catholic Church in the Spanish Civil War.

The "Red Terror" in Spain took on the same character as the Red Terrors in Russia, Ukraine, Hungary, and Italy. The Jewish led Communists launched an orgy of mass murder, rape and destruction. As they had attempted to wipe out Christianity in previous "Red Terrors," they went after the Catholic Church in Spain with a vengeance. Over 20,000 churches across Spain were destroyed, 6,832 Spanish priests were murdered, 3,000 monks, 300 nuns and 13 bishops were killed. In addition, some 4,000 laymen were murdered for helping or hiding nuns or priests. These murders were carried out with the usual torture and mutilation characteristic of other "Red Terrors."

General Francisco Franco, a staunch loyalist, and devout Roman Catholic, stepped up to prevent the country from becoming another

General Francisco Franco saves Spain from the Communists.

victim of Communist revolution. He merged the Falangists and the Carlists (traditional Catholic monarchist rebels) into a united nationalist group and waged civil war against the so-called Republicans who were now controlled by Moscow. In the civil war, he had the support of Antonio Salazar in Portugal, Benito Mussolini in Italy, and Adolf Hitler in Germany. He overthrew the Republican Bolsheviks and saved Spain from Jewish Bolshevism. Franco has been branded a "Fascist" by the international Jewish press, which means only that he opposed Jewish dominance and control of his country. In reality, he was the savior of Spain.

Czechoslovakia in Danger of Communist Takeover

Czechoslovakia was an artificial state created by the Paris Peace Conference after World War I. Its population was made up of several incompatible and contentious nationalities, including Czechs, Germans, Hungarians, Slovaks, Ruthenes, Slavs and Jews, and was therefore unstable from the start. The capital city of Prague was home to 118,000 Jews, most of whom were Communists or Communist sympathizers.

These Prague Jews were highly organized, and openly sympathetic to Bolshevik Russia. The Czechoslovakian Communist Party (under the leadership of Hohumir Smeral, Klement Gottwald, Rudolf Slansky, Vlaclav Kopeky, and Josef Guttmann, et al, all Jews) was a member of the Moscow based Communist International (Comintern) and stood ready to instigate a Communist revolution in Czechoslovakia whenever the opportunity arose.

After the German annexation of the Sudetanland in September, 1938, Czechoslovakia fell apart along ethnic lines with large populations and territories joining surrounding countries. The remaining remnant of the former Czechoslovakia -- Bohemia and Moravia -- with its capital city of Prague, was totally defenseless and extremely vulnerable to a Communist takeover. To prevent such a calamity, Hitler made Bohemia and Moravia a German protectorate.

The war mongers in Britain, France and the United States chose to see this move by Hitler as further proof of his ambitions to dominate all of Europe, and even to conquer the world, instead of seeing it for what it was, a measure to hold Communism in check.

Adolf Hitler saves Czechoslovakia from the Communists. Here he receives an enthusiastic welcome in the city of Prague after making Bohemia and Moravia a "protectorate" of the Reich.

The Comintern's aim? World domination!

All of the European struggles against Communism were of the same pattern, that is, each was a struggle of nationalist forces in each country against revolution instigated and led by Jewish Communists, paid for and supported by the Soviet Union's Communist International (Comintern), which was itself a Jewish organization. World domination as the goal of the Communist International was made clear in its documents, in which it was declared:

"The Communist International is the union of the communist parties of varying lands into a unified communist world party. As leader and organizer of the revolutionary movement of the world proletariat, the Communist International fights for the establishment of a world-wide dictatorship of the proletariat, for the establishment of a world union of socialist soviet republics."

The Communist movement was unequivocally a Jewish movement, directed, controlled and supported out of Moscow by the Jewish Bolsheviks who ruled Russia. Their goal was not only world domination, or at least domination of Western Civilization, but also the complete eradication of Christianity and the deracination of Western culture.

The Russian writer, Dostoevsky had this to say, in his book "Diary of a Writer," published more than 40 years earlier in 1877:

"It is not for nothing that everywhere in Europe the Jews are reigning over the stock exchanges, not for nothing that they control capital, not for nothing that they are masters of credit, and not for nothing, I repeat, that they are the masters of all international politics. What is coming is the complete triumph of Jewish ideas, before which, sentiments of humanity, the thirst for truth, Christian feelings, and the national and popular pride of Europe must bow. And what will be the future is known also to the Jews themselves: Their reign is approaching, their complete reign!" Dostoevsky.

In his 1920 article, "Zionism vs. Bolshevism: A Struggle for the Soul of the Jewish People," Winston Churchill stated his belief that *"International Jews"* were seeking *"a world-wide communistic state under Jewish domination."*

But with the exception of Russia, the Jewish Communist assault on

Western Christian Civilization was unsuccessful in every case where it was attempted, thanks to stalwarts like Horthy, Mussolini, Franco and Hitler. They stopped Communism in its tracks. Instead of being vilified and dismissed as repugnant "Fascists," as they are today, the result of Jewish propaganda, these men should be held up as heroes and champions of Western Christian Civilization, for that is what they were.

It was inevitable that this great contest for the dominance of Europe would eventually culminate in a war between the Soviet Union (representing World Jewry) and Germany (as the champion of Western Christian Civilization). If Britain, France and the United States had given Germany a free hand, or better yet, had supported Germany, then World Communism would have been destroyed in its cradle, in which case, the world would look very different today.

Chapter 7

The Nation of Israel

Jews have lived as alien minorities amongst indigenous majorities in Europe, the Middle East, and North Africa since Roman times. Despite not having a country, or a "state," of their own, Jews nevertheless have always considered themselves to be a single nation with national interests of their own. Long before the advent of the "State" of Israel, the Jews called themselves the "Nation" of Israel. Spread out in numerous other countries (the Diaspora), though they were (and still are), they nevertheless have always maintained highly organized networks that tie the numerous Jewish communities together. There is an international organization of synagogues, for example, through which rabbis travel to and from, and communicate with other synagogues around the world. International Jewish bankers form another highly organized network. Jewish owned newspapers and other journals form another. Both United Press International (UPI) and Reuters, the two primary sources of international news for all newspapers, television and radio news, are owned and controlled by Jews. Hundreds of other Jewish organizations, such as B'nai B'rith, the Anti-Defamation League (ADL), the World Jewish Congress, etc., etc., form tight intertwining and overlapping networks through which Jews everywhere maintain close contact with each other. Jewish leaders are kept abreast of what is happening in Jewish communities throughout the Diaspora. Any Jew from anywhere in the world can always find a congenial stopover at any synagogue or Jewish center in any country and use it as a base for doing business there. That is how St. Paul was able to create all those Christian churches and then maintain communication with them. He did it as a Rabbi communicating through these Jewish networks to the churches he created. As he travelled around the Mediterranean world preaching Christianity, he used synagogues as his base, which also provided him ready-made audiences for his preaching. Christianity at the time of St. Paul was considered a sect of Judaism. Paul's "letters" to these churches, which became such a substantial part of the Christian New Testament, also passed through these Jewish networks.

Jews have never been interested in agriculture and only engaged in it when forced to do so by circumstance. They have always been an urban people, congregating in cities, often in Jewish ghettos, therefore making themselves more visible than their small numbers would indicate. (Venice, Italy is an archipelago of little islands, each with a different name. "Murano" is one of these islands, where Venetian glass is made, hence "Murano glass." "Ghetto" is the name of another Island. The term "Ghetto" originated in Venice -- Ghetto Island, where the Jews lived, by their own choice, incidentally. Later, the term came to mean "The Jewish quarter.") They preferred earning their livings as petty traders, middlemen, shopkeepers, peddlers, shoemakers, tailors, and other similar crafts. Most of them worked for themselves in their own businesses. Out of these small enterprises eventually grew large businesses, such as department store chains. They were also the "money changers." Western Christianity as well as the Muslim world considered "usury" a sin and therefore Christians and Muslims were forbidden to lend money at interest. Yet, money lending is essential for economic growth and development. Jews had no such compunctions about usury and were more than willing to step in to provide that service. Out of such local money lending grew the international banking system, which has always been controlled by Jews.

Jews, generally speaking, are not, and never have been, "wealth creators," in the economies they lived within, rather, they have been wealth "extractors." They are rarely involved in wealth creating industries such as farming, forestry, mining, fishing and manufacturing; preferring to be middlemen and financiers. Even today, wealthy and powerful Jewish financiers don't create wealth, they extract wealth out of the economy, usually in the form of interest, or brokerage fees, or from their "cut" of the profit as middlemen. That is why they have gained a reputation as a parasitic people, living amongst majority populations which serve as their hosts.

As alien minorities in other peoples' countries, Jews congregate together to form closed societies (Ghettos), and tend to view the outside majorities as unsympathetic "others," creating among Jews an "us against them" frame of mind. They form business networks and exclusive trading consortiums between themselves exclusively, and cooperate with each other in competing with the Gentile world outside. Jewish banks extend loans to Jewish businesses that a Gentile under similar circumstances would not be able to obtain, and then they back those Jewish businesses in difficult times to prevent failures. Jews throughout the "Diaspora" have access to international Jewish capital, which gives them a huge advantage in competing with their Gentile neighbors. Jews have a "collectivist" culture, whereas Christians are individualistic. Jews work together for the benefit of all Jews, at the exclusion of non-Jews. The Christian Gentile is the "lone" hunter, while Jews tend to "pack hunt." They gang up to put the lone Gentile out of business by the use of cooperative commercial strategies. Jews thereby tend to achieve monopolies in their fields of endeavor, pushing the Gentiles out. Even the Jewish holy book of laws, the Talmud, does not forbid Jews from taking unfair advantage of Gentiles. The Talmud does require Jews, however, to treat other Jews fairly.

By these methods, Jews have always achieved a dominant position within the traditional societies they happen to live in, and they have shown no qualms about using their elite positions to exploit the host populations. A constant charge against them is that their loyalty to the host country they happen to live in is always secondary to their loyalty to other Jews and to the International Nation of Israel. German Jews, at the time of the Russian Revolution, were accused of being more loyal to Russian Jews than to the nation of Germany in which they lived. That pattern has always been the same. American Jews today are accused of being more loyal to Israel than to America.

During WWII, nearly all of the American spies for the Soviet Union were Jews; Alger Hiss and Whitaker Chambers being notable exceptions. Of the eleven American scientists who built the atomic bomb during World War II, ten were Jews, and the only non-Jew, Enrico Fermi, had a Jewish wife. All had left Europe for America after the Nazis took control, so they were only nominally American. Their loyalty was to the International Jewish Nation, not to the country they lived in -- America. The headquarters of world Jewry at that time was Soviet Russia. Russia's atomic bomb scientists were also Jews. The head of the Soviet atomic bomb project was Solomon Abrahamovich Rebach, a Jew. Atomic bomb development everywhere was totally in the hands of Jews. It should have been anticipated that American atom bomb secrets would be passed to the Jewish scientists in Russia, and that is exactly what happened. Top secret Atomic bomb technological innovations worked out at the Manhattan Project in America were in the hands of Russian Jewish scientists in mere days or weeks afterwards. The information simply passed through the well established international Jewish networks to their fellow Jewish scientists in Russia. All of the atomic spies without exception were Jews, with obvious Jewish names: Ethel and Julius Rosenberg, George Koval, David Greenglass, Morris Cohen, et. al.

Jewish spying for Russia was actually far more extensive than was reported. Even Jews in the movie industry cooperated. The film director Irving Lerner was caught photographing the "cyclotron" at University of California, Berkley in 1944. He was subsequently blacklisted. British Jewish scientists were also a part of the international atomic spy network. But Jewish spying for Russia was by no means limited to atomic secrets. Jewish spies infiltrated every branch of the American government during the Roosevelt administration -- the British government too -- and fed secret information of every kind back to Russia via these Jewish information networks. Even the Jewish undersecretary of the Treasury,

Harry Dexter White (Weise), was a Soviet secret agent. His boss, Henry Morgenthau, Jr., Secretary of the Treasury, was also Jewish. White died before he could be prosecuted; else he would surely have gone to prison. White was the first head of the International Monetary Fund and helped set up the World Bank, both of which have since been controlled exclusively by Jews. Jews are still spying on the United States and passing secret information through these Jewish networks, but now for Israel instead of the Soviet Union.

This issue of doubtful loyalty as well as their aggressive business and financial exploitation of their host populations has been the root of most of the anti-Semitism over the centuries.

History of the Expulsion of Jews

Sooner or later, Jews have invariably provoked the hostility and hatred of their host populations, causing the host populations to turn on them. Over the course of the past 2,000 years Jews have been expelled from virtually every country in Europe and the Middle East at least once and in some cases, multiple times. They were expelled from the German states five times, the last time by the Nazis; from parts of Italy five times; from France four times; from England three times. England expelled the Jews in 1290 and kept them out for 300 years until Oliver Cromwell let them back in. The Jewish Dutch financiers, Manasseh Ben Israel and Moses Carvajal, financed Cromwell's campaign to oust King Charles I. After King Charles was beheaded and Cromwell became "Lord Protector" of England, Cromwell opened England's doors to the Jews again. They quickly rose in power and in 1694 they created the Bank of England for the purpose of lending money to the crown. Jews still control the Bank of England today.

Even in countries where they were permitted to reside, they were usually subjected to sharp restrictions; for example, Jews could not own land in most European countries, belong to guilds or enter the universities. In Germany and Russia, they were not allowed to travel without special permission. In the worst cases over the centuries, they were periodically subjected to attacks and massacres. These expulsions and other measures taken against the Jews were actually defensive in nature, enacted to protect the host populations from exploitation by the Jews. Whenever such restrictions were eventually lifted, usually by some benevolent ruler who wanted to do the right thing, the Jews immediately took advantage and began their exploitative practices again, until the governments felt it necessary to impose new restrictions on them...either that, or to expel them from their country entirely. The Nazi expulsion of the Jews from Germany, beginning in 1934, was by no means a unique event in history; and it was done for the same reasons as all the other expulsions.

Their most recent "expulsion" was from all of the Middle Eastern countries in 1948 as a result of the creation of the Jewish state in Palestine and the Arab/Israeli conflict that followed. The most recent "exodus" of the Jews has been the flight from Russia to Israel and the Unites States, beginning in 1960 to the present. The exodus from Russia was the result of having lost their power under Stalin, after which the Russian people turned on them.

There has got to be a reason that so many disparate peoples have turned against the Jews virtually everywhere in the world Jews have lived. This cannot be attributed to simple bigotry, xenophobia, or to mindless prejudice. Obviously, the Jews bring it on themselves.

In his book, "L'antisemitisme Son Historie Et Ses Causes," published in France in 1894, noted Jewish author, Bernard Lazare, reaches the following conclusion: *"If this hostility, even aversion, had only been shown towards the Jews at one period and in one country, it would be easy to unravel the limited causes of this anger, but this race has been on the contrary an object of hatred to all the peoples among whom it has established itself. It must be therefore, since the enemies of the Jews belonged to the most diverse races, since they lived in countries very distant from each other, since they were ruled by very different laws, governed by opposite principles, since they had neither the same morals, nor the same customs, since they were animated by unlike dispositions which did not permit them to judge of anything in the same way, it must be therefore that the general cause of anti-Semitism has always resided in Israel* [the Jewish people] *and not in those who have fought against Israel."*

Professor Jesse H. Holmes, writing in, "The American Hebrew," stated the following with regard to these expulsions of Jews: *"It can hardly be an accident that antagonism directed against the Jews is to be found pretty much everywhere in the world where Jews and non-Jews are associated. And as the Jews are the common element of the situation it would seem probable, on the face of it, that the cause will be found in them, rather than in the widely varying groups which feel this antagonism."* It is only common sense that for a people to be so universally hated, in whatever society they live, consistently throughout history, they are doing something to provoke it.

The two centers of Jewish world power are now the United States, with approximately 5.2 million Jews, and Israel, with approximately 5.8 million Jews. Previously, Russia was the center of Jewish power, from which Jews tried spreading their Communist ideology around the world using the power of the Russian army. Today, they use the economic and military power of the United States to spread their slightly modified ideology, now of "democracy," around the world, which is the reason the United States has been involved in endless war for the past several decades.

The new Jewish ideology in the United States which is behind our interventionist foreign policy, is the so-called "neo-conservative" movement. Neo-conservatism is not conservative at all, but has its roots in the same old Jewish ideology of Communism. The neo-conservative movement in America is a replication of the Russian Comintern which attempted to spread Communism throughout Western Civilization, and indeed, the world. Both movements, i.e. the Comintern and Neo-conservatism, are Jewish movements. Jews control America today, as they controlled the Soviet Union in the 1920s, 30s and 40s. Since the creation of the Jewish state of Israel, Jews have become more powerful than ever in the world. They now have a state of their own from which to fulfill the interests of the international Jewish nation. They have infiltrated every branch of the American government to the extent that they literally control this country, and they use the power of the United States to further the interests of the International Nation of Israel, including funneling billions of American taxpayer dollars into Israeli coffers.

Chapter 8

Jews in Weimar Germany

After the 1848 Revolution that swept Europe, most of the traditional restrictions placed on Jews were lifted. Germany was particularly generous to the Jews, giving them the same rights as all other citizens. With all restrictions lifted, Jews began to prosper in Germany at a rapid rate. In the rising prosperity that followed Germany's consolidation into a single state in 1871, Jews prospered to a far higher degree than other Germans. Their remarkable ability to work together for the achievement of all Jews at the expense of the Gentile host population, gave them a strong competitive edge. Kaiser Wilhelm kept them out of government for the most part, so they did not acquire significant political power under the Kaiser. That was to change with the advent of the Weimar Republic which followed World War One and the Kaiser's abdication, when restrictions barring Jews from civil service jobs were removed.

East European Jews also began to flood into Germany at this time as the result of the turmoil in that region caused by the war, the Russian Revolution that followed, and the Russian Civil War following that. Large numbers of people wanted to move out of those dangerous areas and cross over into Germany through East Prussia which bordered

Russia. The head of German immigration and naturalization in the early period of the Weimar Republic happened to be Jewish (Herr Badt), who gave preference to Jews wanting to immigrate into Germany. At that same time, other European countries were still maintaining strict limits on Jewish immigration. These newcomers poring over the East Prussian border spread out and joined other Jewish communities which tended to locate in Germany's larger cities. With the Kaiser now gone, and all bars against them lifted, Jews flooded into all government offices of the Weimar Republic. They also systematically invaded the professions and German institutions. Jews stick together as a race and always pull and shove each other up the ranks of institutions and organizations, and pull strings to ensure that members of their race are given first priority at student openings in major universities, and so forth. While Western Christians generally apply the test of "ability" in hiring and promotions, with considerations for ethnicity or religion being secondary, or of no consideration whatever, Jews choose their associates and subordinates primarily based on their being "Jewish," and if they happen to have "ability" at the same time, well, that's OK too. In Jewish controlled organizations in the Weimar Republic, the Gentile did not have a chance in competition for jobs or promotions. Jews always chose other Jews. This intense in-group cooperation and mutual assistance among Jews facilitated their rapid infiltration of every institution in Germany. The pattern has always been the same; once a Jew obtains a position, he brings other Jews in, and in the process, gradually pushes the non-Jews out. It was not long until Jews dominated Weimar Germany. (That same process is occurring in the United States today.)

Sir Arthur Bryant, a respected British historian, explained in his book, *Unfinished Victory*, 1940, that although Jews comprised less than 1% of the German population, they controlled 57% of the metal trade, 22% of grain, and 39% of the textile trade. More than 50% of the Berlin Chamber of Commerce was Jewish, as were an amazing 1,200 of the 1,474 members of the German Stock Exchange. German banking and finance was under the total control of Jews. It was estimated that during the Weimar Republic, the average income of Jews was three times that of non-Jews. In 1928, it was revealed that just fifteen Jews had occupied

718 board positions between them. Of leading positions in industry there were 2 Jews for every non-Jew.

Below is a comparison of the percentage of top positions in Commerce held by Jews in various German cities during the Weimar period with the low percentage of Jews in "blue collar" jobs:

Percentage of Jews in Top Positions in Commerce		Percentage of Jews in Blue Collar Jobs
Berlin	49.4%	2.4%
Frankfurt	48.9%	1.9%
Cologne	49.6%	2.9%
Breslau	57.1%	1.8%

The political influence of the Jews in the Weimar Republic was enormously out of proportion to their numbers in the population. Of the Social Democratic Party's 39 Representatives, 38 were Jews. The membership of The Workers Educational Institutes were 81% Jewish.

Of the 29 legitimate theaters in Berlin, 23 had Jewish directors. In 1931, of 144 film scripts made into movies, 119 were written by Jews, and 77 were produced by Jews. Not less than 75% of all plays were written by Jews.

Joseph Eberle wrote in the journal "Schonere Zukunft," on February 3, 1929, *"The share of Jews in the film industry is so decisive that a very slight percentage is left available for non-Jewish undertakings."*

It gets worse! Of university teachers: in Berlin, in the field of medicine, 45% were Jewish; in Gottingen, 34% of mathematics professors were Jewish, 34% of medical professors were Jewish, 40% in the arts were Jewish, and 47% in law were Jews; in Breslau, in medicine, 45% Jewish; in law, 48% Jewish; in arts, 25% Jewish; In Konigsberg, in arts, 7% Jewish; in law 14% Jewish; in medicine, 25% Jewish.

In 1928, the percentages of lawyers who were Jewish: in Dortmouth 29%, Hamburg 26%, Stuttgart 26%, Dusseldorf 33%, Karlsruhe 36%, Beuthen 60%, Frankfurt 64%, Stettin 36%, Berlin 66%.

Percentage of doctors in private practice who were Jewish (1928): Wiesbaden 20%, Karlsruhe 26%, Cologne 27%, Mainz 30%, Gotha 31%, Beuthen 36%, Berlin 52%.

Percentage of doctors in Berlin hospitals who were Jewish: Moabit Hospital 56%, Friedrichshain Hospital 63%, and Neukolln Hospital 52%.

In his book "Mein Leben als deutscher Jude" (My Life as a German Jew), 1980, Dr. Nahum Goldmann describes the *"phenomenal rise of German Jewry"* as follows: *"German Jewry, which found its temporary end during the Nazi period, was one of the most interesting and for modern Jewish history most influential centers of European Jewry. During the era of emancipation, i.e. in the second half of the nineteenth and in the early twentieth century, it had experienced a meteoric rise.... It had fully participated in the rapid industrial rise of Imperial Germany, made a substantial contribution to it and acquired a renowned position in German economic life. Seen from the economic point of view, no Jewish minority in any other country, not even that in America could possibly compete with the German Jews. They were involved in large scale banking, a situation unparalleled elsewhere, and, by way of high finance, they had also penetrated German industry. A considerable portion of the wholesale trade was Jewish. They controlled even such branches of industry which is in general not in Jewish hands. Examples are shipping or the electrical industry, and names such as Ballin and Rathenau do confirm this statement. I hardly know of any other branch of emancipated Jewry in Europe or the American continent that was as deeply rooted in the general economy as was German Jewry. American Jews of today are absolutely as well as relatively richer than the German Jews were at the time, it is true, but even in America with its unlimited possibilities the Jews have not succeeded in penetrating into the central spheres of industry (steel, iron, heavy industry, high finance, shipping), as was the case in Germany.*

Their position in the intellectual life of the country was equally unique. In literature, they were represented by illustrious names. The theatre was largely in their hands. The daily press, above all its internationally influential sector, was essentially owned by Jews or controlled by them. As paradoxical as this may sound today, after the Hitler era, I have no hesitation to say that hardly any section of the Jewish people has made such extensive use of the

144

emancipation offered to them in the nineteenth century as the German Jews!
In short, the history of the Jews in Germany from 1870 to 1933 is probably
the most glorious rise that has ever been achieved by any branch of the Jewish
people". Dr. Nahum Goldmann

Further, according to Goldmann, *"The majority of the German Jews*
were never fully assimilated and were much more Jewish than the Jews in
other West European countries".

What Goldmann revealed, perhaps inadvertently, was that, precisely
as the Nazis were saying, the Jews had taken control of most of Germany's
institutions. Yet, they numbered less than 1% of the German population,
and as Goldmann also points out, they were never fully assimilated.
This tiny elite were seen by the German people as aliens and not even
German, yet, they literally ran the country. From this perspective,
the rise of Hitler and the Nazi movement and its strong anti-Jewish
sentiments become much easier to understand. Jewish propagandists
today deny that the Jews were so powerful in Germany at that time.

Dr. Nahum Goldmann was an ardent Zionist who was denounced
by the Nazis as a secret Communist agent shortly after the Beer Hall
Putsch. He was stripped of his German citizenship in 1935 and later
emigrated to the United States. He helped Rabbi Stephen Wise establish
the World Jewish Congress and became one of the more active purveyors
of sensational, but false, tales of Nazi atrocities against the Jews.

Jews Undermine German Culture

The Jews in Weimar Germany used their dominance in theater, film
and newspapers to ridicule traditional German culture and German
ideals. Christianity was also targeted for ridicule. (That process is now
occurring in the United States.) This was a period when Berlin gained
an international reputation for decadence, debauchery and pornography,
as depicted in the Broadway musical and later movie, *Cabaret*, for
example. Germany during the Weimar Republic underwent a virtually

The movie Cabaret typified the decadent life of Weimar Berlin

unparalleled period of social and cultural upheaval, to a great extent, a result of the disillusionment over losing the war and the unjust peace treaty which followed. Germans began to question the meaning of life. In Weimar's early years, Germany was a society which had been cut loose from its traditional cultural moorings and set adrift. The old norms and the old rules of social behavior didn't seem to apply anymore. The war also produced a similar result in England and American, though to a much lesser extent, causing a sort of social malaise, as manifested in the so-called "lost generation." The Jews used this climate of cultural uncertainty and loss of confidence among the German people to undermine and destroy what remained of the traditional German culture.

**Homosexuality and lesbianism were openly
flaunted during the Weimar years.**

Debauchery in Weimar Germany

To make matters worse, Germany experienced a "runaway" inflation
in 1923 which nearly destroyed the German economy. During the

inflation, a loaf bread cost four billion Marks. The middle class was wiped out, their life savings gone. People starved. Murder and violence were rampant, including sexual murder, or *lustmord*, which became a sensation in Weimar's tabloids. Women from once respectable families could be seen prostituting themselves, their daughters, and even their sons on the streets of Berlin in order to survive. In the eyes of the world, Weimar Berlin became the epitome of decadence. Women dressed like men and flaunted their lesbian lovers. Nudity was everywhere. The very word "Weimar" conjured up images of cabarets, cross-dressers, open homosexuality and prostitution. Berlin, with other German cities not far behind, became a Mecca of scandal, moral degradation and nudity. Jewish control of the news, information, and entertainment industries was the perceived cause of this breakdown in public morals. It was well established that Jews controlled prostitution and pornography, as well as the white slave trade, during the Weimar years. To use the language of today, the Nazis were "socially conservative," even puritanical in outlook, and saw themselves as the defenders of traditional, conservative, Christian, volkish German values. They denounced the licentiousness which had taken root in the country, and attributed it to Jewish influences. Weimar debauchery was the principle cause of the Nazi crackdown that followed.

Adolf Hitler wrote about it in "Mein Kampf:" *"One needed only to look at the posters announcing the hideous productions of the cinema and theatre, and study the names of the authors who were highly lauded there in order to become permanently adamant on Jewish questions. Here was a pestilence, a moral pestilence from which the public was being infected. It was worse than the Black Plague of long ago. And in what mighty doses this poison was manufactured and distributed. Naturally, the lower the moral and intellectual level of such an author of artistic products the more inexhaustible his fecundity. Sometimes it went so far that one of these fellows, acting like a sewage pump, would shoot his filth directly in the face of other members of the human race....It was a terrible thought, and yet it could not be avoided, that the greater number of Jews seemed specially designed by Nature to play this shameful part. The fact that nine tenths of all the smutty literature, artistic tripe and theatrical banalities, had to be charged to the account of people who formed scarcely one percent of the nation -- that fact could not be gainsaid. It was there. It had to be admitted."*

The Jewish influence in all of this civil discord in Germany was plain for anyone to see. A great majority of the Jews were Communists, which posed a mortal threat to the average German. The German people were fully aware of what had been happening in Russia at the hands of the Bolshevik Jews. Additionally, due to the rampant inflation, for it literally did take a wheel-barrow full of money to buy a loaf of bread, the only people who were able to buy either property or goods were those who could obtain money from outside the country, which, in most cases meant the Jews. In 1914, a German mark was valued at around twenty-five cents of American money. In 1923, four million marks equaled twenty-five cents. During this period many German families were forced to sell everything they had in order to survive. Upper-class Jews with foreign financial connections were able to buy up much of Germany's material wealth for incredibly low prices. So-called Jewish "carpetbaggers" were everywhere, consuming the nation like parasites consume a cadaver. All classes of Jews in Germany advanced themselves during the Weimar years while the economic condition of ethnic Germans steeply declined.

Germany had narrowly avoided a Bolshevik takeover of the country similar to that which had occurred in Russia; saved from this fate, as it were, by the Freikorps, or private militias comprised of soldiers and officers who had recently returned from the front. Nevertheless, from the beginning of the Weimar Republic, a tense bifurcation of political power existed between the Communists on the one hand, and right wing political parties on the other, including the National Socialists. As Germany staggered under the weight of economic chaos, that is, inflation, followed by depression, the Jewish Communists made a relentless, concerted effort to take political control. Under the banner of Communism and through control of finance (two heads of the same dragon), the Jews threatened to take complete control of the country.

An editorial in "The Daily Mail of London" of July 10, 1933 stated: *"The German nation... was rapidly falling under the control of its alien elements. In the days of the pre-Hitler regime there were twenty times as many Jewish government officials in Germany as had existed before the war (WWI). Israelites of international attachments were insinuating themselves into key positions in the German administrative machine."*

Adolf Hitler said: *"If the question is still asked why National Socialism combats the Jewish element in Germany so fanatically, the answer can only be, because National Socialism wishes to establish a real community of the people. Since we are National Socialists, we cannot permit an alien race to impose itself upon our working people as their leaders."*

Chapter 9

Hitler & National Socialists Rise to Power

After World War One, Adolf Hitler, still an Army corporal, joined the German Worker's Party (DAP) in Munich. Though young and inexperienced, he proved himself a mesmerizing public speaker with a mature grasp of the issues of the day, and soon became the party's chairman. Hitler burned with indignation and anger over Germany's humiliation in losing the war and over the vindictive and merciless Versailles Treaty imposed upon Germany afterwards. He dedicated his life to resurrecting Germany's position in the world. Hitler worked hard to build up the party and saw it as a means of acquiring political power. By now, he had become convinced that the Jews were the primary cause of most of Germany's troubles. Opposition to Communism and to Jewish control of Germany became part of the German Worker's Party's political platform.

In a speech at a public meeting on February 24, 1919, Hitler laid out his 25 points for the reclamation of Germany for the German people. These 25 points became, and remained, the platform, or goals, of the National Socialist Party. As can be seen, the platform was both nationalistic and socialistic in nature, hence National Socialism, with the goal of strengthening Germany and resurrecting the German people again. Hitler stressed the principle that "the common weal comes before individual welfare."

Hitler (seated on the right) and fellow soldiers during World War I. The dog was named "Fuchs" and was actually Hitler's pet during the war.

The 25 Points of the National Socialist Party

1. The unity of all German-speaking peoples in one country.
2. The abolition of the Treaty of Versailles.
3. Land and colonies to feed Germany's population (Lebensraum).
4. Only Germans can be citizens. No Jew can be a German citizen.
5. People in Germany who are not citizens, i.e., Jews, must obey special laws for foreigners.
6. Only German citizens can vote, be employed or hold public office.
7. Citizens, i.e., ethnic Germans, are entitled to a job and a decent standard of living. If this cannot be achieved, foreigners (with no rights as citizens) should be expelled.
8. No further immigration of non-Germans must be allowed. All non-German foreigners (which included the Jews) who have come to Germany since 1914 must be expelled.
9. All citizens have equal rights and duties.
10. The first duty of a citizen is to work.
11. All payments to unemployed people should end.
12. All profits made by profiteers during the war must be confiscated (A swipe at the Jews)
13. Nationalization of trusts. (Meaning, the big corporations)
14. Large companies must institute profit sharing plans with their employees.
15. Old age pensions must be increased.
16. Public help for small businesses; large department stores must be closed down (Another swipe at the Jews).
17. Property reform to give small farmers their land.
18. An all-out battle against criminals, profiteers, etc., who must be punished by death.
19. Reform of the law to make it more German.
20. Improve education so that all Germans can get a job.
21. Improve people's health by making a law for people to participate in sports.
22. Abolition of the professional Army, and a new People's Army in its place.
23. German newspapers must be free of foreign (Jewish) influence.
24. Freedom of religion.
25. Strong central government with unrestricted authority.

Among the 25 points was a demand for scrapping the Versailles Treaty and the return to Germany of territories taken away by the treaty. Germany had no moral obligation to abide by the Treaty, because it had been imposed upon Germany by coercion; by force. Any two men will agree that if one man forces another man into slavery by threat of violence or death, the enslaved man has no moral obligation to remain a slave. Anyone would agree that as soon as the enslaved man has the power or the means of escaping his enslavement, he has a moral right to do so. This same moral right also applies to nations. Germany had no moral or legal obligation to remain enslaved by the Versailles Treaty.

Hitler demanded the right of self determination for all Germans (according to President Wilson's 14 Points), which meant the right of Germans outside Germany to be incorporated into the German Reich. This would include the Sudeten Germans, as well as the return of the city of Danzig, and the annexation of Austria, all of whom wished to join Germany. He called for the restoration of equal rights for Germans as compared to those of other European peoples. Hitler also demanded the right of Germany to acquire land for Germany's surplus populations, referred to in other speeches and writings as *Lebensraum*. Britain had solved her surplus population problem by emigration to the colonies, i.e. North America, Australasia, and South Africa. Germany faced the same problem and desperately needed more space for her dense population.

The 25 Points also set the goal of wresting control of German institutions back from the Jews and of sidelining the Jews as a force of power and control in Germany. Toward the goal of creating a German state for the German people, Hitler called for the revocation of the citizenship of all those who did not have German blood, meaning the Jews primarily, and actually expelling all the East European Jews who had entered the country since the war. Revoking the citizenship of Jews would have the effect of sharply limiting the rights of Jews and subsequently, the power of Jews. The East European Jews who had entered Germany beginning in November 1914 were conspicuously non-German aliens, and almost all of them were revolutionary Communists and the primary troublemakers in Germany. Yet, with the help of German Jews, they had quickly insinuated themselves into influential positions throughout Germany. Hitler also called for the destruction of Germany's "bondage of interest," which was another swipe at the Jews. He wanted to create for Germany a new financial system, which, in fact, he did after becoming Chancellor later on.

In this landmark speech, Hitler also announced that the National Socialist Party (DAP) would be renamed the "National Socialist German Worker's Party" (NSDAP, or "NAZI," as the acronym would appear in German). Thereafter, criticism of the Jews became a regular feature of Hitler's speeches. He blamed them for the inflation, the unemployment, the political instability, and for losing the war. But more significantly, he tied the Jews in Germany to "internationalism," accusing them of placing their first loyalty to International Jewry.

The largest communist party in Europe was in Germany, which had a 78% Jewish membership. Germany was under the greatest threat of any European country of succumbing to Jewish, Bolshevik domination and control, and had, in fact, been specifically targeted by the Comintern as the next domino to fall. Had that come to pass, a bloody "red terror" similar to that which was still going on in Russia would surely have followed. It was against this background that Hitler and the National Socialists launched their program to push Jews out of controlling position in Germany.

The Jews were not only in complete control of Russia, they were also very powerful in Britain, France, and the United States, as well as in Germany. They controlled international banking and finance, they controlled the press and the information media, and they controlled movie making throughout Europe, especially in Germany, as well as in Britain and the United States. The Jews saw the upstart Hitler and his fledgling National Socialist party as a developing threat to their power and control in Germany. After Hitler's speech during which he presented his 25 points, the Jews began a virulent, international propaganda war against him and the Nazi party. This propaganda campaign continued relentlessly, growing ever more vitriolic, throughout the Nazi reign. Moreover, it continues even to this day, though the Nazis are long gone.

The Nazi party continued to grow and attract new members. At a public rally held in Munich on October 30, 1923, Hitler called for an end of the leftist Weimar Republic, which he declared was under the control of the Jews. During this rally, he called for a march on Berlin to rid the government of Communism and the Jews. A few days later, on November 8, 1923, Hitler held a rally at a Munich beer hall and proclaimed a revolution. The following day he led 2,000 armed "brown shirts" in an attempt to take over the Bavarian government in Munich. He was joined by a hero of the First World War, General Erich Ludendorff, along with Ludendorff's conservative nationalistic followers. Once they had taken Munich, Hitler and Ludendorff planned to use the Bavarian capital as a base of operations against the national government in Berlin. It turned out that their ambitions exceeded their power and the attempted "putsch" was easily put down by the police.

Hitler and Ludendorff were then arrested for treason, though Ludendorff was immediately acquitted due to his reputation as a war hero, but Hitler went on to trial. The judge in the trial, as it turned out, was sympathetic to Hitler's views, and he permitted Hitler to use the trial as a propaganda forum, which Hitler took full advantage of. Though Hitler was convicted he received the light sentence of 5 years, to be served at Landsberg Prison in comfortable conditions. He only served eight months as it turned out, and he used those eight months very profitably. During his stay at Landsberg, with the help of Rudolph Hess, Hitler wrote his book *Mein Kampf* (My Struggle), The book eventually sold 10 million copies and made Hitler a wealthy man.

In *Mein Kampf* Hitler laid out his views for the future of the German people. He blamed the Jews for Germany's troubles, and also for most of the troubles in the world, as manifested by their murderous regime in Russia, their leadership in the unsuccessful German Communist Revolution of 1918/19, and also the Jewish Communist take-over of Hungary in 1919. Hitler made it plain that he considered the Jews to be the German nation's true enemy. They had no culture of their own, he averred, but perverted existing cultures such as Germany's with their parasitism. As such, he said, they were not a race, but an anti-race.

Another main idea put forward in *Mein Kampf*, an idea previously presented in his "25 Points," was that if Germany was to survive as a state it must acquire "lebensraum," or living space, for its overcrowded population. This, he said, would be found in the East, that is, in Russia and the Ukraine, which was now ruled by Jewish Communists. *"Without consideration of 'traditions' and prejudices,"* he wrote, *"it [Germany] must find the courage to gather our people and their strength for an advance along the road that will lead this people from its present restricted living space to new land and soil, and hence also free it from the danger of vanishing from the earth or of serving others as a slave nation."*

The geopolitical concept of Lebensraum ("living space") was not original with Hitler. It had been advocated by others in Germany long before Adolf Hitler came to power, including Karl Haushofer, Sir Halford Mackinder of Britain, and Friedrich Ratzel. It was Ratzel who coined the term "lebensraum." In 1871, "Lebensraum" was a popular political slogan during the unification of Germany as a single nation-state. At that time, Lebensraum usually meant finding additional "living space" by adding colonies, following the examples of the British and French empires. But Germany's colonies had been taken away after the Great War by the Versailles Treaty, and without colonies to which excess populations could be exported, Germany would have to consider other possibilities. Germany was one of the most densely populated countries in Europe and its population was increasing rapidly. Finding "lebensraum" was seen as a necessity.

The obvious territory for Germany to expand into was always in the East, as Hitler explained in *Mein Kampf*. *"In an era when the earth is gradually being divided up among states, some of which embrace almost entire continents, we cannot speak of a world power in connection with a formation whose political mother country is limited to the absurd area of five hundred thousand square kilometers."*

The "East" was thinly populated compared to the rest of Europe, and Germans, as well as the rest of Europe, thought about it somewhat as Americans thought about the "wild west." In 1926, Hans Grimm's book *Volk ohne Raum* ("A People without Space") was published. This book became a classic on Germany's need for space and the book's title soon became a popular National Socialist slogan. Neither Hitler nor anyone else in Germany ever considered expansion into Western Europe.

Hitler explains the logic of finding lebensraum in the East in order to enlarge Germany within Europe, rather than to seek colonies elsewhere. *"For it is not in colonial acquisitions that we must see the solution of this problem, but exclusively in the acquisition of a territory for settlement, which will enhance the area of the mother country, and hence not only keep the new settlers in the most intimate community with the land of their origin, but secure for the total area those advantages which lie in its unified magnitude."* Adolf Hitler, "Mein Kampf."

Hitler justified a German expansion into Russian territory by pointing out that the Soviet Union was now run by Jews who had killed Russia's best people, the majority of whom were of German blood. The czars of Russia were of German blood, as were most of the aristocracy.

"For centuries Russia drew nourishment from this Germanic nucleus of its upper leading strata. Today it can be regarded as almost totally exterminated and extinguished. It has been replaced by the Jew. Impossible as it is for the Russian by himself to shake off the yoke of the Jew by his own resources, it is equally impossible for the Jew to maintain the mighty empire forever. He himself is no element of organization, but a ferment of decomposition... And the end of Jewish rule in Russia will also be the end of Russia as a state." Adolf Hitler, *Mein Kampf*.

"Lebensraum," in Nazi ideology, meant the settlement of German farmers in the area east of Germany. The Slavic population was to be pushed out as German farmers moved in. This was to be a reprise of America's expansion to the West, during which the Indians had been pushed out. It also parallels modern day Israel's Jewish settlement of Palestine, where the Palestinian owners of the land are pushed out to make way for Jewish settlers. The Nazi theory of Lebensraum became Germany's foreign policy during the Third Reich.

Once released from prison, Hitler decided that the best way to take power was by constitutional means -- that is, by winning elections. A coup or putsch, similar to the one he had just been imprisoned for, was impracticable, he decided. He began to campaign throughout the country, during which he was received enthusiastically by the German people. As the campaign progressed, he drew larger and larger crowds. With his spell binding oratory, he called for the German people to resist the yoke of the Jews and Communism, and to create a new Germany for the German people. He asserted that the Jews were Germany's biggest enemy, accusing them of trying to take over the country to turn it into another Soviet Union, as they had done in Russia, in Hungary briefly, and as they had tried to do in Germany. In one speech, he said, "[The Jews'] *ultimate goal is the denaturalization, the promiscuous bastardization of other peoples, the lowering of the racial level of the highest peoples as well as the domination of his racial mishmash through the extirpation of the volkish intelligentsia and its replacement by the members of his own people.*"

It is the Jews in America today who are behind multiculturalism, open immigration, racial mixing, the denial of the right to "freedom of association," etc. Their intent today is to undermine the once dominant position of white, European Americans, and to reduce them to an ethnic minority in their own country. Hitler's words above is a description of what is going on in America today.

In campaigning for votes, Hitler deliberately appealed to farmers and white collar voters in small towns who were conservative and nationalistic by nature. They were the demographic group who were most antagonistic towards the leftist Weimar Republic. In the election held in September, 1930, the Nazi Party won 18 percent of the votes cast. Suddenly the Nazis were a force to be reckoned with. In 1932, Hitler ran for President and won 30 percent of the national vote, forcing a runoff election between himself and Paul von Hindenburg. Von Hindenburg won the runoff election, but Hitler was not far behind in votes cast. Hitler agreed to enter a coalition government, and in January, 1933, von Hindenburg, who was President of Germany, appointed Hitler to be the Chancellor.

This election put an end to the Jewish controlled Weimar Republic, and marked the beginning of the Third Reich. The election also marked the beginning of a virulent Jewish propaganda war against Germany and the Nazi leadership, and against Adolf Hitler in particular. As a result of this relentless smear campaign, no man in history has been so mischaracterized as Hitler. Despite his impressive accomplishments, he is held up today as the very personification of evil; a madman and a psychopath, demonically intent upon conquering

**President Paul von Hindenburg appoints Adolph Hitler
Chancellor of Germany on January 30, 1933.**

the world. As the decades have passed, this characterization has grown
to mythic proportions, to the extent that for some he now serves as a
modern surrogate for the "Devil" of medieval times.

But this image of Hitler does not square with the way in which he
was described by international statesmen, reporters and other prominent
people at that time, at least up until the beginning of World War Two.
Hitler was not only extremely popular with the German people; he
was widely admired by political leaders throughout the world. Hitler
received high praise from every quarter for all he was able to accomplish
for Germany. When Hitler was elected Chancellor in 1933, he became
the leader of a starving, defeated and demoralized people -- the result of
losing World War One -- and almost miraculously raised them up again
into a prosperous, well fed, highly motivated, industriously advanced
and highly successful nation. Moreover, he was able to do this in the
short span of only five years. Franklin D. Roosevelt became president

of the United States in 1933, at the same time that Hitler was elected chancellor of Germany. The economic problems FDR had to deal with in the United States were mild compared to those in Germany. Yet, by 1938, while Germany under Hitler was booming, the depression in the United States continued unchanged, with an unemployment rate that remained at 19 percent. The depression in the United States only ended when the war began.

The German people adored Hitler and saw him as their redeemer. His unprecedented accomplishments also astonished the world. Hitler provided real leadership for the German nation after a long period of social malaise, and he motivated the German people to unprecedented heights of achievement in every field of endeavor. German industrial production grew spectacularly. Under his leadership Germany became a transformed nation wherein the German people were no longer the humiliated and broken mass he had inherited. An infectious feeling of excitement and expectancy had permeated the country which extended even to Germans living outside the Reich. Ethnic Germans of Austria, Sudetenland, Danzig, etc., all wanted to join Germany and become a part of Third Reich.

These amazing changes did not go unnoticed by prominent visitors to Germany. After a tour through the country in 1936, former Prime Minister of England David Lloyd George wrote an article for the "London Daily Express," in which he said: *"I have never met a happier people than the Germans and Hitler is one of the greatest men. The old trust him; the young idolize him. It is the worship of a national hero who has saved his country."*

Another British leader, Viscount Rothermere, in "Warnings and Predictions," March, 1939, wrote this about Hitler: *"He has a supreme intellect. I have known only two other men to whom I could apply such distinction -- Lord Northcliffe and Lloyd George. If one puts a question to Hitler, he gives an immediate, brilliant clear answer. There is no human being living whose promise on important matters I would trust more readily. He believes that Germany has a divine calling and that the German people are destined to save Europe from the revolutionary attacks of Communism. He values family life very highly, whereas Communism is its worst enemy. He has thoroughly cleansed the moral, ethical life of Germany, forbidden publication of obscene books, and performance of questionable plays and films.*

No words can describe his politeness; he disarms men as well as women and can win both at any time with his conciliatory, pleasant smile. He is a man of rare culture. His knowledge of music, the arts and architecture is profound."

Theodur Huess, a liberal German politician who later served as President of the Federal Republic of Germany after World War Two, said in the late 1930s: *"He [Hitler] moves souls, the will to sacrifice, and great devotion, enthralling and enthusiastically inspiring everyone by his appearance."*

Even after the end of World War II, there were still those who could speak objectively of Hitler. Immediately after the war, future president of the United States, John F. Kennedy was hired by the Hearst Newspaper chain and sent to Germany to travel around and report back on conditions there. Kennedy kept a diary which was recently published. In one diary entry he wrote: *"After visiting these two places (Berchtesgaden and the Eagle's lair on Obersalzberg), you can easily understand how that within a few years Hitler will emerge from the hatred that surrounds him now as one of the most significant figures who ever lived. He had boundless ambitions for his country which rendered him a menace to the peace of the world, but he had a mystery about him in the way that he lived and in the manner of his death that will live and grow after him. He had in him the stuff of which legends are made."* --John F. Kennedy 'Prelude To Leadership - The European Diary of John F. Kennedy - Summer, 1945. (No public figure could get away with expressing such sentiments today.)

General Leon DeGrelle of the Waffen SS was a highly educated Belgian political leader who joined the SS to help save Europe from Communism, which he saw as an existential threat to Western, Christian Civilization. (The Waffen SS was an all-volunteer force, made up of members from every European country. A million foreigners from all over Europe voluntarily joined the SS simply because they believed in what Hitler was trying to achieve. The Waffen SS was the first truly "European" army ever to exist, and it came into being to save Europe from the Communist menace.) DeGrelle was an intellectual, a natural leader, a devout Catholic and a prolific writer, and before the war, he had been personally acquainted with all the heads of state in Europe. He believed that Europe had a unique destiny and that it must unite. He also did all he could to avert a war in Europe. But once the war began, he became a soldier in the life and death struggle against the Communist enemy, the USSR. He joined the Waffen SS as a private but due to his remarkable abilities he was promoted rank by rank up to the rank of general. DeGrelle had only the greatest admiration for Hitler. He wrote after the war from his refuge in Spain:

"Hitler was the greatest statesman Europe has ever known. History will prove that when whipped up emotions have died down. He was more matter of fact, generally more unfolded than Napoleon. Napoleon was more of a vanquishing, empire-founding Frenchman than a true European.

Hitler, in his being a man of his time, dreamed of an enduring, just, honest Europe, unified by the initiative of the victor. A Europe however in which each ethnic group could develop according to their merits and accomplishments. The proof of this is that he offered Petain his hand. Just as Bismarck knew how to outgrow Prussia and become a German, so Hitler soon changed from being a German to being a European. At an early stage he disconnected himself from imperialistic ambition."

SS General DeGrelle

"Without any difficulty he began to think of himself as a European and initiated the creation of a Europe in which Germany - like Prussia in Bismarck's time, was to be the foundation stone. Some comrades of the Fuhrer might still have been short-sighted Pan-Germanists. But Hitler had the genius, the right scale, the absence of bias and the necessary vision to accomplish the terrific task. He had an authority, not to be found a second time in the history of the continent. His success would have established wealth and civilization of Europe for centuries, probably forever. Hitler's plans for Europe would have meant a blessing for us all."

Chapter 10

National Socialism vs. Communism

German National Socialism has usually been characterized as a right wing ideology while Communism is said to occupy the extreme left of the socio-political spectrum. This is the traditional view. But there are those today who say that Hitler's obsessive hatred of Communism was disingenuous because German National Socialism was essentially no different from Communism. Both were totalitarian Socialist creeds. But this is a superficial observation, and the terms, "right" and "left" are insufficient to describe the two systems. It is true that National Socialism contained aspects of socialism, as its name implied, but the differences between National Socialism and Communism were profound. The most obvious difference was that National Socialism supported the concept of private property and a market economy, while Communism abolished private property and the government controlled the economy through "central planning." Under National Socialism the means of production was for the most part in private hands, albeit, "guided" by the state. Under Communism all private property, including farmland, manufacturing, or the means of production, and even private housing, were seized by the state. The only similarity between the two systems was that both were totalitarian in nature, though, between the two, National Socialism was considerably more benign. Under National Socialism, the private rights of "citizens" were respected and protected, while under Communism there were no private rights.

Hitler had this to say about the meaning of "Socialism" for Germany, as printed in an article in the UK's "Guardian, Sunday Express," December 28, 1938: *"'Socialist' I define from the word 'social' meaning in the main 'social equity'. A Socialist is one who serves the common good without giving up his individuality or personality or the product of his personal efficiency. Our adopted term 'Socialist has nothing to do with Marxian Socialism. Marxism is anti-property; true socialism is not. Marxism places no value on the individual, or individual effort, or efficiency; true Socialism values the individual and encourages him in individual efficiency, at the same time holding that his interests as an individual must be in consonance with those of the community. All great inventions, discoveries, achievements were first the product of an individual brain. It is charged against me that I am against property, that I am an atheist. Both charges are false."* Adolf Hitler.

The two systems were also different in their aims. National Socialism under Adolf Hitler was a revolutionary movement in "defense" of Western, Christian civilization, while Communism was a revolutionary movement dedicated to its "destruction." Harold Cox, Member of Parliament in Britain at the time, and a classical liberal scholar, wrote:

"What Socialists (Communists) want is not progress in the world as we know it, but the destruction of that world as a prelude to the creation of a new world of their own imagining...Their ethical outlook is the direct reverse of that which has inspired all great religions of the world...and they deliberately make their appeal to the passions of envy, hatred and malice." Harold Cox.

The Communist Jews who took control of Russia did their utmost to destroy the traditional Christian culture of Russia and they murdered upwards of 40 million of Russia's best people. It has been said that the average IQ for Russia was lowered several points by this slaughter of the "intelligentsia" and all the other successful, achieving people in Russia. Through their "Communist International" (Comintern), they intended to do the same to all of Europe. The long term goal of International

Jewish Communism, which had established its base in Russia, was to destroy the existing political regimes throughout Europe, and replace them, one by one, with Soviet Republics on the Russian model. Once in power, they intended the obliteration of the "possessing classes," that is, to kill them, as they had done in Russia. Europe had every reason to shudder in horror at the prospect of a Communist takeover.

National Socialism (Nazism) developed after 1918 as a counter-movement to the Bolshevik revolution, and to a lesser extent, against the democratic parliamentary system, as manifested in the Weimar Republic. In an article in the Nazi newspaper, "Völkischer Beobachter," May 11, 1933 -- soon after becoming Chancellor -- Hitler wrote: *"For fourteen or fifteen years I have continually proclaimed to the German nation that I regard it as my task before posterity to destroy Marxism, and that is no empty phrase but a solemn oath which I shall follow as long as I live. I have made this confession of faith, the confession of faith of a single man, that of a mighty organization [National Socialism]. I know now that even if fate were to remove me, the fight would be fought to the end; this movement is the guarantee for that. This for us is not a fight which can be finished by compromise. We see in Marxism the enemy of our people which we will root out and destroy without mercy.... We must then fight to the very end those tendencies which have eaten into the soul of the German nation in the last seventeen years, which have done us such incalculable damage and which, if they had not been vanquished, would have destroyed Germany. Bismarck told us that liberalism was the pace-maker of Social Democracy. I need not say here that Social Democracy is the pace-maker of Communism. And Communism is the forerunner of death, of national destruction, and extinction. We have joined battle with it and will fight it to the death."*

National Socialism

National Socialism did not spring fully formed out of Adolf Hitler's head alone, though he made enormous contributions to its formation. It's detractors (Jewish propagandists) characterized Nazi ideology as the shallow fantasies of bigoted psychopaths, but in fact, National Socialism was a coherent, well grounded social philosophy worked out by highly regarded thinkers and scholars. Contrary to his popular image, Hitler, himself, was a thinker and a philosopher of first rank.

History Professor Lawrence Birken of Ball State University in Indiana claims that Adolf Hitler was the most philosophical of all historical leaders. "*Hitler had a gift for presenting his message in an attractive, accessible form.*" Writes Birken: "*The most attractive feature of Hitler's ideology was thus its optimism. It was not merely his mood but his message that carried an infectious excitement. He was a secular messiah proclaiming a Germanic version of the "good news." The possibility of class reconciliation, the plans for a national revival, the identification of a universal enemy whose elimination would usher in the millennium, all stirred his audiences to the very depths. Hitler spoke the language of the [Enlightenment] philosophers, a language that had almost passed out of existence in the rarefied strata of the grand intelligentsia.*

National Socialism's intellectual roots grew out of the philosophical ideas of a variety of popular writers and thinkers of the 19th and early 20th centuries, including the following:

Friedrich Nietzsche's theory of "will to power," the components of which were, achievement, ambition, and striving to reach the highest possible position in life. Nietzsche believed that "will to power" was the main driving force in man.

Arthur de Gobineau's racialist theory of the "Aryan master race." Gobineau was a French aristocrat, novelist, and man of letters who became famous for developing the racialist theory of the Aryan master race in his book, "An Essay on the Inequalities of the Human Races" (1855). Gobineau believed that the white race was superior to other races, manifested by its achievements in developing a civilized culture and in maintaining ordered government. He believed that "race mixing" would result in decline and chaos. Gobineau's views were by no means unusual at the time. They were generally shared by the entire white race.

Houston Stewart Chamberlain, British author of books on political philosophy and natural science. Chamberlain generally supported Gobineau's ideas on the superiority of the Aryan race and also became an advocate of racial "purity." He believed that the Teutonic peoples had profoundly influenced Western civilization, but that other European peoples had also done so. He included not just Germans, but Celts, Slavs, Greeks, Latins, and even Berbers from North Africa into the "Aryan race."

Richard Wagner's "faith in destiny." Wagner, a friend of Nietzsche, developed the idea that the German people should have faith in their destiny for greatness. He also saw the Jew as a parasite on the host populations they lived amongst and the natural enemy of Germany.

Gregor Johann Mendel's theory of genetics and heredity. Mendel was an Austrian scientist and Augustinian friar who was the founder of the science of genetics. He demonstrated that inheritance of certain traits in pea plants follow particular patterns. He developed the laws of "inherited traits" by experimenting on plants, which was then extrapolated to work the same in human beings.

Alfred Ploetz and Harvard Professor Lothard Stoddard both espoused social Darwinism, which led to the development of the science of Eugenics, or race cleansing. Eugenics was widely popular in the early decades of the twentieth century, both in the United States and in Europe. The First International Congress of Eugenics in 1912 was supported by many prominent people, including its president Leonard Darwin, the son of Charles Darwin, honorary vice president Winston Churchill, Alexander Graham Bell, et al.

Karl Haushofer, a German general, geographer and geopolitician who advocated *lebensraum* as the remedy for overcrowding in Germany. (The British, for example, had a similar overcrowding problem which they alleviated with their own version of *lebensraum,* large scale emigration of Britons to the colonies.)

Other influences of Nazi ideology were the ideas of Machiavelli, Fichte, Treitschke and Spengler.

The National Socialist (Nazi) ideology contained these basic points: nationalism, anti-Semitism, anti-Communism, and militarism. Jews were considered racially alien to Europe and the source of most of Europe's troubles, especially as the source of Communist revolution. Hitler called for the defense of the "Blood and Soil" of the German people by, expelling the Jews from Germany, by limiting immigration into Germany only to those of German blood, and by maintaining a strong military. National Socialism emphasized the concept of *das Volk* (the people as a national race), which required the subordination of the individual to the "community," as well as "faith in the leader (Fuhrer)." Hitler believed that Germany, as the largest and most powerful nation state in continental Europe, should be the leader of an economically unified Europe (something like the European Union of today, which, incidentally, is led by Germany). National Socialism emphasized the community of the German Volk, and glorified the comradeship of men in arms as defenders of the German nation. The Nazi movement became a magnet for those who had become disillusioned by the chaos in Germany under the Weimar Republic.

Although he is endlessly castigated as "the most notorious racist of the twentieth century," Hitler's racial views were in perfect harmony with mainstream 19th- and early 20th-century European thinking. Far from being aberrant or bizarre, his views on race were consistent with those of most prominent Westerners in the decades before the Second World War, such as those of Woodrow Wilson and Winston Churchill, for example.

Contrary to popular belief, Hitler never supported any program of breeding a homogenous blond "hyper-Aryan" race. That was just propaganda. He fully accepted the reality that the German population consisted of several distinct sub-racial groups, and stressed the German people's national and social unity. A certain degree of racial variety was desirable, he thought, and too much racial blending or homogeneity could be harmful because it would homogenize and thus eliminate superior as well as inferior genetic traits.

Alfred Rosenberg, Ph. D

The most influential Nazi guidebook, after Hitler's "Mein Kampf," was Alfred Rosenberg's "Myth of the Twentieth Century" (1935). Rosenberg, who held a Ph. D. in architectural engineering, was one of the principal ideologues of the Nazi Party and editor of the Nazi paper

"Volkisher Beobachter." Rosenberg believed that every people, culture and nation has a set of beliefs, or a national "myth," and if and when that myth ever dies, the nation too will die. (A great many comparisons can be made between the period at the end of the Weimar Republic and America today. The American myth, based on Christian belief and the ideals of our founding fathers is under constant attack today, and is being corrupted on a daily basis.) The German national "myth," according to Rosenberg, was in danger of dying, and he made it his mission to resurrect it.

Rosenberg makes a distinction between the "nation," or the "Volk," and the state. The nation is the people or the Volk. The state is the apparatus of government.

"The state," he wrote, *"is nowadays no longer an independent idol, before which everything must bow down; the state is not even an end but is only a means for the preservation of the "Volk".... Forms of the state change, and the laws of the state pass away; the Volk remains. From this alone follows that the nation (Volk) is the first and last; that to which everything else has to be subordinated."*

"No 'Volk' of Europe is racially pure," he wrote, *"including Germany. In accordance with the newest researches, we recognize five races, which exhibit noticeably different types. It is unquestionably true that the Nordic race primarily has borne the genuine cultural fruits of Europe. The great heroes, artists, founders of states have come from this race.... Nordic blood created German life above all others. Even those sections, in which only a small part today is pure Nordic, have their basic stock from the Nordic race. Nordic is German and has functioned so as to shape the culture and human types of the westisch, dinarisch, and ostisch–Baltisch races. Also a type which is predominantly dinarisch has often been innerly formed in a Nordic mode. **This emphasis on the Nordic race does not mean a sowing of 'race-hatred' in Germany, but on the contrary, the conscious acknowledgment of a kind of racial cement within our nationality."*** (Emphasis added.)

". . . On the day when Nordic blood should completely dry up, Germany would fall to ruin, would decline into a characterless chaos. That many forces are consciously working toward this, has been discussed in detail."

"Europe's states have all been founded and preserved by the Nordic man..... In order to preserve Europe, the Nordic energies of Europe must first be revitalized, strengthened. That means then Germany, Scandinavia with Finland, and England. "

". . . Nordic Europe is the fated future, with a German central Europe. Germany as racial and national state, as central power of the continent, safe-guarding the south and southeast; the Scandinavian states with Finland as a second group, safe-guarding the northeast; and Great Britain, safe-guarding the west and overseas at those places where required in the interest of the Nordic Man. "

It is clear from Rosenberg's writings that the Germans, including Hitler, never considered themselves the *Master Race,* and never referred to themselves as such. That accusation was nothing more than Jewish propaganda. The attitude of the British on this matter was identical to that of the Germans. The British were equally as nationalistic as the Germans, and the British considered themselves to be a part of a superior race. Moreover, both the Germans and the British openly acknowledged that the two nations, Britain and Germany, were of the same race and of the same blood. (Yet, Rosenberg was hanged after the Nuremberg Trials for his views, as expressed above.)

Jews Plan Marxist Utopia

While Hitler and the Nazis were busy resurrecting Germany on the basis of the national myth of the German Volk whom they considered the foundation of Western, Christian civilization -- in Russia, the Jews were busy destroying the traditional Russian, Christian culture. Moreover, the very first program initiated whenever Jewish-led Communists took over a country, i.e., Russia, Hungary and Spain, was to try to eradicate the Christian church. They rounded up the priests, nuns and monks by the thousands and shot them, and then burned down the churches and cathedrals. Hitler and the Nazis considered the Jewish Communists as the destroyers of Western, Christian civilization, and they dedicated themselves to Communism's eventual destruction.

The "Communism" which these Marxist Jews who now controlled

Russia dreamed of, and intended to impose on Russia -- and the rest of the world, if they could -- was a strictly theoretical (and completely unproven) system imagined by Karl Marx in which all of society, all of economics and all politics would be combined into one perfect, classless, cultureless, government-less system based on common ownership of all economic means of production (meaning government ownership), with complete social and economic equality, which would, in the end, run itself without the necessity of having a government. Karl Marx and Frederich Engels (both Jews) wrote the "Communist Manifesto" for the purpose of inspiring violent revolution everywhere in order to bring about this Utopian dream. Marxist theory called for the revolutionary overthrow of the *bourgeoisie*, followed by a preparatory stage of *socialism*, alternatively called "The Dictatorship of the Proletariat." Pure Communism, the end goal of Marxist Socialism, would then follow, and would be the theoretical state of "statelessness" in which an un-governed, classless society would live in perfect order.

The remarkable thing about this ideology from the perspective of today, or perhaps any day, is that it was so clearly and obviously stupid that it simply astounds the imagination that intelligent, educated people could have believed in it. But belief in Communism was not limited to these so-called "intellectuals." Marxist Communism became the Jewish secular religion. Communism was a Jewish invention, which sprang naturally out of the collectivist Jewish culture, and was generally accepted at some level by almost all Jews worldwide. Obviously there were non-Jewish adherents to Communism, but Communism was a Jewish movement, created by Jews, led by Jews and propagated by Jews. It would be inaccurate to aver that all Jews accepted Communism as a belief system, but surely the vast majority did.

The obvious flaw in Communist ideology was that it defied human nature. Moreover, it defied common sense. Man simply does not behave in the way required for Communism to work. Yet, Lenin, Trotsky, and all the other Jewish, Marxist revolutionary thinkers and leaders were convinced that they could implement it. The key to doing so, they said, was to kill off the bourgeoisie (Bourgeoisie, for their purposes, was an all inclusive term meaning all those above the peasant and proletariat, or working, class). In the actual application of Communism, they never got beyond the "socialism" stage, or the dictatorship of a Jewish elite. The "dictatorship of the proletariat" never occurred.

Jews considered themselves to be God's chosen people, and innately superior to the Gentiles they lived amongst, yet, over the centuries, they had long been held down, or even expelled by the Gentiles. For that reason, among others, they nourished an intense burning sense of injustice and resentment against Gentiles of all classes, but in particular, the bourgeoisie who had lorded over them. They also despised the ignorant, superstitious, fervently religious Russian peasants, who despised them in return, and who had carried out repeated pogroms against Jews. But now in control of the state, the Jews treated the ethnic Russians as a conquered people, against whom they intended to take their revenge. Vengeance seeking is a basic imperative of Jewish culture. "You kill my cousin; I'll kill your cousin!"

Their goal was to remake Russia into the Marxist Utopia they had long dreamed about. These ideological Bolshevik Jews saw the vast population of Russian peasants and proletarians as a malleable, cultureless mass who could be molded into a "New Soviet Man," through which they could bring about their dream of a communist "heaven on earth," provided, that is, that those wherein the traditional Russian culture resided -- the monarchy, the aristocracy, the educated, the Orthodox Church (collectively, the bourgeoisie) -- could be eliminated. The Jews were not Russians, but an alien people, and they felt no kinship nor compassion for the Russians they intended to kill. They felt only hatred.

In order to create their Utopia in Russia, their first task was to destroy the culture that already existed, including Christianity. To do this, these Bolshevik Jews unleashed the greatest bloodbath in history, far exceeding anything the Mongols did, and a thousand times worse than anything the notorious Nazis did. As an illustration of the bloody mindedness of these Bolshevik Jews, Grigory Zinoviev (real name Hirsch Apfelbaum), as head of the Communist International, wrote in an article in the "Drasnaya Gazeta" in Moscow, September 1, 1918: *"We will make our hearts cruel, hard and immovable, so that no mercy will enter them, and so that they will not quiver at the sight of a sea of enemy blood. We will let loose the floodgates of that sea. Without mercy, without sparing, we will kill our enemies in scores of hundreds. Let them be thousands; let them drown themselves in their own blood! For the blood of Lenin [shot but survived in 1918] and Uritsky [shot and killed in 1918], Zinoviev [shot but lived in 1919] and Voladarsky [shot and killed in 1918], let there be floods of blood of the bourgeois -- more blood! As much as possible."*

These Bolshevik Jews murdered upwards of 40 million ethnic, Christian Russians. The precise number will never be known. This was so horrific that it terrified the traditional ruling classes in the rest of Europe, as they saw the possibility of the same thing happening in their own countries. This was especially true in Germany, still unstable as the result of losing the war, but also with the largest Communist party outside of Russia. The German Communist party was 78% Jewish. Is there any wonder that Hitler and the National Socialists saw Jews and Communism as the mortal enemy of Germany and Western, Christian civilization?

The wonder is that Britain and the United States did not. By allying themselves with the Jewish-led anti-Christian, atheistic, Communist Soviet Union to destroy Christian Germany, Britain and the United States must bear the burden of responsibility for the decline of Western Civilization following World War II.

Chapter 11

Jews Declare War on Nazi Germany

Hitler's election as Chancellor in January, 1933 set off alarm bells throughout International Jewry because he threatened to end the predominating Jewish influence in German affairs.

The Jewish Diaspora, then as now, formed the world's most powerful trading and political bloc. They control, and controlled then, the international press and therefore public opinion, and they control banking and finance, and therefore industry. They provide most of the money with which politicians get elected, and they therefore control the politicians, and by controlling the politicians, they control governments. Hitler's election meant interruption of and interference with the world's commercial and political system which World Jewry dominated. When Hitler and the National Socialists came to power in Germany, the Jews were in complete control of Russia; were very powerful in the United States, Britain and France; and they dominated virtually every institution in Germany. Jewish exclusion from the commercial and political life of Germany, as Hitler planned, meant a breach in the cohesion of the worldwide system which Jews controlled.

Left - Adolf Hitler when he became Chancellor.

Moreover, Hitler stood alone in his defiance of the tidal-wave of Jewish organized Communism which threatened to sweep over Europe. Having seized control of Russia which they used as a base, Jewish Communists were behind all the civil unrest throughout the West, including Eastern Europe, Britain, France, Italy, the Spanish Civil War, and even in the United States. (Communism was introduced into the United States by the wave of East European Jewish immigrants that swarmed into this country at the turn of the twentieth century.) Germany alone repelled and held in check this tsunami of subversion and insurrection. Hitler's election posed an immediate threat to International Jewish power, and they quickly organized economic warfare against Germany as a means of bringing the National socialist state to its knees.

Hitler had spoken out from the day he entered politics against Jewish control in Germany, and had won election in large part due to his promise to free Germany from the Jewish grip. He had made it clear that he intended to impose restrictions on Jewish power in Germany as soon as he was in position to do so. The Jews did not wait for him to begin acting against Jewish interests in Germany. International Jewry made a preemptory strike.

Bernard Lecache, President of the Jewish World League declared at the time: *"Germany is our public enemy No. 1. It is our object to declare war without mercy against her."*

Hans Grimm, a distinguished German writer quoted a leading Jew in Australia, who said to a visiting German admiral: *"Herr Admiral, you have heard that President Hindenburg has assigned the office of Reich Chancellor to the National Socialist Hitler on the basis of the results of the last Reichstag election? Herr, Admiral. I here give you my word, think on it later. We Jews will do everything to erase this event from the world."*

The Jews were not about to tolerate this upstart Hitler without a fight, and fight, they were well prepared to do. It has been said that the pen is mightier than the sword and the Jews were masters of the pen and of the written word. The Jews do not fight their wars with armies of armed men, at least, not armies of armed Jewish men. The Jews control the news media, as well as banking and finance throughout Europe and America, and they fight their wars with propaganda and with their control of capital. They organize boycotts to destroy businesses in their target country; they undermine the economy of the target country through financial manipulation and by cutting off lending which no economy can do without, and they mold and inflame world opinion with manufactured news and propaganda to turn public opinion completely against the target country. Through their control of politicians they manage to pit nations against each other, then use other people's armies to fight their battles. They then reap enormous profits off both sides of the conflict as war profiteers. (This is happening today, as the Israelis and their American fifth column, the Jewish neocons, use American military power to fight their wars in the Middle East.)

The Jews already had an effective anti-Nazi, anti-Hitler propaganda campaign underway, beginning with Hitler's "25 Points" speech in 1921. This campaign intensified with the publication of *Mein Kampf* in 1925. When Hitler became Chancellor, the attacks went into hysteria mode.

Hitler in particular and all Nazi leaders in general immediately became targets of a relentless smear campaign. The Nazis were characterized in the Jewish press as uneducated, low-class, brutish upstarts with crude manners and no sophistication. No smear was too excessive to be used against them. Hitler was said to be nothing more than a wallpaper hanger, and was alleged to spend most of his time either chewing on the carpet or baying at the moon when he was not screaming and gesticulating. It was reported that he only had one testicle and secretly harbored sexually deviant thoughts. It was spread around that Goering was a hedonistic drug addict who wore women's silk underpants. Germany's Foreign Minister, Joachim von Ribbentrop, was accused of being a phony poseur, who was no aristocrat at all as his "von" indicated, but had previously been only a lowly wine salesman. Himmler had been a chicken farmer. Dr. Joseph Goebbels was said to have invented his doctorate credentials. Each Nazi official was attacked and smeared in similar fashion.

Hermann Goering, in reality, was born into a wealthy, aristocratic family and was well educated. His relatives included Count von Zeppelin, producer of the lighter than air dirigibles; the Merk pharmaceutical family; and the Baroness Gertud von Le Fort, among others. He was a flying ace in WWI, won the "Blue Max," and eventually became the commanding officer of the "Red Barron" squadron, after the Red Barron was shot down and killed. He was also an art collector and a lover of opera.

Ribbentrop, the son of a German Army officer, was also well educated, spoke German, French and English fluently, and won the Iron Cross as an army officer in WWI. After the war he married the daughter of a wealthy Champaign producer, eventually becoming a partner in the firm, which made him wealthy. He went on to establish his own "Impegroma Importing Company" and became even wealthier. By all accounts, he was a gentleman of refined tastes and polished manners.

Dr. Joseph Goebbels received a Ph.D. from Heidelberg University. He studied philosophy, history, art and literature and had a reputation for brilliance. He worked as a journalist before entering politics.

Rudolph Hess was born to a prosperous German business man in Alexandria, Egypt, was educated at the Neuchatel University in Switzerland in a Business curriculum. He was a lieutenant and a pilot during WWI. After the war, he studied political science, history, economics and geopolitics at the University of Munich. He was the co-author of *Mein Kampf.*

Heinrich Himmler obtained a degree in agronomy from the University of Munich and was a chicken farmer before entering politics, in the same sense that Jimmy Carter was a peanut farmer.

Reinhard Heydrich came from an upper class family, was educated at the Naval Academy, and served his early years as a Naval officer. He was a talented violinist and a champion fencer and swimmer.

Hjalmar Schacht was a Ph.D. Economist and head of the German National Bank under Hitler.

Albert Speer was an architect and came from a wealthy bourgeois family.

One of Hitler's closest intimates was the Harvard educated Ernst Hanfstaengl.

Baldur von Schirach was an aristocrat who was a published author and a regular contributor to literary journals.

Hans Frank was a lawyer who began his political career as an early member of the German Worker's Party and became Hitler's private attorney.

Alfred Rosenberg was born in Estonia, the son of a wealthy Baltic-German merchant. Rosenberg studied architecture at the Riga Polytechnic Institute, and engineering at Moscow's "Highest Technical School" and obtained his Ph.D. in 1917. He immigrated to Germany in 1918. He became the editor of the Nazi newspaper the *Volkischer Beobachter* (Peoples Observer). He, like Ribbentrop, was fluent in several languages.

It simply was not true that the Nazi regime was comprised of low-class, thuggish, ignoramuses. Most of them, in fact, were educated, cultured and highly capable. But their credentials didn't matter to the Jewish smear bund. They were in the business of discrediting Hitler and the Nazis, and they did it as they have always done, with lies, half truths and distortions. Compare the Nazi leaders, for example, to our own Harry Truman, who never went to college at all and was a failed haberdasher before entering politics; rather low, compared, for example, to the suave, multi-lingual and wealthy Champaign merchant that von Ribbentrop was before he entered politics. The Jewish press never made a point of Truman's low beginnings.

Events in Germany under the Nazis were deliberately misrepresented in the Jewish press. Small events were hysterically exaggerated and blown out of all proportion to their actual significance. Any rumor of an action, or even a slight, against the Jews was trumpeted hysterically, with predictions of mass extermination just around the corner. Any salacious rumor about any Nazi was published as fact, and supported by those famous "eye witnesses" (who later served as the basis for their

"Holocaust" claims, despite the absence of forensic evidence), and given wide publicity.

This propaganda campaign against the Hitler regime was reminiscent of the bogus propaganda campaign against Germany during World War I, in which German soldiers were said to have speared babies on their bayonets, cut off the hands of boys and to have raped and violated young girls; all of which was proven after the war to have been a total fabrication for the purpose of creating hatred against Germany.

Nazi officials indignantly denied the smears and lies propagated in the Jewish media, and even issued official, written protests, but they fell on deaf ears. The Jews had been only too successful in their anti-Nazi, anti-German propaganda campaign because they controlled the mainstream media throughout the western world. Germany had no means of countering the smears, and so the smears were believed. Not only were the minds of the public, especially in Britain and America, poisoned against the Nazis and Germany, but even highly placed public officials, who should have know better, were taken in and became ardent Nazi haters as a result of the propaganda.

President Roosevelt himself became one of the most vituperative German haters of all. He frequently uttered personally insulting and disparaging remarks in public about Hitler and other individuals in the Nazi government, which destroyed any possibility of amicable diplomatic relations between the American and German governments. Roosevelt became virulently anti-German because he was surrounded by anti-German Jewish advisors, including, among others, Hans Morgenthau, Bernard Baruch, and Felix Frankfurter. The historian Arthur M. Schlesinger, Jr. (himself a Jew) noted about President Roosevelt: *"No president had appointed so many Jews to public office. No president had surrounded himself with so many Jewish advisers. No president had condemned anti-Semitism with such eloquence and persistence. Jews were mostly liberals in those faraway days, and a vast majority voted four times for FDR."*

In addition to their anti-German propaganda campaign beginning immediately after the Nazis came to power, Jewish leaders organized mass anti-Nazi demonstrations, not in Germany, but in cities throughout

Europe and Britain, and especially in America. On March 12, 1933, eleven days <u>before</u> passage of the Enabling Act which gave all power to Hitler, and well before any action of any kind had been taken against Jews in Germany, the American Jewish Congress announced a massive anti-Nazi protest to take place on March 27 at Madison Square Garden in New York City. The commander-in-chief of Jewish War Veterans called for an American boycott of German goods. On March 23, a protest rally of 20,000 Jews was staged in front of New York's City Hall. Rallies were also staged outside the North German Lloyd and Hamburg-American shipping lines in New York, and boycotts were organized against German goods in shops and businesses throughout New York City. Up to this point, not a finger had been lifted against the Jews in Germany. Not a single measure had been taken against them. All of the hysterical anti-German activity by the Jews was only in "anticipation" of what the Nazis "might" do.

On March 24, 1933, one day after Hitler became Chancellor, the *Daily Express of London* carried the headline proclaiming that "Judea Declares War on Germany -- Jews Of All the World Unite In Action-- Boycott of German Goods -- Mass Demonstrations." (See below.)

The article describes a planned "holy war" against Germany and went on to implore Jews everywhere to boycott German goods and engage in mass demonstrations against German economic interests.

According to the "Daily Express:" *"The whole of Israel throughout the world* [International Jewry] *is uniting to declare an economic and financial war on Germany. The appearance of the Swastika as the symbol of the new Germany has revived the old war symbol of Judas to new life. Fourteen million Jews scattered over the entire world are tight to each other as if one man, in order to declare war against the German persecutors of their fellow believers. The Jewish wholesaler will quit his house, the banker his stock exchange, the merchant his business, and the beggar his humble hut, in order to join the holy war against Hitler's people."*

The "Daily Express" said that Germany was *"now confronted with an international boycott of its trade, its finances, and its industry...In London, New York, Paris, Warsaw, Jewish businessmen are united to go on an economic crusade."*

An anti-German boycott sign on a store in New York City.

The Jewish War on Germany was declared in 1933 before any action of any kind had been taken against German Jews.

This *Daily Express* report described how Jewish leaders, in combination with powerful international Jewish financial interests, had launched a boycott against Germany for the express purpose of crippling Germany's already precarious economy in order to bring down the new Hitler regime.

"London's Daily Herald carried an interview with a prominent Jewish leader who admitted, 'The leaders are hanging back,' but the Jewish people are 'forcing its leaders on.' Already the boycott has damaged 'hundreds of thousands of pounds of German trade'." (Edwin Black, Jewish author. The Transfer Agreement, p.34)

"In London, almost all Jewish shops in the Whitechapel district were displaying placards denying entry to German salesmen and affirming their anti-Nazi boycott. Teenagers patrolled the streets distributing handbills

asking shoppers to boycott German goods......" - (Edwin Black, Jewish Writer and Author, The Transfer Agreement, p.46/47)

Mass meetings of Jews were held throughout Poland expressing support for the boycott. The largest Warsaw Jewish commercial organizations passed binding resolutions to *"use the most radical means of defense by boycotting German imports."*

After this spectacular declaration of war, it should have been clear to all Jews, and particularly those Jews living in Germany, that such a provocation would produce some kind of backlash. This declaration of war did nothing for the Jews in Germany, except to intensify the German peoples' hostility towards them and to cause the German people to see the Jews in Germany as "an enemy within."

Immediate results of the Jewish boycott could be seen against the German steamship lines in New York, for example, where shipping orders were cancelled and passenger tickets went unsold. International Jewish networking demonstrated its effectiveness when boycott movements quickly developed in Lithuania, France, Holland, Great Britain and Egypt. Jewish controlled trade unions in Britain and America spread signs everywhere that read "Boycott German Goods." Several firms began cancelling their German orders of goods.

The Germans were very worried. Hermann Goering summoned

Reichsmarschall Hermann Goering

the leaders of the three main Jewish organizations in Germany to his office and accused them of being responsible for all the agitation against Germany. He told them that, *"Unless you put a stop to these libelous accusations immediately, I shall no longer be able to vouch for the safety of the German Jews."* Goering wanted them to go to London and to the U.S. to convince the Jewish leaders that nothing was happening to Jews in Germany. In fact, Ernst Wallach, the vice president of the Jewish organization "Central Verein," was already in the United States doing exactly that, and trying to dissuade the American Jewish Congress from its anti-German activities. The leaders of the three German Jewish organizations all agreed to do as Goering had asked.

After the meeting, these Jewish leaders immediately mobilized their organizations to inform the British and American publics that the hysterical reports of ill treatment of Jews in Germany were not true. The three German Jewish leaders then travelled to London and met with Stephen Wise, head of the American Jewish Congress, and begged him to cancel the demonstration scheduled for March 27 in Madison Square Garden. Ernest Wallach from the Central Verein also begged Stephen Wise, that if he could not cancel the demonstration, he should at least try to quiet down the emotions.

Too much momentum had built up due to the hysterical anti-Nazi propaganda spewed out by the Jewish media, so Wise was unable to cancel the rally. The planned protest rally at Madison Square Garden took place, as scheduled, on March 27, 1933 and drew 40,000 people. (New York Daily News headlines: "40,000 Roar Protest Here Against Hitler"). But Wise was able to tone it down a bit with a conciliatory speech at the rally. Similar rallies and protest marches were also held by Jewish groups in other cities.

In spite of the efforts of these Jewish leaders to contain the anti-Nazi hysteria, the announced boycott against Germany began to have its intended effect. Two days after the boycott was announced, an organization called the Jewish War Veterans produced data that showed $2 million (in 1933 dollars --that would be equivalent to $35 million today) in cancelled German orders.

Hitler had previously threatened to boycott Jewish stores in Germany if the International Jewish campaign against Germany did not stop. The day following the March 27 Madison Square Garden rally, Hitler made a speech during which he ordered a one-day boycott of Jewish stores and goods in Germany. This was in direct response to the Jewish boycott against Germany. The boycott was ineffectual, as it turned out, because it was largely ignored by the German people.

Hitler's one-day boycott of Jewish stores and goods is given wide coverage in current history books and in articles written about the period, but the Jewish boycott against Germany which provoked it is rarely if ever mentioned. Though Hitler's boycott of Jewish stores lasted only a day, the Jewish boycott of Germany continued and even intensified for years.

Hitler soon initiated a rapid series of laws to limit Jewish power and control in Germany, as he had promised to do during his election campaign. On April 7 "The Law of the Restoration of the Civil Service" was enacted which limited civil service jobs to ethnic Germans. Jews were less than 1% of the German population, yet, they dominated the Weimar government and filled an inordinate percentage of civil service jobs in pre-Hitler Germany. Under the new National Socialist regime, all Jews holding those positions were either dismissed or forced into paid retirement. As detailed in previous chapters, this tiny Jewish minority also dominated the professions in Germany. On April 22, a law was enacted to reduce Jewish numbers within the professions to somewhere near their percentage within the population of Germany. The April 22 law prohibited Jews from serving as patent lawyers and also from serving as doctors in state-run insurance programs. They were still permitted to practice, but not in government supported positions.

On April 25, a law restricting the number of Jewish children allowed to enroll in institutions of higher learning was enacted. The law limited Jewish enrollment to their percentage in the population.

On May 10, 1933, German students from the universities gathered in Berlin and other German cities to burn books which contained subversive, obscene or un-German themes, especially those by Jewish writers. Propaganda Minister, Joseph Goebbels, declared: *"The soul of the German people can again express itself. These flames not only illuminate the final end of an old era; they also light up the new."*

Part of the Nazis program to clean up Germany was to burn books with subversive, obscene, or un-German themes. Here, in the Operplatz in Berlin, on May 10, 1933, Nazi salutes and anthems accompany the smoldering pile of filth cleaned out of German libraries.

On June 2, Jewish dentists and dental technicians were barred from state-run insurance plans, though they were allowed to continue in private practice, just not in state run programs.

Hostilities toward Jews increased all across Germany as the result of the declaration of war against Germany by International Jewry. Many shops and restaurants refused to serve Jewish people. Placards saying "Jews not admitted" and "Jews enter this place at their own risk" began to appear all over Germany. In some parts of the country Jews were banned from public parks, swimming pools and public transport.

The Jewish boycott almost brought the Third Reich to its knees before it ever got started. Jews controlled much of the world's shipping, so they had the means of blocking German exports and imports.

Moreover, this was the worst possible time for Germany to be a victim of a boycott, as Germany was already deep in a depression with a quarter of her work force out of work.

Hitler demanded an end to the boycott, saying that there was absolutely no justification for it. He appealed to Jewish leaders in Britain and America to condemn the boycott, and many responsible Jewish leaders did so. Lord Reading, a prominent Jew in the House of Commons, and Lord Herbert Samuel, also Jewish, made a joint declaration saying, *"we deprecate exaggerated reports of occurrences in Germany or any attempts to boycott German goods."* Following that, the British Foreign Minister John Simon gave the German ambassador a letter supporting that declaration. Yet, the International Jewish war against Germany continued unabated with accusations and charges against Germany becoming ever more salacious and sensational.

In July, 1933 in Amsterdam, Holland, an International Jewish Boycott Conference was organized and assembled under Samuel Untermeyer's leadership. Untermeyer was elected President of the "International jewish Federation to Combat the Hitlerite oppression of the Jews." He had also been elected President of the "World Jewish Economic Federation." This belligerent organization had been set up to counter the Third Reich's program of restricting Jewish power and control in Germany.

The conference was a call to International Jewry to wage total war against Germany with all means at their disposal, including propaganda, financial manipulation, and an intensification of the boycott, while at the same time protecting Jewish interests in Germany.

On his return to the United States, Untermeyer gave a radio address over station WABC in New York City, during which he announced his declaration of war. The text of this address was then published in the New York Times' August 7, 1933 edition, and is presented in its entirety below.

Untermeyer's inflammatory speech was a blatant misrepresentation of what was happening in Germany. His claims of Nazi atrocities against Jews were simply not true. Untermeyer hyperbolically described Nazism as a *"curse that has descended upon benighted Germany, which has thereby been converted from a nation of culture into a veritable hell of cruel and savage beasts."* In comparison, he described the Jews as the "aristocrats of the world."

Untermeyer declared that Germany intended to "exterminate" the Jewish race. This was 1933! No one in Germany had ever uttered such a threat. Untermeyer proclaimed a "holy war" against Germany to destroy Germany's very existence. Jews all over the world were ordered not to buy German goods, not to patronize German merchants, not to deal with or buy from firms that did business with Germany, and not to ship goods on German ships. Jewish bankers were told not to lend money to Germans. Untermeyer, speaking officially for all the Jews of the world, said, *"what we are proposing and what we have already gone far toward doing...is to undermine the Hitler regime and bring the German people to their senses by destroying their export trade on which their very existence depends."* Thus a "holy war" of revenge was begun and was already under way by August 7, 1933, the day of Untermeyer's speech.

Untermeyer's speech was a landmark speech in that it was the first to accuse Nazi Germany of the intention to "exterminate" the Jewish people, though no such threat had ever been made by anyone in Germany. He accused the Nazis of committing unspeakable cruelties and atrocities against the Jews inside Germany, though, in reality, nothing whatever had happened to the Jews by the time he gave his speech. This kind of inflammatory, though baseless, accusation of German atrocities against the Jews was to continue, and even intensify, right through the Nazi period in the 1930s, right through the war, and into the Nuremburg Trials after the war. It could be said that the March 24, 1933 Jewish declaration of war on Germany, followed by the International Jewish Boycott Conference of July, 1933, was the real beginning of World War Two.

The German government protested this speech but it fell on deaf ears in America and Britain who had already been conditioned to believe the worst about Germany as a result of the relentless anti-German propaganda campaign spewing out of the Jewish press since 1921.

Untermeyer's entire speech is presented below so that the reader may judge its inflammatory nature for himself.

Left - Jewish leader, Samuel Untermeyer.

<u>Text of Untermeyer's Speech in New York City after his return from Amsterdam</u>

My Friends: What a joy and relief and sense of security to be once more on American soil! The nightmares of horrors through which I have passed in those two weeks in Europe, listening to the heartbreaking tales of refugee victims, beggar description.

I deeply appreciate your enthusiastic greeting on my arrival today, which I quite understand is addressed not to me personally but to the holy war in the cause of humanity in which we are embarked. Jews and non-Jews alike, for we are equally concerned that the work of centuries shall not be undone, and that civilization shall not be allowed to die.

It is a war that must be waged unremittingly until the black clouds of bigotry, race hatred and fanaticism that have descended upon what was once Germany, but is now medieval Hitlerland, have been dispersed. If we will but enlist to a man and persist in our purpose, the bright sun of civilization will again shine upon Germany, and the world will be a safer place in which to dwell.

As our ship sailed up the bay today past our proud Statue of Liberty, [a gift to the U.S. from the Grand Orient - Illuminati - Lodge of France] I breathed a prayer of gratitude and thanksgiving that this fair land of freedom has escaped the curse that has descended upon benighted Germany, which has thereby been converted from a nation of culture into a veritable hell of cruel and savage beasts.

The World's Concern

We owe it not only to our persecuted brethren but to the entire world to now strike in self-defense a blow that will free humanity from a repetition of this incredible outrage. This time the Jews are the victims, next time it may be the Catholics or the Protestants. If we once admit, as is brazenly insisted by the German Government, that such fiendish persecution of the people of one race or creed is an internal domestic affair and not a world concern, how are we to know whose turn will be next?

Now or never must all the nations of the earth make common cause against the monstrous claim that the slaughter, starvation and annihilation, by a country that has reverted to barbarism, of its own innocent and defenseless citizens without rhyme, reason or excuse is an internal affair against which the rest of the world must stand idly by and not lift a hand in defense.

I have seen and talked with many of these terror-stricken refugees who have had the good fortune to escape over the border, though forced to leave their property behind them, and I want to say to you that nothing that has seeped through to you over the rigid censorship and lying propaganda that are at work to conceal and misrepresent the situation of the Jews in Germany begins to tell a fraction of the frightful story of fiendish torture, cruelty and persecution that are being inflicted day by day upon these men, women and children, of the terrors of worse than death in which they are living.

When the tale is told, as it will be some day if the impotent League of Nations ever sufficiently awakens from its Rip Van Winkle slumbers to the realization of its power and duty to prosecute an investigation into the facts, the world will confront a picture so fearful in its barbarous cruelty that the hell of war and the alleged Belgian atrocities will pale into insignificance as compared to this devilishly, deliberately, cold-bloodedly planned and already partially executed campaign for the extermination of a proud, gentle, loyal, law-abiding people — a people who love and have shed their blood for their Fatherland, and to whom Germany owes in large part its prosperity and its great scientists, educators, lawyers, physicians, poets, musicians, diplomats and philosophers, who are the backbone of its past cultural life.

Back to Dark Ages

But why dwell longer upon this revolting picture of the ravages wrought by these ingrates and beasts of prey, animated by the loathsome motives of race hatred, bigotry and envy. For the Jews are the aristocrats of the world. From time immemorial they have been persecuted and have seen their persecutors come and go. They alone have survived. And so will history repeat itself, but that furnishes no reason why we should permit this reversion of a once great nation to the Dark Ages or fail to rescue these 600,000 human souls from the tortures of hell as we can with the aid of our Christian friends, if we have the will to act.

Protests and pleas from all corners of the earth, from the leaders of all creeds, having proven as vain and unavailing as was the idealistic dream of our martyred President of making the world safe for democracy and of protecting minorities, what then are to be the lines of our defensive campaign against these atrocities, on which we are already actively embarked? Are we right in our plan? If so, what steps shall now be prosecuted to attain success?

Our campaign is twofold — defensive and constructive. On the defensive side will be the economic boycott against all German goods, shipping and services. On the constructive side will be an appeal to the League of Nations to construe and enforce the labor union provisions of the Versailles Treaty and the written promises made by Germany, while the treaty was under negotiation, to protect its minorities, which have been flagrantly violated by its disfranchisement and persecution of the German Jews.

What Boycott Means

As in the boycott, strange to say a mere handful in number, but powerful in influence, of our thoughtless but doubtless well-intentioned Jews seem obsessed and frightened at the bare mention of the word "boycott". It signifies and conjures up to them images of force and illegality, such as have on occasions in the past characterized struggles between labor unions and their employers. As these timid souls are capitalists and employers, the word and all that it implies are hateful to their ears.

In point of fact, it signifies nothing of the kind. These gentlemen do not know what they are talking or thinking about. Instead of surrendering to their vague fears and half-baked ideas, our first duty is to educate them as to what is meant by a purely defensive economic boycott, and what we are doing and proposing.

Admittedly, the boycott is our only really effective weapon. These gentlemen who are taking counsel of their groundless fears to the exclusion of their reason have done nothing and have no program except to attempt to arouse world opinion, which is and has been from the outset on our side, as it was bound to be because of this brutal, senseless, unprovoked assault upon civilization.

It is not necessary to belittle or underrate that accomplishment, if their aimless, fruitless endeavors in that direction may be so dignified in recognition of their good intentions, barren of results as they have been.

It is sufficient that their efforts have proven unavailing and that the campaign of Schreckligheit not only goes on unabated in the face of unanimous world opinion; but that it is increasing in intensity and that the masses of the German people, misled by government propaganda and suppression of free speech and of the press, are either voluntarily, or through fear of punishment at the hands of their despotic rulers, supporting their government in this hellish campaign.

What then have these amiable gentlemen accomplished and what do they hope or expect to accomplish in the way of stemming this conflagration of civilization by their "feather-duster" methods? You cannot put out a fire, and especially that kind of a fire, by just looking on until the mad flames, fanned by the wind of hate, have destroyed everything.

What we are proposing and have already gone far toward doing, is to prosecute a purely defensive economic boycott that will undermine the Hitler regime and bring the German people to their senses by destroying their export trade on which their very existence depends.

Force Them to Learn

They have flaunted and persisted in flaunting and defying world opinion. We propose to and are organizing world opinion to express itself in the only way Germany can be made to understand. Hitler and his mob will not permit their people to know how they are regarded by the outside world. We shall force them to learn in the only way open to us.

Revolting as it is, it would be an interesting study in psychology to analyze the motives, other than fear and cowardice, that have prompted Jewish bankers to lend money to Germany as they are now doing. It is in part their money that is being used by the Hitler regime in its reckless, wicked campaign of propaganda to make the world anti-Semitic; with that money they have invaded Great Britain, the United States and other countries where they have established newspapers, subsidized agents and otherwise are spending untold millions in spreading their infamous creed.

The suggestion that they use that money toward paying the honest debts they have repudiated is answered only by contemptuous sneers and silence. Meantime the infamous campaign goes on unabated with ever increasing intensity to the everlasting disgrace of the Jewish bankers who are helping to finance it and of the weaklings who are doing nothing effective to check it.

The Hitler regime originated are fiendishly prosecuting their boycott to exterminate the Jews by placarding Jewish shops, warning Germans against dealing with them, by imprisoning Jewish shopkeepers and parading them through the streets by the hundreds under guard of Nazi troops for the sole crime of being Jews, by ejecting them from the learned professions in which many of them had attained eminence, by excluding their children from the schools, their men from the labor unions, closing against them every avenue of livelihood, locking them in vile concentration camps, starving and torturing them, murdering and beating them without cause and resorting to every other conceivable form of torture, inhuman beyond conception, until suicide has become their only means of escape, and all solely because they are or their remote ancestors were Jews, and all with the avowed object of exterminating them.

Appeal to Mankind

As against this, the foulest boycott in the annals of time, we are appealing to all mankind to enforce a counter-boycott. That appeal is meeting with the conviction that idealism and justice are still alive.

There is nothing new in the use of the economic boycott as an instrument of justice. The covenant of the League of Nations expressly provides in these identical words for its use to bring recalcitrant nations to terms. President Roosevelt, whose wise statesmanship and vision are the wonder of the civilized world, is invoking it in furtherance of his noble conception for the readjustment of the relations between capital and labor under the terms of the sweeping Industrial Recovery Act, to the end that labor shall receive a more just share of the wealth it creates. He is about to enlist the consumers of the country in a national campaign in which they pledge themselves to boycott all manufacturers, jobbers and retailers who fail to subscribe to the codes and to buy only from those who have assented and who are thereby privileged to fly the blue eagle of NRA [National Recovery Act]. What more exalted precedent do our timid friends want?

With this explanation of our aims, I appeal to the American Jewish Committee, whose public spirit and good intentions I do not for a moment question, but the wisdom of whose judgment I challenge, no longer to hold aloof but to rid themselves of their timid and ill-considered prejudices and join in actively pressing this boycott as our only weapon except the appeal to the League, which I shall discuss at a later time.

I purposely refrain from including the American Jewish Congress in this appeal because I am satisfied that 95 per cent of their members are already with us and that they are being misrepresented by two or three men now abroad. Of them I ask that, prior to the meeting to be held this month in Prague by their executive committee, they instruct these false leaders in no uncertain terms as to the stand they must take on this all-important subject and demand that they shall either openly represent their views or resign their offices. One of them, generally recognized as the kingpin of mischief makers, is junketing around the Continent engaged in his favorite pastime of spreading discord, asserting at one time and place that he favors and supports the boycott and at another that he is opposed or indifferent to it, all dependent on the audience he is addressing; but always directly or indirectly delivering a stab in the dark.

Progress So Far Made

There is not time now, but I hope and expect in the near future to be able to report to you the steps that have been taken and that are already under way, and the surprising and gratifying progress already made in many countries toward the success of the economic boycott in which we are engaged. Although considerable progress in that direction has already been made in Great Britain and in the United States, you will be surprised to learn that they are the least advanced and as yet the most inadequately organized of all the countries that were represented at the Amsterdam World Economic Conference, where the boycott was unanimously and enthusiastically approved by formal resolution by a rising vote.

With us in America the delay has been due in part to lack of funds and the vast territory to be covered, but it is hoped, and expected, that this condition will soon be corrected. The object-lesson we are determined to teach is so priceless to all humanity that we dare not fall.

Each of you, Jew and Gentile alike, who has not already enlisted in this sacred war should do so now and here. It is not sufficient that you buy no goods made in Germany. You must refuse to deal with any merchant or shopkeeper who sells any German-made goods or who patronizes German ships or shipping.

To our shame be it said that there are a few Jews among us, but fortunately only a few, so wanting in dignity and self-respect that they are willing to travel on German ships where they are despised and meet with the just contempt of the servants who wait upon them and of their fellow passengers. Their names should be heralded far and wide. They are traitors to their race.

In conclusion, permit me again to thank you for this heartening reception and to assure you that, with your support and that of our millions of non-Jewish friends, we will drive the last nail in the coffin of bigotry and fanaticism that has dared raise its ugly head to slander, belie and disgrace twentieth century civilization. **The end.**

Untermeyer's speech was inflammatory by any standard, filled with hyperbole, exaggeration and falsehood, though it was to prove to be only typical of Jewish commentary on Nazi Germany from that time forward until Germany's final defeat. Jews wage war with propaganda, not armed soldiers, at least, as already mentioned above, not their own armed soldiers, and they were waging a full scale war against Nazi Germany at this time, no less than Britain, Russia and the USA waged war against Germany somewhat later, with armed men. A joke making the rounds at the time was that the Jewish national anthem ought to be "Onward Christian Soldiers." It is also a cultural characteristic of Jews to wildly exaggerate their troubles and woes and to protest loudly and melodramatically, any slight, either real or imagined, against them. They even have a word for it -- *kvetching.*

Untermeyer spoke of the "fiendish torture and cruelty" Jews were being subjected to day-by-day in Germany, and of "terrors worse than death." Nothing of the kind was happening in Germany, except in his fevered imagination. Untermeyer referred in the early part of his speech to "the holy war in the cause of humanity in which we are embarked." He went on to develop this theme at great length. He described the Jews as the "aristocrats of the world." He made a call to action: "Each of you, Jew and Gentile alike, who has not already enlisted in this sacred war should do so now and here." Those Jews who did not wish to join in his "holy war," he denounced, declaring: "They are traitors to their race."

The Jewish Persecution Myth

In his 1952 book, "Behind Communism," Frank L. Britton explains the phenomenon of the Jewish persecution myth. Britton says that the persecution myth is the "adhesive and cement of Judaism; without it Jews would have long since ceased to exist" as a nationality. He says that though Jews do not always agree among themselves, in the presence of their enemies, real or imagined, Jewish thinking crystallizes into unanimity. Through 25 centuries, he says, the Jewish mind has been conditioned by the shrill refrain of "persecution!" Every accident of fate is chronicled, enhanced, and passed on to succeeding generations as another example of gentile cruelty to the Chosen People. Any opposition to Jewish aspirations and ambitions, he says, is also translated into these same terms of persecution, and all Jewish aggression and exploitation of others in the pursuit of their aspirations is excused on the same basis.

To be sure, the Jewish people have suffered numerous hardships in the course of their history, but this is also true of other peoples. The primary difference is that the Jews keep score. They never forget and they never forgive. They have cultivated within the collective Jewish mind an exaggerated sense of self-righteousness and a compulsion for vengeance seeking. Gentiles move on and put their misfortunes behind them, but the Jews have made a tradition of nurturing their memories of persecution. They nurse and savor every grievance and store them away in Jewish cultural memory. A slaughter of a few thousand Christians is remembered by no one in 50 years time, but a similar incident in which Jews are killed is preserved forever in Jewish histories, embellished and amplified in the retelling. They recite and bewail their woes not only to themselves, but seek sympathy by declaiming them in exaggerated form to the world. A sort of leitmotif of "Jews as eternal victims" runs through Jewish story-telling, to the point that Jewish history seems like a bizarre comic version of a Wagnerian opera. Part of the Jewish psyche is the suspicion that Gentiles are planning their extermination. This has been a constant refrain throughout Jewish history. (Even today, they loudly and repeatedly declaim that Iran intends to "wipe Israel off the map.") The three motivating factors of Jewish culture which seem to most influence their outlook on the world, and which govern their relationship with their Gentile hosts amongst whom they live, are, 1) the persecution myth, 2) the extermination fantasy, and 3) vengeance seeking.

Untermeyer's speech, as well as all of the hysterical anti-German Jewish propaganda should be seen in this light. Jewish Holocaust claims should also be seen in this light. The Jews claim 6 million of their people were killed in the Holocaust. But the number "6 million" seems more like a metaphor than an actual number, used again and again in Jewish historical story-telling. Surely the actual number was only a fraction of that.

1902 -- On page 482 of the article on "Anti-Semitism" in the 10th Edition of the Encyclopedia Britannica (1902), for example, is found the words: "While there are in Russia and Rumania six millions of Jews who are being systematically degraded...". This reference precedes references to the 6 million of WWII by approximately 40 years.

1906 -- In the New York Times, March 25, 1906 edition, an article titled "Dr. Nathan's View of Russian Massacre," worried about the "condition and future of Russia's 6 million Jews..." The article goes on to say "...the Russian Government's studied policy for the 'solution' of the Jewish question is systematically and murderous extermination."

1911 -- Max Nordau, co-founder of the World Zionist Organization, warns of the "annihilation of 6 million" at the Zionist Congress in Basle, Switzerland. This was 22 years before Hitler came to power.

1919 -- In the American Hebrew Magazine of October 31, 1919, there appeared an article entitled "The Crucifixion of Jews Must Stop!" By Martin H. Glynn, former governor of the state of New York. This article begins: "From across the sea, six million men and women call to us for help ...". The article goes on to include passages such as, "...when six million human beings are being whirled toward the grave...," "Six million men and women are dying...," "...and a bigoted lust for Jewish blood." "In this threatened holocaust...," ad infinitum. The article was published approximately 20 years before the outbreak of WW2.

1921 -- In the Chicago Tribune, July 20, 1921, an article headlined: "Begs America Save 6,000,000 in Russia." The article claims, "Russia's 6,000,000 Jews are facing extermination."

1936 -- In the New York Times, May 31, 1936, an article headlined "Americans Appeal For Jewish Refuge," appealed to Britain to "...throw open the gates of Palestine and let in the victimized and persecuted Jews escaping from the European holocaust."

1940 -- In the Palm Beach Post, June 25, 1940, an article reported Dr. Nahum Goldman, administrative committee chairman of the World Jewish Congress, said today that if the Nazis should achieve final victory 6,000,000 Jews in Europe are doomed to destruction."

1943 -- The Polish Jew Rafael Lemkin, in his book "Axis Rule in Occupied Europe," published in New York in 1943, claimed that the Nazis had already killed millions of Jews, "perhaps as many as 6 million," he said. This would have been a remarkable feat by 1943, since the alleged extermination of Jews, according the Jews themselves, only began in 1942.

1945 -- In a New York Times article of January 8, 1945, four months before the war in Europe ended, and before anyone could possibly have known how many Jews, if any, had died, it was reported that 6,000,000 Jews were dead.

1945 -- An article in the Pittsburg Press, May 13, 1945 headlined "Nazis Destroy Six Million Jews."

Obviously, Jewish claims of persecution and predictions of extermination cannot be taken seriously.

****

Jews all around the world answered Untermeyer's call for war against Germany. Bernard Baruch, another powerful American Jewish financier, called for all out war against Germany, even pointing out the benefits to Britain of a such a war. *I emphasized that the defeat of*

Germany...and [her] elimination from world trade would give Britain a tremendous opportunity to swell her foreign commerce in both volume and profit," he said. Bernard Baruch was a presidential advisor to Wilson, Roosevelt and Truman.

In June, 1934, the Jew Emile Ludwig Cohn, in the French journal, "Les Annales," wrote, *"Hitler will have no war* (does not want war), *but we will force it on him, not this year, but soon."*

David A. Brown, National Chairman, United Jewish Campaign, 1934, said, *"We Jews are going to bring a war on Germany."*

Henry Morgenthau, Jewish Secretary of the U.S. Treasury said, in September, 1933, *"War in Europe in 1934 was inevitable."*

In January, 1934, Ze'ev Jabotinsky wrote in the "Natcha Retch," in Palestine, *"The fight against Germany has been carried out for months by every Jewish conference, trade organization, by every Jew in the world. . . we shall let loose a spiritual and a material war of the whole world against Germany."*

L - Ze'ev Jabotinsky was an ardent Zionist and virulent anti-Nazi.

In the "Jewish Daily Bulletin" in Palestine on July 27, 1935, Jabotinsky wrote, *"There is only one power which really counts. The power of political pressure. We Jews are the most powerful people on earth, because we have this power, and we know how to apply it."*

The "Jewish Chronicle" of February 22, 1935, reporting on J.E. Marcovitch, the Jewish newspaper magnate in Cairo who virtually controlled the Egyptian press, wrote: *"He had converted the whole Egyptian Press into a real battlefield against Hitlerism."*

Louis Marschalko, Hungarian Jewish journalist and author, wrote, *"National Socialism was condemned to war because it was a system which inevitably made enemies of Bolshevism and world capitalism* [both controlled by Jews]."

The French Jewish journalist Paul Dreyfus wrote in "La Vio de Tanger" on May 15, 1938, *"Before the end of the year, an economic bloc of England, Russia, France and the U.S.A. will be formed to bring the German and Italian economic systems to their knees."*

An article in the British journal "Sunday Chronicle" of January 2, 1938: *"£500,000,000 FIGHTING FUND FOR THE JEWS . . . The battle will be fought on the world's stock exchanges. Since the majority of the anti-Semitic states are burdened with international debt, they may find their very existence threatened. A boycott throughout Europe of their export products by way of the retailer may undermine the present uncertain economic stability of several of the anti-Semitic countries."*

International Jewry justified its war on Germany because Germany was "persecuting" Jews inside Germany, with plans to eventually "exterminate" them entirely. (And today, the Iranians plan to exterminate them.)

Effect of boycott on the German economy

Between January and April 1933, Germany's exports dropped by 10%. As the boycott organized by World Jewry spread, German trade was hit particularly hard and during the first quarter of 1933, Germany's vital exports were less than half its 1932 trade. The worldwide Jewish boycott of Germany continued relentlessly year after year.

In 1941 the International Conference of Jews held in Moscow called for intensified economic pressure on Germany: *"Jewish brothers of the whole world: Let the holy flame of vengeance burn more and more brightly in your hearts with every hour! Be ready to act at any minute! You must do everything in your power to destroy the economic resources of the fascists, no matter in what part of the world you live. Go among the most vital sections of the death-bringing industries of the Hitlerian hangmen and cripple them with every means at your disposal. Boycott their products everywhere! Struggle together with the noble, self-sacrificing partisans! Develop everywhere a fully effective propaganda for solidarity with, and an active support for the Soviet Union. Mankind wants to be freed of the brown plague. Do your duty in this holy war."*

Edwin Black, Jewish author of "The Transfer Agreement" wrote, *"How many months could Germany survive once the boycott became global, once commerce was re-routed around Germany: The boycotters adopted a slogan, 'Germany will crack this winter'."*

Jewish exaggerations are contradicted by many

At the same time that international Jewish wailing and *kvetching* was filling international newspapers, this is what the Englishman, G.E.O. Knight, had to say about what was going on in Germany, in his brochure, "In Defense of Germany," published in July, 1934: *"My private conversations with Jews* [inside Germany] *were illuminating. They did not bear out what the British newspapers suggested. Mountains had been made out of molehills; melodrama out of comic opera. The majority of the 'assaults' were committed by over-zealous youths, and in nearly every instance consisted of 'ratting' unfortunate men who were not particularly respectful of the new regime. Physical harm very little, mental, probably much."*

"This is what I learned from my Jewish friends, who are staying in Germany and have no intention of leaving the country, nor have they ever been asked to leave the country. Those who wish to leave and return may do so at their own pleasure. The laws relating to the freedom of Jews are substantially the same as those of other people."

"The trouble that has risen has nothing to do with the domiciled Jew, many of whom are still employed by government in various spheres of usefulness. There are about 80,000 undesirable Jews that Germany wants to get rid of for all time, and willingly would she deport them all to Great Britain or the United States of America if the request was made."

"These are Jews who since the Armistice [1918] have penetrated the country and created a situation that has wrought considerable social and political harm in Germany. Among these undesirables are murderers, ex-convicts, potential thieves, fraudulent bankrupts, white slave traffickers, beggars of every description, and political refugees. Many have come from Baltic states, others from Poland, and not an inconsiderable number from Russia."

He went on to write: *"Before the revolution of last March* [when Hitler and the National Socialists came to power], *the Jews in the Reich overran every government department, and enjoyed the highest privileges in every profession and calling. They were the principle organizers of the Communist Party, and became identified with every one of the seventy-two warring political sects in the country."*

"In every way they proved themselves eminently capable businessmen and politicians. Many had grown very wealthy. Nearly every German war profiteer was a Jew; the native German seems to have regarded with feelings of shame and horror the idea of making money out of his country during times of great stress. . "

"That one per cent of the population of Germany should impose their rule and culture -- however eminent that culture may be -- on more than sixty-million native born Germans is unreasonable, to use no stronger word. . ." "So when the Nazi worm turned, and the services of many Jews were dispensed with, Jewry throughout the world rose in arms and through the medium of the Press here, and public meetings in London and the provinces, denounced the German Government in violent terms. "

"The Germans have assumed control of their country, and for weal or woe they mean to maintain their position. The German people are perfectly entitled to possess what form of government they please; it ill becomes us to dictate to them."

The Jewish war on Germany caused the Germans to clamp down even harder on Jews living in Germany, which, in turn, produced even shriller wailing and kvetching amongst International Jewry. On September 29, 1933, Jews were banned from all cultural and entertainment activities including literature, art, film, and theater. Hitler had spoken many times about *"the endless filth coming out of the Jewish film, theater and entertainment industries,"* but also about the insidious Jewish effort to undermine German culture by ridiculing German morals, German values, German traditions, and by their attacks upon Christianity. He was determined to put an end to it. In October, 1933, Jews were barred from journalism and all newspapers were placed under government control. Hitler's intent was to break the Jewish hold on German institutions and to encourage them to emigrate out of Germany, not to harm them.

Chapter 12

The Nazis and the Zionists actually work together for Jewish Emigration out of Germany

The story of the emigration of the Jews from Germany has been totally distorted and misrepresented in contemporary historiography. The emigration of Jews from Germany is typically depicted as some sort of secret undertaking in which those Jews who wished to leave had to escape in the middle of the night, sneaking across borders, crossing over mountain ranges, and leaving behind all their goods and property. Other dramatizations describe the ruinous price the Jews had to pay for an exit visa. All of these poignant tales are nothing more than a stupid fantasy.

There is no doubt that the German government wanted the Jews to leave Germany, and that it applied increasing pressure to persuade them to do so. The anti-Jewish legislation of the Third Reich is a matter of historical fact which cannot be denied; and the hardship imposed upon the Jews was real. But contrary to all the hyperbolic tales and adventure stories contained in Jewish memoirs, Jewish emigration from Germany was a legal event carried out in accordance with established, published procedures.

German government offices and Jewish organizations worked hand in hand to facilitate the emigration. Jews interested in emigrating were extensively counseled and received considerable aid. All talk about a dangerous escape from Germany in the middle of the night is sheer nonsense. The National Socialists wanted to create a nation-state of ethnically pure Germans. The German government wanted the Jews to leave Germany. The Germany government did not stand in the way of Jewish emigration. To have done so would have undermined its own program.

Intrinsic to National Socialism was the precept that the Germans were a distinct race, and that they had every right to an ethnically and religiously homogeneous homeland. The Zionists were no less nationalistic than the Nazis and likewise declared the Jews to be a distinct race, even superior to others, i.e., the "Chosen People of God," as they called themselves. The Zionists wanted to make Palestine into an ethnically and religiously homogeneous homeland for Jews, just as the Nazis wanted Germany to be a homogeneous land of Germans. To that extent, Israel today is no different from Germany of the 1930s. "Nationalism" was an accepted concept throughout Europe during the Nazi era, meaning that each "nationality" or "ethnic group" had a natural right to create a nation-state of its own. President Wilson's concept of "self determination for all peoples," was a confirmation of the concept of "nationalism." The aim of the National Socialists to have a German nation-state exclusively for ethnic Germans was not an aberration, nor was it even unusual for the time. For the Germans to hold their own ethnic group in high regard was also not exceptional for that time.

Except for their tiny Jewish minority, Germany was almost entirely homogeneous in the 1920s and 30s. Encouraging the Jews to emigrate out of Germany became a national policy, though no Jew, at least, before World War Two began, was actually forced to leave. This policy served two purposes; first, to "cleanse" Germany of its alien element, and second, to wrest control of German institutions out of Jewish hands to turn them back over to Germans.

Germany's policy of encouraging Jewish emigration also served the purposes of the Zionists who wanted to create a Jewish homeland in Palestine. Toward this end, the Zionists and the Nazis joined forces and actively collaborated in facilitating the emigration of the Jews out of Germany into Palestine. The Zionist Federation of Germany (an organization of Zionist Jews inside Germany) submitted a detailed memorandum to the new Nazi government which served as a "review" of German/Jewish relations and also formally offered Zionist support to the Nazis in their program of encouraging Jewish emigration out of Germany. The first step, the memo suggested, had to be a frank recognition of fundamental national differences between Germans and Jews. The memorandum stated the following:

"...Our acknowledgment of Jewish nationality provides for a clear and sincere relationship to the German people and its national and racial realities. Precisely because we do not wish to falsify these fundamentals, because we, too, are against mixed marriage and are for maintaining the purity of the Jewish group and reject any trespasses in the cultural domain, we -- having been brought up in the German language and German culture -- can show an interest in the works and values of German culture with admiration and internal sympathy ...

For its practical aims, Zionism hopes to be able to win the collaboration of even a government fundamentally hostile to Jews, because in dealing with the Jewish question not sentimentalities are involved but a real problem whose solution interests all peoples and at the present moment especially the German people ...

Boycott propaganda -- such as is currently being carried on against Germany in many ways -- is in essence un-Zionist, because Zionism wants not to do battle but to convince and to build ...

We are not blind to the fact that a Jewish question exists and will continue to exist. From the abnormal situation of the Jews severe disadvantages result for them, but also scarcely tolerable conditions for other peoples."

Hitler was very favorably disposed toward cooperation with the Zionists and they with him. According to British historian David Irving, the two largest contributors to the Nazi Party were the general managers of two of the largest Berlin banks, both of them Jewish, and one of them the leader of Zionism in Germany. Irving uncovered this fact in a letter written by Dr. Heinrich Bruning, Chancellor of Germany before Hitler, to Winston Churchill in 1949, while researching for his book "Churchill's War."

Hitler wanted to cooperate with the Zionists because he wanted to be rid of the problem of Jewish predominance in German affairs. The Zionists were working to set up an independent Jewish homeland in Palestine and wanted all of Germany's Jews to immigrate to Palestine, if possible. On August 25, 1933 Hitler entered into a pact with representatives of the Jewish Agency, whose members would eventually become the leaders of Israel. The pact was called the *Haavara* Agreement, or *Transfer* Agreement, which was a program for moving the Jews out of Germany to Palestine. "Haavara" in Hebrew means to move, or to relocate. The German Interior Ministry was put in charge of the logistics for the program and the Reichsbank and the German Treasury were responsible for financing the mass emigration. By November, 1933 the program was in full swing and it kept functioning until well into 1942. The aim was to conduct a peaceful and painless transfer of Jews out of Germany to Palestine with as little inconvenience to the Jews as possible. Coercive measures were used to push those who were unwilling to go. The Zionists even offered suggestions on ways to speed up the emigration process out of Germany. It was a Zionist idea, for example, to force the Jews in Germany to wear the yellow stars. The more pressure applied on the Jews, they reasoned, the more likely they were to leave Germany.

Contrary to popular myth today, Germany's Jews were permitted to leave with practically all of their possessions and all of their wealth, provided that Jews deposited all of their assets in one of two Jewish owned banks in Germany which had branch offices in Tel Aviv and Jerusalem. Upon arrival in Palestine thy could withdraw their assets according to the terms of the agreement. The German capital of these two Jewish banking firms was guaranteed by the German government. Even after the war these assets were fully available to the Jewish owners or their representatives. Even those Jews who decided to remain in Germany for the time being could transfer all of their assets out of Germany to Palestine through these two banks.

Some 40 camps were set up throughout Germany where prospective settlers were trained for their new lives in Palestine. Special schools were established for Jewish students who had been barred from German schools, and Jewish teachers, some even from Palestine, were hired to

Jewish children gathered for a sporting event in a summer
camp organized by the Reich Union of Jewish Frontline
Soldiers. Germany, between 1934 and 1936.

The Reich Union of Jewish Frontline Soldiers organized
summer camps and sports activities for Jewish
children. Germany, between 1934 and 1936.

teach in them. In these camps, they held meetings and seminars, sports meetings, went sailing, and hiking through the countryside, and were allowed to hand out leaflets about Zionism. The first kibbutz farms were set up in Germany (collective farms) to teach agriculture to the prospective Jewish settlers. Some of these camps were in operation as late as 1942. These camps flew the blue and white flag with the star of David, which eventually became the national flag of Israel. All of this was paid for by the German government at considerable cost. In addition to the cost of running this program, massive amounts of material and equipment were also sent to Palestine by the German government. This included coal, iron and metal products and machines for desalinating sea water. From 1933 to 1941 around 100 Jewish settlements were build in Palestine with German help. The Haavara (Transfer) Agreement, which was financially supported by the German government, saved the Jewish Agency from bankruptcy. According to Dr. Nahum Goldmann, co-founder of the World Jewish Congress, the Transfer Agreement was an indispensible factor in the creation of the state of Israel.

In 1933 and 1934, SS Untersturmfuhrer Leopold von Mildenstein from the SS Office for Jewish Affairs, travelled to Palestine on fact finding missions and was accompanied on these tours by Zionist officials. His final tour lasted 6 months, during which he was a welcome guest at many Kibbutz farms. His report after returning to Germany was so filled with praise and compliments about the work being done by the German Jewish settlers in Palestine that Goebbels had a special coin minted in honor of the joint effort between the Nazis and the Zionists. The coin had a Star of David on one side and a Swastika on the other. In recognition of this coin, Palestine's largest fruit growing firm decorated their advertisement for Jaffa oranges with a portrait of King David flanked by Swastika flags.

**Coin minted to honor the joint Nazi/Zionist effort
to move Jews out of Germany to Palestine.**

The Nuremberg Laws - 1935

Meanwhile, Hitler proceeded with his program to reduce the influence and control of Jews in Germany and to marginalize them as a race. The Nuremberg Laws, which changed the legal status of Jews in Germany, became the law of the land on September 15, 1935 soon after they were presented to the German people in a Speech by Hitler at the annual Nazi Nuremberg Rally.

The Nuremberg Laws consisted of two laws; (1) "The Law of the Reich Citizen," and (2) "The Law for the Protection of German Blood and German Honor."

The first law stripped Jews of their German citizenship and made them "subjects of the Reich," that is, legal residents in Germany, but not citizens. Only those with German blood could be citizens of the Reich. The second law forbade marriage or sexual relations between Jews and those of German blood, or even the employment of German women (under age 45) in Jewish households. The stated purpose of the law was to protect the purity of German blood, which was deemed necessary to preserve the German race.

Jews were no longer allowed to vote or to hold public office since they were no longer citizens. Their movements and activities inside Germany were restricted, and a large red J was stamped on their passports. The Nuremberg laws caused Jews to want to leave Germany for friendlier shores, which is precisely what Germany wanted them to do. It should be pointed out, however, that the Jews were never actually forced to leave Germany until well after World War II began, and a great many Jews remained in Germany, unmolested, throughout the war.

These laws had the unexpected result of generating a lot of confusion and heated debate among Nazi bureaucrats as to how a Jew should be defined because there were a great many people with mixed blood. The Nazis settled on defining a "full Jew" as a person with three Jewish grandparents. A mixed Jew or *Mischlinge* was defined in two degrees. The first degree Mischlinge had two Jewish grandparents, while the second degree Mischlinge had only one grandparent. Mischlinges who practiced Judaism were considered full Jews. Full Jews were subject to the full extent of the law, while Mischlings were subjected to the law in lesser degrees, depending on their degree of Jewishness. Mischling civil servants as well those in some other jobs were allowed to stay on.

Surprisingly, many German Jews reacted to the Nuremberg Laws with a sense of relief, because their status was now clarified. They would be required to suffer some inconveniences, but they could now get on with their lives. Instead of being offended by these laws, the head of the German Jewish community and the head of Germany's Zionist movement, Georg Kareski, actually supported them. In an interview with *Angriff* magazine, in its December 23, 1935 edition, he said he had been trying for years to find a method to keep the two races (Germans and Jews) separate, and he considered the race laws to be beneficial to Jews. The Jews were no less interested in keeping their race pure than the Germans were. The Jews in Germany had long worried about being gradually subsumed or absorbed into the larger German population and thus losing their distinct Jewish identity, and Jewish leaders had long tried to prevent marriage outside the Jewish race.

After enactment of the Nuremberg Laws, things quieted down for the Jews in Germany and remained so for the next four years, that is, until the beginning of World War II, and were likely to have remained so if the war had not occurred.

Such were the relations between the Nazis and the Zionists, though information about this cooperative relationship will not appear in the main stream media, nor in official historiography today. On the contrary, such information today is carefully suppressed.

The Zionist Movement

The *Zionist Movement* itself was formally established in 1897 by the Austro-Hungarian journalist Theodor Herzl after publication of his book *Der Judenstaat,* in which he called for a Jewish homeland in Palestine, then under Ottoman rule. Though the movement formally began with Herzl, the idea of a Jewish homeland in Palestine had been incubating for some time prior to that.

Zionism as a movement, advocated the "return" of the Jewish people, scattered as they were around the world (the Diaspora), to "their homeland" with the "resumption" of Jewish sovereignty in the Land of Israel. World Jewry was divided over the issue of Zionism. Some Jews supported it but many did not. Moreover, there were several things wrong with the precept of Zionism. First, most of the Jews of the world had no ancestral roots in the Land of Israel because around 85% of the world's Jews are descendants of the Khazars who lived north of the Black Sea, not the Semitic tribes of Palestine. But leaving that aside, a great many Jews at that time did not want to take up residence in Palestine because they liked it just fine where they were, especially those who had immigrated to America. Most American Jews believed that America was the "New Jerusalem," though there were notable exceptions, such as Louis Brandeis who was an ardent Zionist. Jews had done very well in America, to the extent that the center of world Jewish power had shifted to America. They had no reason whatever to want to leave. But they were doing well in Europe too, and International Jewish power over all Western countries depended on having as many Jews there as possible. They reasoned that creation of a Jewish homeland in Palestine and attracting millions of Jews to it would have the effect of weakening Jewish power in America and Europe. Rich, powerful Jews, particularly in America, began using their influence to try to sabotage the Transfer Agreement. The anti-Zionist Jews in America and Europe were the source of most of the anti-Nazi propaganda. The Zionist Jews tended to cooperate with German Nazi leaders because they wanted all German Jews to move to Palestine, while Jews who were opposed to Zionism carried on a virulent anti-German propaganda campaign, and even declared a war against Germany.

By 1939, more than two thirds of Germany's Jews had emigrated voluntarily in a peaceful process whereby they were permitted to take their wealth with them. Germany's "Jewish problem" was two thirds solved - peacefully - by the time World War Two began, but Jewish immigration to Palestine (Israel) was stopped by the British who were having political trouble with the Palestinians, else, most of the rest of the Jews might have left Germany too. By October, 1941 only around 160,000 Jews remained in Germany, and 40,000 in Austria.

With the help of the Transfer Agreement, hundreds of thousands of Jews emigrated from Europe to Palestine. In September 1940 the Jews news agency in Palestine, "Palcor," reported that 500,000 Jewish emigrants had already arrived from the German Reich, including Austria, the Sudetenland, Bohemia-Moravia, and German ruled Poland. Nevertheless, after 1950 it was claimed that the total number of Jewish emigrants to Palestine from all European countries was only about 80,000. What happened to the other 420,000 Jews? In 1940 they probably had no idea that later on they would be reported to have been "gassed"!

Chapter 13

Life in Germany under Hitler

When Hitler came to power, Germany was hopelessly bankrupt and deeply in debt. The Treaty of Versailles had imposed crushing reparations requirements on the German people, demanding that Germany pay all the costs incurred by the Allied nations during the war. This was totally unrealistic because the combined costs of the war totalled three times the value of all property in Germany, completely beyond Germany's ability to pay. At the same time that the Treaty required Germany to pay these unrealistic reparations, other measures in the Treaty, i.e. taking her coal mines, her merchant fleet and her richest farmlands and giving them to other countries, reduced her ability to pay even further. As unrealistic as these demands were, France nevertheless demanded that they be paid, and paid on time, and then sent the French army in to occupy the Rhineland for the purpose of enforcing these reparations payments. The German army was limited by the Treaty to only 100,000 men, too small to resist an invasion, or to even effectively police the country.

Germany was in a double bind. She had no choice but to pay the reparations, but pay with what? To meet the scheduled payments, the

German government resorted to printing money, which, predictably, created inflation. Once inflation began, private currency speculators jumped in to try to make money off the inflation by selling the mark short. This caused the German mark to plummet in value, setting off an inflationary spiral which quickly zoomed out of control. The Jews totally dominated finance and the financial markets in Germany, and nearly all of these currency speculators were Jews. Their role in setting off the inflation received wide publicity and was therefore well known by the German people. The inflation went out of control, to the point that at its worst, a wheelbarrow full of marks could not buy a loaf of bread.

The thrifty German middle class who had always been careful savers, were ruined *en masse* by the inflation, as their life savings simply evaporated before their eyes. The value of the mark decreased so rapidly that prices were adjusted upwards several times a day. To compensate, employers began to pay their employees twice a day. With their pay in hand, these poor German people literally ran to a store, any store, to purchase almost anything of value before the price was adjusted upwards

**Sweeping up worthless German Marks
during the 1923 hyper inflation.**

again. Almost any item or real asset was preferable to their handfuls of marks which were losing their value by the hour. This wild consumer spending set off an economic boom in Germany for a time, though that soon deflated. Due to the velocity of the inflationary spiral, prices went up so fast that people could not buy enough food with the wages they earned. They began desperately selling off all their personal possessions just to buy enough food to keep themselves and their families alive as wages and salaries lagged far behind the rapidly increasing prices. Pawn shops proliferated. Countless homes, farms and commercial buildings were lost to private banks. Those with access to foreign capital, especially dollars, began buying up property all over Germany for pfennigs on the mark. The private banks and the pawn shops were owned almost entirely by Jews, and the Jews were the ones who had access to foreign capital. The Jews, as a result, grew rich off the inflation, while ordinary Germans were reduced to living in hovels, and in many cases, starving to death.

According to the British historian Sir Arthur Bryant in "Unfinished Victory," 1940:

"It was the Jews with their international affiliations and their hereditary flair for finance who were best able to seize such opportunities. They did so with such effect that, even in November 1938, after five years of anti-Semitic legislation and persecution, they still owned, according to the Times correspondent in Berlin, something like a third of the real property in the Reich. Most of it came into their hands during the inflation. But to those who had lost their all this bewildering transfer seemed a monstrous injustice. After prolonged sufferings they had now been deprived of their last possessions. They saw them pass into the hands of strangers, many of whom had not shared their sacrifices and who cared little or nothing for their national standards and traditions.. "

The 1923 inflation resulted in the largest transfer of wealth from one group to another -- that is, from the Germans to the Jews -- in all of German history, and, as might have been expected, feelings of bitter resentment developed toward the Jews because of it.

As if this were not enough, the inflation was soon followed by a global depression which hit the already fragile German economy especially hard. Germany's unemployment rate at the depth of the depression was the highest in Europe at 30%; even higher than that of the United States, which stood at 24%. Germany's depression was not just worse than America's Great Depression, it was *much* worse. Anguished parents in Germany watched helplessly as their children starved to death. People lost their homes. Shanty towns of hovels constructed of shipping crates and the like sprang up all around Germany's cities and in the forests. To keep alive, they made communal pots of soup out of anything they could scrounge up, such as turnips, potatoes, and even grass.

By the beginning of 1933, the misery of the German people was virtually universal. At least six million unemployed and hungry workers roamed aimlessly through the streets looking for anything to eat or any way to earn a few pfennigs with which to buy food. The government paid unemployment benefits, but only for six months, after which, nothing, and what it paid was pitifully inadequate. These unemployed men had families to feed, so that altogether some 20 million Germans, a third of the population, were at the point of starvation.

Line at the unemployment office in Hanover, Germany in 1930

The cost of welfare amounted to 57% of the total revenue taken in by the government. The entire society was at the point of collapse. Those lucky enough to still have jobs were not much better off, as their salaries and wages had been sharply reduced. The intellectuals were hit as hard, or harder, than the working class. The unemployment rate of university graduates was 60%. Well educated people could be seen on the streets of Berlin with signs on their backs saying they would accept any kind of work. But there was no work. Hardest hit of all were the construction workers, 90% of whom were unemployed.

Farmers had also been ruined by the two economic disasters; the inflation followed a few years later by the depression. Many had been forced to mortgage their homes and land, but then, when the economy "crashed," the value of real estate declined to the point that by 1932, to use the parlance of today, they were "under water" in loan to value ratio. Those who could not meet the interest payments saw their homes and farms auctioned off, the result of which was that those with access to foreign currencies (again, mainly Jews) grew rich off the misery of the hapless ordinary Germans. In 1931 and 1932, 17,157 farms, with a combined total of 1.15 million acres, were liquidated in this way.

Germany's industries, once the envy of the world, saw drastic reductions in production. Thousands of factories had closed down, resulting in a 50 percent decrease in gross industrial production compared to what it had been in 1920. Exports had also dropped by an astounding 75 percent. Germany's central bank, the Reichsbank, was in danger of collapse due to the growing number of outstanding loans going into the red, while at the same time foreign loans were being called in.

It was estimated during that time that no more than around 100,000 people in all of Germany were able to live without financial worries. Germany was a nation of 65 million people living in gut-wrenching misery caused by a variety of problems, including the imposed burdens of the Versailles Treaty, industrial stagnation, horrific unemployment, and serious political instability. The situation became so bad that between 1929 and 1933 some 250,000 Germans committed suicide out of despair and hopelessness. The birth rate in Germany dropped from 33.4 per thousand to just 14.7 per thousand. Even this birth rate was achieved only because of the higher birth rate in the countryside. In the 50 largest cities, there were more deaths than births. In Berlin, deaths exceeded births by 60 percent. This morass of misery caused many to submit to the allures of Communism, making a Communist takeover of the country a real possibility. The Weimar government proved itself totally incompetent to deal with this multiplicity of crises, with its various factions squabbling impotently as Germany teetered on the brink of disaster.

Germany's situation was further aggravated by the unrestrained competition of its 25 regional states whose governments were often in direct conflict with policies of the central Reich government. These states, such as Bavaria, Prussia, Wurttemberg and Saxony, had ancient origins, and only a few years before, that is, before the 1871 consolidation of Germany, they had been independent, sovereign monarchies. Not surprisingly, they jealously guarded the power and privileges which still remained. Germany was a federation, with a weak central government and each of the 25 states was still ostensibly sovereign. Getting them to work together for the greater good of Germany was nearly impossible. Germany had become a country that was ungovernable.

March 21, 1933, Hitler strolls toward the Garrison Church in Potsdam (Suburb of Berlin) for a ceremony to open the new Reichstag session. Hitler became Chancellor in January, 1933.

These were the conditions that existed in Germany when Hitler and the National Socialists came to power in 1933. But as if the situation were not bad enough, conditions were made worse by the worldwide Jewish boycott of German goods which immediately followed Hitler's election to the Chancellorship. The immediate result of the boycott was a precipitous 10% drop in German exports, which were already disastrously low, which then threw even more people out of work. The boycott also attempted to strangle the German economy by cutting off funding from international Jewish banks. International Jewry had declared war on Germany with the intention of undermining and destroying the already fragile German economy in order to discredit and destroy the National Socialists (Nazis) who had just been elected into office. Germany was already at the point of collapse, and the boycott might well have been the proverbial straw that broke the camel's back.

After assessing the situation, Hitler gave a speech to the German people in which he said that the difficulties facing Germany were so dire that he needed emergency dictatorial powers in order to confront them. *"German people, give us four years time, after which you can arraign us before your tribunal and you can judge me!"*

Hitler speaks to the German people and asks for 4 years of dictatorial power to cure Germany's ills.

The Reichstag responded overwhelmingly. On March 23, 1933, the Reichstag voted 441 to 84 to pass the Enabling Act into law, which gave Hitler the 4 years of emergency dictatorial powers he said he needed to resurrect Germany's economy. *"The great venture begins,"* Hitler said. " *The day of the Third Reich has come."*

Hitler knew from the start that the task he had set for himself would be immense and difficult to accomplish. He knew that Germany would have to be transformed from top to bottom, beginning with the very structure of the state. The old class structure would have to go and a new German society, imbued with a new civic spirit would then take its place. He also intended to free Germany from foreign hegemony (the Versailles Treaty) and to restore German honor in the world. But the first and most immediate task would be to put the six million unemployed back to work.

Hitler intended not only to put men back to work, but to give prestige and honor to the concept of "work," itself. Germany had traditionally been stratified by "class," with a privileged class at the top, including the industrialists, and the working class at the bottom, who were considered by the upper class to be nothing more than "instruments of production." In the eyes of the capitalists, "money" was the important element in a country's economy. To Hitler's way of thinking, that conception was upside down. Hitler believed that "money" was only an instrument, and that "work" was the essential element in an economy. Work was man's honor, blood, muscle and soul, Hitler believed.

"All work which is necessary ennobles him who performs it. Only one thing is shameful -- to contribute nothing to the community."

"Nothing falls into a man's lap from heaven. It is from labor that life grows."

"Social honor recognizes no distinction between the employer and the employed. All of them work for a common purpose and are entitled to equal honor and respect." Adolf Hitler

Hitler wanted to put an end to the class struggle and to reestablish the priority of the human being as the principle factor in production. Germany could do without gold to finance industry, he believed. In any case, Germany was broke and didn't have any gold. Other things

221

could be used to finance industry, and he would find them, but "work" was the indispensable foundation for industry and for the economy. The worker had been alienated from society in Germany because he had traditionally been treated with disdain and contempt. Hitler believed that to restore the worker's trust in the fatherland, he would from now on have to be treated as an equal, not as a socially inferior "instrument of production." Hitler argued that under previous so-called democratic governments, those who ran these governments failed to understand that in the hierarchy of national values, "work" is the very essence of life. Mere matter, either steel, or gold, or money of any kind, is only a tool.

What Hitler intended was a total revolution. *"The people,"* he said, *"were not put here on earth for the sake of the economy, and the economy does not exist for the sake of capital. On the contrary, capital should serve the economy, and the economy in turn should serve the people."* It would not be enough to reopen the thousands of closed factories, put the people back to work and continue with business as usual. Unless things were drastically changed, the workers would remain, as they had been before, nothing more than living machines, faceless and interchangeable. Hitler was determined to establish a new moral balance between the workers and capitalism. He was determined that capital was to be used in its proper function as a tool to facilitate what the workers create with their labor. *"It will be the pride of my life,"* Hitler said, *"if I can say at the end of my days that I won back the German worker and restored him to his rightful place in the Reich."*

Hitler knew that such a revolution could not be achieved as Germany was presently structured. The 25 different states that made up Germany continued to compete with each other and to initiate policies that conflicted with those of the central government in Berlin. No coherent national program for economic recovery could be initiated as long as this condition existed. The revolution could also not succeed as long as there were dozens of political parties and thousands of deputies of every conceivable stripe, all squabbling and competing with each other. There would have to be centralization and control if the revolution were to succeed. There were also the Communists who continued assiduously in their efforts to undermine the German state and turn it into a Russian style Soviet Socialist Republic. The Communists would also have to be dealt with.

Hitler took a series of steps to secure absolute power over Germany which was necessary to impose a coherent recovery program. First, he abolished the independent local governments of the 25 states in Germany and replaced them with Reich Commissioners answerable only to Hitler and the National Socialist regime.

Jewish prisoners at Dachau, 1938.

Then he cracked down on the Communists. The SA and the SS rounded them up by the thousands and locked them up in the newly constructed "re-education center" at Dachau near Munich -- later called a "concentration camp." 78% of the membership of the Communist Party in Germany was Jewish. Therefore, to arrest a Communist was almost always to arrest a Jew. It was not that Jews were being singled out for arrest because they were Jewish. They arrested the Communists who almost all happened to be Jews. Hitler saw the Communists as enemies of the German people.

By centralizing federal power in Berlin, and by locking up the Communists, Hitler put an end to the constant squabbling and working at cross purposes among the states and began to create rational, consistent policies and programs necessary for national recovery. Step by step, Hitler implemented his plan.

On May 2, 1933, Hitler outlawed the trade unions and ordered the SA to arrest the trade union leaders, who also happened to me mostly Jews. These too went to Dachau. Hitler then established the "German Labor Front" as the only labor organization allowed in Germany, and placed Dr. Robert Ley in charge. Ley, an intelligent and industrious man, had been an aviator in the war and worked as a chemist before joining the Nazi Party. Ley confiscated the money of the labor unions and used it to fund his "Strength Through Joy" program, a broad based program to improve the working and living standards of Germany's workers. As part of his program, Ley ordered two new cruise-liners to be built which were used to take German workers on foreign holidays. In 1938 an estimated 180,000 people went on cruises to places such as Madeira and the Norwegian fjords. Others were given free holidays in Germany.

Left - Hitler with Dr. Robert Ley, new head of the German Labor Front.

The Strength Through Joy program also built sports facilities, paid for theatre visits, and financially supported travelling cabaret groups. Although the German worker paid for these benefits through compulsory deductions, the image of people being given holidays and subsidized entertainment was of great propaganda value for the Nazi government. It also vastly improved the lives of German workers.

The Strength Through Joy program also subsidized the development of the People's Car, known as the Volkswagen. The American auto maker, Henry Ford, was an enthusiastic supporter of Hitler in his plan to reshape the German culture in favor of the working man. In fact, Hitler said, in 1931, *"I regard Henry Ford as my inspiration."* Hitler's (and Ley's) mass production of the Volkswagen car was modeled on Ford's formula of mass production, low prices, and high wages for workers. Ford also shared Hitler's opinion of the Jews.

By abolishing the labor unions, Hitler was able to hold down wages to give industry a chance to prosper and grow. It has been said that labor unions are in the business of extortion. They extort ever higher wages out of factory owners by strikes and threats of strikes, by slowdowns and often by sabotaging machinery and equipment, all of which is extremely deleterious to industrial growth and development. The aims of labor unions can be summed up by a comment made by the American labor leader, Samuel Gompers. When asked what the labor unions wanted, he said, "More." Even though self-defeating in the end, labor unions never stop demanding ever higher wages and benefits, until eventually they put the company out of business. By outlawing the labor unions and establishing the government controlled "German Labor Front," Hitler was able to maintain a fair wage level for all German workers, not just the members of trade unions, and at the same time to end the strangulation effect of the trade unions on German industry.

On July 14, 1933 the Communist Party and the Social Democrat Party were banned. Party activists still in the country were arrested and sent to the concentration camp. Hitler decided that while they were at it, they would clean up Germany in other ways, as well. The Gestapo began arresting and incarcerating beggars, prostitutes, homosexuals, alcoholics and anyone who refused to work, or who was "work shy," as they put it. A law was then enacted banning all political parties except for the Nazi Party.

All of these measures were met by hysterical propaganda diatribes in the international Jewish press in which events were exaggerated out of all proportion to their actual significance. Labor unions, the Communist party and all other left wing movements and organizations had been specifically targeted by Hitler and the Nazis as "enemies of the German people." As Jews were highly disproportionately represented in the labor unions and all other left wing movements and organizations, they were disproportionately arrested and incarcerated at Dachau. This was described in the international Jewish press as an attack upon the Jews. The Nazis were accused of specifically singling out and arresting Jews, simply because they were Jews. In reality, there was, at this time, no specific Nazi program to target Jews, per se. Nevertheless, international Jewry made the most of this opportunity in their anti-German propaganda campaign.

Night of the Long Knives

The greatest threat to Hitler's survival during the early years of the Third Reich came from the SA, a huge and powerful organization within the Nazi Party, around 3 1/2 million strong, led by its Chief of Staff, Ernst Rohm. The SA was largely responsible for putting Hitler into power, but now in power, things changed. If he was to succeed in implementing his programs, Hitler now needed the support of the industrial and military leaders. The German General Staff despised and detested the SA. The Industrialists who had financed Hitler, also detested the SA and saw them as a dangerous bunch of hooligans. Rohm had made matters worse for himself by indiscreet remarks about absorbing the German army into the SA with himself as the commander. The SA was at that time much larger than the Army. This further set the General Staff's teeth on edge.

Several of the SA leaders, including Rohm, had also been vocal about their socialistic, anti-capitalist sentiments, which neither Hitler, the industrialists nor the army approved of. The SA Brown Shirts were also not very popular with the average Germany citizen because of their gangster-like, thuggish behavior. Critical and derisive remarks made indiscreetly by Rohm about Hitler, personally, also got out. Rohm began to be seen as a "loose cannon" whose loyalty could no longer be trusted, and who might even be a threat to Hitler's leadership. General von Bloomberg and President Paul von Hindenburg advised Hitler that he had to do something about Rohm and the SA or they would no longer be able to support him. The industrialists were telling him the same thing. Both Hermann Goering and Heinrich Himmler had already been warning Hitler of a possible coup by Rohm's SA against Hitler, himself. Hitler finally decided that he had to act against Rohm and the SA.

Hitler began by ordering all the SA leaders to attend a meeting in the Hanselbauer Hotel in the city of Wiesse. There was no explanation of what the meeting was about. Meanwhile Goering and Himmler were drawing up a list of political enemies outside the SA whom they wanted eliminated. On June 29, 1934, Hitler, accompanied by the SS, arrived at Wiesse where he personally arrested Ernst Rohm. During the next 24 hours 200 other senior SA officers were arrested on their way to Wiesse. Several were shot as soon as they were captured but others were taken into custody for further consideration. Hitler personally liked Rohm and decided to pardon him because of his past services to the Nazi movement, but both Goering and Himmler argued against it, advising Hitler that he was making a dangerous mistake. Hitler finally relented and decided that Rohm must die, but insisted that he be given the chance to commit suicide. When Rohm refused, he was shot by two SS men.

Chief of the SA, Ernst Rohm

All together, around 77 of these "unreliables," including Rohm, were "officially" shot, putting an end to all opposition to Hitler and the National Socialists. Unofficial estimates of the number executed range much higher, however. In a speech following the executions, Hitler explained his actions to the German people. *"In this hour I was responsible for the fate of the German people, and thereby I became the supreme judge of the German people. I gave the order to shoot the ringleaders in this treason."* The Night of the Long Knives was a turning point in the Nazi regime, making Hitler the supreme, unchallenged ruler of Germany.

An article in the *Daily Mail* of London was full of praise for Hitler's actions. *"Herr Adolf Hitler, the German Chancellor, has saved his country. Swiftly and with exorable severity, he has delivered Germany from men who had become a danger to the unity of the German people and to the order of the state. With lightening rapidity he has caused them to be removed from high office, to be arrested, and put to death.*

The names of the men who have been shot by his orders are already known. Hitler's love of Germany has triumphed over private friendships and fidelity to comrades who had stood shoulder to shoulder with him in the fight for Germany's future." Daily Mail, London, July 2nd 1934.

Victor Lutze was appointed to head the SA in Rohm's place. Under Lutze, the SA gradually dwindled and lost its power as the SS under Himmler grew rapidly to take its place as the dominant force in Germany.

On August 2, 1934, President von Hindenburg died and Hitler took over the office of President and thereby became Commander in Chief of the army. Hitler, thereafter called himself the "Fuhrer," or leader.

On August 19, 1934, an election, called a "plebiscite," was held in which the German people could express either their approval or disapproval of Hitler and his regime. About 95 percent of registered voters went to the polls, and 90% of them voted for Hitler. The election was internationally supervised, and by all accounts, was a fair and open election without voter intimidation of any kind. Hitler now had the overwhelming support of the German people.

1934 Annual Nazi Rally at Nuremberg

The Nazis held their annual rally at Nuremberg in September, 1934, just two weeks after the plebiscite, during which the Fuhrer's grand proclamation was read: *"The German form of life is definitely determined for the next thousand years. The Age of Nerves of the nineteenth century has found its close with us. There will be no revolution in Germany for the next thousand years."*

The Jewish American journalist William L. Shirer ("Inside the Third Reich") attended the rally to see what Nazi pomp and pageantry was all about. He wrote: *"I am beginning to comprehend some of the reasons for Hitler's astounding success. Borrowing a chapter from the Roman Catholic Church, he is restoring pageantry and color and mysticism to the drab lives of 20th century Germans. This morning's opening meeting...was more than a gorgeous show; it also had something of the mysticism and religious fervor of an Easter or Christmas Mass in a great Gothic cathedral. The hall was a sea of brightly colored flags. Even Hitler's arrival was made dramatic. The band stopped playing. There was a hush over the thirty thousand people packed in the hall. Then the band struck up the Badenweiler March...Hitler appeared in the back of the auditorium and followed by his aides, Goring, Goebbels, Hess,*

Himmler and the others, he slowly strode down the long center aisle while thirty thousand hands were raised in salute."

To Shirer, the intoxicating atmosphere inside the hall was such that *"every word dropped by Hitler seemed like an inspired word from on high."*

**The 1934 Nazi rally at Nuremberg during which
Hitler proclaimed the "thousand year Reich."**

In his speech before the Nuremberg Rally, Hitler absolved the SA Brown shirts from any complicity in the events precipitating the blood purge (night of the long knives) which had just occurred, and acknowledged their unwavering loyalty to him and the party. The 50,000 Brown shirts assembled for the occasion responded with a full throated chorus of "Seig Heils." There was no longer any question of SA loyalty.

The Nuremburg Rally was held annually in the month of September until 1938 when it was suspended. The Rallies were intended to show the world a German nation-state in lock step with its leader and his ideology. They also energized the nationalistic pride of the German people. Hitler obtained the services of the German film actress and director, Leni Riefenstahl, to make a documentary of the 1934 Nuremberg rally.

Leni Riefenstahl had made a name for herself in the German film industry by appearing in a series of so-called *mountain films* directed by Arnold Franck. In these films, she played the part of a prototypically

Mass gymnastics at the Nuremburg Rally during "Day of Community." Hitler and the National Socialists promoted unity, discipline, health and vigor for the German "volk."

fit and healthy German girl with a properly Aryan face. This film genre would soon become associated with the nationalistic aspirations of the emerging Nazi party. She went on, in 1932, to write, direct and perform in her own *mountain film*, "The Blue Light." Despite her lack of experience, the film was remarkably sophisticated in its visual effects. In the whiteness of its snow and the robust Teutonic energy of its heroines, *The Blue Light* was a celebration of the spirit and vitality of the Aryan *Volk*, a theme which was central to Nazi ideology.

It was no accident that Riefenstahl was hand-picked by Hitler to direct a series of documentary films that would cast National Socialism in a favorable light. The first and most influential of these films was *Triumph of the Will*, which was shot in commemoration of the 1934 rally at Nuremberg. This film has been called the most dazzling and successful propaganda film ever made.

Hitler with Leni Riefenstahl at Nuremberg

Hitler Revives the German Economy

In a very short period of time, Hitler engineered what was and remains probably the greatest economic turnaround in history. People went from starving to full employment, and became so prosperous that ordinary workers were given vacations abroad, paid for by the German Labor Front, the government's labor organization. Germany went from hopelessly bankrupt to massively restoring, and even expanding, its infrastructure. The world's first superhighway system, the "Autobahn," was a shining example. Mass production of the Volkswagen, which literally means "people's car," was another. General Eisenhower was so impressed by the German Autobahn system that when he became president years later, he initiated the superhighway system for American -- a direct replication of the German Autobahns. Hitler also pursued a policy of "autarky," meaning, national "self sufficiency." That is, Germany would limit imports and produce its own consumer goods, in so far as possible. Hitler transformed Germany from a seemingly irreversible deep depression into the most vibrant economy in Europe.

The Volkswagen (people's car) begins mass production.

Hitler's government had reduced unemployment from 6,014,000 in January 1933, when he became chancellor, to less than 338,000 by September 1936. At the same time, wages also dramatically increased. German trade was prospering, and deficits of the cities and provinces had almost disappeared. **Contrary to official historiography, expenditures for armaments had been minor up to this point, and played no part in Germany's economic recovery. That came later.**

Unemployment was eliminated at first, primarily by increased government spending on public works. Germany's basic infrastructure, such as railways, roads, and public building projects, were improved and expanded. There was also indirect government support to private works projects. At the same time, taxes were sharply reduced to create an incentive for hiring more workers. The effect was an injection of increased wages into the national economy, followed by increased consumer spending, which itself led to job increases. Hitler's policy of "autarky" (national self-sufficiency) had the effect of creating "wealth creating" jobs in manufacturing which was necessary to sustain long term economic growth. By 1936 there was a labor shortage, especially in the building and metallurgical trades.

Charles Lindbergh and his wife Anne Morrow Lindbergh travelled widely in Germany at this time. In his book *Autobiography of Values*, Charles Lindbergh wrote, *"The organized vitality of Germany was what most impressed me: the unceasing activity of the people, and the convinced dictatorial direction to create the new factories, airfields, and research laboratories..."*

His wife drew similar conclusions. *"...I have never in my life been so conscious of such a directed force. It is thrilling when seen manifested in the energy, pride, and morale of the people--especially the young people,"* she wrote in *"The Flower and the Nettle."*

To counter the effects of the international Jewish boycott of Germany, including the financial strangulation, Hitler simply went around the international bankers by creating a new currency issued by the German government instead of borrowing it from the Jewish owned central bank. This new currency was not backed by gold, but by the credibility of the German government. The new mark was essentially a receipt for labor and materials delivered to the government. Hitler said, *"For every mark issued, we required the equivalent of a mark's worth of work done, or goods produced."* The government paid workers in these new marks and the workers spent them on other goods and services, thus creating more jobs for more people. In this way the German people climbed out of the crushing debt imposed upon them by the International bankers (read, Jewish bankers). Within two years Germany was back on her feet again. It had a solid, stable currency with no debt and no inflation.

Germany even managed to restore foreign trade, despite the international bankers' denial of foreign credit to Germany and despite the global boycott by Jewish owned industries and shipping. Germany got around the boycott and the capital strangulation by exchanging equipment and commodities directly with other countries using a barter system that cut the bankers completely out of the loop. The Jewish boycott actually boomeranged. While Germany flourished -- because barter eliminates national debt, interest on the debt, and trade deficits -- Jewish financiers were deprived of the money they would have earned on these activities. This, of course, only intensified International Jewry's determination to undermine and destroy the Nazi regime.

"Through an independent monetary policy of sovereign credit and a full employment public works program, the Third Reich was able to turn a bankrupt Germany, stripped of overseas colonies, into the strongest economy in Europe within four years, even before armament spending began." (Henry C.K. Liu, "Nazism and the German Economic Miracle," Asia Times (May 24, 2005).

Hitler becomes the most popular leader in the world

The German economic miracle did not escape the notice of foreign leaders who heaped praise on Hitler at every opportunity. David Lloyd George, Prime Minister of Britain wrote:

"I have now seen the famous German leader and also something of the great change he has affected. Whatever one may think of his methods -- and they are certainly not those of a parliamentary country, there can be no doubt that he has achieved a marvelous transformation in the spirit of the people, in their attitude towards each other, and in their social and economic outlook.

"He rightly claimed at Nuremberg that in four years his movement had made a new Germany.

"It is not the Germany of the first decade that followed the war -- broken, dejected and bowed down with a sense of apprehension and impotence. It is now full of hope and confidence, and of a renewed sense of determination to lead its own life without interference from any influence outside its own frontiers.

"There is for the first time since the war a general sense of security. The people are more cheerful. There is a greater sense of general gaiety of spirit throughout the land. It is a happier Germany. I saw it everywhere, and

Englishmen I met during my trip and who knew Germany well were very impressed with the change.

"One man [Hitler] has accomplished this miracle. He is a born leader of men. A magnetic and dynamic personality with a single-minded purpose, a resolute will and a dauntless heart.

"He is not merely in name but in fact the national Leader. He has made them safe against potential enemies by whom they were surrounded. He is also securing them against the constant dread of starvation which is one of the most poignant memories of the last years of the War and the first years of the Peace. Over 700,000 died of sheer hunger in those dark years. You can still see the effect in the physique of those who were born into that bleak world.

"The fact that Hitler has rescued his country from the fear of repetition of that period of despair, penury and humiliation has given him an unchallenged authority in modern Germany.

"As to his popularity, especially among the youth of Germany, there can be no manner of doubt. The old trust him; the young idolize him. It is not the admiration accorded to a popular leader. It is the worship of a national hero who has saved his country from utter despondence and degradation.

"To those who have actually seen and sensed the way Hitler reigns over the heart and mind of Germany, this description may appear extravagant. All the same it is the bare truth. This great people will work better, sacrifice more, and, if necessary, fight with greater resolution because Hitler asks them to do so. Those who do not comprehend this central fact cannot judge the present possibilities of modern Germany.

"That impression more than anything I witnessed during my short visit to the new Germany. There was a revivalist atmosphere. It had an extraordinary effect in unifying the nation.

"Catholic and Protestant, Prussian and Bavarian, employer and workman, rich and poor, have been consolidated into one people. Religious, provincial and class origins no longer divide the nation. There is a passion for unity born of dire necessity.

"The divisions, which followed the collapse of 1918, made Germany impotent to face the problems, internal and external. That is why the clash of rival passions is not only deprecated but temporarily suppressed.

"I found everywhere a fierce and uncompromising hostility to Russian Bolshevism, coupled with a genuine admiration for the British people with a profound desire for a better and friendlier understanding of them. The Germans have definitely made up their minds never to quarrel with us again, nor have they any vindictive feelings towards the French. They have altogether put out of their minds any desire for the restoration of Alsace-Lorraine.

"But there is a real hatred and fear of Russian Bolshevism, and unfortunately it is growing in intensity. It constitutes the driving force of their international and military policy. Their private and public talk is full of it. Wherever you go you need not wait long before you hear the word 'Bolshevism', and it recurs again and again with a wearying reiteration.

"Their eyes are concentrated on the East as if they are watching intently for the breaking of the day of wrath. Against it they are preparing with German thoroughness.

"This fear is not put on. High and low they are convinced there is every reason for apprehension. They have a dread of the great army, that has been built up in Russia in recent years.

"An exceptionally violent anti-German campaign of abuse printed in the Russian official Press and propelled by the official Moscow radio has revived the suspicion in Germany that the Soviet Government are contemplating mischief." -- David Lloyd George, Daily Express, 9/17/1936

Winston Churchill, who would later become Hitler's most obstinate enemy when German economic power began to again challenge that of Great Britain, had this to say in 1935 -- (before he became the front man for the Jewish Focus group):

"In fifteen years that have followed this resolve, he [Hitler] has succeeded in restoring Germany to the most powerful position in Europe, and not only has he restored the position of his country, but he has even, to a very great extent, reversed the results of the Great War. . . the vanquished are in the process of becoming the victors and the victors the vanquished. . . whatever else might be thought about these exploits they are certainly among the most remarkable in the whole history of the world."

". . . and the achievement by which the tables have been turned upon the

complacent, feckless and purblind victors deserves to be reckoned a prodigy in the history of the world and a prodigy which is inseparable from the personal exertions of life thrust on a single man. . .

"Those who have met Hitler face to face in public, business, or on social terms, have found a highly competent, cool, well-informed functionary with an agreeable manner, a discerning smile and few have been unaffected by a subtle personal magnetism.

"Nor is this impression merely the dazzle of power. He exerted it on his companions at every stage in his struggle, even when his fortunes were in the lowest depths. . .

"One may dislike Hitler's system and yet admire his patriotic achievement. If our country were defeated I should hope we should find a champion as indomitable to restore our courage and lead us back to our place among the nations." -- Winston Churchill, 1935

Douglas Reed, British journalist, playwright, novelist and author of many books about Europe between the wars and after World War Two provided the following observation about the economic transformation of Germany under Hitler:

"Germans in their country are not less well cared for than the English people in theirs, but better. You are faced with a country immensely strong in arms and immensely strong in real wealth -- not in gold bars in a vault of the national bank, but industry, agriculture, the thrift and energy of the work people, and the conditions of life they enjoy.

"In Germany now they have a mighty organization, equipped with full powers, for improving the lot of the work people in factories and workshops. Their engineers and social workers and artists go into the factories and see what needs to be done. They say that a shower room, recreation room, a restaurant, a medical clinic, a dental clinic is needed and these are provided. They have a civic sense, a social conscience, a feeling of the community of German mankind -- in spite of the bestial concentration camps -- which you lack."

John L Garvin, editor of the London Sunday paper, "The Observer," wrote:

"Last May, I returned, bringing my family for another sojourn, after two years spent in other European countries. I found a Germany which has

advanced miraculously from the point of 1933. I found political solidarity, a wholesome tone in the life of city dweller and country dweller alike.

"I found living costs materially reduced and an unmistakable optimism on every hand. In every quarter I found the same answer to my questioning: Profound belief in the genius of the Leader, love and admiration for him as an individual. My observations have covered a wide range of social classification.

"I have talked with the humblest type of laborers, with merchants, professional men. I have yet to discover a dissenting voice to the question of loyalty to the Fuehrer. My two young daughters are attending German public schools and are receiving an education which in thoroughness could be equaled in few countries."

And this from Lord Lothian, British Ambassador to Washington, written June 29, 1937: *"I think that it must be admitted that National Socialism has done a great deal for Germany. It has undoubtedly cleaned up Germany in the ordinary moral sense of the word. The defeatism, the corruption so manifest a characteristic in the days after the war has disappeared, at any rate from public view. It has given discipline and order and a sense of purpose to the great majority of young people who in earlier days did not know where to go or what they were living for."*

In an article which appeared in the New York Times on July 12, 1935, John H. Holmes, Pastor of Community Church wrote:

"The spectacle of Germany today is a tremendous experience. Fifteen years after the war in which the allied powers thought they had destroyed her, Germany is on her feet again. As compared with 1922 and 1931, when I last saw Germany, the change is miraculous. The people are confident, enthusiastic and courageous. They have recovered their morale. In 1931 the German people were going to pieces. But now they are themselves again, no doubt about that! The masses of the people are increasingly with Hitler. I have been fooling myself all along that this was not so, but now I know it is so."

In his book, *Defense of Germany*, British scholar G.E.O. Knight wrote:

"Last July, feeling that the Press of this country was willfully lying and conducting a political campaign against Germany, I resolved to go to Berlin and make free and independent investigation. I was determined to

do pretty much as I pleased when I got there, and no one interfered with my movements.

I found Germany, comparatively speaking, a free country, much freer than some of its neighbors. My own views were not always acceptable to my many friends, among whom I can count Jews and Gentiles, Nazis and Communists, Democrats and Socialists. Soon I found that being a Nazi does not preclude one holding views that few Labor men in my own country would dare to express to their 'comrades' of the national Labor Party."

The general improvement in the standard of living of the German people under Hitler's regime put Germany well ahead of all other nations at that time, including the United States. The Nazi regime implemented a viable social security program for retirement. The working conditions were drastically improved, and the German people were provided opportunities for leisure and recreation after work. The same level of prosperity and social benefits for all its citizens have rarely been achieved anywhere in the world, either before or since then.

German society under Nazi rule was also very democratic, with regular elections of representatives to a legislature. It was not democratic in the same sense as in the United States today. The German form of democracy, as an expression of the popular will, was assured by the right to organize plebiscites to express the desires of the people.

"The result of the revolution [National Socialist revolution] in Germany has been to establish a democracy in the best sense of the word. We are steering towards an order of things guaranteeing a process of a natural and reasonable selection in the domain of political leadership, thanks to which that leadership will be entrusted to the most competent, irrespective of their descent, name or fortune. The memorable words of the great Corsican [Napoleon] that every soldier carries a Field Marshal's baton in his knapsack, will find its political complement in Germany." -- Adolf Hitler

"In England, under democracy, you do not put experts in charge of your affairs, but distribute favors among men of a small class without especial qualification for the posts they receive. This is the misuse of democracy in the interest of class, the betrayal of democracy, and it is the cause of our woes, past, present and to come." -- Douglas Reed, in "Disgrace Abounding"

"What the German nation has ardently desired for centuries is henceforth

a reality; one single, fraternally united people, liberated from the mutual prejudices and hindrances of past times." -- Adolf Hitler

"The will of the people is the will of the government, and vice versa. The new political structure raised in Germany is a kind of ennobled democracy; i.e., the government derives its authority from the people, but the possibility of misinterpreting the peoples will or of sterilizing it by the intervention of parliamentary methods has been eliminated altogether."-- Dr. Joseph Goebbels

"The movement was consolidated together in one Reich a people who were hitherto kept in disunion but various lines of division. . . religious divisions, class divisions, professional divisions, political divisions and the territorial divisions into the various autonomous federal states. This unification is now an historical fact. Nationalism has founded a genuine folk community.

"Formerly the votes of the people were distributed among several political parties. Eventually the number of these parties came to thirty-six. They had no great common platform to offer to a people who were struggling to live. They carried on their political campaigns against one another in a quarrel over paltry and selfish issues.

"Today the people of Germany vote for one leader and one party in a consolidated unity that has never before been dreamed of. Following the disappearance of the political parties, which fought only for their own ends and kept the nation divided, great and common vital problems were presented to the people so that they might understand which ideals were worth striving for and for which sacrifices would have to be made. The whole of Germany was aroused to struggle for these great questions which are of vital importance to a nation's existence." -- Rudolf Hess.

"The parliamentary principle of decision by majorities only appears during quite short periods of history, and those are always periods of decadence in nations and States." -- Adolf Hitler

". . . Hitler has repeatedly taken the opportunity of consulting the nation and has each time obtained its wholehearted approval of his policy and methods of government." -- Cesare Santoro, *"Hitler Germany, Vivisection"*

"I myself was and still am a child of the people. It was not for the capitalists that I undertook this struggle; it was for the German working man that I took my stand." -- Adolf Hitler

The following photos show Hitler interacting with the German people, especially children. Hitler is the most popular national leader in the world at this time.

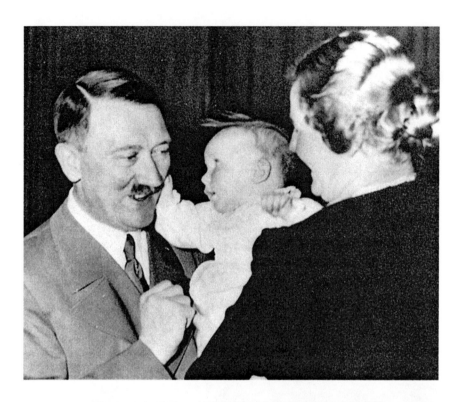

Flowers for the Fuhrer

**Contrary to the propaganda, Hitler was a Catholic
and a Christian believer. Here, he is photographed
leaving the Marine Church in Wilhelmshaven.**

It has been made out by those whose intent was to slander and
smear Hitler that he was an atheist, an occultist, that he believed in
astrology, that he engaged in pagan ritualism, etc., ad nauseam. The
History Channel is currently running a documentary asserting these
very absurdities. But this is how Hitler described his beliefs in *Mein
Kampf*. *"First, I believe in Almighty God... and I solemnly declare that*

Almighty God has chosen me for this task." He said further, *"We wish to fill our culture once more with the spirit of Christianity - but not only in theory."*

Hitler saw Christianity as an essential cultural institution for Germany: *"The German Government, which regards Christianity as the unshakable foundation of the ethical life of the German nation, attaches the greatest importance to the maintenance and development of friendly relations with the Holy See* [The Pope]. *The national government regards the two Christian confessions* [Protestantism and Catholicism] *as the most important factors of the maintenance of our ethical personality. The Government will adopt a just and objective attitude towards all other religions."* -- Adolf Hitler

In numerous utterances by Adolf Hitler and about Adolf Hitler, he hardly comes across in the way he was described above. In his 25 Point Speech of 1920 (point 24), Hitler said, *"The Party as such advocates a positive Christianity without binding itself to any particular church."*

"In this hour I would ask of the Lord God only this: that, as in the past, so in the years to come, He would give His blessing to our work and our action, to our judgment and our resolution, that He will safeguard us from all false pride and from all cowardly servility, that he may grant to us to find the straight path which His Providence has ordained for the German people, and that He may ever give us the courage to do the right, never to falter, never to yield before any violence, before any danger." -- From a speech by Adolf Hitler

"I believe in the Holy German people inside and outside the German frontiers. I believe in Adolf Hitler, who by the grace of God, was sent to give the German people faith in themselves once more." -- German Faith Movement

"Adolf Hitler gave us back our faith. He showed us the true meaning of religion. He has come to renew for us the faith of our fathers and to make us new and better beings. . . just as Jesus Christ made his twelve apostles into a faithful band to the martyr's death whose faith shook the Roman Empire, so now we witness the same spectacle again. Adolf Hitler is the true Holy Ghost." -- Hanns Kerrl. German Minister for German Affairs

It was international Jewish propaganda that made Hitler out to be an atheistic, murderous monster. His Nazi regime did not persecute the German people, nor deprive them of their rights. On the contrary, as can be seen by the statements and comments of world leaders at that time, Hitler devoted his life and all his energies toward improving the lot of *his* German people, and the German people responded with an outpouring of love and devotion for *their* Fuhrer rarely seen in history. The police actions of his regime were directed against the enemies of the German people, which included the Communists and other Leftist organizations whose members were generally not ethnic Germans. Both Hitler and the German people saw what the Jews in Russia had done to that country, and knew that they intended to do the same to Germany if they ever got the chance. Hitler had these leftist revolutionaries rounded up and locked away to make sure they never got the chance. That the vast majority of these people were Jews was only coincidental. They were locked away because they were Communists and revolutionaries, and therefore a dire threat to Germany. Judging by what they did in Hungary, Italy and Spain, he had every justification for his actions.

The International Jewish press blew these events all out of proportion and accused the Nazi regime of "persecuting" the Jews in Germany for no reason except that they were Jews. They repeatedly and relentlessly accused the Nazi regime of the intent to "exterminate" the Jews, beginning with the Untermeyer Speech in New York in 1933. That simply was not true. Most Jews lived unmolested in Germany right up until the beginning of World War II, and a great many lived unmolested in Germany right through the war. It was the Communists, who happened to be Jews, who were harshly dealt with. A number of German Army officers, including a couple of field marshals, Field Marshal Erhard Milch, for example, were Jewish. Milch oversaw the development of the Luftwaffe.

At the same time that the comments and observations of statesmen, historians and journalists presented above in this chapter were being made describing Germany as a land of happy, prosperous people with a benign government dedicated to their well being, international Jewry continued its virulent anti-German propaganda campaign portraying Germany as a charnel house of repression, brutality, and murder. In March, 1935 the National Council of Jewish Women in New York

City proclaimed Hitler a "world menace." At precisely the same time in Germany, Julius Streicher, publisher of "Der Sturmer" newspaper, was comparing Hitler to Jesus Christ. A professor Hauser made the news by declaring that God had revealed himself to Germany through Hitler, and Dr. Reinhardt Krause declared that Hitler alone had "God's order" for the Germany nation. The National Socialists claimed that the international hostility toward Hitler was entirely Jewish inspired. While the German people adored Hitler and saw him as the savior of Germany, many outside Germany had been conditioned by Jewish anti-German propaganda to regarded him as a menace to mankind.

Hitler had been elected in large part on his promise to reclaim territories taken away from Germany by the Versailles Treaty, and to create a single German state to include all German people. British, French and Soviet leaders refused to recognize Germany's aims as legitimate, but chose instead to regard Hitler's revanchist goals as international aggression. Representatives of Britain, France and Italy met at an Italian village (Stresa) on April 11, 1935 to reaffirm their opposition to Germany absorbing Austria or the Sudetenland of Czechoslovakia. Hitler denounced these reaffirmations as hostile to Germany, declaring that his aims were legitimate and that Germany did not want another war. He spoke of the absurdity of war and of the "*follies*" of the past. Wars of revenge, he said, were out of date. *"A deliberate maker of war may have been a patriot in the old days,"* he said, *"but today such a person would be a traitor." "We are not imperialists,"* he added, and said that all the German people wanted was *"equal rights for all,"* and its honor restored. All the German people wanted, he said, was to be treated like everyone else, and among other things, that meant the return of German territory.

Despite the dogged anti-German propaganda, there remained support for Hitler's aims from reflective, thoughtful men. On June 6, 1935, Britain's leading cleric, the Archbishop of Canterbury, expressed sympathy for Germany's position among nations, declaring that Germany *"must be recognized as a nation entitled to an equal place among other nations."*

Yet, the average American or Englishman was made to believe

that Germany was a world menace and should be controlled and held in check. They were made to believe through the Jewish controlled media that Germany was an evil, brutish country with an oppressive, totalitarian government that kept a terrified population under strict control with secret police forces and concentration camps. Nothing could have been further from the truth.

The "holy war" declared on Germany by international Jewry continued relentlessly, and the propaganda campaign of deliberate lies, smears and misrepresentations was succeeding in turning the world against Germany. The contrast between life inside Germany as it actually was, and the way in which it was depicted in the International Jewish press could not have been greater.

Following is a series of photographs taken during the Nazi period showing the Germans to be a clean-cut, handsome, intelligent and civilized people, not unlike those of any other European country at the time.

This was the real face of Germany during the Nazi period

**A German army officer and a soldier (above) A young soldier
(below left) and a young German officer (below Right).**

A German Officer and his dog

Young men of the "Hitler Youth" Movement (like Boy Scouts).

Young women of the Nazi Youth Movement (Girls' equivalent of the boys' Hitler Youth).

More German Youth Movement Girls

German farm girl, 1930s   **German city boy of the 1930s**

A 1930s German street (before it was bombed)

German public swimming pool -- 1930s

Strolling the children.

An elegant German couple of the 1930s.

Below is the face of Germany as depicted in Jewish propaganda.

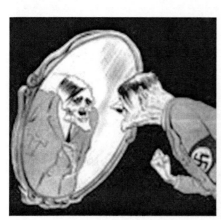

"Propaganda" Nazis

Chapter 14

Hitler Begins Reclamation of German Territory

One of Hitler's goals as Chancellor of Germany was to make Germany whole again. He was determined to regain control of lands taken from Germany by the Versailles Treaty but also to bring ethnic Germans living outside the Reich back into Germany. If his plans were to have any chance of succeeding, however, it would first be necessary for Germany to re-arm. The Versailles Treaty had limited Germany to a total of 100,000 men at arms, a pitifully inadequate military force to support his ambitions. After mulling over what to do, Hitler convened a meeting with the Army's General Staff and members of his Cabinet on March 15, 1935 and announced his decision that Germany would openly defy the military limitations set by the Versailles Treaty and re-arm. Not a single person present objected. All enthusiastically approved.

Propaganda Minister Joseph Goebbels held a press conference the very next day and announced to the world that the Fuhrer had decided that Germany would reintroduce military conscription and build a new Army consisting of 36 divisions, totaling 550,000 men. This was a brazen violation of the Versailles Treaty, and an open invitation for retaliation by France and Britain.

The German leaders then waited anxiously to see how Britain and France would react. Some of the more cautious generals were worried that France might attack Germany immediately. After all, France was well armed, with the largest army in Europe and Germany would have been powerless to defend itself. But nothing happened; absolutely nothing. Hitler had gambled and won!

Hitler knew that France was struggling with internal political problems and that Britain was still in the depths of the depression. Neither country, he wagered, had the stomach to take military action against him, and he turned out to be right. Hitler also had moral suasion on his side. Any sovereign country, including Germany, has an intrinsic right to the means of self defense and of defending its sovereignty. It was obvious that Germany could not do so with a military force limited to 100,000 men. In a positive light, Hitler's decision to re-arm Germany could be seen as the "responsible" thing for a national leader to have done.

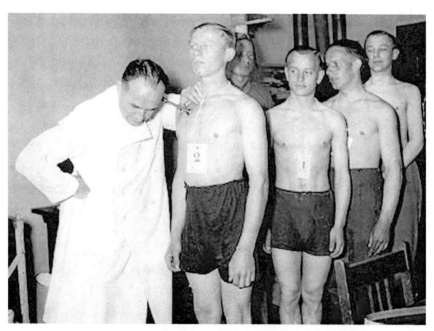

June 1935 - Hitler re-arms Germany. Here, new recruits line up for their enlistment physicals.

But Hitler was smart enough to understand that he needed to follow up his proclamation by being conciliatory. A couple of months after the conscription announcement, he spoke before the Reichstag and declared that, "Germany wants peace...None of us means to threaten anybody." And surely, he meant it. He wanted to reclaim Germany's lost lands, but he did not want war.

He announced before the Reichstag a thirteen-point peace program. He said that Germany would respect all other provisions of the Versailles Treaty, including the demilitarization of the Rhineland. Germany is ready, he said, to cooperate in a collective system for safeguarding European peace. He further stated that Germany was ready to conclude pacts of non-aggression with her neighbors.

This seemed to soothe the nerves of his gun-shy neighboring countries. This method of diplomacy set a pattern which Hitler was to follow thereafter; a forceful announcement on a Saturday (Hitler's Saturday surprises), followed by a conciliatory speech. After each such initiative, he permitted time to lapse so that everything could settle back down before making his next move. He knew what he wanted and knew what he was doing, and he played his hand very carefully.

He let a year pass before he took his next big gamble; the reoccupation of the Rhineland. Early Saturday morning on March 7, 1936, three German Army battalions crossed the bridges over the Rhine and entered the industrial heartland of Germany known as the Rhineland. This demilitarized area, the Rhineland, included all territory west of the Rhine River, stretching over to the French border, as well as a section east of the river. The Rhineland included the cities of Cologne, Dusseldorf and Bonn.

Hitler's Foreign Minister, Constantin von Neurath, summoned the French, British and Italian ambassadors to his office at 10 A.M. the same morning and handed them a memorandum which stated that the German government had "restored the full and unrestricted sovereignty of the Reich in the demilitarized zone of the Rhineland." This, of course, was also a violation of the Versailles Treaty.

At noon on the same day, Hitler appeared before a hastily called Reichstag assembly and announced what had happened. The totally surprised Reichstag members jumped to their feet in jubilation and began cheering wildly, with shouts of "heil" to the Fuhrer.

When they calmed down and returned to their seats, Hitler continued speaking. He said, *"First, we swear to yield to no force whatever in the restoration of the honor of our people, preferring to succumb with honor to the severest hardships rather than to capitulate. Secondly, we pledge that now, more than ever, especially for one with our Western neighbor nations... We have no territorial demands to make in Europe!...Germany will never break the peace."*

Saturday, March 7, 1935 - German troops cross a bridge over the Rhine River and enter the Rineland.

Hitler and his generals again waited nervously to see how France and Britain would react. The German troops even had orders to immediately abandon the Rhineland and cross back over the bridges if France were to attack. But, as before, nothing happened. The French and the British did nothing. The horrors of the First World War were too fresh in their memory, and the French in particular simply did not have the stomach for another war with Germany. The British did not act because most British leaders had already come around to the belief that the Versailles Treaty was unreasonable in many aspects and most of them sympathized with Hitler's position.

This had been a tremendous gamble for Hitler because the French, with their one hundred division army could easily have overwhelmed the 30,000 lightly armed German troops now in the Rhineland, in which case Hitler could have lost everything. Hitler was later to admit, *"The 48 hours after the march into the Rhineland were the most nerve wracking in my life. If the French had marched into the Rhineland, we would have had to withdraw with our tail between our legs..."*
Several of Hitler's generals were extremely fearful of the bold move, but his Foreign Minister, von Neurath, had calmly assured him, *"You can risk it. Nothing will happen."* Hitler learned to ignore the trepidations of his generals and use his own judgment in such matters.

The German people in the Rhineland welcomed the troops with jubilation. The soldiers were met by German priests who conferred blessings upon them. Women threw flowers in their path. The people in Cologne went wild with joy. Inside Cologne's magnificent cathedral, Cardinal Schulte lavishly praised Hitler for what he had done.

A few weeks later, on March 29th, another plebiscite was held. 99% of the registered voters went to the polls, and 98.8% voted approval of Hitler's reoccupation of the Rhineland. Hitler had become the most popular man in Germany.

With this accomplishment securely in the bag, Hitler then went back to Berchtesgaden, his retreat in the Bavarian mountains, to relax while things calmed down, but also to ponder his next move, for he had many more moves to make in implementing his plan of irredentism for Germany.

Meanwhile, in Berlin and throughout Germany, preparations were underway to host the coming Summer Olympics. The Berlin Olympics would be a big opportunity for the Nazis to show off the new Germany they had created to people from all over the world.

Chapter 15

The 1936 Olympics

Berlin won the bid in April 1931 to host the 1936 Olympic Games over Barcelona, its number one contender. The bid for the games had been won two years before the Nazis were elected into office in Germany. When the Nazis came to power, American Jewish organizations immediately demanded that some other venue be chosen for the games other than Berlin. The American Jewish Congress and the Jewish Labor Committee staged rallies to oppose America's participation in the games if the games were not moved out of Berlin. Avery Brundage, President of the American Olympic Committee, to his very great credit, decided, despite this pressure, that America would participate in the Games in Berlin as scheduled. International Jewry already had a propaganda campaign under way against the Nazis long before they came into office, and Brundage took the view that the attempted boycott of the Olympic Games was just another "Jewish-Communist conspiracy" against Germany, which, of course, it was. He stated that Jewish athletes were not being treated unfairly in any way by anyone. The Jews were nevertheless relentless.

The story most repeated about Hitler and the Olympic Games in

Berlin, is that Hitler refused to shake the hand of the American black athlete Jesse Owens after he had won a race. This myth is widespread, and appears as fact in many journals and publications today, including, for example, in Microsoft's Encarta Encyclopedia.

What actually happened is that Hitler personally attended the first day of the track and field competition on August 2, 1936, and personally congratulated the German athlete Hans Wollke, who was the first German to win a gold medal in the Olympics since 1896. Throughout the rest of the day, Hitler continued to receive Olympic champions, both German and non-German, in his VIP box.

The next day, August 3, the chairman of the International Olympic Committee, Comte Bailet-Latour, approached Hitler early in the morning and told him that he had violated Olympic protocol by personally congratulating each Olympic winner. Hitler duly apologized and said that he would hence forward refrain from shaking the hands of the winners. Later in the same day, when Jesse Owens won his gold medals, Hitler did not shake his hand...or anybody else's, during the remainder of the games.

It is, therefore, utterly false to claim that Hitler deliberately chose to snub Owens. In his autobiography, "The Jesse Owens Story," 1970, Owens recounted how Hitler had stood up and waved to him: *"When I passed the Chancellor,"* he wrote, *"he arose, waved his hand at me, and I waved back at him. I think the writers showed bad taste in criticizing the man of the hour in Germany."*

During the afternoon of the first day, Hitler and his entourage left the stadium early because rain threatened. In fact, it had already begun to sprinkle. Coincidentally, the American black, Cornelius Johnson, had just barely beaten his American teammate in the high jump to win a gold medal shortly before Hitler left the stadium. The anti-German propagandists reported through the International Jewish press that Hitler had "stormed out" of the stadium in a tantrum because a black man had won an event. Hitler was much too sensitive to world opinion to have left himself open to negative publicity by any such inappropriate behavior.

But the facts would never stand in the way of a good anti-Nazi story. The Jewish owned *New York Times* carried on its front page, "Hitler greets all medalists except Americans," the day after the first

The Baltimore *African-American* newspaper, *August 8, 1936*.

competitive events. The headline on the next day's paper read, "Hitler ignores Negro medalists." Not by coincidence, the *New York Times* had earlier led the movement to boycott the Berlin games. Other newspapers picked up the story. "Hitler Snubs Jesse," read the huge, bold headline of a black Cleveland paper, *Call and Post*. The *Baltimore Afro-American* carried the headline "Adolf" Snubs U.S. Lads. These were deliberate lies. Nothing of the kind had happened.

Another story spread around about the 1936 Olympics by the anti-German press was that Owens' victory "disproved the Nazi master race theory." If anything, the Games supported that idea, if, in fact, such an idea even existed. Germany won 89 medals, while the United States, with two and a half times Germany's population, won 56.

That Germany claimed to be the "master race" is another myth with no basis in fact; just more anti-German propaganda from the International Jewish press. The Nazis never made any such claim (though the Jews do claim to be God's chosen people), and Hitler never used the term, "master race," or anything close to it to describe the German people. Hitler used the term "Aryan" to represent all the Germanic peoples of Europe, including the British, Dutch, Swedes, Norwegians, Fins, Swiss, and all the other peoples of Europe of Germanic origin. Hitler believed that the Aryan people were culturally superior to most of the rest of mankind as manifested in all their achievements. He wrote in *Mein Kampf*: *"All the human culture, all the results of art, science, and technology that we see before us today, are almost exclusively the creative product of the Aryan..."* This idea was generally accepted by all Europeans at the time, and could hardly be disputed given the fact that almost all civilizational advances were accomplished by these people. The British have always considered themselves to be a superior race. The anti-German international Jewish press deliberately misinterpreted these general concepts to mean that the Germans considered themselves alone to be the "Master Race." In fact, no such claim was ever made.

In what was to become an act of extreme irony, President Franklin D. Roosevelt, then running for re- election and concerned about the reaction of the southern states, refused to see Jesse Owens at the White House. Owens was later to remark that it was Roosevelt, not Hitler, who snubbed him.

Jesse Owens was the citizen of a country whose racism would have made Hitler blush. In Hitler's Germany, Jesse Owens could share a bus or tram ride with white people. Treated equally in all respects before the law, he could sit in a movie theater next to whites, use public toilets, dine in restaurants, and stay in hotels without any discrimination being shown towards him. There were many things he could do in Hitler's Germany that were forbidden at home in the United States. In the United States black athletes were required to eat separately from their white fellow athletes. If they were allowed to share the same hotel at all, which was unlikely, it would be necessary for them to use the service entrance. There were no blacks on any major league baseball team and there were no black swimmers. This was in the enlightened north. In the southern states there was no possibility of a black being allowed to participate in any sport, except to compete with other blacks. For the Jewish press to have smeared Hitler and the German people in general as "racists" was hypocritical in the extreme.

Jesse Owens evidently enjoyed his time in Hitler's Germany

immensely. In Germany he received a lot of pre-Olympic media hype and the German people idolized him. *"Once at the stadium, the mere appearance of Jesse Owens' head from some pit below the stands would cause sections of the crowd to break out in chants of, 'Yes-sa Ov-enss! Yes-sa Ov-enss!'* "-- Richard D. Mandell. "The Nazi Olympics."

"Some mornings at the Olympic village the athletic hero of the hour was awakened by amateur photographers who flocked outside his bedroom window to click at the athlete before he could gather poise for one of his many appearances before the mobs in Berlin." -- Richard D. Mandell. "The Nazi Olympics."

"Jesse Owens was cheered as loudly as any Aryan." -- Lawrence N. Snyder; Jesse's coach. Saturday Evening Post Nov. 7th, 1936

When Jesse Owens first returned to the states, he denied that he had been snubbed by Hitler or that he had been mistreated in any way. But he learned soon enough that he could use the "snub myth" to his own advantage. In his postwar interviews, postwar public addresses, and in his "ghosted" articles and books, he began to claim that Hitler had, indeed, refused to shake his hand, and he also began to repeat the lie that Hitler "left the stadium in a tantrum" when a black athlete won a medal, because that is what people wanted to hear. As he discovered that anti-Hitler stories resonated well with American audiences, he began to exaggerate his "mistreatment" stories even further. Such exaggerations finally became the central feature of his talks as he described how emotionally torn apart he was by the "snubs" and other mistreatment by Hitler and the Nazis. The reality is that Jesse Owens was given the warmest ovation of his life by the German spectators, including Hitler.

Yet another myth still commonly believed as the result of the anti-German propaganda is that American blacks "ran away" with the gold medals during the Berlin games. It is true that Owens won four gold medals, but outside of track and field, the Germans dominated the Olympic Games of 1936 by winning more medals than all other participants combined.

These are only some of the flagrant distortions about Nazi Germany created by the International Jewish propaganda campaign. Since the victors write the historical accounts of events, Nazi Germany has been permanently smeared with these blatantly false stories.

Hitler's "Film Expert to the National Socialist Party," Leni Riefenstahl, made a documentary of the 1936 Olympic Games, called, *Olympia,* which nearly matched her earlier film, *Triumph of the Will,* in its propaganda value to the Third Reich. The film won many international awards.

Leni Riefenstahl shooting the 1936 Olympic Games in Berlin

Germany scored a huge propaganda coup with the 1936 Olympic games, despite all efforts of the International Jewish press to denigrate it. The world was able to see firsthand "the new Germany" which had been created by Nazi rule. German hospitality won high praise from visitors from all over the world, and Adolf Hitler was seen as the man of the hour. Despite efforts being made by international Jewry to discredit Nazi Germany in every way possible, most objective reports were favorable to Germany as a result of the Games. Frederick Birchall

Hitler at the opening ceremony of the 1936 Olympic Games.

Berlin's Olympic Stadium

reported in the *New York Times* that the Games put Germany *"back in the fold of nations,"* and even made them *"more human again."*

But Jewish reporters consistently took only the most sinister interpretation of everything occurring in Germany. The Jewish journalist William Shirer, for example, regarded the *"Berlin glitter on display for the world to see as merely hiding a menacing, racist, militaristic regime. ...I'm afraid the Nazis have succeeded with their propaganda,"* he wrote. *"First, the Nazis have run the Games on a lavish scale never before experienced, and this has appealed to the athletes. Second, the Nazis have put up a very good front for the general visitors, especially the big businessmen."* The most well intentioned and even the most praiseworthy activities of the Germans were seen by Shirer and other Jewish reporters only as a *"front."*

The Jewish propaganda of that time was designed to smear and discredit Germany and the Nazis, not to present an accurate picture of actual events. Every event was deliberately twisted in the Jewish press to mean something it didn't. Every word and gesture of Hitler or any Nazi was deliberately misinterpreted to cast them in the worst possible light. Sinister motives were attributed to every act and deed. When Hitler behaved in a courteous, considerate, statesmanlike manner, it was reported in the Jewish press that he was *"wearing a false face,"* and that he was *"cynically manipulating world opinion for his own sinister purposes."*

Despite all that is now known to be true about the circumstances surrounding the 1936 Olympic Games, especially the personal conduct of Hitler himself, Jewish writers and historians continue, even to this day, to trot out the same old propaganda lies of the 1930s and 40s.

Shirley Povich, (July 15, 1905 -- June 4, 1998) Jewish sports writer for the Washington Post newspaper.

A good example of this is an article written by the Jewish sports writer Shirley Povich for the Washington Post on July 6, 1996, titled, "Berlin, 1936: At the Olympics, Achievements of the Brave in a

Year of Cowardice." The article was written to commemorate the sixtieth anniversary of the 1936 Berlin Olympic Games. (It is worth mentioning that the Washington Post is a Jewish owned newspaper, and was an enthusiastic participant in the international Jewish smear campaign against Germany during the 1930s and 40s. The Washington Post also participated in the effort to boycott the Berlin Olympic Games.) He begins his article by writing: *"It is about the 1936 Olympics in Berlin that Adolf Hitler turned into a sickening pageant of Nazi propaganda, supported by submissive U.S. Olympic officials and craven American track and field coaches who, like Nazi cousins, kicked their only two Jewish athletes off the 4x100-meter relay team. And it is about Hitler's snub of America's victorious black Olympians in their triumph."*

Povich's description of the 1936 Olympic Games in Berlin is simply astonishing in view of what is known to be the real story about the Games today. The Nazis were defeated and destroyed in 1945, yet half a century later the preposterous Jewish anti-German propaganda campaign continues unabated.

In the article, he repeats the lie that our "own Jewish athletes were kicked off the team, in order to placate Hitler." He also repeats the lie that Hitler snubbed Jesse Owens and the other black American athletes. He preposterously states that Hitler "already had the killing of six million Jews in mind." He wrote that Germany did not permit German Jews to participate in the games. That was a lie. The Jewess Helene Mayer, for example, was a member of the German fencing team.

In the article, Povich accused Avery Brundage, head of U.S. Olympic Committee, of cowardice for refusing to participate in the attempted boycott of the Olympic Games. Povich claims that prominent Catholic, Protestant, as well as Jewish individuals and groups in the United States, were loudly clamoring for a boycott, as were, he says, trade unions and civic organizations. That was not true. The campaign to boycott the Olympics was a purely Jewish campaign. Catholics and Protestants had nothing to do with it, and did not support it. Trade unions did support it, but trade unions were totally dominated and controlled by Communist Jews.

Povich states in the article that Germany was humiliated by the

American black athletes. In reality, Germany, at less than half of the population of the United States, won 89 medals to America's 56.

Povich claims that two Jews were removed from the American team simply because they were Jews. Not so! The two Jews that were removed were replaced by two blacks who outperformed them.

Povich's article was a reiteration of the blatant anti-Nazi propaganda spewed out of the Jewish controlled media during the Nazi era, without a word of truth in it. The article totally mischaracterized events as they actually occurred, yet, his version of events has become the official history of the 1936 Olympic Games, the history taught to children in school.

Chapter 16

"Anschluss." The unification of Austria and Germany

Beginning with his 25 Points speech of 1919, one of Hitler's overriding goals was the unification of all German people into a single nation-state. Hitler was an Austrian, but always called himself a German, and he considered Austria to be part of Germany. The giant multi-ethnic Austro-Hungarian Empire had been dismembered after World War I by the Paris Peace Conference and Austria was left as a small rump state of 6.8 million people, mostly ethnic Germans. As part of the Austro-Hungarian Empire, Austria had been an integral part of a relatively self-sufficient economic system, but now, having been carved out of that giant empire and made into a tiny independent state, Austria was no longer an economically viable entity. She had been cut off from sources of raw materials which had been available to her from the Austro-Hungarian Empire, and also from markets for export. Austria was a German speaking, German state, and it would have been only logical for Austria to combine with Germany after the Austro-Hungarian Empire no longer existed. Moreover, there was strong support for that in both Austria and Germany, but the Versailles Treaty specifically forbade it. World War I had been fought primarily to reduce the size and power of Germany, and the Versailles Treaty was designed to prevent Germany from ever becoming a super power again. For that reason, the victors of the war were steadfastly opposed to the union of Austria with Germany.

As it became more and more clear that Austria was not an economically viable state, popular support for union with Germany steadily increased. By the early 1930s popular support for union among both the German and Austrian populations was overwhelming. It was estimated that at least 80 percent of the Austrian people favored unification with Germany, and nearly as high a percentage of Germans also favored it. As a preliminary measure, an attempt was made in 1931 to create a customs union between Austria and Germany to permit free trade and unrestricted travel between the two countries, but the agreement was blocked by outside forces, notably France and Czechoslovakia, who saw it as an attempt to circumvent the Versailles Treaty. With a 25% unemployment rate and a starving population, Austria was desperate to find a means of increasing trade and productivity, but all such attempts were blocked by these outside forces. Union with Germany would have solved all of Austria's problems, and it would also have partially fulfilled the aspirations of the National Socialists for a single German state.

Austria was politically divided during this period by a struggle between left wing and right wing groups. Traditional, mostly rural Austrians, along with the bourgeoisie, supported the conservative, Catholic Christian Social Party (CS), while the workers and labor unions, mainly in the cities, supported the Social Democratic Party. The Communist Party (KPO) and the National Socialist Party (Nazi) were marginal groups at first. The Communist Party was composed mostly of Jews, but it was small and failed to gain traction in Austria as it had in Germany. Most of Austria's Jews belonged to the Social Democratic Party, and most of these Jews were avowed Marxists. The leader of the party, Otto Bauer, was a Jew, and Jews filled all of the leadership positions in the party, though the rank and file were mostly Austrian laborers and members of Jewish led labor unions.

During the early 1930s, 192,000 Jews were resident in Austria, almost all of them in Vienna. Jews represented 2.8 percent of the Austrian population, but nearly 10 percent of the population of Vienna. The population of Vienna was just under 2 million. Despite their small numbers, Jews totally dominated the capital city. Jews owned two thirds of all newspapers and banks. They owned 60 percent of all large businesses and industries. Over 50% of lawyers, doctors and dentists in Vienna were Jewish, and nearly a third of university professors were Jewish.

Through their control of the Social Democratic Party, Vienna's largest party, Marxist Jews dominated the city government of Vienna, giving it the reputation of "Red Vienna." They held a majority of seats on the City Council, and they controlled the labor unions. The Jewish controlled Social Democratic Party was traditionally anti-clerical and given to anti-religious rhetoric, which the Catholic clergy used to label them "godless, Jewish-Bolshevists."

The conservative Christian Social Party (CS), which had the support of the Catholic Church in Austria, managed to gain control of the Austrian government in 1932 through a coalition with other conservative parties. It's leader, Englebert Dollfuss, became the Austrian Chancellor. While the Jewish dominated Social Democratic Party (SDP) controlled the government of Vienna, the Christian Social Party (CS) controlled the national government.

By this time, a branch of Germany's Nazi party had established itself in Austria. The members wore the same uniforms as their German colleagues and adhered to the same doctrines of anti-Marxism and anti-Semitism. They were recruited mainly from the lower bourgeoisie and the peasantry and their main political goal was the union of Austria and Germany. The movement grew slowly and no Nazi had as yet managed to get elected to the national parliament. In the provincial elections of 1932, however, the Nazis won a number of seats in several of the local diets. After Hitler became Chancellor in Germany in 1933, the Austrian Nazis, led by Dr. Alfred Frauenfeld, began immediately to concentrate their energies to bring about Anschluss, or union with Germany. The Austrian Nazis considered themselves a part of the Nazi movement in Germany, and took their orders from Hitler.

Though Dollfuss had previously favored Anschluss, he changed his mind and decided that the best path for Austria was independence. Dollfuss was a devout Catholic and he wanted to build up an alternative to Nazism -- a Catholic, anti-socialist, authoritarian, Austrian movement. He was supported in his opposition to Anschluss by the Social Democratic party under Jewish, Marxist control, but he wanted nothing to do with them either. He was as much opposed to the Reds as to the Nazis.

The Christian Social Party was now in a four way struggle with the Nazis, the Communists, and the Social Democrats. In order to assert control, the Dollfuss regime dissolved parliament, banned the Austrian Nazi and Communist parties, and centralized power in the office of the Chancellor who now had dictatorial powers to rule the country. Many of the Nazi leaders were thrown in jail. A brief civil war ensued in which the Dollfuss government was victorious. A concordat was soon announced with the Holy See (the Pope), which essentially made Catholicism the official religion of Austria.

Dollfuss didn't last long, however. He was soon assassinated by the Nazis in a failed coup attempt as the political struggle in Austria continued. Kurt Schuschnigg, who succeeded Dollfuss as Chancellor, made up his mind to destroy the Austrian Nazis and immediately began to initiate actions against them, including rounding them up and locking them up in internment camps. The oppressive Schuschnigg regime was not popular with the Austrian people, the majority of whom actually favored the Nazis because the Nazis supported union with Germany. The Christian Social Party (CS) under Schuschnigg, which now controlled the national government, and the Social Democratic Party (mostly Jewish) which now controlled the government of Vienna, became strange bedfellows as they united in their opposition to union with Germany, though in little else. The Austrian people, on the other hand, were 80 percent in favor of unification with Germany.

On February 12, 1938, Hitler summoned Schuschnigg to his villa at Berchtesgaden in Bavaria to discuss Schuschnigg's problems with the Austrian Nazis. During the meeting, Hitler was very condescending toward the Austrian Chancellor, and virtually instructed him to lift the ban on political parties in Austria, to reinstate full party freedoms, to release all imprisoned members of the Nazi Party and to permit them to participate in the government. When Schuschnigg indicated reluctance to comply with these instructions, Hitler threatened military action. Schuschnigg had no choice but to comply, as Austria's military power was no match for that of Germany. Moreover, Austrian public opinion was against the Austrian Chancellor.

After returning to Austria, Schuschnigg, in compliance with Hitler's instructions, appointed Arthur Seyss-Inquart, a lawyer and member of the Nazi Party, as Interior Minister. He also removed General Alfred Jansa as Chief of Staff of the Austrian Army, also at Hitler's instruction, because Jansa had expressed his intention to resist any attempted German entry into Austria by armed force. Hitler wanted to avoid any such confrontation at all costs.

But safely away from Hitler's intimidating presence, Schuschnigg began reverting back to his recalcitrant position on union with Germany and continued to oppose it. He also continued his oppressive measures against the Austrian Nazi Party which advocated union with Germany. The mostly Jewish Social Democrats agreed on very little with the Christian Socialists, but they turned out in force to support Schuschnigg in opposition to union with Germany. Groups of these Social Democrats (mostly Jews) went all around the city of Vienna painting slogans on the sidewalks and on the walls of buildings in support of Austrian independence and against Austrian union with Germany. Austria's Jews vehemently opposed Hitler and the Nazis, including Austrian Nazis, and they wanted nothing to do with Hitler's Germany, certainly not union with it. This put them in direct opposition to the Austrian people and served only to inflame the already rampant anti-Semitism in Austria.

In contravention of Hitler's instructions Schuschnigg immediately announced a plebiscite (a national vote) to be held on Austria's Independence day of March 13, 1938, to determine whether or not Austria would unite with Germany. He then set out on a tour of Austria to try to whip up patriotic feelings and to persuade the Austrian people to vote for an independent Austria, and against union with Germany.

Schuschnigg's plebiscite was to be open to all Austrian voters, but was to be restricted only to those over the age of 24. It was Austria's youth -- those under 24 years of age -- who were most overwhelmingly in favor of union with Germany. Various other devices were also to be employed to stack the vote against union with Germany. One device he used to influence the vote was to write the wording of the plebiscite in a confusing way so that the voters would be voting for independence while believing they were voting for unification.

Arthur Seyss-Inquart, (L) with Hitler, replaces Kurt Schuschnigg (R) as chancellor of Austria.

Hitler was furious with Schuschnigg and declared that he would not permit the plebiscite to go forward under those circumstances. Hitler described Austria as: *"A country which for many years had no elections at all, where there were no means of determining who were qualified to vote, and then announces an election which is to take place in less than three and a half day's time. There are no lists of voters,"* Hitler said, *"there are no voting cards, there are no means of testing a person's right to vote, there is no obligation to maintain the secrecy of the ballot, there is no guarantee that the election will be conducted with impartiality, there is no security that the votes will be properly counted – and so on."*

Hitler sent an ultimatum to Schuschnigg on March 11, demanding that he step down as Chancellor and hand over all power to the Austrian National Socialists (Nazis), or face invasion. Unable to gain support from either Italy, France or Britain, and with little support from the Austrian people, Schuschnigg resigned as Chancellor. Seyss-Inquart, the Nazi Minister of the Interior, then became Chancellor, and the Nazi Party now controlled the government in Austria.

Rioting had broken out all over Austria over the issue of unification with Germany, so the new Chancellor, Seyss-Inquart, sent a request to Hitler to send in German troops to restore order. Whether they were actually needed or not is not clear, but this was the necessary pretext for German troops to enter Austria. The next day, on the morning of March 12, the German 8th Army crossed into Austria. They faced no resistance whatever, but were greeted by crowds of cheering Austrians instead. Hitler entered Austria by car in the afternoon of the same day. His first stop was at Braunau, his birthplace. In the evening he entered Linz where he grew up. At both stops, he received an overwhelming reception.

Hermann Goering, who had accompanied Hitler into Austria, made a telephone call that evening back to party officials in Germany, and stated: *"There is unbelievable jubilation in Austria. We ourselves did not think that sympathies would be so intense."*

Hitler then made a triumphal tour through Austria which ended in Vienna. A huge crowd totaling more than 200,000 filled the Heldenplatz (Heroes Square) in Vienna to hear him proclaim that Austrian was now a part of Germany. *"This is the moment of the greatest accomplishment of my life,"* he said. *"The German Reich, as it stands today, can never be broken by anyone again."*

The Anschluss was made immediately effective, subject to ratification by a plebiscite. Following proper registration of Austria's voting population, elections were held in both Germany and Austria on April 10, 1938. The Anschluss was approved by the Austrian people with a 99.75% "yes" vote, and by the German people with a 99.2 % "yes" vote.

Hitler wrote in *Mein Kampf,* "*People of the same blood should be in the same Reich.*"

Austrians cheer as German troops enter.

Hitler is warmly greeted as he enters Austria.

Hitler enters Vienna.

Austrians are overjoyed by arrival of German troops.

Cardinal Theodor Innitzer, a political figure in the Austrian Christian Social Party (CS) declared on March 12: *"The Viennese Catholics should thank the Lord for the bloodless way this great political change has occurred, and they should pray for a great future for Austria. Needless to say, everyone should obey the orders of the new institutions."*

Robert Kauer, President of the Protestants in Austria, greeted Hitler on March 13, as *"saviour of the 350,000 German Protestants in Austria and liberator from a five-year hardship."*

Karl Renner, Austria's first post-war chancellor in 1918, announced his support for the Anschluss and appealed to all Austrians to vote in favor of it on April 10.

"Hitler had a plausible case to argue when he claimed that the Anschluss was only the application of the Wilsonian principle of self-determination." - Alan Bullock -- Historian.

"The crisis of March, 1938 (which led to the Anschluss) *was provoked by Schuschnigg, the Austrian Chancellor, not by Hitler."* - A.J.P.Taylor. British Historian.

"He (Chamberlain) *had no difficulty in recognizing where this injustice lay. There were six million Germans in Austria to whom national reunification was still forbidden by the Peace Treaties of 1919. Three million Germans in Czechoslovakia whose wishes had never been consulted; three hundred and fifty thousand people in Danzig who were notoriously* **German.***"* - A.J.P.Taylor. British Historian.

"The German Army was invading Austria, or rather was marching in to the general enthusiasm of the people." - A.J.P.Taylor, British Historian.

"The pull of sentiment, language and history, reinforced by the material advantages offered by becoming part of a big nation, was strong enough to waken a genuine welcome when the frontier barriers went down and the German troops marched in garlanded with flowers.... there was a widespread sense of relief, even amongst those who were far from being Nazis." - Alan Bullock. Historian.

As might have been expected, Jewish writers took a different view. The Jewish historian William L. Shirer, in his book *The Rise and Fall of the Third Reich,* calls the Anschluss *"the rape of Austria."*

Hitler later commented: *"Certain foreign newspapers have said that we fell on Austria with brutal methods. I can only say: even in death they cannot stop lying. I have in the course of my political struggle won much love from my people, but when I crossed the former frontier* (into Austria*) there met me such a stream of love as I have never experienced. Not as tyrants have we come, but as liberators."*

Austrian Economy Revived

Prior to the *Anschluss*, Austria's economy was in a catastrophic condition with nearly a third of Austrians out of work. Just across the border in Germany, unemployment had been eliminated, living standards and working conditions had vastly improved, and economic, social and cultural life was flourishing again. Before Hitler became Chancellor, economic conditions in Germany had been the same as Austria's. Following Austria's incorporation into the Reich, conditions also improved dramatically in Austria. Within six months after Anschluss, the total number of unemployed was reduced from 401,000 to only 99,865. By 1940, the unemployment rate in Austria was only 1.2 percent.

By the end of 1938, during which the Anschluss occurred, the weekly income of industrial workers in Austria rose 9 percent. The Austrian GNP experienced a 12.8 percent growth rate in 1938, and 13.3 percent in 1939. Seldom in history has a country experienced such rapid, dramatic economic growth.

Shortly after the Anschluss, Germany's National Labor Law and its comprehensive social security system were introduced in Austria. Basic rights in the workplace were thereby guaranteed, and workers were protected from arbitrary dismissal. By these measures, relief was also quickly provided to more than 200,000 desperately poor people, and health care benefits were extended to the working class. A large-scale construction program was immediately launched to provide affordable housing. Cultural life was greatly encouraged, with energetic promotion of music, the fine arts and literature. The result of all of this was an increase in prosperity and optimism, but also a jump in the Austrian birthrate. The Austrian people believed that union with Germany was the best thing that ever happened to Austria, and they believed that Hitler was a miracle worker.

According to Professor Evan Burr Bukey of the University of Arkansas, in his book, "Hitler's Austria," *"Hitler enjoyed a frenzied acclimation among the Austrian people seldom seen since the days of the Caesars."*

Austria's Jews

In 1938, prior to the Anschluss, 192,000 Jews lived in Austria, almost all of them in Vienna, a city of nearly 2 million. In spite of their relatively small numbers, Austria's Jews wielded vast and disproportionate wealth and power. For this reason, and all the other reasons that Jews have been universally despised by their host populations, Austrian Jews were extremely unpopular with the Austrian people.

Professor Evan Bukey wrote, *"The predominant position of the Jews in an impoverished country only intensified the fear and loathing of the Austrian masses. As we have already seen, Jewish businesses and financial institutions managed much of the country's economic life. At the time of the Anschluss three-quarters of Vienna's newspapers, banks and textile firms were in Jewish hands ... The extraordinary success of the Jews in the learned professions also inspired jealously and spite. Over 50 percent of Austria's attorneys, physicians and dentists were Jewish."*

Yet, Jews were only 2.8 percent of the Austrian population. Moreover Jews isolated themselves within a closed society in Austria, with intense in-group cooperation and mutual assistance between themselves, at the total exclusion, and expense, of non-Jewish Austrians. Many of them dressed differently. They were regarded by Austrians as an alien, parasitic elite who exploited non-Jewish Austrians for the benefit of Jews alone. They also avoided physical work and treated ordinary Austrians with condescension.

According to Professor Bukey, large numbers of Austrians, especially of the Catholic faithful, viewed baptized Jews, as well as all other Jews, with a hatred *"so tightly woven into the fabric of Austrian society that it constituted a Sorelian political myth, immune to empirical falsification."* (Georges Sorel, a French philosopher averred that "myth" was a powerful motivator in people's lives.)

Jews on the streets of Vienna prior to Anschluss.

This seething, barely contained hatred of the Jews boiled over on March 11, 1938, as crowds gathered to welcome Hitler into Vienna where he was to announce the Anschluss. Professor Bukey writes that *"Untold thousands of Viennese took to the streets of their city like mad persons, dragging anyone who "looked Jewish" from vehicles, clubbing and beating victims, desecrating synagogues, robbing department stores, and raiding Jewish apartments. They compelled rabbis to scrub toilet bowls with prayer shawls and stole whatever cash, jewelry, and furs they could find. An SS correspondent would later write admiringly, 'The Viennese have managed to do overnight what we have failed to achieve in the slow-moving, ponderous north up to this day. In Austria, a boycott of the Jews does not need organizing the people themselves have initiated it.'"*

Once Austria had been incorporated into the Reich, Germany's laws automatically became Austria's laws, including the Nuremberg Race Laws. The intent of the Nuremberg Laws, as well as the other anti-Jewish laws, was to break the Jewish grip on the economic, cultural, and social life of Germany and to encourage Jewish emigration. After

Anschluss, when these laws applied in Austria, the Austrian Jews became disenfranchised over night. What had taken 5 years to accomplish in this regard in Germany was done within days in Austria.

By March 18 the authorities had closed down the offices of the Jewish community and Zionist organizations in Vienna and sent their officers to Dachau. During the first weeks after the Anschluss, Jews were fired from their jobs in theaters, community centers, public libraries, and universities. Throughout Austria, Jews were arrested and imprisoned.

Local Nazis rounded up Jews in the city of Vienna and forced them to scrub the streets and walls with brushes. The photo below was widely publicized at the time as an example of the cruelty and pointless humiliation Jews in Vienna were subjected to, but there was also a rational explanation for what took place which is not usually reported. Prior to the Anschluss, when Chancellor Schuschnigg was campaigning against Austrian unification with Germany, the Social Democrats in Vienna turned out in large numbers to support him. Most of Vienna's Jews belonged to the Social Democratic Party, and as Jews, they were fervently against union with Germany. International Jewry, after all, was engaged in a "holy war " against Germany, which included an economic boycott campaign, and an anti-German propaganda campaign in the international Jewish press. This "holy war" had the enthusiastic support and participation of Austria's Jews. The last thing Austrian Jews wanted was unification with Germany.

In support of Schuschnigg's campaign, Jewish Social Democrats painted anti-unification slogans on the sidewalks and walls of buildings throughout the city of Vienna. This angered the non-Jewish Austrians, the vast majority of whom supported unification with Germany. It was the Jews who painted the slogans all over the walls and sidewalks, so it was the Jews who were made to scrub them off. That fact was left out of the international anti-German propaganda. The sidewalk cleaning project may well have been humiliating, but it was not without justification; at least an explanation. But it is also true that the Austrian people took unseemly pleasure in the humiliation of these wealthy and formerly powerful Jews as they were being forced to clean up the sidewalks. Crowds gathered, hissed, and spat abuse at them as they scrubbed.

**Jews are forced to clean painted slogans off the sidewalks
of Vienna. The slogans had been previously painted
on the sidewalks by Jews opposing Anschluss.**

At the same time, Jewish stores were plundered by SA men who sometimes (cynically but with a pretense of legality) left a receipt. Jewish businesses were Aryanized, that is, Jewish owners were forced to sell their businesses to Austrians, or Aryans, in transactions that were decidedly one sided and invariably a big financial loss to the Jew. The greed in Vienna ran out of control as Austrians stepped on one another to get at Jewish wealth. The American journalist William Shirer, who was Jewish, witnessed all of this and described it as *"an orgy of sadism."*

Jews began leaving Austria in massive numbers. In August 1938 the "Reich Central Office for Jewish Emigration" was set up in the Rothschild palace in Vienna, for the purpose of cutting through the red tape and facilitating rapid Jewish emigration out of Austria. SS Captain Adolf Eichmann was assigned there as one of the administrators. By June 1939 the office had aided in the emigration of 110,000 Austrian Jews. An assembly line process was established through which the Jews passed in one day's time, relinquishing one document (and piece of property) at every step of the way until the end when he and his family received visas out of the country. Eichmann employed the services of the local Jewish leadership to process the this emigration -- much of it to Palestine.

In late June, 1939, the remaining Jews, as well as all non-Jews married to Jews, still working in the private sector, were fired from their jobs and "encouraged" to leave the country. By this time, hundreds of Jewish owned factories and thousands of businesses had been closed or confiscated by the government.

The population of Jews in Germany in 1933 was approximately 500,000, and in Austria, 192,000. By 1940 only 160,000 remained in Germany and 40,000 remained in Austria, for a total of 200,000 in Germany and Austria combined. All the rest had emigrated.

Anschluss could now be checked off of Hitler's checklist of things he had avowed to accomplish.

Chapter 17

Germany annexes the Sudetenland

Czechoslovakia was a creature of the peace treaties following World War One; a new state cobbled together out of some of the remnants of the now defunct Austro-Hungarian Empire. The population of this new state was made up of 7,450,000 Czechs, 2,300,000 Slovaks, 720,000 Magyars (Hungarians), 560,000 Ruthenes, 300,000 Jews, 100,000 Poles..., and 3,200,000 Germans who comprised nearly a fourth of the country's entire population.

Czechoslovakia was the antithesis of Woodrow Wilson's concept of "self determination for all peoples," which, ideally, would have manifested itself in ethnically homogeneous nation states. Combining all of these disparate nationalities into a single state had instability and conflict built into it from the outset. (One wonders why "multiculturalism" is such a popular idea today, since it has proven again and again to be unworkable.)

The German population of Czechoslovakia was clustered mainly on its western border adjacent to Germany in a region known as the Sudetenland. These Sudeten Germans or *Sudetendeutsche* had lived in the region for centuries, and had become very prosperous under the

SUDETENLAND: Czech Territory ceded to
Germany at Munich, September 30, 1938

**The dark shaded area surrounding Bohemia and Moravia was the
German area of Czechoslovakia, known as the Sudetenland.**

Austro/Hungarian Empire. These industrious, meticulous Germans
developed a well ordered society over time, with prosperous farms
throughout the region and a highly productive mining and timbering
industry. The Sudetenland also became highly industrialized during the

A prosperous Sudeten German farm

nineteenth century and early twentieth century, with huge chemical works, and lignite mines, as well as numerous textile, china, and glass factories. The Sudetenland was the wealthiest and most productive part of the old Austro-Hungarian Empire, and the Sudeten Germans were by far the most successful and wealthy ethnic group. This remained true in the new state of Czechoslovakia. Within the Sudetenland, 39 percent of the population was employed in industry with only 31% in agriculture, compared to the rest of the country, where a majority were rural farmers. All the big factories were owned by Germans and controlled by German owned banks.

This region had been ruled for centuries by the German Hapsburgs, so the ruling nationality had always been German and the official language had always been German. Though the Czechs and the Germans had lived together for centuries in this region, formerly known as Bohemia, and Moravia, they had developed separate cultural, educational, political and economic institutions which kept them isolated from each other. The two groups did not mix well, and the region had seen constant strife between the Czechs and the Germans for a hundred years or more . The new artificial country of Czechoslovakia, created by the Treaty of St. Germain in 1919, was now ruled by the majority Czechs, which essentially reduced the 3.2 million Germans to being ruled by their former subjects. The Czechs took great satisfaction in lording it over their former German betters, and conditions for the Germans became very harsh very quickly. During 1919, some 600,000 Germans were uprooted and forced to leave their settlements of centuries, to make way for Czechs who were being moved in by the new government.

The Sudeten Germans never wanted to be separated from Austria and included in this newly created country in the first place. Now, their worst fears were becoming a reality as they became a suppressed minority in essentially a foreign country. Claiming the right of self-determination according to number ten of President Wilson's Fourteen Points, they demanded that their homeland be re-combined with Austria, which was, of course, also ethnic German. The Czech army (now the Czechoslovakian army) was already moving in to occupy the Sudeten region with large numbers of Czech speaking troops. This region had been solidly ethnic German for centuries, and the sudden Czech occupation produced an explosive situation.

On March 4, 1919, almost the entire population of Sudeten Germans staged a peaceful demonstration against the Czech occupation and for self-determination. This demonstration was accompanied by a one day general strike. The Czech army quickly moved in and brutally dispersed the demonstration, killing 54 Germans and wounding 84 others. The Germans were shocked by the brutality of the Czechs, but they were law abiding, so they ended the strike and returned to work, but continued to harbor a seething, smoldering resentment against the Czechs which threatened at any time to explode into violence. These brutal killings of Germans by the Czechs only intensified nationalist and separatist sentiments among the Sudeten Germans. They wanted to separate themselves from Czechoslovakia and re- join Austria or to be annexed by Germany; or barring that, to obtain as much autonomy for themselves as possible. But the Treaty of St. Germain of September 10, 1939 specifically forbade union of the Sudetenland with either Austria or Germany and reconfirmed that it would remain a part of Czechoslovakia. If this decision defies common sense, it must be born in mind that the very purpose of these treaties was to break Germany apart, and to prevent the Germans from re-combining into a European super power. Therefore, the Sudeten Germans would not be allowed to join either Austria or Germany, but would be forced to remain subjects of Czechoslovakia against their will.

To make matters worse, a constitution for the new republic of Czechoslovakia was drawn up in 1920 without Sudeten German participation. The new constitution included provisions which were extremely prejudicial to Sudeten German interests, such as measures to redistribute German wealth to its various other ethnic groups. Land was confiscated from the wealthy German farmers and redistributed to other ethnic groups, mainly Czechs. The government also confiscated one fifth of all paper money to pay for other redistributive schemes, and since the Germans were by far the wealthiest, this fell hardest on them. Policies intended to protect the security of the Czechoslovak state and the rights of Czechs also worked to the disadvantage of Germans, which created local hostilities. Border forestland, considered the most ancient Sudeten German national territory, was expropriated for security reasons. The Czechoslovak government settled Czechs in areas of German concentration in an effort to moderate German nationalism, but the policy produced just the opposite effect. Czech schools were built in German districts for the same reason. Sudeten Germans, in possession of a large number of subsidized local theaters, were required to put these at the disposal of the Czech minority one night a week, which produced another cause for hostility. All efforts were made to dissolve the cohesive German society and to promote their assimilation into the other ethnic groups. All of these measures only further alienated the German population from the rest of the country and increased friction and strife between the Sudeten Germans and the Czechs.

When the Depression hit Europe in 1931, it hit the Sudeten Germans particularly hard, as they depended more than the rest of Czechoslovakia on international trade, especially with Germany. During the depression, the Czechoslovakian government took measures to protect its Czech citizens at the expense of the Sudeten Germans. As a result, the unemployment rate among the industrialized Sudeten Germans was five times that of the rest of Czechoslovakia. Tension between the two groups increased. Fighting broke out. The Czech army and Czech police sided with the Czechs and numerous atrocities were committed against the German population.

In 1931 the Sudeten German Peoples Party was created, led by Konrad Henlein, with the central objective of Sudetenland annexation with Germany. Henlein established communications with the Nazi Party in Germany and sought their support for annexation. After becoming Chancellor in 1933, Hitler openly called for annexation of the Sudetenland and eventually began providing financial support for the Sudeten German Peoples Party to help them towards that goal.

Though Henlein's demand had almost unanimous Sudeten German support, it was vigorously opposed by the Czech government. If the Germans were allowed to secede from the Czech state, what about all the other nationalities? The very idea posed an existential threat to the state of Czechoslovakia. Moreover, the Sudetenland held some of

Czechoslovakia's richest resources, large deposits of coal in particular, and also its most productive industries. The Czech government was ready to fight, if it came to that, in order to prevent the loss of this wealthy region.

The Czechoslovakian army was one of the most powerful, well trained and best equipped in Europe at the time and could have withstood a German invasion attempt without outside assistance. The German army had not yet rebuilt itself. Nevertheless, President Benes entered into alliances with France and the Soviet Union as additional insurance, but the Germans saw this as an attempt at encirclement of their country. Even though the Soviet Union had entered the alliance, they asserted that they would not go to war against Germany unless France did also, and France was unprepared for war, so the alliances were essentially worthless.

In 1938 both the British and the French people were very opposed to war, though a belligerent faction among British leaders existed who did want war, including Winston Churchill, Anthony Eden, Duff Cooper, and Lord Halifax. This group called for war against Germany in the event of any attempt to annex the Sudetenland. Instead of viewing Hitler's annexation of German peoples into the Reich as a limited goal of pan-Germanism, as was the case, they accused Hitler of wanting to create a super state in order to dominate the world, yet, there was no evidence that that is what Hitler wanted to do. Chamberlain, who was not a part of this group of British war mongers, happened to believe that the Sudeten Germans' grievances were well founded and believed that Hitler's intentions in the matter were limited. Both Britain and France, therefore, advised Czechoslovakia to give the Sudeten Germans the autonomy they sought, and then let them decide what they wanted to do. Czech President Benes, however, strongly resisted this proposal.

As the political situation worsened, security in the Sudetenland deteriorated. Armed clashes began to occur between bands of Sudeten Germans and the police and border forces. In a few instances, the Czech army was called out to pacify the situation. Leaders in Germany expressed their concern for their fellow Germans in the Sudetenland. Henlein and his Sudeten German Party then presented the Prague government with an eight point demand. Henlein demanded complete autonomy, ideologically as well as politically, and reparations for damages caused by the "injustices inflicted since 1918" on Sudeten Germans. Despite pressure from London and Paris to accept it, the Prague government rejected these demands out of hand. When fighting broke out in the Sudeten area and rumors of German troop movements across the border were passed around (which turned out to be untrue), the Czechoslovak army mobilized on May 20, 1918. Mobilization at that time was universally seen as a provocation, and war between Czechoslovakia and Germany seemed certain. A war between the two states was even egged on by Winston Churchill and his group.

Prime Minister Chamberlain stepped in and offered to mediate to try to settle the matter peacefully. He sent Vicount Runciman in to work things out between Germany and Czechoslovakia short of war. Runciman was unable to bring the two sides together in any kind of an agreement, however, so he returned to England. Upon his return to England, he presented the following report to the British government which was very sympathetic to the Sudeten Germans:

"Czech officials and Czech police, speaking little or no German, were appointed in large numbers to purely German districts; Czech agricultural colonists were encouraged to settle on land confiscated under the Land Reform in the middle of German populations; for the children of these Czech invaders Czech schools were built on a large scale; there is a very general belief that Czech firms were favoured as against German firms in the allocation of State contracts and that the State provided work and relief for Czechs more readily than for Germans. I believe these complaints to be in the main justified. Even as late as the time of my Mission, I could find no readiness on the part of the Czechoslovak Government to remedy them on anything like an adequate scale ... the feeling among the Sudeten Germans until about three or four years ago was one of hopelessness. But the rise of Nazi Germany gave them new hope. I regard their turning for help towards their kinsmen and their eventual desire to join the Reich as a natural development in the circumstances."

Czechoslovakian President Benes proposed a compromise plan, but it was too little, too late, and Henlein turned it down. He then instructed the Sudeten Germans to prepare for self defense in case of attack. On

September 15, 1938 Henlein flew to Germany and met with Hitler. He then issued a proclamation demanding Sudetenland annexation with Germany. Riots and clashes with police broke out in the Sudetenland which were brutally put down by the Czech army. German newsreels showed evidence of widespread atrocities against Sudeten Germans. Hitler threatened to send in German troops to protect them.

Left - Konrad Henlein, leader of the Sudeten German People's Party, with Adolf Hitler in Germany.

Chamberlain went to Berchtesgaden on September 15 and met with Hitler. During the meeting, Hitler demanded the swift annexation of the Sudetenland by Germany or he threatened to invade in order to protect the Sudeten Germans, whom he claimed were being slaughtered by the Czechs. There was plenty of evidence from outside sources that what Hitler claimed was indeed occurring. Both the British and French governments accepted Hitler's argument and supported his demand for annexation.

Predictably, however, the war mongering element among the British leadership opposed the settlement. Winston Churchill immediately issued a statement to the press denouncing Chamberlain's policy:

"The partition of Czechoslovakia under pressure from England and France amounts to the complete surrender of the Western democracies to the Nazi threat of force. Such a collapse will bring peace or security neither to England nor to France. On the contrary, it will place these two nations in an ever weaker and more dangerous situation. The mere neutralization of Czechoslovakia means the liberation of 25 German divisions, which will threaten the Western front; in addition to which it will open up for the triumphant Nazis the road to the Black Sea.

"It is not Czechoslovakia alone which is menaced, but also the freedom and the democracy of all nations. THE BELIEF THAT SECURITY CAN BE OBTAINED BY THROWING A SMALL STATE TO THE WOLVES IS A FATAL DELUSION. The war potential of Germany will increase in a short time more rapidly than it will be possible for France and Great Britain to complete the measures necessary for their defense."

But Hitler was not satisfied to simply annex the Sudetenland. He wanted to solve Czechoslovakia's ethnic instability problem once and for all, and insisted that claims of Poland and Hungary for the return of their ethnic minorities from Czechoslovakia also be satisfied.

The *Times of London* editorialized that Hitler was right and supported the annexation of the Sudetenland by Germany. The editorial also supported the demands of Hungary and Poland.

Churchill, of course, took issue with this editorial of *The Times*. *"In this single paragraph,"* Churchill wrote, *"The Times gave support to the most extreme of Nazi demands, the complete cession of the Sudetenland, a demand which, if met, would have condemned Czechoslovakia to disintegration, and placed a majority of the Sudeten Germans under the grim rigors of Nazi rule."* Churchill ignored the fact that the overwhelming majority of Sudeten Germans demanded annexation with Germany. That same day, the Foreign Office publically disassociated itself from Churchill.

Chamberlain requested a conference with Hitler which would also include France and Italy to make a final decision on the matter. On September 29, 1939, Hitler met at Munich with the heads of government of France, Italy, and Britain. The Czechoslovakian government was not invited. From this meeting, the Munich Agreement was signed by all present, agreeing to all of Hitler's demands. The Agreement stipulated that the Sudetenland be ceded to Germany, effective immediately. By this act, 3.25 million Sudeten Germans then became citizens of the Reich, along with approximately 38 percent of the territory of Bohemia and Moravia. Hungary received 11,882 square kilometers of Southern Slovakia and southern Ruthenia along with their Hungarian populations, and Poland received Tesin and two minor border areas in northern Slovakia along with their Polish populations. This was accomplished peacefully, without firing a shot. British historian A.J.P. Taylor wrote: *"The Munich Pact...was a triumph for all that was best and most enlightened in British life."*

**Hitler greets Chamberlain at the Munich
conference of September 29, 1938**

Chamberlain flew back to London to a hero's welcome. As he got off the plane, he held aloft an agreement signed by Adolf Hitler which stated the German leader's desire never to go to war with Britain again. Chamberlain proclaimed that he had secured "peace for our time." As the jubilant crowd applauded and cheered, Chamberlain expressed his desire to find a peaceful solution to the Fuhrer's wish to create an enlarged German homeland in Europe to include all Germans. He then read a further passage in the Agreement in which Hitler stated: *"We are determined to continue our efforts to remove possible sources of difference and thus to contribute to assure the peace of Europe."*

British Prime Minister Neville Chamberlain proclaims "Peace for our time," after the Munich Agreement permitting the German annexation of the Sudetenland.

Winston Churchill, quite expectedly, took the opposite view. He made a speech in the House of Commons in which he stated that the British Government, in approving the Munich Agreement, had *"sustained a total and unmitigated defeat,"* and that *"a disaster of the first magnitude has befallen Great Britain and France."* Churchill had for some time called for a "Grand Alliance" between Britain, France, the United States, and the Soviet Union to *"stop Hitler."*

But Churchill was a war monger of the first rank, and his statements about Germany were often inaccurate or gross exaggerations, and intended only to inflame public opinion against Germany. If the cause of World War Two could be pinned on a single person, it should be pinned on him; and if not on him alone, then on him and Roosevelt. He was also an opportunist. Churchill had been an ardent anti-Bolshevist from the start and blamed the Russian Revolution and all that came after it on the Jews. But then, when it suited his purposes, he jumped on the Zionist bandwagon, stating that Zionism (which advocated the creation of a Jewish homeland in Palestine) would deflect European Jews away from social revolution to partnership with European imperialism in the Arab world.

In 1936, Churchill became associated with the informal London Jewish pressure group known as "The Focus," (of which, more in the following chapter). The purpose of The Focus was to "open the eyes of the British public to the one great menace, Nazi Germany." In reality, Germany was never a threat to Britain, and Hitler had done all he could to win Britain's friendship. The Focus became Britain's main contributor to the international Jewish propaganda campaign against Nazi Germany, and Churchill became its Gentile front man. Churchill was useful to The Focus in its campaign to destroy Hitler and the Nazis, and The Focus was useful to Churchill in bringing him back to power after years "in the wilderness," as he put it. The Focus was lavishly funded by these wealthy British Jews and Churchill, as its front man, lived a lavish life as a result. (Churchill also received an excessively large payment from the Czechoslovakian government, which cast doubt on the genuineness of his opposition to the annexation of the Sudetenland by Germany.) In his role as Gentile front man for the Focus, Churchill began berating the British government for its "blindness to the Nazi threat," and he especially went after Prime Minister Neville Chamberlain for his efforts to maintain the peace. In his articles and speeches, Churchill greatly exaggerated the extent of German rearmament and distorted the rearmament's purpose by harping on German production of heavy bombers. In fact, Germany had never focused on heavy bombers, but Churchill used this lie to support his contention that Germany intended to eventually attack Britain. Hitler wanted only peace and friendship with Britain, not war, and said so repeatedly. Moreover, Hitler had made clear that his goal was to reconstitute the German state which had been dismembered by the Versailles Treaty. That plan was no secret to anyone, including Churchill. But Churchill and his fellow alarmists treated each of Hitler's actions to fulfill that plan as a new and unexpected act of aggression, and further proof of his intent to conquer

Europe. Churchill was determined that Britain would eventually go to war with Germany for his own reasons. While others worked feverishly to avoid war, Churchill and his fellow alarmists worked feverishly to bring it about. Was he deliberately channeling British power towards the service of the international Jews who were paying him through "The Focus," or was he deluding himself that he was serving England? That question will probably never be answered.

The British publicist, F.S. Oliver, said this about Winston Churchill's character: *"From his youth up, Mr. Churchill has loved with all his heart, with all his mind, with all his soul, and with all his strength, three things: war, politics and himself. He has loved war for its dangers, he loves politics for the same reason, and himself he has always loved for the knowledge that his mind is dangerous –dangerous to his enemies, dangerous to his friends, dangerous to himself. I can think of no man I have ever met who would so quickly and so bitterly eat his heart out in Paradise."*

Germany Annexes the Sudetenland

**German troops enthusiastically welcomed
into Sudetenland, Oct 1, '38**

On October 1, 1938, the German army marched unopposed into the Sudetenland where they were received with jubilation. Czechoslovakia was an artificial and unworkable state created by intellectuals and supported by the victors of WWI. In reality, it had no chance of succeeding, and its demise was no tragedy. The remainder of the country, left over after the Munich Agreement, began immediately to fall apart along ethnic lines. On March 14, 1939, Slovakia declared its independence, followed soon after by Carpatho-Ukraine (Ruthenia). After these areas were gone, all that remained of the former Czechoslovakia were parts of Bohemia and Moravia. The situation was an open invitation for a Communist takeover.

The overwhelming threat to Western Christian Civilization at that time was Communist revolution instigated and supported by the Soviet Union. The Jewish Bolsheviks who controlled the Soviet Union had set up the Communist International (Comintern) for the specific purpose of taking control of all of Europe. They tried taking over Germany in the revolution of 1918 but were defeated by the Freikorps. They had even succeeded for a time in establishing the Soviet Socialist Republic of Bavaria, until also brought down by the Freikorps. They took Hungary briefly in 1919 but were thrown back by forces under Nicholas Horthy. They tried taking Italy in the 1920s but were defeated and driven out by Mussolini. They started a civil war in Spain in 1936 and nearly succeeded in creating a Soviet style Communist dictatorship in that country, but with the help of Mussolini and Hitler, the devout Catholic General Francisco Franco, after three years of bloody war, defeated the Communists and drove them out of Spain. Soviet Russia stood ready with a watchful eye to create and support Communist revolution in any European country that seemed vulnerable.

Czechoslovakia's capital city, Prague, had a large Jewish population who had built an active Communist revolutionary party, ready at any time to act as the Soviet Union's fifth column to take control of what remained of the former Czechoslovakia. Hitler made it known that he would not allow this to happen. The new president of Czechoslovakia, Emil Hacha, was himself concerned about this, and wanted to meet with Hitler. Hitler invited him to Berlin for talks. When he arrived at the train station with his daughter, he was met by Foreign Minister von Ribbentrop, who had a bouquet of flowers for the daughter. Hitler had also sent a box of chocolates. During the late night meeting, Hitler harangued Hacha relentlessly, until he finally signed an agreement making his country a protectorate of Germany.

When Hitler came out of the meeting, he was ecstatic. He told his two middle-aged secretaries; "Children, quickly, give me a kiss! Quickly!" The ladies kissed him on both cheeks. Hitler said: "It is the greatest triumph of my life! I shall enter history as the greatest German of them all!"

Hitler had every reason to be satisfied with himself. So far, he had brought into Germany the Saar, Austria and the Sudetenland, and now he had made Bohemia and Moravia a protectorate. He had also essentially nullified the Versailles Treaty; and he had done it all through diplomacy, without firing a shot.

That same day, March 15, the German army moved in, meeting no resistance. On March 16, Hitler went to Prague and from the Hradcany Castle officially proclaimed that Bohemia and Moravia were now a German protectorate. Bohemia and Moravia were placed under the supervision of Reich Protector Baron Konstanin von Neurath and German officials manned government departments in a similar capacity as that of cabinet ministers. The Gestapo assumed police authority. Hitler was remarkably considerate of the existing Czech civil servants, allowing most of them to remain in their posts and permitting them to retire with pensions.

Not to have occupied Bohemia and Moravia (the remnants of the former Czechoslovakia), would have invited disaster. Germany stood as the bulwark for all of Europe against the Communist menace. Only Germany held the Communists at bay and prevented them from sweeping over Europe. A Communist takeover of Bohemia and Moravia was out of the question.

Bohemia and Moravia contained 118,000 Jews at the beginning of the German occupation, most of whom resided in Prague. When the Germans moved in, Jews were dismissed from the civil service and placed in an extralegal position. The international Jewish press, of course, reacted with an intensified outpouring of vitriolic hyperbole against the Nazis. But what should Hitler have done? World Jewry was still engaged in a "holy war" against Germany. It would have been idiotic under the circumstances for Germany to retain large numbers of Jews in the Czechoslovakian government who would surely have cooperated with the Comintern to undermine and sabotage German control. Communism was banned and Czech communists, most of whom were Jews, fled the country. Large numbers of Jews who were not overtly affiliated with the Communist Party also left.

Hitler saves Czechoslovakia from the Communists by making it a protectorate of Germany. The sign on the marquee in the Czech city of Brno, reads "We thank our Fuhrer." He gets an enthusiastic welcome.

As the victors of World War I, Britain and France assumed the role of enforcers of the Versailles Treaty, as well as all other treaties resulting from the war. The United States had withdrawn from Europe and took no such role. Germany had never willfully accepted the terms of the Versailles Treaty, and only signed it under duress. The Treaty had been imposed upon Germany by force, and Germany therefore acknowledged no moral obligation to abide by it. Moreover, the onerous terms of the treaty had been ruinous for Germany, and continued to have a deleterious effect on the lives of the Germany people by the time Hitler came to power. It would have been unreasonable to have expected that the burdensome terms of the Versailles Treaty would have continued in perpetuity, or to have expected Germany to continue to accept them without protest. Sooner or later, they would have had to come to an end, Hitler or no Hitler. Hitler avowed when he assumed the Chancellorship that he would abnegate the Treaty despite Britain's and France's determination to enforce it. He believed that the treaty was unfair and unjust and therefore had no moral force, and he was not alone in believing that. Numerous people of prestige and influence sided with Germany in the matter. George Bernard Shaw, for example, had this to say:

"It was evident that Germany needed only a resolute and clear-headed leader to denounce the [Versailles]*Treaty; declare her determination to assert her full equality with the Powers, and refuse to be disarmed, plundered and chastised under the pretext of reparations and 'war guilt', to rally to him every living soul whose native language was German, and at the same time take a great step towards peace in Europe by proving that neither France nor England nor the United States dare outrage humanity by attempting military occupation of her territory on the model of the old partitions of Poland; in short, that instead of Europe being plunged into war she would be dragged back from the brink of it by Germany."*

Britain and France, against common sense, took the position that any violation of the terms of the Versailles Treaty would be a provocation for war. This irrational position was aggressively promoted by the "war party" in Britain, including Winston Churchill, Anthony Eden, Lord Halifax, Duff Cooper, Robert Vansittart, and a few others, but just as many believed there was just cause for Hitler's actions. Hitler continued his defiance of the Treaty, gambling that neither Britain nor France had the stomach for another bloody war.

The intent of the Versailles Treaty was to reduce the size and power of Germany and to keep Germany down. Those clamoring for war with Germany on the basis of justice for Czechoslovakia were being disingenuous and were using the German occupation as a pretext for war. At the same time that the German occupation of the Sudetenland created consternation among the anti-German elements (International Jewry in particular), Poland's invasion of Cesky/Tesin in Bohemia aroused no concern whatever. These two territories of Czechoslovakia contained majority Polish populations, and Poland occupied them for the same reason Germany occupied the Sudetenland. Likewise, when, at the same time, Hungary occupied southern Slovakia, which contained a majority Hungarian population, it created hardly a stir. Yet, Germany's actions were promoted as a cause for war.

Polish tanks invade Cesky/Tesin in Czechoslovakia in 1938. Though Germany was severely criticized for invading the Sudetenland, Poland was not, for doing the exact same thing.

No one in either England or Germany wanted war except for Winston Churchill and his gang of war mongers and the Jewish war hawks who controlled him. When Prime Minister Chamberlain returned from a meeting with Hitler, he announced to the Parliament that "there will be no war." While the people in both England and Germany were thanking God and celebrating that fortunate outcome, the scheming war mongers, including Churchill, got to work to undermine it. Inside of a week, the Jewish controlled press began smearing Chamberlain and tearing him down.

Chapter 18

War with Poland

The international jubilation over the peace pact between Prime Minister Chamberlain and Chancellor Hitler resulting from the Munich Agreement, did not last for long. Public opinion outside Germany soon began to cool again and turn against Hitler and the Nazis; the result of the relentless anti-Hitler, anti-Nazi propaganda. Propaganda is a powerful weapon and it was used to its fullest potential to turn public opinion against Nazi Germany, and to create pretexts for war, both in Britain and the United States. This hate campaign was controlled and managed mainly by the Jews who spared no effort to undermine the Nazi regime.

British historian Nesta Webster wrote in her book, *Germany and England,* published in 1938, shortly before World War II began:

"Britons in the past have not been easily worked up to hate, but this insane hatred of two men, Mussolini and Hitler, is being instilled in them by the Jews and those who benefit by them, and acting like a poison in the life blood of our people.

Germany is under a visible anti-Jewish dictatorship. We are under an invisible Jewish dictatorship, but a dictatorship that can be felt in every sphere of life, for no one can escape from it.

*Already the Jews can make or break the career of any man as they please. Once war breaks out we cannot doubt that they will be found in every key position and will hold us at their mercy. Then the real purpose of the world war will become apparent. **As long as the Jews do not hold Germany they can never realize their final aim – world domination.** Therefore Hitler must be overthrown and Jewish power restored."* (emphasis added)

In this atmosphere of hate, distrust and bellicosity created by the anti-Hitler propaganda, the Western leaders were preconditioned to take the worst possible interpretation of any foreign policy initiative by Hitler. He had been made out to be an aggressive psychopath by the Jewish press and was therefore given no credit for having legitimate claims for Germany.

After the Munich conference, personal control of British foreign policy passed from Prime Minister Chamberlain to his Foreign Minister, Lord Halifax, who thereafter waged a relentless campaign to provoke a war with Germany. Halifax and certain British leaders on both the left and the right joined together to castigate Hitler and the Nazis and push for war. Principle among these was Sir Robert Vansittart, Chief Diplomatic Advisor to the British Government, who made anti-Nazi radio broadcasts. Vansittart's radio broadcasts were intended to awake the British public to "The Nature of the Beast" -- to the habits of militarism, aggression and blind obedience which, according to Vansittart, had been inculcated into the Germans since the time of Tacitus, and which made them uniquely dangerous to their neighbors. Vansittart used the metaphor of the butcherbird he had observed years before on the Black Sea, ruthlessly eliminating its unsuspecting prey one by one. In Vansittart's view, Nazism was no aberration but the logical outcome of German history. Vansittart and the others characterized each foreign policy move by Hitler as a new "surprise" and declared that he could not be trusted and had to be "stopped." Vansittart's broadcasts were very effective in inflaming British public opinion against Germany.

In reality, Hitler had made it clear from the beginning of his chancellorship that he intended to reclaim those territories taken away from Germany by the Versailles Treaty. His plan for a single German state that would include all Germans was also made clear from the beginning. *"Ein Reich, ein volk, ein fuhrer ,"* (one country, one people, one leader) he repeated again and again. So far, he had remilitarized the Rhineland, annexed Austria, and annexed the Sudetenland -- all peacefully. The majority German city of Memel had also been returned to East Prussia from Lithuania. The only remaining pieces of the puzzle were Danzig and the Polish Corridor. It was obvious that they were next on the agenda. Hitler had already made that clear. But he also renounced any claim to the provinces of Alsace and Lorraine which had been returned to France at the end of World War I. Hitler stated his plan clearly and then followed that plan, step-by-step, precisely as he said he would do. Moreover, numerous world statesmen, journalists and academics concurred with Hitler's demand for reclamation of these German territories, and declared that his demands were both reasonable and just. The Versailles Treaty was based on the "War Guilt" clause which assigned blame for starting WWI to Germany. Revisionist historians had already disproved the war guilt allegation against Germany, so there was no longer any basis for the onerous terms of the Versailles Treaty and it should have been scrapped long before Hitler was elected to office. It was simply disingenuous for Churchill, Halifax, Vansittart, and the other members of the British "war party" to characterize Hitler's moves as "aggression" or "surprises." To say that his word could not be trusted was not true.

The Polish Problem

The Versailles Treaty had taken a large swath of German territory, along with its German inhabitants, to create the new sovereign state of Poland. This included a strip of land across Germany to give Poland access to the Baltic Sea, called the Polish Corridor. The main problem of the Corridor was that it split Germany in two, separating East Prussia from the rest of Germany. For Germans to travel back and forth between East Prussia and the rest of Germany, they were required to go around the Corridor by ship. They were not allowed to cross the Corridor. The German City of Danzig had also been taken from Germany and placed under the supervision of the League of Nations as a "free city" for the purpose of providing Poland with her port facilities. Around one and a half million ethnic Germans now lived as second class citizens in this Polish controlled territory.

This territory, along with its residents, had been German for centuries and its people made it clear from the start through countless mass demonstrations that they did not want to be separated from Germany. Danzig had been a member of the old Hanseatic League, and was one of the most German of German cities. It's population was 96 percent German, and in a plebiscite they voted overwhelmingly to be returned to Germany. The ethnic Germans living in this region were now a minority in a hostile Polish state, under Polish rule, and suffered the same kind of discrimination and repression that the Germans had suffered in the Sudetenland. Germany had a just claim for the return of all of the territory taken from it by force by the Versailles Treaty, and many world leaders openly acknowledged that. A prominent British authority on Germany and German affairs, William Harbutt Dawson, wrote in "Germany Under the Treaty," 1933:

"*. . . no factor in the life of Europe today offers so grave and certain a menace to peace than the Corridor, which cuts Germany into two parts, and severs Danzig, one of the most German of cities, from the fatherland. Can Europe afford to ignore this menace and allow matters to drift? To do so would be tantamount to inviting and hastening catastrophe, for instead of improving, the conditions in the Corridor after and because of 12 years of Polish occupation, are steadily growing worse.*

Because it is now abundantly clear that all the needs of Polish trade, present and future, can be satisfied without the corridor, and because good relations between Germany and Poland, which are so essential to the settlement of peace in Europe, will be impossible so long as that political monstrosity continues. The greater part of the territory should go back to the country to which it owes its civilization."

Halifax and the "war party," however, refused to acknowledge the justification of Germany's claims, and characterized each of Hitler's revanchist actions as naked aggression and proof of his intent to take over the world. They claimed that he even had designs on Britain itself. There was no basis in fact for either of these claims. President Roosevelt was at the same time, preposterously warning the American people of a possible German invasion of the United States through South America.

Hitler's Proposal to Poland

Poland had traditionally harbored hostile feelings towards Germany and for all German people, so Hitler proceeded with caution in attempting to settle this last territorial dispute. He was moderate in his approach and displayed considerable generosity in recognizing Polish interests. British Ambassador to Berlin, Sir Neville Henderson, acknowledged Hitler's reasonable approach. *"Of all the Germans,"* Henderson said, *" believe it or not, Hitler is the most moderate as far as Danzig and the Corridor are concerned."*

On October 24, 1938, Hitler had his foreign minister, von Ribbentrop, propose the following four step plan to Polish Ambassador Lipski that would have rectified the injustices of the Versailles Treaty and which should also have eliminated all sources of friction between Poland and Germany.

1). The return of the Free City of Danzig to the Reich, but without severance of its economic ties to the Polish State. This offer would guarantee to Poland free port privileges in the city of Danzig, as well as extra-territorial access to the harbor.

2.) Germany would make no demand for the return of its former territory, now called the Polish Corridor, but Germany should be allowed to build a highway and a railroad across the Polish Corridor in order to reunite Germany with East Prussia.

3.) Mutual recognition of the location of the borders between Germany and Poland would be permanently settled. In other words, Germany would not demand return of any remaining territory ceded to Poland by the Versailles Treaty.

4.) The German-Polish Pact of 1934 would be extended from ten to twenty-five years. (In the German-Polish Pact of 1934, both countries pledged to resolve their problems through bilateral negotiations and to forgo armed conflict for a period of 10 years. The pact effectively normalized relations between Poland and Germany, which were previously strained by border disputes arising from the Treaty of Versailles.)

In his negotiations with Poland, Hitler could not have been more reasonable.

Kristalnacht

While these negotiations were going on an unfortunate event known as "Kristaslnacht" (night of broken glass) occurred in Germany which had the effect of further turning international public opinion against Germany. It could not have occurred at a worse time. The trigger for Kristalnacht was the murder of the German diplomat, Ernst vom Rath, in Paris by a young Jewish man named Herschel Grynszpan, on November 9, 1938. Grynszpan's family, along with approximately 15,000 other Jews who had entered Germany from Poland after 1914, and who were not German citizens, had been expelled out of Germany back to Poland on October 27, 1938. Seventeen year old Herschel Grynszpan, who was living in Paris with an uncle at the time, shot and killed vom Rath inside the German Embassy in revenge for the deportations, though vom Rath personally had nothing to do with it. News of the murder was in all the German papers.

Anti-Jewish feeling was already running high as a result of the Jewish "holy war" against Germany, and the German people reacted angrily over vom Rath's murder. On the nights of November 9 and 10, gangs of youths roamed through the Jewish neighborhoods breaking windows of Jewish businesses and homes and setting fire to synagogues. Uniformed SA men also participated. The official German position on these events was that these were spontaneous outbursts of angry German citizens over the murder of a German diplomat by a Jew, but the international Jewish press accused Nazi officials, specifically Goebbels, of orchestrating the event. That seems doubtful, however, because early in the morning following the Kristalnacht events, Dr. Goebbels announced in a radio broadcast that any action against Jews was strictly prohibited and warned of severe penalties for disobeying this order. Numerous people were also arrested for violence against Jews. Government and Nazi Party officials were furious over what had happened because of the negative propaganda against Germany which would obviously follow. Hitler was also furious when he first heard about it and ordered a telex message to be sent to all Gauleiter offices, which read: *"By express order from the very highest authority, arson against Jewish businesses or other property must in no case and under no circumstances take place."*

Unfavorable international reaction was impossible to avoid, and popular opinion of Nazi Germany declined dramatically as a result of Kristalnacht. The British historian, Martin Gilbert, himself a Jew, writes that *"no event in the history of German Jews between 1933 and 1945 was so widely reported as it was happening, and the accounts from the foreign journalists working in Germany sent shock waves around the world."*

The Times of London wrote at the time: *"No foreign propagandist bent upon blackening Germany before the world could outdo the tale of burnings and beatings, of blackguardly assaults on defenseless and innocent people, which disgraced that country yesterday."*

There was no need to exaggerate what had happened. The violent rampage against Germany's Jews was truly a disgrace. But in typical fashion, the international Jewish press *did* exaggerate the event out of all proportion to what actually happened, providing their usual "eye witness" accounts. An orgy of brutal beatings, rapes, and murder of large numbers of innocent Jews all across Germany, as well as extensive damage to Jewish property was alleged. These exaggerated reports had the effect of poisoning international public opinion against Germany, as they were intended to do. Yet, it makes no sense that the German government or the Nazi Party could have orchestrated this pogrom, as the negative publicity resulting from it hurt Germany and the Nazis far more than it did the Jews. Already sensitive to the hysterical anti-Nazi propaganda campaign being waged against them, German officials were being very careful not to create incidents, such as Kristalnacht, for which they could be criticized further. It is more likely that Kristalnacht was a spontaneous pogrom against the Jews, caused by the buildup of hostility over the International Jewish "holy" war against Germany, and triggered by the vom Rath murder.

In the aftermath of Kristalnacht, the world press became overwhelmingly sympathetic to the Jews, and bitterly hostile towards Germany. In France, Britain and the United States, calls for war against Germany became increasingly bellicose as a result of Kristalnacht.

German-Polish Talks Continue

On January 5, 1939, Poland's Foreign Minister, Josef Beck, met with Hitler at Berchtesgaden. Hitler reiterated to Beck a clear and definite guarantee that Germany would make no claims on the Polish Corridor, and reaffirmed that he only wanted to build a railroad and a highway across it. The following day, January 6th, in a meeting with Polish officials in Munich, von Ribbentrop confirmed Germany's willingness to guarantee, not only the Corridor, but all Polish territory. This friendly, generous offer was repeated again by von Ribbentrop during a state visit to Warsaw on January 23, 1939. During this state visit von Ribbentrop appealed for a final all-inclusive settlement of German-Polish territorial points of contention.

A settlement in accord with the "four points" outlined above would have taken nothing away from Poland. Danzig was not a Polish city, but a "free city," supervised by the League of Nations. Germany's four point offer would have permitted Poland to continue to use Danzig's port facilities, as before. Germany did not demand a return of its lost territory, now known as the Polish Corridor, only the right to build a highway and a railroad across it in order to reconnect with East Prussia. There was nothing unreasonable in Germany's demands.

Yet, on March 21, 1939 French President LeBrun and British Prime Minister Chamberlain met in London and proposed a French-British-Polish alliance to contain Germany. This proposal was then sent on to Polish officials, which had the effect of further steeling their resistance to Hitler's demands. Despite Germany's best diplomatic efforts, the Poles were now refusing to concede anything.

The popular view today is that an overwhelmingly powerful Germany was threatening and intimidating a weak and impotent Poland, but in reality, that was hardly the case. Poland had a long military tradition and maintained a powerful, well trained army. The Polish army had only recently (1920) defeated the Russian "Red" army. Polish military leaders were not in the least intimidated by the power of Germany. It should be remembered that German armed forces had been reduced to only 100,000 men by the Versailles Treaty, and that Germany at the time of the crisis with Poland was still in the process of rebuilding her military forces. Not only was Poland not intimidated by Germany, she was even belligerent.

These Polish tanks were the equal of anything in the German army.

In October 1930, the influential Polish newspaper, *Die Liga der Grossmacht*, carried the following declaration:

"A struggle between Poland and Germany is inevitable. We must prepare ourselves for it systematically. Our goal is a new Grunewald (The Battle of Tannenberg on July 15th, 1410 when the Teutonic Knights were defeated). However, this time a Grunewald in the suburbs of Berlin.

"That is to say, the defeat of Germany must be produced by Polish troops in the centre of the territory in order to strike Germany to the heart. Our ideal is a Poland with the Oder and the Neisse as a border in the West. Prussia must be re-conquered for Poland, and indeed, Prussia as far as the Spree.

"In a war with Germany there will be no prisoners and there will be room

neither for human feelings nor cultural sentiments. The world will tremble before the German-Polish War. We must evoke in our soldiers a superhuman mood of sacrifice and a spirit of merciless revenge and cruelty."

At around the same time, Poland's Marshall Rydz-Smigly said, *"Poland wants war with Germany and Germany will not be able to avoid it even if she wants to."*

Edvard Rydz-Smigly, Marshall of Poland

Jews influence both Roosevelt and Churchill

As the result of restrictions placed on them in Nazi Germany, Jews involved in theater and the movie business left Germany *en masse* for Hollywood where they were quickly made welcome by the Jews who ran the motion picture industry. These German émigré Jews then joined the Hollywood Jews in making anti-Nazi movies (usually with pro-Communist undertones) for American audiences. The stereotype Nazi officer, complete with monocle, cigarette holder, arch aristocratic manner, impeccable uniform, erect, arrogant bearing, and an evil sneer or a sinister smile on his haughty face, became a stock character in these movies.

The mass information and entertainment media in Britain and the United states was almost entirely under Jewish control, so a very one-sided picture of events in Germany was presented to the British and American people. Hitler and the members of his Nazi government were relentlessly smeared as guttersnipes, murderers and psychopaths, in total contradiction of the actual facts, thus public opinion in both countries was turned against Nazi Germany.

In 1940 and 1941 appeared Jewish made, pro-war films such as Charlie Chaplin's burlesque of Hitler and Mussolini, *The Great Dictator*, as well as *Man Hunt*, directed by German Jewish émigré Fritz Lang, *The Mortal Storm*, *A Yank in the R.A.F.*, *Sergeant York*, *I Married a Nazi* and numerous other such movies. These movies were an integral part of the vigorous campaign by various elements to get the United States into a war with Germany.

Once the United States was at war with Germany, the studios churned out one anti-Nazi potboiler after another. An audience today is likely to snicker at such "classics" as *Hillbilly Blitzkrieg*, *Women in Bondage*, *The Devil with Hitler*, *I Escaped from the Gestapo*, *Hitler's Children*, *That Nazi Nuisance*, *Strange Death of Adolf Hitler*, *Enemy of Women*, *Hitler's Madman*, *The Master Race*, *The Hitler Gang*, *Hotel Berlin* and *Tarzan Triumphs*.

A summary of the plot of *Tarzan Triumphs* will illustrate the flavor of these potboilers. Nazi agents parachute into Tarzan's peaceful kingdom and occupy a fortress, hoping to exploit oil and tin. Johnny Weissmuller, a slightly flabby but still commanding noble savage, rallies his natives (all of whom are white) against the Axis. "Kill Nadzies!" Tarzan commands the natives. They nod eagerly. The Germans are so despicable even the animals turn against them. Tarzan chases the head of the Nazi troops into the jungle, and, just as the fear-crazed German officer frantically signals Berlin on his shortwave radio, Tarzan kills him. In Berlin the radio operator recognizes the distress signal and rushes out to summon the general in charge of the African operation. While Tarzan, Boy, and Jungle Priestess laughingly look on, Cheetah the chimp chatters into the microphone of the transmitter. Ignorant of the fatal struggle in the jungle depths, the general hears the chimp on the radio, jumps to his feet, salutes, and yells to his subordinates that they are listening not to Africa but to Der Führer.

The roles of the sadistic, sex-crazed, bullet-headed, Nazi "Krauts" in these Jewish made anti-German movies were played by such Hollywood "heavies" as George Siegman, Erich von Stroheim, Walter Long and

Hobart Bosworth. Actor Bobby Watson was kept busy throughout the war playing the part of Adolf Hitler.

The American public, inundated with this kind of anti-German propaganda, was brainwashed to hate Germany and the German people. Anything our brave and noble armed forces could do to them was less than they deserved. Bomb their cities, kill their women and children. But destroy evil Germany by all means possible!

British and American political leaders under Jewish influence

The political leaders in both Britain and America were also under the controlling influence of the Jews. Both Roosevelt and Churchill had surrounded themselves with Jewish advisors, to the exclusion of almost anyone else, and relied on Jewish money to support their campaigns for office. Jews were 2% of the American population, but of the 15 members of Roosevelt's "Brain Trust," 8 of them were Jews. The Jews therefore had control of the political leaders of both Britain and America, as well as control of public opinion in both countries.

A partial list of Jews surrounding FDR included: Bernard Baruch, Felix Frankfurter, David E. Lilienthal, David Niles, Louis Brandeis, Samuel I. Rosenman, Henry Morgenthau, Jr., Benjamin V. Cohen, Rabbi Stephen Wise, Francis Perkins, Sidney Hillman, Herbert H. Lehman, Jesse I. Straus, Harold J. Laski, Charles E. Wyzanski, Samuel Untermyer, Edward Filene, David Dubinsky, Mordecai Ezekiel, Abe Fortus, Isador Lubin, Harry Dexter White (Weiss), David Weintraub, Nathan G. Silvermaster, Harold Glasser, Irving Kaplan, Solomon Adler, Benjamin Cardozo, Anna Rosenberg...and numerous, numerous others, almost to the exclusion of Gentile advisors.

As a consequence, Roosevelt was enveloped in a milieu of Jewish hate and hostility for Germany, to the extent that he eventually became a part of it himself, habitually making malicious anti-Hitler and anti-Nazi remarks in public. These indiscreet public remarks by Roosevelt foreclosed any possibility of amicable diplomatic relations between Nazi Germany and the United States.

Moreover, these Jews were, to a man, sympathetic to Stalin and the Communists and acted essentially as the Soviet Union's agents within the American government. These Communist leaning Jews proliferated in every branch of Roosevelt's government and spied routinely for the benefit of the Soviets. Roosevelt warmly regarded Joseph Stalin and referred to him as "Uncle Joe."

Churchill likewise surrounded himself with Jewish advisors. Churchill enjoyed living high on the hog though he had very little money. He was accused more than once during his long career of taking Jewish money in exchange for advocacy of policies which favored them. Churchill supplemented his salary as a public servant by writing as a journalist and by writing books, though these combined amounts were inadequate to finance his lavish life style. During his "wilderness years," as he called them, between 1930 and 1939 when he was out of government, though still a Member of Parliament, Churchill was supported by a slush fund set up by a secret anti-German pressure group known as "The Focus." Focus membership was composed of wealthy British Jews, like Sir Robert Mond, a directory of several chemical firms, and Sir Robert Waley-Cohen, the managing director of Shell Oil, who employed Churchill as their Gentile front man. The American Jew Bernard Baruch also made significant contributions to Churchill's well being. Churchill's assigned task was to fight Germany; to start warning the world about Nazi Germany. Churchill was a brilliant orator and a superb writer, and he did his job splendidly.

Jewish money, primarily through "The Focus," paid for Churchill's lavish life style, got him into the British cabinet, and eventually made him Prime Minister. From his position as a Member of Parliament, and subsequently as a member of the cabinet, Churchill, doing the bidding of The Focus, began loudly and belligerently berating Nazi Germany and sternly criticized first Stanley Baldwin's and then Neville Chamberlain's alleged blindness to the threat to Britain posed by Nazi Germany. He began to clamor for war. Both Roosevelt and Churchill became Gentile front men in international Jewry's war on Germany.

**A German Cartoon of Winston Churchill, depicting him
as the paid front man of the Jews. In fact, he was paid
lavishly by the Jewish group called "The Focus."**

Churchill, in a speech before the House of Commons on October 5, 1938, said: *"...but there can never be friendship between the British democracy and the Nazi power, that Power which spurns Christian ethics, which cheers its onwards course by a barbarous paganism, which vaunts the spirit of aggression and conquest, which derives strength and perverted pleasure from persecution, and uses, as we have seen with pitiless brutality the threat of murderous force."* He was, of course, only repeating the super-heated, hysterical exaggerations and outright lies of international Jewish propaganda against Nazi Germany.

Contrary to Churchill's warnings, Germany had no designs on Britain, whatever. Hitler actively sought an alliance with Britain, which the British rejected. Hitler even offered to provide German military assistance if it were ever needed to protect Britain. Hitler believed, and often stated, that the British Empire, and the Catholic Church, were international institutions which were absolutely essential to world peace and to world stability. Hitler was an open Anglophile who yearned to be accepted by the British and did everything he could to forge an alliance between Britain and Germany. He often said, as many British did also, that the British and German peoples were the same race; the same people actually, divided only by language. Hitler wanted only peace and friendship with Britain.

Hitler was dismayed by the steady stream of invective and hate propaganda directed at Germany by these British war mongers. In a speech given in Saarbrucken on October 9, 1938 he said: *"...All it would take would be for Mr. Duff Cooper or Mr. Eden or Mr. Churchill to come to power in England instead of Chamberlain, and we know very well that it would be the goal of these men to immediately start a new world war. They do not even try to disguise their intents, they state them openly..."*

In the post-World War II world, Churchill has become almost God-like in the common mythology about the war, but the common mythology is so far from the truth that even an ardent Churchill sympathizer, Gordon Craig, felt obligated to write:

It is reasonably well-known today that Churchill was often ill-informed, that his claims about German strength were exaggerated and his prescriptions impractical, that his emphasis on air power was misplaced.

In "Rethinking Churchill," 1998, Dr. Ralph Raico wrote: *"For all the claptrap about Churchill's "far-sightedness" during the 30s in opposing the "appeasers," in the end the policy of Chamberlain's government to rearm as quickly as possible, while testing the chances for peace with Germany was more realistic than Churchill's."*

Roosevelt's Contribution to Hostilities

The attitude of President Roosevelt and his entourage toward Germany was even more extreme than that of the British leaders. Roosevelt was predisposed from the beginning of his career in public office to a deep antipathy for the German people in general, probably stemming from the anti-German propaganda of WWI, and there is no doubt that he personally despised Adolf Hitler. According to Professor David L. Hoggan ("The Forced War" - 1961): *"Roosevelt's hatred for Hitler was deep, vehement, passionate -- almost personal. This was due in no small part to an abiding envy and jealousy rooted in the great contrast between the two men, not only in their personal characters but also in their records as national leaders."*

The public lives of Roosevelt and Hitler had many similarities. Both assumed the leadership of their respective countries at the beginning of 1933 and then proceeded down parallel tracks. They both faced the enormous challenge of mass unemployment during a catastrophic worldwide economic depression. Each became a powerful leader in a vast military alliance during the most destructive war in history, albeit on opposite sides. Both men died while still in office within a few weeks of each other in April 1945. Though there were many similarities, the contrasts in their lives were enormous.

Roosevelt was born into one of the wealthiest families in America, and his life was completely free of economic worry. He, like Hitler, served in the First World War, but in an entirely different way. Roosevelt spent the war in an office in Washington as Under Secretary of the Navy. Hitler was born into a provincial family and grew up in semi-poverty. As a young man he worked as a manual laborer and lived hand-to-mouth. He served in the First World War as a front line soldier in the hell of the Western Front, never higher in rank than corporal. He was wounded several times and was decorated for bravery.

Despite his Ivy League education, his confident, aristocratic manner and persuasive rhetoric, Roosevelt was unable to solve the enormous economic problems existing in the United State which he inherited when he became president. Throughout his presidency, he was never able to reduce unemployment or to get the economy moving again. At the end of his first four years as president, millions of people remained unemployed, undernourished and poorly housed in a country rich in all the resources required for incomparable prosperity. Roosevelt's New Deal was plagued from beginning to end with bitter strikes and bloody clashes between labor and industry.

The story unfolded very differently in Germany under Hitler. When Hitler became Chancellor, he was faced with all the problems facing Roosevelt, multiplied many times over. Yet, Hitler rallied his people behind a radical program that transformed Germany within a few years from an economically ruined land on the verge of civil war, into Europe's powerhouse. Germany underwent a social, cultural and economic rebirth without parallel in history.

The contrast between the personalities of the two men was also stark. Hitler tended to be straightforward in his relationship with others and unambiguous in communicating his intentions. He had a conservative sense of Christian morality and was not a liar. Roosevelt put on a front of *bon homme,* but behind the big smile he was devious and calculating, and he manipulated others by misleading them. He was very probably a sociopath, devoid of a conscience, as many successful politicians are. Hitler, on the other hand, was truly a man of the people who genuinely wished to elevate the German people out of their "slough of despond" to the realization of their full potential as a people and as a nation. In contrast to Hitler, there was much of the cynical politician in Roosevelt who may have cared about the people in an abstract way, but he believed that only he knew what was best for them and that they were incapable of understanding such matters themselves. He manipulated the American people through devious and deceitful means, such as lying about his true intentions about taking America to war. He even admitted his devious and contradictory nature. He once said, *"I never let my left hand know what my right hand is doing."*

Roosevelt had worked in the Wilson administration during the First World War and was impressed by Wilson's boundless idealism, and also by the way he was idolized by people around the world for his high-minded approach to the peace settlement after the war. Like Wilson before him, Roosevelt had an exaggerated, messianic view of himself as uniquely qualified for national leadership, and believed that he had been called upon by providence to reshape the world. He was convinced, as so many American leaders have been, that the world could be saved only by remodeling itself after the United States.

Presidents like Wilson and Roosevelt, and George W. Bush most recently, view the world not as a multiplicity of different nations, races, and cultures who must mutually respect each others' separate collective identities in order to live together in peace. They look at the world from a self righteous missionary perspective which divides the nations of the world into two groups -- those representing "good" on one side (our side), and those representing "evil" on the other (This is known as a "Manichean" world perspective.). They also see America as providentially ordained as the permanent leader of the forces of "good" in the world, with the mission of either destroying or converting the forces of "evil." (Luckily, this view just happens to correspond to the economic and political interests of those who wield power in the United States.) Nazi Germany, in Roosevelt's view, represented the forces of "evil," with whom normal relations were impossible, and with whom one could not even reason; and so, he refused to try. He regarded Nazi Germany with total hostility.

Roosevelt most certainly did not see himself as an evil man, though his actions certainly made him one. He sincerely believed that he was doing the right and noble thing in pressuring Britain and France into a war against "evil" Germany. He was St. Michael the archangel leading the world in an existential struggle against the forces of Satan. The result of his vision of himself as the leader of the forces of righteousness, and his view of Germany under the Nazis as the force of evil in the world constantly threatening the forces of righteousness, produced an atmosphere of war hysteria and war psychosis among those who surrounded him and who ran his administration, to the extent that any utterance or action of this "force of evil," that is, Nazi Germany, was given the worst possible interpretation, and evil designs were imputed to them however benign their actual intentions. The Jews who surrounded him and advised him, and who hated Hitler's Germany for their own reasons, fed Roosevelt's delusions about himself and his role in the world, and validated his Manichean view of the world.

To illustrate the war psychosis which had seized American political leaders during this time, Assistant Secretary of State F.B. Sayre exclaimed to British Ambassador Sir Ronald Lindsay on September 9, 1938, "...*at such a time, when war is threatening and Germany is **pounding at our gates**, it seems to me tragic that we have not been able to reach and sign an agreement* [against Germany]." To imagine Germany "pounding at the gates" of America in 1938 was totally absurd. Germany lacked the means to pound at the gates of Britain, just across the English Channel. Moreover, Hitler and the Nazis had no motive or reason in

1938 to view America with hostility; only with dismay at America's baseless bellicosity towards Germany. If anything, it was the United States "pounding at the gates" of Germany.

In this atmosphere of false urgency, America's Jewish secretary of the Treasury, Henry Morgenthau, Jr., telephoned the Jewish French President, Leon Blum, and suggested freezing German bank accounts in France, in hopes of pushing France into war with Germany. Roosevelt, himself, became increasingly belligerent towards Hitler, and repeatedly made personally insulting remarks about him in public. (Rather like the current war hysteria over Iran, but more extreme.)

William C. Bullitt was the American Ambassador to France at the time, as well as Ambassador at Large to all other European countries. Like Roosevelt, Bullitt "rose from the rich." He was born into a wealthy Philadelphia banking family and was descended from Jonathan Horwitz, a German Jew who had immigrated to America. Bullit was especially close to Roosevelt and shared Roosevelt's enthusiasm for "Uncle Joe" (Stalin) and the Soviet Union, as well as his enthusiasm for war with Germany. Bullitt was used by Roosevelt to transmit messages to other American Ambassadors, including Joseph P. Kennedy, Ambassador to London (father of President John Kennedy), and Anthony Biddle, Ambassador to Warsaw, and those messages consistently expressed Roosevelt's belligerence towards Germany.

In 1919 Bullitt was an assistant to President Wilson at the Versailles Peace Conference. That same year, Bullitt was sent to Russia to meet with Lenin to determine if the new Bolshevik government deserved recognition by the Allies. Bullit was impressed with what he saw in Bolshevik Russia, and upon his return to Washington, urged recognition of the new regime. He was very sympathetic to Communist aims. In 1923 Bullitt married Louise Bryant Reed, the widow of American Communist leader John Reed (The movie, "Reds," starring Warren Beatty, 1981, was about John Reed). When Roosevelt became president in 1933, he brought Bullitt back into diplomatic service. Throughout his career, Roosevelt had consistently maintained close relations with people who were either Communists or Communist sympathizers. In 1938, all U.S. envoys in Europe were subordinated to Bullitt who was based in Paris. Roosevelt bypassed the State Department and frequently spoke with Bullitt directly by telephone, often daily, giving him precisely detailed and ultra-confidential instructions on how to conduct America's foreign policy. Bullitt had access to Roosevelt by telephone at any hour of the day or night. Roosevelt and Bullitt were close friends and saw eye to eye on all foreign policy issues, and were especially in consonance in their hostility to Germany. Both were aristocrats and thorough internationalists with a shared view on how to remake the world, and both saw themselves as destined to bring about that grand reorganization. In Europe, Bullitt spoke with the voice and the authority of President Roosevelt himself.

President Roosevelt riding in a car with his "agent provocateur" Ambassador William C. Bullitt

The Polish Ambassador to Washington, Count Jerzy Potocki, reported back to Warsaw that William C. Bullitt had informed him that President Roosevelt was determined to bring America into the next European war. Bullitt predicted that a long war would soon break out in Europe. *"Of Germany and her Chancellor, Adolf Hitler, he* [Bullitt] *spoke with extreme vehemence and with bitter hatred,"* Potocki reported. *"He* [Bullitt] *suggested that the war might last six years, and he advocated that it should be fought to a point where Germany could never recover."*

Potocki asked Bullitt how such a war might begin, since it was very unlikely that Germany would attack either France or Britain. Bullitt said that it would likely begin with a war between Germany and some other country, and that the Western Powers would then intervene against Germany. Bullitt predicted an eventual war between Germany and the Soviet Union, which Germany would probably win, but would then be so worn out that it would have to capitulate to the Western Powers. Bullitt assured Potocki that the United States would participate in any such war if Britain and France made the first move. When Bullitt asked about the German-Polish problem, Potocki said that Poland would fight rather than give in to German demands, and Bullitt and Roosevelt were both encouraging Poland in this stance. Potocki attributed the belligerent American attitude toward Germany solely to Jewish influence. He reported to Warsaw again and again that American public opinion was merely the product of Jewish manipulation.

In a report from Washington back to the Foreign Ministry in Warsaw, dated February 9, 1939, he wrote:

"The pressure of the Jews on President Roosevelt and on the State Department is becoming ever more powerful ...

... The Jews are right now the leaders in creating a war psychosis which would plunge the entire world into war and bring about general catastrophe. This mood is becoming more and more apparent.

In their definition of democratic states, the Jews have also created real chaos: they have mixed together the idea of democracy and communism and have above all raised the banner of burning hatred against Nazism.

This hatred has become a frenzy. It is propagated everywhere and by every means: in theaters, in the cinema, and in the press. The Germans are portrayed as a nation living under the arrogance of Hitler which wants to conquer the whole world and drown all of humanity in an ocean of blood.

In conversations with Jewish press representatives I have repeatedly come up against the inexorable and convinced view that war is inevitable. This international Jewry exploits every means of propaganda to oppose any tendency towards any kind of consolidation and understanding between nations. In this way, the conviction is growing steadily but surely in public opinion here that the Germans and their satellites, in the form of fascism, are enemies who must be subdued by the 'democratic world.' "

Lord Halifax Beats the War Drums

Britain's Foreign Minister, Lord Halifax, continued to maintain a hostile attitude toward Hitler and Germany, and was determined to provoke a war with Germany. He circulated rumors both at home and abroad which presented the foreign policy of Hitler in the worst possible light. He would have found fault with Hitler no matter which direction he turned or what he did. Halifax dispatched a message to President Roosevelt on January 24, 1939 in which he claimed to have received *"a large number of reports from various reliable sources which throw a most disquieting light on Hitler's mood and intentions."* He falsely claimed that Hitler harbored a fierce hatred for Great Britain. Hitler had, in fact, consistently expressed only admiration for Great Britain and had pursued a goal of Anglo-German cooperation. Regardless, Halifax continued to claim the opposite. Halifax claimed that Hitler wanted to establish an independent Ukraine, and that he intended to destroy the Western Powers in a surprise attack before moving Eastward. He claimed that not only British intelligence but *"highly placed Germans who are anxious to prevent this crime"* had furnished him evidence of this evil conspiracy. No German had furnished any such thing to him. He made it up. Hitler had not the remotest intention of attacking either Great Britain or France.

How to explain the desire of these men to have a war with Germany? These men, Churchill, Halifax, Cooper, Eden, Vansittart, et al, were conservative men devoted to the British

Churchill and Halifax were determined to have a war with Germany.

Empire and to its dominant position in the world. But they were also nervously aware that British power was waning. Churchill had been one of the most vocal advocates for war against Germany before World War I. He, and the others, were now advocating war with Germany for the same reason as before -- Germany was becoming too powerful, both commercially and militarily, and therefore threatened to eclipse the dominance of the British Empire. These conservative British leaders were devoted to the old balance of power principle worked out after the Napoleonic Wars. Preventing any one power from becoming dominant on the European continent had always been an overriding foreign policy principle of Great Britain. Germany's defeat in a war would serve the interests of both Britain and International Jewry. Vilifying Hitler and deliberately misinterpreting his actions and intentions served only as pretexts for a war they were determined to bring about for their own reasons.

These advocates of war with Germany were well aware that Britain could not defeat Germany without bringing the United States in on her side, as in World War I. At the same time that they were developing pretexts for war against Germany, they were propagandizing President Roosevelt to make sure he was behind them, though little propaganda was needed, as Roosevelt was already in their corner. To fan the flames, Halifax made the most dire, though unfounded warnings to Roosevelt concerning Germany's intentions. He told Roosevelt in a telegram that Hitler planned to invade Holland and give the Dutch East Indies to Japan. (Japan needed its oil.) Germany had no such plan. He told

Roosevelt that he was certain that Germany would soon give Britain an ultimatum. Halifax added that the British leaders expected a surprise air attack from Germany before the ultimatum actually arrived. He claimed to have knowledge that Germany was mobilizing for such an attack as he was composing the telegram and that the attack could occur at any moment. These were preposterous inventions.

Hitler was preoccupied at the time with the Polish matter and had not given a thought to attacking Britain. But Halifax was determined. He went on to emphasize *"Hitler's mental condition, his insensate rage against Great Britain and his megalomania."* He confided that Britain was greatly increasing her armament program, and he believed that it was his duty to enlighten Roosevelt about Hitler's intentions and attitudes *"in view of the relations of confidence which exist between our two governments and the degree to which we have exchanged information hitherto."* Halifax claimed that Chamberlain was contemplating a public warning to Germany prior to Hitler's annual Reichstag speech on January 30, 1939, and suggested that Roosevelt should do the same without delay. Chamberlain gave no such warning, but Halifax hoped to goad Roosevelt into making another alarmist and bellicose speech.

Halifax had sent Anthony Eden to the U.S. in December 1938 to spread rumors about sinister German plans, and Roosevelt responded with a provocative and insulting warning to Germany in his message to Congress on January 4, 1939. Halifax hoped for a repeat performance from Roosevelt as a result of his most recent telegram. Halifax was preparing a war propaganda campaign for the British public and such a warning from Roosevelt would feed into his purposes. All of these machinations of Lord Halifax amounted to sheer fantasy, but Roosevelt, already predisposed toward war with Germany, swallowed it whole. Halifax only told him what he already wanted to hear.

Secretary of State, Cordell Hull, another strident advocate for war, sent a message to Halifax stating that *"the United States Government had for some time been basing their policy upon the possibility of just such a situation arising as was foreshadowed in your telegram."* This was the Roosevelt administration's way of informing Britain that it supported the idea of war with Germany despite American public opinion, which was totally against it.

Roosevelt wanted a war to distract attention from his failed economic policies. He also wanted war because he cherished the idea of himself as an heroic wartime president. The Jews who surrounded Roosevelt, such as Henry Morgenthau, Jr., as well as all the other officials in the

Henry Morgenthau, Jr.

Roosevelt administration, worked themselves into a fever fantasizing about Nazi Germany's malevolent intentions.

According to David L. Hoggan, in his paper, "President Roosevelt and the Origins of the 1939 War, "*...anyone within Roosevelt's and Hull's circle who did not declare that Hitler was hopelessly insane was virtually ostracized."*

On January 4, 1939, Roosevelt told Congress that U.S. neutrality policy must be re-examined. He wanted a freer hand to act against Germany. At this same time (the next day, in fact) Poland's foreign minister, Beck, joined Hitler at Berchtesgaden in an amicable meeting during which Hitler stressed German-Polish cooperation in settling the matter of Danzig and the Polish Corridor. Though cordial, the conversations were unproductive and nothing concrete was settled. Hitler made clear, however, that as Danzig was a German city, sooner or later it would have to be returned to Germany.

The contrast between Hitler's calm, diplomatic approach in his talks with Polish officials, and the deranged, hysterical, confrontational manner imagined of him by officials surrounding Roosevelt, could not have been greater.

American Charge d'Affaires in Berlin, Prentiss Gilbert, reported back that the situation between Poland and Germany was not as incendiary as Washington officials imagined. He reported to the State Department on February 3, 1939 that Hitler's basic policy in the East was friendship with Poland. It seemed certain according to Gilbert that Beck would be willing to allow the return of Danzig to Germany in exchange for a 25 year Pact, and for a German guarantee of the Polish Corridor. That is not, however, what Roosevelt and his officials wanted to hear. But had Britain and America stayed out of it, that is most likely what would have happened.

Germany Occupies Bohemia and Moravia

Meanwhile, what remained of Czechoslovakia after the German annexation of the Sudetenland, soon fell apart, as described in the previous chapter. All that remained of the former Czechoslovakia was parts of Bohemia and Moravia, and on March 15, 1939, with the consent of the Czecho-Slovak president, Emil Hacha, Germany occupied Bohemia and Moravia and proclaimed it a German protectorate in order to prevent its being taken over by the Communists. In any case, Bohemia and Moravia had existed under German rule for most of its thousand year history, so this was nothing new. Czechoslovakia was a new, artificial creation of the Peace Conference after WWI, which now had already fallen apart. The entire region had a German character. Mozart premiered his opera "Don Giovanni" in Prague. Pilsen, Bohemia's fourth largest city, is known worldwide for Pilsner beer, a German beer. Another Bohemian city with a German name, Budweis, is best known for the original Budweiser beer (the European brand).

Britain initially accepted the German occupation, reasoning that her guarantee of Czechoslovakia was rendered invalid by the collapse of the Czech state. But Prime Minister Chamberlain had been under attack by Churchill, Halifax, Duff Cooper, and Vansittart, among others, for his "appeasement" of Hitler through the Munich Agreement. After Germany occupied Bohemia and Moravia, the attacks on him intensified, and were egged on even further by Roosevelt. Chamberlain became flustered and defensive. In a speech on March 17, he declared that he wished to correct a misapprehension of weakness on his part. He said that Munich had been the right policy, but now Hitler had broken that agreement by occupying Czechoslovakia (Bohemia and Moravia). From that point on, Chamberlain stated, Britain would strenuously oppose, even to the point of war, any further territorial moves by Hitler, no matter how justified.

The occupation of Bohemia and Moravia caused a greater outburst of hostility towards Germany in Washington, D.C., than it did in Britain, or for that matter, in any other capital in the world, though the reason for it is not clear. The occupation in no way affected American interests. Nevertheless, the head of the German Embassy in Washington reported back to Berlin that a violent press campaign against Germany had been launched throughout the United States. President Roosevelt also pressured Lord Halifax to adopt an *"outspoken anti-German policy,"* in Britain, as well. Halifax replied by promising Roosevelt that the British leaders were *"going to start educating public opinion as best they can to the need for action."* In other words, they would launch an anti-German/pro-war propaganda campaign.

Roosevelt pushes for war

Ambassador Bullitt informed the Poles that both he and President Roosevelt were counting on Polish willingness to go to war over Danzig if necessary. On March 19, 1939, Bullitt informed the Poles that Roosevelt was prepared to do everything possible to promote a war between the British and the French against Germany. Halifax, meanwhile, was attempting to create a broad anti-German front and an encirclement of Germany by proposing an alliance to include Britain, France, Poland and the Soviet Union. The Poles distrusted the Soviets as much as they did the Germans, and backed away from any such agreement that would bind Poland to the Soviet Union.

Both Lord Halifax and President Roosevelt began to vigorously encourage the Poles in their refusal to accept the German demands regarding Danzig. Bullit finally told the Poles that he regarded an alliance between Britain, France and Poland, without the Soviet Union, to be the best possible arrangement. He said that British leaders hoped that there would be a war between Germany and the Soviet Union, and that they were not eager to make commitments to the Soviet Union for that reason. The Soviet Union was also becoming ever more distrustful of Britain and France.

On March 26, Bullitt contacted Ambassador to London Joseph P. Kennedy and instructed him to tell Prime Minister Chamberlain that the United States hoped that Great Britain would go to war against Germany in event of hostilities over Danzig. Britain then announced a doubling in size of its army. On March 31, 1939 Prime Minister Chamberlain announced in Parliament a "blank check" guarantee to Poland in event of war between Poland and Germany, that is, that Britain would declare war on Germany if Germany were to invade Poland. France joined Britain and made the same guarantee.

Ambassador Kennedy was appalled at the idea of a war with Germany, and only reluctantly carried out his duties as Ambassador when that possibility was involved. To this extent, he was out of step with the Roosevelt administration, as well as with the British government. Both Roosevelt and Bullitt disliked and distrusted Kennedy and Kennedy disliked and distrusted both of them. In a letter to his wife, he wrote: *"I talk to Bullitt occasionally. He is more rattlebrained than ever. His judgment is pathetic and I am afraid of his influence on FDR because they think alike on many things."*

Anti-war movement becomes active

Meanwhile, back in the United States, the anti-war movement was growing in strength. One of the leading voices in that movement was that of Hamilton Fish, a leading Republican congressman from New York. Fish made a series of radio speeches to expose Roosevelt's march to war while claiming that he only wanted peace. On January 6, 1939, Fish told a nationwide radio audience:

"The inflammatory and provocative message of the President to Congress and the world [given two days before] *has unnecessarily alarmed the American people and created, together with a barrage of propaganda emanating from*

high New Deal officials, a war hysteria, dangerous to the peace of America and the world. The only logical conclusion to such speeches is another war fought overseas by American soldiers.

All the totalitarian nations referred to by President Roosevelt ... haven't the faintest thought of making war on us or invading Latin America.

I do not propose to mince words on such an issue, affecting the life, liberty and happiness of our people. The time has come to call a halt to the warmongers of the New Deal, backed by war profiteers, Communists, and hysterical internationalists [meaning Jews], *who want us to quarantine the world with American blood and money.*

He [Roosevelt] *evidently desires to whip up a frenzy of hate and war psychosis as a red herring to take the minds of our people off their own unsolved domestic problems. He visualizes hobgoblins and creates in the public mind a fear of foreign invasions that exists only in his own imagination."*

In another radio address of April 5, 1939, Congressman Fish said:

"The youth of America are again being prepared for another blood bath in Europe in order to make the world safe for democracy.

If Hitler and the Nazi government regain Memel or Danzig, taken away from Germany by the Versailles Treaty, and where the population is 90 percent German, why is it necessary to issue threats and denunciations and incite our people to war? I would not sacrifice the life of one American soldier for a half dozen Memels or Danzigs. We repudiated the Versailles Treaty because it was based on greed and hatred, and as long as its inequalities and injustices exist there are bound to be wars of liberation.

The sooner certain provisions of the Versailles Treaty are scrapped the better for the peace of the world.

I believe that if the areas that are distinctly German in population are restored to Germany, except Alsace-Lorraine and the Tyrol, there will be no war in western Europe. There may be a war between the Nazis and the Communists, but if there is that is not our war or that of Great Britain or France or any of the democracies.

New Deal spokesmen have stirred up war hysteria into a veritable frenzy. The New Deal propaganda machine is working overtime to prepare the minds of our people for war, who are already suffering from a bad case of war jitters.

President Roosevelt is the number one warmonger in America, and is largely responsible for the fear that pervades the Nation which has given the stock market and the American people a bad case of the jitters.

I accuse the administration of instigating war propaganda and hysteria to cover up the failure and collapse of the New Deal policies, with 12 million unemployed and business confidence destroyed.

I believe we have far more to fear from our enemies from within than we have from without. All the Communists are united in urging us to go to war against Germany and Japan for the benefit of Soviet Russia.

Great Britain still expects every American to do her duty, by preserving the British Empire and her colonies. The war profiteers, munitions makers and international bankers [meaning Jews] *are all set up for our participation in a new world war."*

The hero aviator, Charles A. Lindbergh, was also a leading opponent of Roosevelt's war aims, and went around the country speaking out against going to war with Germany. In his diary entry of May 1, 1941, Lindbergh wrote:

"The pressure for war is high and mounting. The people are opposed to it, but the Administration seems to have 'the bit in its teeth' and [is] hell-bent on its way to war. Most of the Jewish interests in the country are behind war, and they control a huge part of our press and radio and most of our motion pictures. There are also the 'intellectuals,' and the 'Anglophiles,' and the British agents who are allowed free rein, the international financial interests, and many others."

Roosevelt's motives for wanting a war with Germany have long been the subject of debate. As America's interests were not threatened in any way by Germany, nor would they be served by a war, Roosevelt's determination to have a war made little sense..., that is, unless one takes into account Roosevelt's intimate ties to organized Jewry. As Jewish historian Lucy Dawidowicz noted: *"Roosevelt himself brought into his immediate circle more Jews than any other President before or after him. Felix Frankfurter, Bernard M. Baruch and Henry Morgenthau were his close advisers. Benjamin V. Cohen, Samuel Rosenman and David K. Niles were his friends and trusted aides."*

Roosevelt was totally in thrall to the Jews, owed his political career to the Jews, and had so surrounded himself with Jews, almost to the exclusion of all others, that he essentially became one of them. Their attitudes, motives and goals became his. They hated Germany, so he hated Germany. They were determined to destroy Germany, so he was determined to destroy Germany.

In the summer of 1939 Polish ambassador to Washington, Count Jerzy Potocki returned to Warsaw on leave and was astonished at the calm mood in Poland, compared to the war psychosis that had gripped the West. In a conversation with Polish Foreign Ministry Under-Secretary, Count Jan Szembek, about the growing war psychosis that had gripped the West. Potocki said to Szembek:

"In the West there are all kinds of elements openly pushing for war: the Jews, the super-capitalists, the arms dealers. Today they are all ready for a great business, because they have found a place which can be set on fire: Danzig; and a nation that is ready to fight: Poland. They want to do business on our backs. They are indifferent to the destruction of our country. Indeed, since everything will have to be rebuilt later on, they can profit from that as well." From the diary of Count Szembek.

Poles murder German Nationals within the Corridor

Reports of increased hostilities breaking out between Poles and ethnic Germans in Polish controlled territories created a feeling of urgency in Germany. For several months before Germany's invasion of Poland, ethnic Poles, protected by the Polish Army, launched a reign of terror against German nationals living within the Polish Corridor. (Formerly part of Germany where Germans had lived for several hundred years.) It is estimated that some 58,000 German nationals were killed during this period by marauding mobs, encouraged by the Polish government. The German government lodged dozens of formal complaint with the League of Nations, but with no results. Hitler became increasingly distressed about it and said to the British Ambassador Sir Neville Henderson on August 25, 1939: *"Poland's provocations have become intolerable."*

Typical of these massacres was that which occurred in the German town of Bromberg, in the Polish Corridor. In this massacre, called "Bloody Sunday," 5,500 ethnic Germans were slaughtered like pigs. Children were nailed to barns, women were raped and hacked to death with axes, men were beaten and hacked to death. 328 Germans were herded into Bromberg's Protestant church, after which the church was set on fire. All 328 burned to death.

William Joyce, nicknamed Lord Haw Haw by British propaganda, became a German citizen and took up Germany's cause against Poland. He described the horrible conditions of the Germans who lived in the former German territory which was now a part of Poland, in his book, "Twilight Over England." The following is his description of what happened in Bromberg:

"German men and women were hunted like wild beasts through the streets of Bromberg. When they were caught, they were mutilated and torn to pieces by the Polish mob. . . . Every day the butchery increased. . . . Thousands of Germans fled from their homes in Poland with nothing more than the clothes that they wore.. On the nights of August 25 to August 31 inclusive, there occurred, besides innumerable attacks on civilians of German blood, 44 perfectly authenticated acts of armed violence against German official persons and property."

According to historian John Toland in his book "Adolf Hitler," when Hitler first learned of the Bromberg slaughter, at first he refused to believe that such a number had been killed, but, when Berndt (the German public official who had brought the matter to his attention) replied that it may have been somewhat exaggerated but something monstrous must have happened to give rise to such stories, Hitler shouted *"They'll pay for this! Now no one will stop me from teaching these fellows a lesson they'll never forget! I will not have my Germans butchered like cattle!"* At this point, according to Toland, the Fuhrer went to the phone and, in Berndt's presence, ordered Keitel to issue "Directive No. 1 for the Conduct of the War." That may well have been the actual trigger for the war, though the causes of the war were multiple.

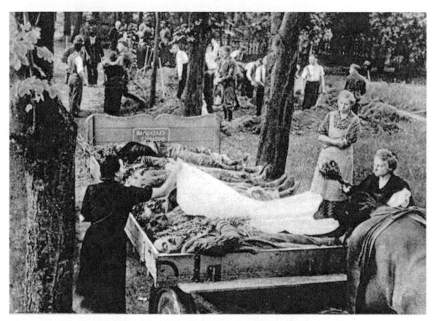

**Murdered Germans before their burial in the
Protestant cemetery of Bromberg.**

**German woman weeping over the murder of her
husband in Bromberg by marauding Poles.**

On August 24, 1939, a week before the outbreak of hostilities, Sir Horace Wilson, advisor to Chamberlain, went to Ambassador Kennedy with an urgent appeal from Prime minister Chamberlain to President Roosevelt. He wanted Roosevelt to "put pressure on the Poles" to open negotiations with Germany in order to avert a war. Chamberlain was already regretting Britain's "guarantee" to Poland. Kennedy telephoned the State Department and said that the British *"felt that they could not, given their obligations, do anything of this sort but that we could."* Roosevelt rejected Chamberlain's plea out of hand. When Kennedy reported this back to Chamberlain, Chamberlain, according to Kennedy, said: *"The futility of it all, is the thing that is frightful. After all, we cannot save the Poles. We can merely carry on a war of revenge that will mean the destruction of all Europe."*

Kennedy sent a telegram to Roosevelt urging him to intervene on behalf of peace. *"It seems to me,"* Kennedy wrote, *"that this situation may crystallize to a point where the President can be the savior of the world. The British government as such certainly cannot accept any agreement with Hitler, but there may be a point when the President himself may work out plans for world peace. Now this opportunity may never arise, but as a fairly practical fellow all my life, I believe that it is entirely conceivable that the President can get himself in a spot where he can save the world."*

Joseph P. Kennedy, Sr., U.S. Ambassador to Britain under Roosevelt.

Roosevelt rejected Kennedy's efforts and called Kennedy's plea *"...the silliest message to me that I have ever received."* Roosevelt told Henry Morgenthau that Kennedy was a *"pain in the neck."* *"Joe has been an appeaser and will always be an appeaser,"* Roosevelt said. *"If Germany and Italy made a good peace offer tomorrow, Joe would start working on the King and his friend the Queen and from there on down to get everybody to accept it."* Angered by Kennedy's stubborn attempts to prevent a war in Europe, Roosevelt essentially instructed him to cease and desist, and told him that any American peace effort was completely out of the question. Kennedy resigned shortly thereafter under pressure.

Deep distrust was developing between the British government and the Soviets. The British had made strong efforts to create a mutual pact against Germany that would include Britain, France, Poland and the Soviet Union, and had finally obtained the Soviets' agreement to a joint declaration. But when Chamberlain gave his blank check guarantee to the Polish government, he did it without consulting the Soviets. The Soviets were bewildered that the British would go ahead with a new plan without consulting them, and took it as an insult. The Soviets were already convinced that France and Britain were scheming against them. The Poles, for their part, were deeply distrustful of the Russians, and the British/French guarantee of Poland strengthened Polish resistance to Soviet participation in any kind of alliance in which they themselves took part. The British/French guarantee antagonized the Russians but at the same time did not have the effect of restraining Hitler.

Unable to reach a collective agreement with Britain and France against Germany, the Soviets began to fear that that they might face a war with Germany alone, so they began searching around for a change of policy. On May 3, 1939, Stalin fired Foreign Minister Maksim Litvinov, who was Jewish and an advocate of collective security with Britain and France, and replaced him with Vyacheslav Molotov, who soon began negotiations with the Nazi foreign minister, Joachim von Ribbentrop. The Soviets, at the same time, continued negotiations with Britain and France, but in the end Stalin decided to reach an agreement with Germany. In so doing, he hoped to avoid a war with Germany until such time that he could re-build the Soviet Military which had been severely weakened by the purge of the Red Army officer corps in 1937. For his part, Hitler wanted a nonaggression pact with the Soviet Union so that his armies could invade Poland without winding up in a two front war. After the Polish matter was settled, Hitler believed that he would then be able to deal with Britain and France from the stand point of a fait accompli regarding Poland. Hitler did not believe that Britain and

France would follow through on their guarantee to Poland and actually declare war on Germany. It made no sense to him that they would take such a step when they were manifestly in no position to act upon it.

The Molotov-Ribbentrop Pact was signed in Moscow on August 23, 1939. Formally a nonaggression pact, the agreement also included a secret provision to divide Northern and Eastern Europe into German and Soviet spheres of influence. Poland was to be divided between Germany and the Soviet Union. The Soviet Union was to take back the region of Poland that it had controlled since 1772. The Baltic states, Finland, Estonia, Latvia, Lithuania, Bessarabia, Northern Bukovina and the Hertza region (on the Romanian border in Southern Ukraine), were ceded to Soviet control.

Soviet Foreign Minister Molotov signs the Nazi-Soviet Non-aggression Pact while German Foreign Minister von Ribbentrop and Stalin look on.

The news of the Pact was met with utter shock and surprise by government leaders and media worldwide, most of whom were unaware of the negotiations which had been going on between the Soviet Union and Germany. They were aware only of the ongoing negotiations between the Soviets and Britain and France. Jews around the world, who looked upon the Soviet Union as the base of International Jewry, were particularly shocked by the agreement. They saw it as a sell out by the Soviets. In reality it was only a ploy to buy time by both Stalin and Hitler, and neither side saw it as permanent.

During the months leading up to the outbreak of war, Polish armed forces repeatedly violated German borders. Numerous altercations occurred between Polish irregulars and regular or auxiliary Germans all along the Polish/German border; in each case, on German territory. Poland in 1939 was highly militarized with an army larger than the German army. Moreover, Poland's new leaders were military men with an aggressive attitude towards Germany. Poland even underwent a partial mobilization in March, 1939, and on August 30, 1939, ordered a total mobilization. (According to the Geneva Convention, mobilization is equivalent to a declaration of war.) On August 31, 1939, Polish irregular armed forces launched a full scale attack on the German border town of Gleiwitz.

The next day, September 1, 1939, German forces invaded Poland. On that same day, Hitler addresses the Reichstag. *"For months we have been suffering under the torture of a problem which the Versailles Diktat created – a problem which has deteriorated until it becomes intolerable for us. Danzig was and is a Germany city. The Corridor was and is German. Both these territories owe their cultural development exclusively to the German people. Danzig was separated from us, the Corridor was annexed by Poland. As in other German territories of the East, all German minorities living there have been ill-treated in the most distressing manner.*

...proposals for mediation have failed because in the meanwhile there, first of all, came as an answer the sudden Polish general mobilization, followed by more Polish atrocities. These were again repeated last night. Recently in one night there were as many as twenty-one frontier incidents; last night there were fourteen, of which three were serious. I have, therefore, resolved to

speak to Poland in the same language that Poland for months past has used towards us.

This night for the first time Polish regular soldiers fired on our territory. Since 5:45 a.m. we have been returning fire, and from now on bombs will be met by bombs. Whoever fights with poison gas will be fought with poison gas."

The invasion of Poland occurred one week after the Molotov-Ribbentrop Pact was signed. On September 3, 1939, to Hitler's great surprise, Britain and France declared war on Germany, though they totally lacked the means of intervening in Poland.

On September 3, also, Winston Churchill was returned to the cabinet by Prime Minister Chamberlain as First Lord of the Admiralty, the job he had had in WWI. Churchill's bellicose warnings against Hitler leading up to the war now made him seem prescient and far sighted to many. On September 17, the Soviet Union invaded Poland from the other side. The Soviet invasion of Poland produced no reaction from Britain and France, though the Soviets had done precisely the same thing the Germans had done, albeit, without Germany's justification of reclaiming lost territory. This gave the lie to Britain's reason for declaring war on Germany. Germany's invasion of Poland provided only Britain's needed pretext for war. It was not a *casus belli*. The war with Poland ended on October 6, 1939, after which Germany and the Soviet Union divided and annexed Poland.

As in interjection, we shall mention here the reaction of Poland's Jews to the Russian invasion of Poland. Jews throughout Europe saw the Soviet Union as "good for the Jews," and were very favorably disposed towards the Soviet Union. Alexander Solzhenitsyn, in his book "Two Hundred Years Together," wrote that when the Soviets invaded Poland, *"Polish Jews, and the Jewish youth in particular, met the advancing Red Army with exulting enthusiasm"* (as they had also done during the Soviet invasion of 1919). The enthusiastic welcome of the Soviet invaders by Poland's Jews angered Polish patriots and became a major aspect of Polish anti-Jewish attitudes in later years. Jews welcomed the Soviet troops in the very same way when they later invade Lithuania, the other Baltic States, and other central and east European countries. After the

347

war when the Soviet Union took control of all of Eastern and Central Europe, all-Jewish regimes were installed in each of these countries.

Hitler's invasion of Poland is known as the beginning of World War II, though that is not what Hitler intended. Hitler did not even want a war with Poland, much less a world war. Hitler had made every attempt to settle diplomatically the dispute with Poland over the return of Danzig and a highway across the Polish Corridor. In fact, Hitler wanted more than to simply settle the dispute with Poland; he wanted an alliance with Poland in his anti-Comintern pact against the Soviet Union, which he had already concluded with Japan. Poland saw the Soviet Union as her enemy and the anti-Comintern pact would actually have served Poland's interests. They were foolish, indeed, to have rejected it.

The Poles had stubbornly refused to negotiate with Germany for a number of reasons. First, the Poles and the Germans had shared a mutual hostility for centuries. The military officers who ruled Poland were a proud lot with an exaggerated confidence in their military power. Britain, France and the United States all pressured Poland to resist Hitler's demands; and finally, British Prime Minister Chamberlain had insanely given the Poles an unsolicited war guarantee, promising to declare war on Germany if Hitler invaded, and he talked France into doing the same. From March to August, 1939, Hitler did his best to negotiate a settlement with Poland over Danzig, and his demands were far from unreasonable. But the Poles, confident in their British and French war guarantee defiantly refused. Finally, at wits end, Hitler made a deal with Stalin and the two invaded and divided Poland.

What would it have cost Poland to have concluded a peaceful settlement with Hitler? The German city of Danzig, which was under the supervision of the League of Nations, and did not belong to Poland, would have been returned to Germany. Germany would also have been allowed to build a highway and a railroad across the former German territory, the Polish Corridor, to reconnect with East Prussia. That's it! A peaceful settlement of the dispute would have taken nothing away from Poland. But the cost of refusing to settle the dispute peacefully was a world war in which millions of Poles were killed, much of their country destroyed, followed by 50 years of Nazi and Soviet occupation. If Poland had yielded, there would have been no World War II, no Cold War, no Korean War, and no Vietnamese War, and Eastern Europe would have escaped the horrific occupation and domination by the Soviet Union.

Chapter 19

The Phony War

Hitler was convinced that the future of Western civilization depended on the close cooperation of Germany with other European states, but particularly with her Aryan cousins, Britain and America. To Hitler, the big existential threat to Western civilization was Communist Russia, which he regarded as the base of Jewish world ambitions. He came to this conclusion as a young man when he first became interested in politics. He watched as the Bolshevik Jews took control of Russia and then launched their Red Terror. He watched as Jewish-led Communist revolutions sprang up all over Europe, which were organized and funded by the Comintern based in Russia, and backed by international Jewish banks. He came to power in Germany as an anti-Communist, and saw it as his life's mission to fight Communism and to raise Germany up as a bulwark against the tidal wave of Jewish Communism which threatened to sweep over Christian Europe. He made every attempt to forge alliances with Britain and to have good relations with the United States, and was dismayed that his overtures were spurned at every turn. He was distressed and saddened that the threat to Western civilization posed by Communist Russia was not as obvious to the leaders of Britain and the United States as it was to him.

Hitler saw it as inevitable that Germany would eventually end up in a war with Communist Russia. It was only a matter of when, not whether. Soviet leaders were of the same mind. Hitler was convinced that Communist Russia would invade Europe, Germany first, at some time in the not too distant future whenever the Soviets felt strong enough to do so. When that day came, what he wanted more than anything was to avoid another two front war. Hitler had every interest from that standpoint alone in establishing and maintaining friendly relations with the other Western powers, particularly with Britain and the United States, in order to avoid any such likelihood. But he also wanted good relations with the other European nations because he believed that they each, like Germany, were an integral part of Western Christian Civilization, under siege by atheistic Jewish Bolshevism. The last thing Hitler wanted was a war with Britain and France. Pulitzer Prize winning author Louis Kilzer confirms this in his book, "Churchill's Deception - Simon & Schuster, 1994):" *"Hitler did not want a world war, and had no stomach for fighting England,"* he wrote. But powerful forces in Britain and France wanted a war with Germany.

Though Britain and France were in no position to intervene in Poland, they wasted no time in initiating military actions against Germany. The very next day after Britain and France declared war on Germany (September 3, 1939), RAF bombers bombed German warships in the Helgoland Bight (where the Elbe River flows into the North Sea). On September 7 the French crossed into the Rhine River Valley with 40 divisions to begin the "Saar Offensive," but that effort was only half hearted and the offensive stopped just short of Germany's defensive positions, known as the Siegfried Line, with only a few insignificant skirmishes taking place. The German army was preoccupied with the Polish war and did not mount a counter attack. No effort was made to oppose Germany's occupation of Poland. So began an interlude variously known, in America as the Phony War, in Britain as the Twilight war, and in Germany as the Sitzkrieg, which began in September, 1939 and lasted until April, 1940. At times the situation seemed almost like a truce. Nothing was happening on land, though a ferocious sea war was underway which became known as the Battle of the Atlantic. Britain's great strength was her navy and she, along with France, immediately set up a total naval blockade to prevent shipments of any kind from either entering or leaving Germany. This was similar to the total blockade of World War I, which starved Germany into submission. Germany retaliated against the blockade with her submarine force.

The first shot of the Battle of the Atlantic was fired on September 3, 1939 when a German U-boat sank the British liner, the SS Athenia, off the coast of Ireland. When France and Britain declared war on Germany, Hitler was still hopeful of a diplomatic resolution. He believed that after the Polish campaign was completed and matters settled down again that he might be able to dissuade France and Britain from war. For that reason, he wanted to avoid provocations of any kind, and issued strict orders forbidding U-boat attacks on non-military ships. Unfortunately, the first ship to be sunk by a U-boat was the passenger liner Athena, which was a violation of Hitler's order. As Hitler had expected, this produced outrage among the Allies, as well as in neutral countries. The sinking of the Athena created the false impression that Germany intended to engage in unrestricted submarine warfare, as she had done during the First World War. But the sinking was done in error at dusk when it was difficult to see. The U-boat commander believed that the Athena was a warship. Hitler was furious, but the damage was done and no action was taken against the submarine captain.

On September 18, another German submarine sank the British aircraft carrier Courageous off the Scottish coast.

When the war in Poland came to a quick end on September 27, 1939, Hitler made a peace offer to Britain and France, but it was rejected by both. Churchill by now was back in the government in Britain as the First Lord of the Admiralty, and openly clamored for all out war against Germany. He held Germany's invasion of Poland up as proof that he had been right all along in warning of the Nazis plan to conquer the world. But, as described in previous chapters, Hitler had no such intention, and had no designs whatever on any West European state. Churchill and his gang of war mongers, including Duff Cooper, Lord Halifax, Anthony

Eden, Robert Vansittart, and the Jewish controlled press, were working overtime whipping up war hysteria, nevertheless.

The Allied strategy during the Phony War was to hold defensive positions on land while maintaining its naval blockade to weaken the German economy, and to wage naval war. The British and French continued to re-arm at a rapid rate, and a sizable British expeditionary force was sent over to France. Belgium and the Netherlands were determined to stay out of the war. They maintained strict neutrality and refused to submit to pressure from Britain and France to move their troops into their countries.

On the 8th of October three U-boats were sunk by the British and another was sunk on October 13. On October 14, in retaliation, a German U-boat entered Scapa Flow and sank the British battleship Royal Oak while it was at anchor. Nothing was happening as yet on land, though the air and naval war expanded furiously. German U-boats stepped up their attacks on British merchant shipping, causing worrying losses. The pocket battleship Admiral Graf Spee conducted a particularly destructive raid in the southern Atlantic ocean, destroying nine merchant ships in the fall of 1939. The British cruisers Exeter and Ajax and the New Zealand cruiser Achilles damaged the Graf Spee in a battle off the coast of Uruguay on December 13. The German ship took refuge in the neutral port of Montevideo, Uruguay, where, the Uruguayans insisted, it could remain for only 72 hours. Faced with certain destruction by the Allied ships waiting in international waters just outside the harbor, the captain of the Graf Spee ordered it scuttled in the harbor on December 17.

Russo-Finnish War

Despite the German/Soviet non-aggression pact, Stalin did not trust the Germans, and worried about Russia's vulnerability to a possible German attack through the Baltic countries. In September and October, 1939, Stalin set about to close off this route by pressuring the tiny countries of Estonia, Latvia, and Lithuania into agreeing to permit Soviet troops to be stationed in their territories. On October 7 the

Soviets demanded that Finland give up some of its territory for stationing of Russian troops and also demanded the use of Finland's Hang naval base, all in exchange for Soviet territory on Finland's eastern border. Finland agreed to everything except for the use of her naval base, but Russia persisted. These negotiations ended on November 30 when the Soviet Union invaded Finland.

Although outnumbered and poorly equipped, the Finns were tough and well trained, and to everyone's surprise, threw back the much larger Soviet forces. It turned out that Stalin's purge of his military officers in 1937, during which approximately 30,000 Russian officers were murdered, had severely weakened the Soviet army, a point which Hitler took careful note of. But the Soviets reorganized, and in January, 1940 mounted another offensive, this time with more success. On March 12, 1940, Finland signed a peace treaty and was forced to surrender all the Soviets had originally demanded, plus more. Finland gained nothing in the end by resisting the Soviet demands. Britain and France were working out ways to come to Finland's aid against the Soviets but before plans were completed, Finland had capitulated.

The Norway/Denmark Campaign

When Britain and France declared war on Germany on September 3, 1939, Norway, Sweden, Denmark and Finland immediately announced their neutrality. By so doing, these Scandinavian countries were following a policy they had adhered to since the mid-nineteenth century. In response, the German government formally agreed to respect Norway's neutrality, but added that it would not tolerate infringement of Norway's neutrality by a third power, meaning, of course, Britain.

Germany's economy depended on the 11 million tons of iron ore imported from Sweden each year, about half of which passed through the ice-free Norwegian port of Narvik. As long as Norway remained neutral, German ore ships could travel safely from Narvik to Germany, remaining inside Norwegian waters by wending their way through the numberless islands fringing the Norwegian east coast. They were thereby unhindered by the British blockade. But the Altmark incident of February 16, 1940, during which Norwegian gunboats stood by and allowed a British destroyer to board a German transport ship -- the Altmark -- within Norwegian waters, caused Hitler to doubt that Norway could maintain her neutrality in the face of British determination and aggressiveness.

The head of the National Socialist Party in Norway, was the German sympathizer Vidkun Quisling, who repeatedly warned the Germans of Britain's intention to invade and occupy Norway. A British invasion of Norway, which could then easily be extended into Sweden, would completely cut off Germany's essential iron ore supply, thus crippling Germany's manufacturing industry. As First Lord of the Admiralty, Winston Churchill was now openly proposing an invasion of Norway, though Prime Minister Chamberlain, who was far less enthusiastic for war than Churchill, was still indecisive in the matter. On April 8, 1940, as First Lord of the Admiralty, Churchill unilaterally took it upon himself to order the mining of Norwegian coastal waters for the purpose of blocking these German iron ore shipments. This was a flagrant violation of Norway's neutrality, and it posed an intolerable threat to Germany.

Germany had already worked out a contingency plan for just such an eventuality and reacted swiftly once it occurred. On April 9, the next day after Churchill's order to mine the Norwegian coastal waters, German troops began to pour into Denmark, overwhelming the surprised Danes who quickly surrendered. Germany invaded Denmark because she needed the northern Danish airports to facilitate her simultaneous invasion of Norway.

German invasion of Denmark and Norway

Troop laden German transports, escorted by Luftwaffe aircraft, immediately sailed for Oslo, and German paratroopers were dropped on Norwegian airfields. The paratroopers quickly seized control of all the airfields around Oslo and German planes began pouring in, while German naval forces landed troops in numerous locations along the Norwegian coast, including Narvik. The German landings were mostly unopposed because immediately after the Germany invasion began,

German sympathizer Vidkun Quisling, head of the Norwegian National Socialist party, proclaimed himself the new head of government, and ordered the Norwegian armed forces to stop resisting. The entire operation went off without a hitch, and was a testament to the quality and skill of Germany's military leadership, and to the efficiency and discipline of German military personnel.

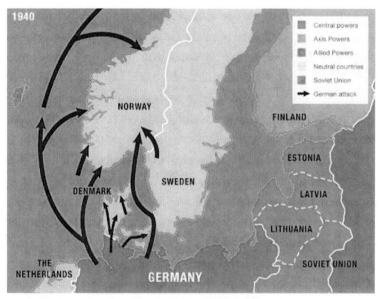

(L) Map showing invasion of Denmark and Norway.

German troops boarding a plane for Norway

German troops off-load at Norwegian ports

Troop laden Luftwaffe planes entering Norway

Vidkun Quisling, head of the Norwegian National Socialist Party, welcomes German troops to Norway.

****

The sea battle went a little differently, however. The first German losses occurred at Oslo Fjord, where Norwegians opened fire from coastal defense batteries at close range. On the first morning of the sea war, the German heavy cruiser Blucher was sunk with the loss of most of her crew. Another German cruiser was also damaged, and a German torpedo boat was sunk. At Narvik, a naval engagement on April 10 between British and German ships resulted in the sinking of two German destroyers, with 5 others seriously damaged. The British also lost two destroyers in the engagement.

Three days later a British naval force consisting of a battleship, an aircraft carrier and several destroyers destroyed the remaining German ships with surface and air attacks. Despite this naval disaster, 2,000 German troops got ashore and took Narvik. The British landed troops and clashed with the Germans at different locations, but the British lost at every contested point. In the end the British were forced to retreat and then withdraw from Norway entirely. On June 10, 1940, Norway capitulated and fell under the control of Germany. Germany was thus assured of an uninterrupted supply of iron ore, but the occupation of Norway also enabled Germany to protect her exposed northern flank against an Allied invasion.

Churchill takes Chamberlain's place as Prime Minister

The most significant casualty of the Norwegian campaign was Prime Minister Neville Chamberlain. The British disaster in Norway triggered a two day Parliamentary debate, which took place on the 7th and 8th of May, to decide what to do about the matter. In the debate, those who had long been clamoring for war accused Chamberlain of vacillation and indecisiveness, and of being too weak to "stand up to Hitler." He was blamed for the Norway blunder, even though the entire operation had been exclusively in Churchill's hands, and if anyone was to be held accountable, it should have been him. (Churchill's entire career in fact had been marked by a series of such military blunders.) A mood of war hysteria was created in the debate by Churchill and his supporters, and it was resolved that "Germany had to be stopped! " Churchill and those clamoring for war characterized Germany's invasion of Denmark and Norway as just more irrefutable evidence of Hitler's plan to conquer the world, as they had already repeatedly warned about. In reality their warnings had been only self-fulfilling prophecies. Britain was the relentless provocateur. Germany's military initiatives in all cases were "reactive" in nature. Germany would have preferred not to have invaded Denmark and Norway and only did so because Britain was planning to do so and because of Britain's violation of Norway's neutrality. Germany's vital iron ore supply had to be protected at all cost. Moreover, Britain was conducting a blockade of Germany, not the other way around.

As a result of the debate, it was generally resolved that Germany had to be stopped, but it was also agreed that Chamberlain was not the man to do it. At the end of the debate, Chamberlain received a no-confidence vote, and subsequently stepped down as Prime Minister. The next day Winston Churchill took his place, and formed a coalition government to include all political parties. Churchill asserted that all political parties must work together to support the war effort.

Chapter 20

Germany invades France through the Low Countries. The Phony War Ends.

On May 10, the same day Churchill became Prime Minister, Germany invaded Belgium, Holland, and Luxembourg, as the only viable pathway into France, which was Germany's primary goal. This must also be seen as a pre-emptive strike, as Britain had already sent large numbers of troops into France, and a combined British/French army of 500,000 men was at that moment being organized for an invasion of Germany. Since their declaration of war on Germany, both Britain and France had been frantically building up their military forces in preparation for an all out offensive against Germany. Germany, as previously discussed, had tried to avoid a war with Britain and France, and even made a formal peace offer to both countries after the Polish war ended, but it was rejected out of hand. Not only did Britain and France reject Germany's offer of peace, but went even further and began a relentless naval campaign against Germany, known as the Battle of the Atlantic, which included a naval blockade of German ports. It was clear that a land attack on Germany would follow as soon as the Allied military build-up was ready.

The Maginot Line
·············· *Weak fortifications*
▬▬▬▬ *Strong fortifications*
Locations featured in this photo collection
are displayed in blue.

What was Germany to do, wait helplessly for the inevitable invasion? Again, Hitler seized the initiative and beat them to the punch with his invasion of the Low Countries on May 10 and his rapid push into France. France's impregnable Maginot Line blocked a German invasion across the German/French border, but the Maginot Line extended only to the Luxembourg border. The border between France and Belgium, and France and Luxembourg was unfortified all the way to the English Channel. An invasion of France would have to go around the Maginot Line, through the only route available, and that would be through the Netherlands, Belgium or Luxembourg. Again, Hitler's initiative was "reactive" in nature, and essentially "defensive" as opposed to "offensive." All of Hitler's military initiatives were of this nature; all the result of Allied provocations or of Allied threats. Britain, led by Churchill, was the provocateur throughout.

Three days after becoming Prime Minister, and three days after the German invasion of the Low Countries, Churchill addressed the House of Commons and made his melodramatic "blood, sweat and tears" speech. In the speech, he declared British war aims as, "Victory. Victory at all costs. Victory in spite of all terror. Victory, however long and hard the road may be, for without victory there is no survival." Churchill deliberately ignored the fact that Adolf Hitler had made numerous peace overtures to Britain, had repeatedly expressed his admiration for the British Empire, had even offered German military assistance if needed by the British Empire, and had made repeated attempts to establish friendly relations with Britain, all of which were spurned. Germany had no designs on Britain and wanted above all else to avoid a war. It should also be remembered that Britain and France declared war on Germany, not the other way around. Germany's occupation of Norway, as well as the invasion of the Low Countries, were actually defensive in nature though Churchill and his "war party" held them up as the ultimate proof of Germany's plan to conquer the world. Perhaps they even believed it. Churchill's life dream had at last come true. He was now Prime Minister of England, fulfilling his imagined destiny of heroically leading the British Empire to victory in war. Making peace with Germany was the farthest thing from his mind.

On May 10, 1940, German bombers hit air bases in France, Luxembourg, Belgium, and the Netherlands, destroying large numbers of Allied planes on the ground and crippling Allied air defenses. Elite squads of German paratroopers were dropped onto fortified Allied points along the front, neutralizing a key element of France's defense strategy.

On the ground, German forces advanced in two directions: one through the Netherlands and northern Belgium (as Britain and France had expected) and the other, larger force to the south, through Luxembourg and into the Ardennes Forest on a path that led directly into the French heartland (which was completely unexpected). Unaware of the German advance to the south through the Ardennes Forest, Britain and France sent the bulk of their troops to Belgium.

During the first days of the attack, German progress toward Brussels and The Hague was slowed unexpectedly by the formidable resistance of the Dutch forces. On May 14, when the Dutch forces refused to surrender, the German Luftwaffe was unleashed for a massive bombing attack on central Rotterdam. Efforts were made to call the bombers back when the Dutch suddenly agreed to negotiate, but only a few of the

German pilots received the message and turned back. The remaining bombers continued on and dropped their bombs on the city, killing more than 800 civilians. The Netherlands surrendered that same day.

The British and French plan to defend Belgium was to make a stand at a line of forts between the cities of Antwerp and Liege. Unaware that these forts had already been captured by German paratrooper units on the first night of the invasion, the British and French armies found themselves under attack on May 13. At the same time, the second German offensive to the south emerged from the Ardennes Forest, to the complete surprise of the Allies. Over the next few days, the main Allied armies were trapped between the two German forces, able neither to protect Paris nor to stop the Germans from advancing to the English Channel. Then, when the German troops to the south moved between the French and British forces, the Allies were divided and thus weakened still further. The Allied defense of Belgium turned out to be an unequivocal disaster.

German tanks emerge from the Ardennes Forest

While the main French army was trapped between the two German armies, the British Expeditionary Force (BEF) was pushed to the coast near the French port of Dunkirk. Over 200,000 British and 140,000 French, 340,000 in all, were trapped on the beaches of Dunkirk; sitting ducks for the German forces pressing in on them.

With the BEF cornered and its back to the sea, and with little hope of reuniting with French forces, the British government decided that the BEF had to be evacuated. The evacuation, called Operation Dynamo, began on May 27, 1940, and took a full week to complete. Using more than 800 civilian and military sea vessels, all 340,000 men were brought back across the English Channel to British soil, all the while under constant attack by the Luftwaffe. The Dunkirk evacuation has gone down as one of the most heroic events of British history. At least that is the official story. The real story is somewhat different.

British and French troops trapped on the beaches of Dunkirk.

The real story is that Adolf Hitler halted the German panzers just at the point where they could have swept down and either destroyed or captured what amounted to the bulk of the entire British army as they were stranded indefensibly on the beaches of Dunkirk. If they had done so, Britain would thereafter have been defenseless against a German invasion and World War II would have been over in the West.

But Hitler did not want to destroy the British army. He wanted only peace and friendship with Britain. In his book, The "Other Side of the Hill," published in1948, which deals with the invasion of France and the Dunkirk event, British military historian Sir Basil Liddell Hart quotes the German General von Blumentritt concerning Hitler's halt order:

"He (Hitler) then astonished us by speaking with admiration of the British Empire, of the necessity for its existence, and of the civilization that Britain had brought into the world. He remarked, with a shrug of the shoulders, that the creation of its Empire had been achieved by means that were often harsh, but 'where there is planing, there are shavings flying'. He compared the British Empire with the Catholic Church saying they were both essential elements of stability in the world. He said that all he wanted from Britain was that she should acknowledge Germany's position on the Continent. The return of Germany's colonies would be desirable but not essential, and he would even offer to support Britain with troops if she should be involved in difficulties anywhere.."

The "miracle at Dunkirk" was in fact an extraordinary peace overture to England.

Louis Kilzer quoted Hitler, in his book "Churchill's Deception," 1994: *"The blood of every single Englishman is too valuable to shed. Our two peoples belong together racially and traditionally. That is and always has been my aim, even if our generals can't grasp it."* Adolf Hitler.

According to Kilzer, Hitler was trying to convince the British to make peace. Hitler even offered to pull out of France, retreat from the Low Countries, retreat from Norway and Denmark and to give up much of Poland in exchange for peace with Britain. Hitler wanted an alliance with Britain in order to fight Bolshevik Russia.

British historian David Irving, in his book "Hitler's War," quoted the renowned Swedish explorer Sven Hedin who knew Hitler: *"Hitler felt he had repeatedly extended the hand of peace and friendship to the British, and each time they had blacked his eye in reply."* According to Hedin, Hitler said: *"The survival of the British Empire is in Germany's interests too because if Britain loses India, we gain nothing thereby."*

Martin Allen, in his book, "The Hitler Hess Deception," (Harper Collins - 2003) quotes Hitler's legal advisor, Ludwig Weissauer. According to Weissauer, Germany contacted the British ambassador in

Sweden, Victor Mallet, during the invasion of France, through Sweden's Supreme Court judge Ekeberg, who was an acquaintance of Weissauer. According to Weissauer, Ekeberg told the British ambassador that *"Hitler feels himself responsible for the future of the White race. He sincerely wishes friendship with England. He wishes peace to be restored..."*

These are the peace terms Hitler offered:

1. The British Empire retains all its colonies and delegations

2. Germany's continental supremacy won't be questioned

3. All questions concerning the Mediterranean and its French, Belgian and Dutch colonies are open to discussion

4. Poland. A Polish state must exist

5. Czechoslovakia must belong to Germany

Ekeberg understood that implied in this peace offer was that all European states occupied by Germany would see their sovereignty restored. Germany's occupation of these states was defensive in nature and the result of military threats against Germany.

Churchill the War Lover

Dr. Ralph Raico, wrote, in his 1997 paper titled "Rethinking Churchill":

"But while Winston had no principles, there was one constant in his life: the love of war. It began early. As a child, he had a huge collection of toy soldiers, 1,500 of them, and he played with them for many years after most boys turn to other things. They were 'all British,' he tells us, and he fought battles with his brother, Jack, who 'was only allowed to have colored troops; and they were not allowed to have artillery.' He attended Sandhurst, the military academy, instead of the universities, and 'from the moment that Churchill left Sandhurst...he did his utmost to get into a fight, wherever a war was going on.' All his life he was most excited..., only really excited by war. He loved war as few modern men ever have. He even 'loved the bangs,' as he called them, and he was very brave under fire. For Churchill, the years without war offered nothing to him but 'the bland skies of peace and platitude.'"

In 1911, Churchill became the First Lord of the Admiralty, and was now in his element. He quickly sought out others in the government who favored war, and during the build up to World War I, he constantly fanned the flames for war. Churchill was the only member of the cabinet who backed war from the start, and did so enthusiastically. Prime Minister Asquith wrote about him: *"Winston very bellicose and demanding immediate mobilization...Winston, who has got all his war paint on, is longing for a sea fight in the early hours of the morning to result in the sinking of the Goeben. The whole thing fills me with sadness."*

It was Churchill who established the hunger blockade around Germany during WWI and maintained it for nearly seven months after the war was over, which resulted in the starvation death of a million German civilians, even though doing so was a violation of international law. But throughout his career, international law and the conventions by which men have tried to limit the horrors of war meant nothing to Churchill. He was strangely unmoved by the massive deaths of innocents and of the destruction of ancient centers of culture which resulted from his whims. Churchill was a manic-depressive, and referred to his bouts of depression as "the black dog." He thrived on the rush of war and cared little for ordinary people.

Beatrice Webb, a baroness and co-founder of the Fabian Society, sat next to Churchill at dinner. She wrote : *"First impression; restless, almost intolerably so...egotistical, bumptious, shallow minded and reactionary but with a certain personal magnetism...More of the American speculator than the English aristocrat. Talked exclusively about himself and his electioneering plans..."*

It is almost certain that Churchill arranged the sinking of the Lusitania, which was the trigger that brought the United States into World War I.

Now back in power, on his first day as Prime Minister, May 10, 1940, Churchill ordered a bombing raid on the defenseless university town of Freiberg, killing a number of German civilians. The bombing raid on Freiberg had no military purpose. After the fall of France, Churchill wrote Lord Beaverbrook, Minister of Air Production; *"When I look round to see how we can win the war, I see that there is only one sure* *path ... an absolutely devastating, **exterminating attack** by very heavy bombers from this country upon the Nazi homeland* "(emphasis added).

Having been given the gift of Dunkirk by Hitler, Churchill refused to acknowledge it, and instead painted the evacuation of British troops off the beaches of Dunkirk back to Britain as an heroic miracle pulled off by the British navy. He became more bellicose than ever in his determination to go on with the war.

The Fall of France

With the British out of the way, the Germans began their final push against France. By June 12, German tanks had broken through the main fronts along the Somme River and the fortified Maginot Line, moving ever closer to their goal, Paris. During this time, the British vigorously encouraged France to resist at all costs. Winston Churchill, now Prime Minister, even flew to Paris himself to offer his personal encouragement, though he did not offer British military assistance.

By this time, the size of the French army had been reduced by roughly half, and French leaders became resigned to an inevitable surrender. The French government abandon Paris, declaring it an open city. This allowed the Germans to enter on June 14 without resistance. The French government under Premier Rayaud fled south to Bordeaux, after which Rayaud resigned. A new government was formed under the premiership of WWI hero Marshall Petain. Petain's first move was to ask for an armistice. On June 17, Petain made a radio broadcast ordering a cessation of all resistance, and he then surrenders the French army to the Germans.

On June 22, 1940, France signed an armistice with Germany. After all that France had done to Germany since Germany's defeat in 1918, Hitler was in a mood to humiliate the French as pay back. He insisted that the armistice be signed in the same railway car in a forest in Compiegne, in which Germany had surrendered to France in 1918 to end World War I. The terms of the 1940 armistice divided France into an occupied and an unoccupied zone, with a rigid boundary line between the two. The Germans would directly control two thirds of the

Hitler with some of his ministers and officers outside the railway car in the forest near the city of Compiegne in which the armistice with France was signed on June 22, 1940. It is the same railway car in which the Germans signed the armistice to end WWI.

country, an area that included northern and western France and the entire Atlantic coast, while the remaining part of the country would be administered by the French government at Vichy under Marshal Petain

Other provisions of the armistice included disbanding the French army except for a force of 100,000 men to maintain domestic order. (This was identical to the requirement imposed upon Germany by the Versailles Treaty. It could not have been a coincidence.) The 1.5 million French soldiers captured by the Germans were to remain prisoners of war. The French government also agreed to stop members of its armed forces from leaving the country and instructed its citizens not to fight against the Germans. Finally, France was required to pay the occupation costs of the German troops.

On June 23, Hitler, along with architect Albert Speer, sculptor

Arno Breker, architect Herman Giesler, and others, flew to Paris for a brief sightseeing tour of the occupied city. Tour stops included the Eifel Tower, the Paris Opera, the Arc de Triomphe and the Tomb of

Adolf Hitler tours Paris after the fall of France. Albert Speer is to his left in the photo.

Napoleon. The three hour tour ended with a visit to the church of Sacré-Cœur on Montmartre. Hitler had never visited Paris before. *"It was the dream of my life to be permitted to see Paris,"* Hitler told Speer. *"I cannot say how happy I am to have that dream fulfilled today."*

Hitler makes peace offer to Britain

After the fall of France, Hitler again made a peace offer to Britain, only to have it rudely rejected by Churchill. As he had fought against a negotiated peace with Hitler after the war with Poland, now as Prime Minister, Churchill obstinately resisted any suggestion of peace negotiations with Hitler under any circumstances. This, more than anything else, is supposed to be the foundation of Churchill's greatness -- that he bravely held out against Hitler against all odds -- seemingly irrationally. At wit's end, after being rebuffed again and again in trying to make peace with Britain, Hitler did the only thing left to do, and that was to prepare for an invasion of Britain. On August 1, 1940 he resignedly ordered the Luftwaffe to put the Royal Air Force out of business as a prelude to a seaborne invasion of Britain.

According to British historian, Sir Basil Liddel Hart, having issued the order, Hitler subsequently took almost no part in the air battle, which came to be known as the Battle of Britain, leaving it entirely in the hands of Reichsmarshal Hermann Goering who headed the Luftwaffe. Hitler had been an ardent admirer of Britain all his life, did not want war with Britain, and never seemed to have his heart in this project to subjugate Britain. If Goering could bring it off, all well and good, but the fact that he was not "bringing it off" never seemed to bother Hitler all that much. The whole project was a nuisance to him. His real project was an invasion of the Soviet Union. He would come back to the subject of what to do about Britain after he had disposed of the Soviet Union. According to Liddel Hart, in his book, "The Other Side of the Hill," 1948:

"At the time we believed that the repulse of the Luftwaffe in the "Battle over Britain" had saved her [Britain]. *That is only part of the explanation, the last part of it. The original cause, which goes much deeper, is that Hitler did not want to conquer England. He took little interest in the invasion preparations, and for weeks did nothing to spur them on; then, after a brief impulse to invade, he veered around again and suspended the preparations. He was preparing, instead, to invade Russia."*

By late 1940, wrote historian Paul Johnson, *"British bombers were being used on a great and increasing scale to kill and frighten the German civilian population in their homes."* Churchill was ordering mass armadas of heavy bombers to bomb, not military targets, but city centers in Germany and particularly dense residential areas in order to kill as many civilians as possible and to de-house the rest.

Germany finally bombed non-military targets in London on September 7, 1940, which killed 306 people. Up to then, Hitler had ordered the Luftwaffe not to target civilians, but was finally goaded into doing so by repeated British attacks on German cities, including

Berlin. While Hitler was trying to convince the British to make peace, British air attacks on German cities intensified.

There was a group of pro-German elitists in Britain known as the "Clivenden Set" which included the Duke of Windsor (formerly King Edward VII), Lady Astor, Geofrey Dawson (editor of the London Times), Lord Lothian, the Duke of Manchester, the Duke of Hamilton, et al. The Clivenden Set favored friendly relations with Germany, and the Nazis had maintained long standing channels of communication with these people.

According to Louis Kilzer, in his book, "Churchill's Deception," Rudolph Hess, the Deputy Leader under Hitler, was in contact with the Clivenden Set and flew to England on May 10, 1941, at Hitler's behest, to try to negotiate a peace agreement with Britain through the Clivenden Set.

The official propaganda of the event claims that a mentally deranged Hess decided on his own initiative to fly a Messerschmitt to Scotland in May, 1941 on a whimsical, Quixotic mission to reach the Duke of Hamilton to set peace talks with Churchill. When he parachuted down in Renfrewshire, just 8 miles from the duke's estate, he was arrested by a farmhand with a pitchfork, and then taken to prison. Hitler reportedly went into an enraged, ranting, raving fit when he first heard of Hess's foolish mission, and was reported to have even scrambled aircraft to try to shoot down his plane to stop him.

Kilzer says that that isn't so. Hitler, according to Kilzer, was in on the mission and Hess was his dutiful agent in the daring peace mission. After the collapse of the Soviet Union in 1991, a 28 page notebook that belonged to Major Karlheinz Pintsch, a long time adjutant to Hess, was found in the Russian archives, which backs up Kilzer's version of events. In the notebook Pintsch wrote that Hitler hoped an *"agreement with the Englishmen would be successful."* Pintsch noted that Hess' task -- five weeks before Germany's invasion of Russia -- was to *"bring about, if not a military alliance of Germany with England against Russia, then to bring about a neutralization of England."*

Pintsch was captured at the end of the war by the Russians and held prisoner for years, where he was subjected to brutal torture during interrogations that left him crippled for life. He could never hold a knife or fork afterwards. Pintsch's interrogation transcripts found in the same archive as the notebook show that Hitler was not surprised when news came through of Hess's capture...nor did he rant and rave about what Hess had done. Instead, Hitler calmly commented upon the risk and danger of Hess' mission, and read a letter out loud that Hess had sent him before taking off. From Hess' letter, Hitler read: *"And if this project... ends in failure...it will always be possible for you to deny all responsibility. Simply say I was out of my mind."*

The mission *did* end in failure and both Hitler and Churchill claimed that Hess was deranged. The mission was a failure because Churchill had no intention whatever of making peace with Germany. Hess was interrogated by British army officers, at which time he told them that he had a *"secret and vital message for the Duke of Hamilton"* and that he must see him immediately. The Duke met with Hess, and then briefed CHURCHILL on his conversation with Hess.

Hess was then hustled off to prison and was not allowed to talk with anyone thereafter. Hess' flight, but not his destination or his final fate, was first reported by Munich Radio in Germany on May 12. Hess' capture by the farmhand also received wide coverage in Britain, though his mission was not explained. He was dismissed in both Britain and German as a deranged man.

Hess spent the duration of the war in a British mental institution under constant guard, and was sentenced to life imprisonment at the Nuremberg Trials after the war. But for what? He had not killed anyone, nor had he ordered anyone killed. He did not even participate in the war. He was just another tragic victim of Jewish vengeance, which was what the Nuremburg Trials were all about. Hess died in Spandau prison at age 93 under suspicious circumstances, where he had spent 40 years under constant, close guard. He was never allowed to talk to anyone or to write anything, and was not even allowed to touch his son when he came to visit him once. This was cruel beyond belief.

On June 22, 1941, Germany began the invasion of the Soviet Union, called Operation Barbarossa. Hitler considered the invasion a "pre-emptive" strike, as both Germany and the Soviet Union seemed to understand that sooner or later a war between the two powers was inevitable; a matter of when, not whether. The Soviet Union had for some time been building up its forces, including vast number of tanks and warplanes; for what?, except to eventually invade Germany.

Germany was now fighting on two fronts, against the Soviet Union on one side and in the Battle of Britain on the other. On September 14, 1940 a conference was held at Hitler's headquarters. Hitler concluded that air superiority had not yet been established over Britain and "promised to review the situation on September 17, for possible landings in Britain on September 27 or October 8. But 3 days later when the evidence was clear that the German Air Force had greatly exaggerated the extent of their successes against the RAF, Hitler postponed Operation Sea Lion indefinitely to concentrate on the war with the Soviet Union.

Even after prevailing in the Battle of Britain, Lloyd George, Halifax, and other officials in the government, understood that Britain could not defeat Germany alone. Churchill's aim of total victory over Germany, especially after the fall of France, could only be achieved under one condition, and that was if he could draw the United States into the war on Britain's side. He had to have been highly confident that he could do that, else he would have had no choice but to accept Hitler's peace offer.

President Roosevelt was of the same mind as Churchill regarding war with Germany, and was more than willing to be drawn into it. In blatant violation of diplomatic protocol, Roosevelt began a secret exchange of letters with Churchill as soon as Churchill became First Lord of the Admiralty, instead of communicating with his co-equal, Prime Minister Chamberlain. In this exchange of letters Churchill made clear that he wanted to draw the United States in on Britain's side in an eventual war with Germany, and in return, Roosevelt made clear that that was his aim too. In Roosevelt, Churchill found a willing co-conspirator. Both men ardently wished for the same thing -- war with Germany.

Roosevelt even made it obvious to those around him by his words and actions that he was intent upon a war with Germany. But since he could not take the country into a war without a formal declaration from Congress, he was determined to do it by devious means. He and Churchill plotted together to bring America into the war without consulting Congress. By now, Roosevelt had purged his administration of those who opposed war and surrounded himself only with those who supported it, including Harry Hopkins, among others.

In January, 1941, Harry Hopkins, one of Roosevelt's closest advisors and troubleshooters, visited Churchill in London. Later on, Churchill wrote about his 1941 meeting with Hopkins: *"With gleaming eye and quiet, constrained passion he said 'The President is determined that we shall win the war together. Make no mistake about it. He has sent me here to tell you that at all costs and by all means he will carry you through, no matter what happens to him there is nothing that he will not do so far as he has human power.' There he sat, slim, frail, ill, but absolutely glowing with refined comprehension of the Cause. It was to be the defeat, ruin, and slaughter of Hitler, to the exclusion of all other purposes, loyalties and aims."*

Churchill sent a British agent, William Stephenson, code named "Intrepid," to the United States in 1940 with orders to do everything possible to bring the United States into the war. Stephenson and 300 or so other British agents set up in the Rockefeller Center in New York City, rent free, and *"intercepted mail, tapped wires, cracked safes, kidnapped...rumor mongered"* and incessantly smeared the *"isolationists"* who were opposed to the United States entering the war. This went on with the full knowledge and cooperation of Roosevelt, and with the collaboration of federal agencies. In fact, Stephenson served as a direct conduit between Churchill and Roosevelt.

As described in previous chapters, the Jews, both in Britain and America, were conducting a full scale propaganda war against Nazi Germany, and Stephenson and his "Operation Intrepid" joined them in this effort. In working toward their goal of bringing America into the war, Stephenson and his men worked hand in hand with American Jews, including the Hollywood Jews.

Gore Vidal, in his book "Screening History," 1992, (which is about how America's self image is determined and controlled by the movie industry in Hollywood), reported that beginning in 1937, Americans were subjected to one film after another glorifying England and the

The Myth of German Villainy

warrior heroes who built the British Empire. A key figure in generating all these pro-British movies was the Hungarian Jew, Alexander Korda. Korda began working in films in Budapest before WWI. When the Communist Jew Bela Kuhn took over the Hungarian government in 1919 and installed his all Jewish regime, he installed Korda as the head of the now nationalized Hungarian film industry. When the Kuhn regime was driven out by Admiral Horthy a few months later, Korda was imprisoned briefly, but soon released. He then went to Berlin to establish himself in the film industry there, but eventually moved on to London under pressure from the Nazis. In London, Korda founded the Denham film studio on a 165 acre estate outside London, and established his own roster of contract actors including Leslie Howard, Merle Oberon (who became the second Mrs. Korda in 1939), Wendy Barrie, Robert Donat, Maurice Evans, and Vivien Leigh. Korda became a leading figure in the British film industry, the founder of London Films, as well as the Denham studio, and the owner of British Lion Films, a film distributing company. (Only a Jew could start with nothing and build up an empire such as Korda's in such a short time, because a penniless Gentile would not have had his access to Jewish capital.)

As previously described herein, Churchill was well connected to Jews in Britain. At the beginning of the war, Churchill sent Korda to Hollywood to set up a movie studio there. Like Stephenson, Korda became Churchill's agent and propagandist in Hollywood. His movie studio began producing a steady stream of films about "brave little England standing up to the evil Nazis." But Korda was not the only one producing pro-British, anti-Nazi movies in Hollywood. As also previously described herein, Hollywood was owned and controlled by Jews, and concurrent with Korda's films, every Hollywood studio cranked out a steady stream of pro-British, anti-German films without any prompting from Churchill. The Hollywood Jews, in coordination with other powerful Jews, were already fully engaged in the propaganda war against Germany. But Korda's case was unique because he was virtually an agent of the British government and an integral part of the highly coordinated, highly controlled propaganda organization in America, whose purpose was to bring America into the war on Britain's side.

Churchill understood the power of the Jews in both Britain and America. He had become Prime Minister primarily as the result of the backing of his Jewish support group, The Focus. According to Professor Michael J. Cohen, in his book, "Churchill and the Jews:"

"[Churchill] believed that the Zionist movement commanded powerful political and economic influence, particularly in the United States. As late as in December, 1939, he lectured his cabinet colleagues on the important role Zionists could play in mobilizing American resources to the British war effort. He told them that it had not been for light or sentimental reasons that the Government had issued the Balfour Declaration in 1917, but in order to mobilize American support. In 1939, Churchill believed that history would repeat itself, that the Zionists, via their proxies across the Atlantic, could be influential in accelerating the vitally needed early entry of the Americans into the war."

Though the American public was staunchly opposed to entering the war, Roosevelt was determined to find a way in. The published minutes of an August, 1941 War Cabinet meeting in London contain Churchill's report to the War Cabinet. Churchill said: *"He* [Roosevelt] *obviously was determined that they* [the United States] *should come in* [to the war]. Included also in the minutes was this Churchill comment: *"The President had said he would wage war but not declare it and that he would become more and more provocative. If the Germans did not like it, they could attack American forces...Everything was to be done to force an incident."* But Germany refused to take the bait and was very careful to avoid any incident which could be used as a pretext by the United States to enter the war.

On July 5, 1941, Admiral Little, of the British Naval Delegation in Washington, wrote to Admiral Pound, the First Sea Lord: *"The brightest hope for getting America into the war lies in the escorting arrangements to Iceland, and let us hope the Germans will not be slow in attacking them."* Little added, perhaps jokingly: *"Otherwise I think it would be best for us to organize an attack by our own submarines and preferably on the escort!"* A few weeks earlier, Churchill, looking for a chance to bring America into the war, wrote to Pound regarding the German warship, *Prinz Eugen: "It would be better for instance that she should be located by a U.S.*

*ship as this might tempt her to fire on that ship, thus providing the incident
for which the U.S. government would be so grateful.*" Incidents in the North
Atlantic did occur, increasingly, as the United States approached war
with Germany.

Between August 9 and 12, 1941, before America entered the war,
President Roosevelt met with Churchill on board the British battleship
Prince of Wales anchored off Argentia, Newfoundland. Together they
drafted the Atlantic Charter setting out their aims for war and peace.
U.S. Navy involvement in the ongoing Battle of the Atlantic was also
discussed. The U.S. Navy was already involved in escorting convoys of
war material across the Atlantic to Britain, an act of war according to
the international rules of war, but after the Newfoundland meeting, the
U.S. Navy began actively confronting German submarines. By now, the
U.S. was already in an undeclared, de facto war with Germany; a war
Germany did not bring about, did not want, and a war which Germany
desperately tried to avoid.

But Roosevelt wanted to be all the way in against Germany and
that would require a Congressional declaration of war, though, so far,
Germany had managed to avoid providing a pretext for that. Germany
had entered into a Tripartite Agreement with Italy and Japan, one of the
terms of which was that if one of its members were to wind up in a war,
then all three would be in the war. Since Roosevelt was unsuccessful
in provoking the Germans into a war, he turned his attention to Japan.
By provoking a war with Japan, he would then have the war he wanted
with Germany. Both Joseph E. Persico, in his book, "Roosevelt's Secret
War," and Robert B. Stinnett, in his book, "Day of Deceit," prove beyond
a shadow of a doubt, based on years of research of scores of previously
classified documents, that Roosevelt provoked the Japanese into attacking
our fleet in Hawaii, but also that he refused to warn the commanders
in Hawaii of the impending Japanese attack, though he knew precisely
when and in what force the attack would come. After the Japanese attack,
public opinion swung from strongly against, to strongly in favor of war.
Congress wasted no time in formally declaring war against Japan. The
Tripartite Agreement brought Germany into a war with the United
States. Both Churchill and Roosevelt had accomplished their aim.

Since Roosevelt had goaded Japan into war only to have the war he really wanted with Germany, he announced that the war against Germany would have first priority over Japan. When Germany was defeated, Roosevelt said, then we would turn our full attention to defeating Japan. But first, Germany. On February 15, 1942, Churchill said this about America's entry into the war: *"This is what I have dreamed of, aimed at, worked for, and now it has come to pass."* Thirty years earlier, Churchill had told Lord Asquith that...his life's ambition was *"to command great victorious armies in battle."*

****

The brutal war with the Soviet Union continued apace. The Soviet Union and Germany represented two gigantic opposing forces with conflicting political, social, economic, religious and cultural systems, which one day were bound to clash. Hitler saw himself as the defender of Western Christian Civilization against a rapacious foe which threatened to sweep over and obliterate Europe. He had done his best to settle matters with Britain and the West before launching his attack on the Soviet Union, but Britain and the United States refused to cooperate. In his decision to invade the Soviet Union, Hitler calculated that time was running out for Germany. The Soviet Union was becoming more powerful by the day. If Germany had waited to attack, then it might have been too late. In retrospect, it appears almost insane that Britain and the United States chose to ally themselves with Jewish controlled, Communist Russia against their own brethren -- Christian Germany.

But we did more than simply "ally" ourselves with Soviet Russia. According to U.S. Congressman Hamilton Fish, in his book, "Tragic Deception: FDR & America's Involvement in World War II," Under the Lend-Lease Act, FDR sent Russia 20,000 aircraft, 400,000 trucks, thousands of tons of munitions, vast quantities of leather for shoes, cloth for uniforms, hundreds of miles of barbed wire and telephone lines, thousands of locomotives and automobiles, much needed food, supplies of all kinds on a huge scale, and equipment for setting up new industrial plants to replace those destroyed by the Germans. If not for this endless cornucopia of war materiel, Russia would have been defeated.

Chapter 21

The Allied Goal? Destruction of Germany!

"You must understand that this war is not against Hitler or National Socialism, but against the strength of the German people, which is to be smashed once and for all, regardless whether it is in the hands of Hitler or a Jesuit priest." Winston Churchill, 1940, as quoted in Emrys Hughes book, "Winston Churchill, His Career in War and Peace."

Frederick Lindemann, later known as Lord Cherwell, was a Jew born in Baden-Baden, Germany but raised in England. He went back to Germany to obtain a Ph.D. in physics from the University of Berlin, after which, he returned to England. Lindemann was an early pioneer of British aviation technological development, and when Churchill became Prime Minister, he appointed Lindemann as the British government's (and his) leading scientific advisor. As a Jew, Lindemann harbored a pathological hatred, not only of the Nazis, but of Germany and the German people. Vengeance against the Germans motivated his every action and opinion. He was a leading advocate from the start of "area bombing" of German cities, and devised a "plan" to carry it out.

The Lindemann plan proposed that Britain should forget military targets and concentrate air attacks on Germany's civilian population in order to break the morale of the German people. After their morale was broken, Lindemann believed, and Churchill believed also, the German public would demand an unconditional surrender to the Allies. His plan proposed that *"bombing must be directed to working class houses. Middle class houses have too much space round them, so are bound to waste bombs."*

"It should be emphasized," Lindemann said, *" that the destruction of houses, public utilities, transport and lives, the creation of a refugee problem on an unprecedented scale, and the breakdown of morale both at home and at the battle fronts by fear of extended and intensified bombing, are accepted and intended aims of our bombing policy. They are not by-products of attempts to hit factories."* In other words, killing massive numbers of civilians should be the primary aim of the bombing raids.

Lindemann was not writing in a vacuum when he created the Lindemann Plan. Professor Solly Zuckerman and Professor Desmond Bernal, both Jews, also did studies on the effects of area bombing on structures and people, and both became strong advocates of massive bombing of Germany. Bombing cities as a means of waging total war had already become an accepted strategy among the members of Britain's "war party." Britain began developing and building long range, heavy bombers as early as 1933. The United States did the same. The Lancaster, the B17 and the B24 were built for no purpose except to destroy cities and inflict massive casualties on the German population. Military operations require small, fast, "tactical" planes. Thousand plane armadas of four-engine, heavy "strategic" bombers had no military purpose. Colonel (later Brigadier General) Robin Olds, a highly respected officer and USAF fighter pilot who served in both WWII and Vietnam, stated more than once that the so-called strategic bombing program was ineffective, wasteful and pointless. It is generally acknowledged today that the strategic bombing program did not shorten the war by a single day, and that in the end, it served no military purpose. After all, Germany reached her highest level of war production in the last months of the war when the bombing was most intense.

Colonel Olds, among many others, was of the opinion that fighter bombers carrying a single bomb flying low and fast would have been far more effective against German military and strategic targets. He said that a single Mustang could have dropped a five hundred pound bomb through the window of any factory in Germany. It was impossible to hit a factory with a huge formation of bombers flying at 25,000 feet without destroying everything for miles around it. He also emphasized that this would have greatly minimized civilian casualties. Perhaps the colonel was naive. Perhaps he did not understand that the very purpose of "strategic bombing" was to *maximize* civilian casualties. In a word, the purpose of "strategic bombing" was genocide!!

While Britain and the United States were building thousands upon thousands of four-engine, long range, heavy bombers, designed for no other purpose than the destruction of cities and the slaughter of massive numbers of civilians, Germany built only light, maneuverable, low altitude bombers designed for ground support. These planes were unsuitable for genocidal terror bombing. Hitler only undertook the bombing of British civilian targets reluctantly, three months after the RAF began a campaign of carpet bombing German cities. Hitler would have been willing at any time to stop the slaughter.

Churchill's War Cabinet adopted the Lindemann Plan in March, 1942, which then became Britain's official policy. This decision of the War Cabinet was kept a closely guarded secret from the British public throughout the war and for many years afterwards. The British people were told that only military and industrial targets were bombed, and any damage beyond that was unintentional. The true nature of British bombing of German cities and civilians was revealed in 1961 in a book titled *Science and Government* by the physicist and novelist, Sir Charles Snow. The following passage from the book was immediately translated and published in several languages:

"Early in 1942 Professor Lindemann, by this time Lord Cherwell and a member of the Cabinet, laid a cabinet paper before the Cabinet on the strategic

bombing of Germany. It described in quantitative terms the effect on Germany of a British bombing offensive in the next eighteen months (approximately March 1942–September 1943). The paper laid down a strategic policy. The bombing must be directed essentially against German working-class houses. Middle-class houses have too much space round them and so are bound to waste bombs; factories and "military objectives" had long since been forgotten, except in official bulletins, since they were much too difficult to find and hit. The paper claimed that—given a total concentration of effort on the production and use of aircraft—it would be possible, in all the larger towns of Germany (that is, those with more than 50,000 inhabitants), to destroy 50 per cent of all houses."

Angus Calder wrote, in his book, "The Peoples' War," 1969: *"It may be Inconvenient History but England rather than Germany initiated the murderous slaughter of bombing civilians thus bringing about retaliation. [Neville] Chamberlain conceded that it [bombing of civilians and cities]was "absolutely contrary to International law." It began in 1940 and Churchill believed it held the secret of victory. He was convinced that raids of sufficient intensity could destroy Germany's morale, and so his War Cabinet planned a campaign that abandoned the accepted practice of attacking the enemy's armed forces and, instead made civilians the primary target. Night after night, RAF bombers in ever increasing numbers struck throughout Germany, usually at working class housing, because it was more densely packed."*

Britain devoted more of her resources to RAF Bomber Command than to all the other branches of the British military combined. Having discovered early in the war that it was nearly impossible to hit a small target such as a factory or a runway from high in the air, Bomber Command decided to concentrate entire air wings into bomber raids of a thousand planes at a time on German cities. To avoid airplane losses to German fighter planes and anti-aircraft fire from the ground, these massive attacks were flown only at night at high altitude. The British gave up on military targets early in the war and decided to concentrate entirely on Germany's cities, using the city centers as their aiming point. The city centers were the oldest part of the cities, dating back to the middle ages and beyond. In the city centers the streets were narrow and the buildings were close together, constructed mostly of highly flammable wood, covered with plaster, which ignited easily and burned furiously. The people in these old cities suffered agonizing deaths as they were fried, cooked, and broiled by the fires, or blown to pieces by the explosions.

****

The United States entered the air war in Europe in September, 1942 with air groups of B-24s and B-17s flying out of Britain. The United States at first did not attack civilians directly but attempted to carry out precision bombing of German factories and military installations. Whereas the British flew all their raids at night, the Americans did their bombing runs during daylight, to improve bombing accuracy. But "precision bombing" at high altitude was a fantasy, whether done during the day or at night, as more bombs invariably fell on areas surrounding the target than on the target itself. After a time, the Americans gave up on "precision bombing" and joined the British in "area bombing," that is, targeting entire cities.

By the end of the war, 1,000 German cities and towns had been bombed, with some 160 of the largest reduced to rubble. These cities and towns were among Europe's oldest and finest; similar in artistic and cultural value to Florence, Paris or Rome. These destroyed cities contained the accumulated cultural treasures of centuries, including art, art galleries, statuary, architecture, libraries, museums, palaces, bridges, guild halls, churches and cathedrals. The accouterments of this highly developed culture which took a thousand years to build and accumulate were obliterated in minutes by the bombs.

Of course, there was plenty of objection at the time to what was happening, though the vast majority of the public supported it. The liberal Catholic weekly *Commonweal*, hardly a pacifist organ, early in 1944 denounced the policy of strategic bombing as *"the murder of innocent people and the suicide of our civilization."*

The London Times Review on the British official History of the Strategic Air Offensive, commented: *One closes these volumes feeling uneasy, that the true heroes of the story they tell are neither the contending Air Marshalls, nor even the 58,888 officers and men of Bomber Command who were killed in action. The heroes were the inhabitants of the German cities under attack; the men, women and children who stoically endured and worked on among the flaming ruins of their homes and factories, up till the moment when the Allied Armies overran them.*

This kind of savagery became self-perpetuating during the course of the war until all pretence of complying with the traditional "Rules of Civilized Warfare" was finally abandoned, as both sides tacitly adopted the principle that any act was justifiable if it held out even a remote possibility that it might stave off the awful consequences of defeat.

But another factor was also at work in the pointless and senseless continuation of carpet bombing German cities and towns, even after victory was certain, and that was simple "inertia." The massive bombing raids continued because that was what Bomber Command and the United States Army Air Force had been organized to do. Like any complex, dynamic organization, after a time the entire military industrial complex took on a life of its own and sort of ran itself. The aircraft assembly lines, both in Britain and America, cranked out a steady stream of new bombers. The bomb manufacturers ran their bomb assembly lines day and night. The aircraft fuel supply system functioned automatically, delivering aircraft fuel on time at points needed. The training commands continued to produce thousands of new pilots and air crewmen. Staff officers assigned to pick targets and to brief the bomber crews before takeoff continued to do their jobs. The entire military/industrial complex designed and organized to deliver thousands of tons of bombs daily on German cities worked like a giant machine on auto-pilot. No one had to tell it to do its job. Just the reverse. Someone in high authority would have had to tell it to stop. Even if someone had told it to stop, he would have met tremendous bureaucratic resistance. Moreover, those in command of the giant bombing apparatus, Churchill, Roosevelt, Air Marshall Harris, and General Hap Arnold, were inclined to continue the bombing, justified or not.

Both Germany and Japan would have ended the war at any time with an armistice if they had been given the chance to do so, even as early as the spring of 1943. If that had been allowed to happen, the greatest majority of death and destruction would have been avoided. But the unconditional surrender policy of Roosevelt, supported by Churchill, made such an end impossible. The demand for unconditional surrender guaranteed that the long, grinding struggle which left much of Western Europe in ruin, with millions dead, would continue to the bitter end. Churchill and Roosevelt, not Hitler, were responsible for that. In the summer of 1943 when Churchill was about to leave London to meet Roosevelt at a conference in Quebec, a reporter for Time magazine asked Churchill, "Will you offer peace terms to Germany?" Churchill, in a jovial voice, answered back, "Heavens, No! They would accept immediately." Everyone laughed.

Near the end of the war, most of the big cities and towns in Germany had already been destroyed so small towns and villages were now being targeted for no reason except that they had not been bombed before. Thousands of innocent German civilians suffered horrific deaths every day and every night for no reason except the whim of the staff officer who more or less arbitrarily chose their town as that day's target. Everyone employed within the giant bombing apparatus continued to do the job they had been assigned to do, and no one in authority told them to stop, so the bombing continued, day after day, night after night.

Norman Stone, Professor of Modern History at Oxford, wrote in the Daily Mail: *"Already, by 1944...(W)e went on bombing German cities months and months after it had been clear that we would win, and that Stalin would be as potentially deadly an enemy. Some of the bombing was just pointless. In the last days of the war, we struck at the old gingerbread towns south of Wurzburg, where there was no military target at all . . . just refugees, women and children. Of these acts of gratuitous sadism, the worst was the bombing of Dresden."*

Dresden! Dresden was one of the most beautiful cities in Europe before it was bombed, a cultural center filled with elegant palaces, cathedrals and statues. It was a fairy tale city, with winding cobblestone streets, church steeples and gingerbread houses. It had no military significance whatever. In the last year of the war, it had been a hospital city, caring for thousands of wounded German soldiers. Not a single German military unit was stationed there. In the early weeks of 1945, the coldest winter in a century, hundreds of thousands of refugees had flooded into Dresden to escape the advancing Russian army. The inhabitants of Dresden took in as many of these poor souls as possible, but it was not possible to take them all in. Hundreds of thousands of frightened, hungry, desperate refugees concentrated in the Old Town, camping out on the sidewalks and in every garden and every city park. They slept on the ground and huddled together to keep from freezing to death. Children whimpered and begged for food. City social services were overwhelmed, though they did all they could to try to feed them and care for them. Then the bombers came.

The first wave of bombers were British, which arrived over the city at 10 PM on February 13, 1945, dropping thousands of huge, high explosive bombs on the Old Town, thick with refugees, to blast the roofs off buildings in preparation for incendiary bombs which were to follow close behind. The high explosive bombs knocked out the air raid warning system, destroyed the fire stations, broke the water mains and caused massive destruction and death. The crowds of refugees had no place to run to and no place to hide. Then came the bombers loaded with incendiary bombs which turned the Old Town into a howling ocean of fire. Air temperatures rose to 1,100 degrees Fahrenheit. Winds up to 100 mph sucked all oxygen into the center of the storm. Scores of thousands were burned alive. This late in the war, the science of bombing had been well worked out. The pattern of bombs dropped by the British were designed to produce a "firestorm," and the Dresden firestorm was one of the most spectacular of the war.

Thousands suffocated in cellars as the oxygen was sucked out by the flames outside. Thousands more were hurled into the air like rag dolls and sucked by the ferocious winds right into the inferno. The air suction of the firestorm was so strong that it uprooted trees and lifted roofs from houses miles away. Utter panic struck the people. Horses reared and ran into the crowds. Wild animals such as lions and tigers escaped from the broken enclosures of the zoo and ran into the terrified crowds. Huge snakes slithered between the feet of those fleeing. Hospital trains, still filled with wounded soldiers from the front, were burning and tried to pull out of the station, and in the process severing limbs from young children who had sought cover from the bombs underneath the trains.

The next wave of bombers came three hours later with high explosives and anti-personnel bombs. The spacing of the waves of bombers, as well as the types of bombs dropped, had been carefully calculated to produce the highest kill rate possible. This third wave of bombers caught the emergency crews and fire crews, as well as throngs of those escaping the fires out in the open, as planned. The result was a slaughter.

The next day, the American 8th Air Force completed the destruction of the city. During the bombing, a total of 1,300 British and American heavy bombers dropped nearly 4,000 tons of high explosive bombs and incendiary devices on Dresden. The most disgraceful episode of the aerial attack on Dresden was the American Mustang fighter planes that followed the wave of B-17 bombers. Swarms of people fleeing the bombs and seeking refuge on the banks of the Elbe River were strafed by the Mustang fighters. Piles of bodies were lying everywhere along the banks as a result of the strafing. This is how one eye-witness described it: ". . . scores of Mustang fighters diving low over the people huddled on the banks of the Elbe, as well as on the larger lawns of the Grosse Garden, in order to shoot them up."

The city was completely destroyed, and there were so many dead bodies that the Germany army sent units in to gather them up, pile them onto funeral pyres made from lengths of railroad tracks and burn them. American POWs held in the city were brought in to assist. Kurt Vonnegut, the American author of "Slaughterhouse Five," was one of them. They went through the cellars and pulled out all those who had suffocated or burned to death and then burned them. There were so many bodies that it took weeks to finish the job. They piled up dead soldiers, young and old women, boys in short pants, girls with long braids, Red Cross nurses, babies. These pyres burned day and night. No one will ever know the total number of civilian casualties resulting from the bombing of Dresden because of the countless refugees who had taken refuge in the city, but estimates have ranged as high as 500,000. British historian David Irving, who wrote the first authoritative book on the bombing of Dresden estimates that 135,000 were killed.

There was no military necessity for the bombing of Dresden. It was simple mass murder of a people we had grown to hate as the result of Jewish anti-German propaganda. Yet, the bombing of cities and towns continued, even as the Reich was collapsing. Those who planned and carried out these bombing raids were and are war criminals by anyone's definition! While the Simon Wiesenthal's and other Jewish Nazi hunters are still combing the geriatric wards around the world for German "war criminals," who may only have served their country at war, one should think about the crime of Dresden, and the hundreds of other cities and towns blown to bits and burned to the ground, for no reason except malice. *"Those innocents who lost their lives in Dresden were killed - not because of something they had done, but because of an accident of birth. Those who died in the Dresden Holocaust on February 13-14, 1945 were simply Germans."* --Ingrid Rimland, Ed.d.

On February 16, just two days after the bombing of Dresden, British bombers attacked the tiny town of Pforzheim, known only for producing crockery and dinnerware, and killed half of its 63,000 inhabitants. These attacks continued right up to the day Germany surrendered.

In the early days of the development of the bomber as a weapon of war, Winston Churchill said: *"The air opened paths along which death and terror could be carried far behind the lines of the actual enemy; to women, children, the aged, the sick, who in earlier struggles would perforce have been left untouched."* Churchill's chillingly detached vision of the capabilities of war from the air were finding their fruition in Britain's air campaign against Germany.

Estimates of civilians killed in the bombing of Germany range to well over a million, possibly as high as two million, with millions more suffering horrible injuries. Near the end of the war when Germany was essentially defenseless and the bombing was most intense, German cities and towns, especially in the east, were teeming with masses of uncounted refugees fleeing the advancing Russian army. No one knows how many refugees even to the nearest million. Scores of thousands of these poor people were simply burned to a cinder in the fires resulting from the bombing, with no trace left behind, and therefore could not be counted. There has been a tendency in recent years to reduce the estimated number killed in deference to "political correctness." Coming clean about the true nature of Allied atrocities against the Germans during the war is not a popular thing to do today. After all, we were the "good guys."

B-17s bombing a German city.

German civilian corpses after an Allied bombing raid.
This was indiscriminate slaughter of innocents.

Stacks of bodies after the bombing of Dresden.

They have cleared the streets and civilians try to go on with their lives after their city was destroyed. What choice did they have?

Essential transportation is restored in the midst of rubble

Germany was filled with feral children whose parents had been killed in the bombings. They wandered the streets searching for food.

**Another German city burns to the ground
after being fire bombed by the Allies.**

**This is the enemy Churchill and Lindemann went
after with their massive bombing raids.**

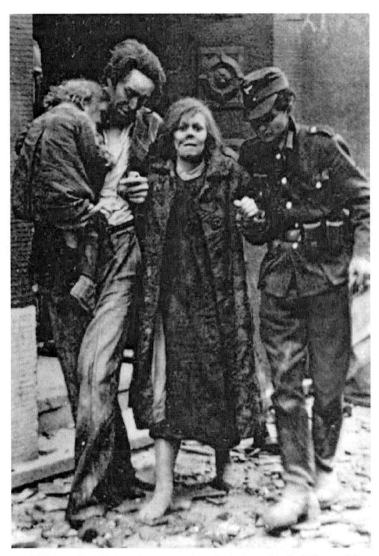

Churchill and Lindemann decided that the RAF would
concentrate its attacks on civilian instead of military targets.
This is the result. A million innocent German civilians like these
were baked, fried, broiled or blown to bits by the Allied bombing
campaign, the great majority of whom were women, children and
old people. The point was to kill as many of them as possible.

These women and children were the lucky ones; they got out alive. Their homes were deliberately targeted by Britain's Lindemann Plan.

Not long before, this was a thriving neighborhood.

This was a single bomb hit. By the time the raid was over, these
buildings and all the other buildings in this German town,
including the thousand year old fountain, were flattened

An elderly German woman looks sadly upon
a pile of dead school children.

This stately building is still standing, but thousands like it were either gutted (as this one was) or destroyed completely all over Germany by Allied "strategic bombing." The British bombing campaign specifically targeted Germany's built up cities and towns instead of military targets. The aim was to destroy Germany and kill as many people as possible. This building contained a hospital.

160 German cities and towns were destroyed by British and
American bombing raids. This was done to "terrorize" the German
people. Destroying these cities served no military purpose
and did not shorten the war by a single day. The purpose was
to destroy Germany and kill as many Germans as possible.

Bombed out and nowhere to go.

****

**Let us not forget that we did this…, to people
who were exactly like ourselves!!!**

****

Professor Frederick Lindemann, author of the Lindemann Plan for the mass murder of German civilians by aerial bombardment, was also an enthusiastic supporter of the "Morganthau Plan," a plan to dismantle Germany's industry after the war and reduce Germany to a medieval, peasant society. Morganthau wrote in his diary, p.11, *"Germany must be turned into a wasteland, as happened there during the 30-year War."* Morganthau was Roosevelt's Secretary of the Treasury and a close friend and advisor to Roosevelt.

Morganthau's assistant in the Treasury was the Communist Jew, Harry Dexter White (Weiss). It was actually he, White, who drafted the Morganthau Plan. According to John T. Flynn, in his book, "The Roosevelt Myth," 1948 and revised in 1956, White was a secret agent of the Soviet Union and served as a conduit for top secret information to the Soviets. (This was proved to be true after *perestroika* when access was gained to Soviet archives.) According to Flynn, Communists who were totally loyal to the Soviet Union held key positions in every department and agency of the Roosevelt administration, almost all of them Jews, who passed every secret immediately to the Soviets. They also received orders directly from Stalin. One of these Jewish agents of the Soviets, Nathan Silvermaster, who had worked in the Agriculture Department, was appointed by Roosevelt to be the head of the Near East Division of the Board of Economic Welfare. He formed the "Silvermaster Group," a Soviet spy agency, which consisted of highly placed officials within the Roosevelt administration, including Harry Dexter White. (The Silvermaster Group included Nathan Silvermaster, his wife Helen, Schlomer Adler, Norman Bursler, Frank Coe, Bela Gold, Sonia Steinman Gold, Lauchlin Currie, Irving Kaplan, George Silverman, William Ullman, Anatole Volkov and Harry Dexter White -- all Jews and all Communists, and all highly placed officials within the Roosevelt administration.) White had unlimited access to the most secret information of the government. The "Secret Service" was an agency of the Treasury Department and as Assistant Secretary of the Treasury, White had complete inside information, which he assiduously passed to the Jews who controlled the Soviet Union. Harry Dexter White's personal secretary was a Communist Jewess, Sonia Gold, supplied to him by Nathan Silvermaster.

In the spring of 1944, according to Flynn, the Silvermaster Group in Washington received instructions from the Kremlin outlining Russia's plan for Germany after surrender. The instructions were clear: destroy Germany's capacity as an industrial nation and reduce her to the level of a mere agricultural country. The Silvermaster Group passed these instructions on to Harry Dexter White for implementation. White was given the job because of his relationship with Morganthau, and because of Morganthau's relationship with Roosevelt. White got to work immediately and produced the infamous Morganthau Plan.

The Morganthau Plan called for Germany to be partitioned into small independent states, with part of Germany to go to Russia and parts to other countries, including Poland. Germany's main industrial centers, including the Saar area, the Ruhr area, and Upper Silesia, were to be internationalized or annexed by neighboring countries. All of Germany's industrial equipment was to be taken down and shipped to the Soviet Union. What couldn't be taken away was to be destroyed. The mines were to be destroyed by flooding them. Germany was a thoroughly industrialized country. The Morganthau Plan would obviously have resulted in millions of starvation deaths in Germany, as they well knew.

When Roosevelt left for the Quebec Conference on September 12, 1944 to meet with Prime Minister Churchill, he took neither Secretary of State Hull nor Secretary of War Stimson with him as protocol would have required, but took only his Secretary and Assistant Secretary of the Treasury Hans Morganthau, Jr. and Harry Dexter White. Roosevelt already had some foreknowledge of the Morganthau Plan and knew that Hull and Stimson would stalwartly oppose it, so he left them at home. At the conference, Morganthau and White presented the plan that White had drawn up to Roosevelt and Churchill.

Churchill reacted with anger and indignation when the Plan was presented to him, as did his Foreign Minister Anthony Eden. But in the end, Churchill agreed to the Plan. It was subsequently revealed that Morganthau offered him $6.5 billion in Lend Lease money which Churchill was in no position to refuse. Britain was broke and desperately needed the money, so he withdrew his objections in exchange for the money and the Plan became the doctrine of the Allies.

The final paragraph of the Plan called for withdrawing American and British armed forces out of Germany as soon as possible after the surrender, leaving Germany under the control of the Soviet Union. When Roosevelt returned to Washington, he made no announcement concerning this momentous agreement, and he told neither Hull nor Stimson. They only learned that the Morganthau Plan had been adopted by reading it in the newspapers several days later. They also read that Churchill was to get the $6,500,000,000 as a *quid pro quo* for withdrawing his objections to the Plan. Both men called the Plan "blind vengeance," and both were outraged over it. When they confronted Roosevelt about it, Roosevelt at first denied it. It nevertheless became American and Allied policy.

The Morganthau Plan was actually a Russian Plan. The Kremlin had issued orders to its agent in the American government, Harry Dexter White, who drew up the plan according to the Kremlin's specifications, then handed it over to Hans Morganthau, Jr., who then presented it to a sick and enfeebled Roosevelt, who then made it American policy. Churchill was bribed to go along. The Jews had prevailed again! The Jews who controlled the Soviet Union had combined their efforts with the Jews who controlled the Roosevelt Administration and produced a plan which was enthusiastically embraced by the British Jew Frederick Lindemann, to destroy their nemesis, Nazi Germany, completely, and for all time. International Jewry, whether in the Soviet Union, the United States or in Britain, possessed a pathological hatred for the German people and harbored a burning desire for vengeance. They combined their efforts, not in the interest of the countries they represented, but to achieve the aims of world Jewry. Now, they would have their vengeance upon the hated Germans. The Germans, of course, obtained a copy of the Morganthau Plan, a plan for their total destruction, from which they came to understand that they had no choice but to fight on.

In January, 1943, Prime Minister Churchill and President Franklin D. Roosevelt had met at the City of Casablanca, Morocco at what is known as the Casablanca Conference. Joseph Stalin did not attend. The most notable development to come out of the Casablanca Conference was Roosevelt's proclamation of "unconditional surrender" as the policy of the Allies. Roosevelt and Churchill also decided at the Conference to increase the strategic bombing of German cities. Faced with the demand for unconditional surrender, after which they would be subjected to the destructive and murderous Morgnathau plan, the Germans faced only two options: fight on and be destroyed, or surrender and be destroyed. Fighting on seemed the more honorable path to take.

In the end a watered down version of the Morganthau Plan, known as Joint Chiefs of Staff Directive 1067, or JCS-1067, became the Allied occupational doctrine. JCS-1067 was only slightly less onerous than the original Morganthau Plan.

****

Hitler had repeatedly tried to reach a peace agreement with Britain, first after the war with Poland, and second after Dunkirk, only to have his peace overtures rejected. He had also sent Rudolph Hess on a Quixotic mission during the Battle of Britain to try to arrange a peace agreement, but Churchill refused to even listen to Hess. He had had him thrown into prison where he remained for the duration of the war.

The British wanted only to destroy Germany and had no interest in making peace. Hitler, on the other hand, would have welcomed any chance to reach a peace agreement with both Britain and the United States at any time during the war. "Unconditional surrender" was Roosevelt's and Churchill's answer. At the same time that they refused to accept anything short of unconditional surrender, Britain and the United States continued relentlessly to destroy one German city after another by massive bomber raids.

The Nuremburg Trials were conducted after the war in which the Nazi leaders were found guilty of war crimes and executed or given long prison sentences. But those who sat in judgment of the Germans were no less guilty. The so-called "Holocaust" was invented at the Nuremburg trials, to the absolute astonishment of the accused, who claimed to a man that they never heard of any such thing until the trials began. Considerable doubt has been cast upon Holocaust claims in recent years, but even if the so-called Holocaust were true in every detail, it would not compare as a war crime to the bombing of Germany. The word "genocide" is used against the Germans, but the bombing of Germany was the true genocide. It was also a culturecide. The bombing campaign was carried out to destroy Germany completely, and to kill as many Germans as possible. German civilians were killed in their masses, not because they were guilty of anything, but only because they were Germans. That is the very definition of "genocide."

The great 13th-century Catholic theologian St. Thomas Aquinas and the Dutch Protestant Hugo Grotius of the 17th century worked out a "Just War Theory" to determine the morality of a particular war. For a war to be just, they said, first of all, it must be defensive in nature.

Prisoners taken in war must be protected. The war must be publically declared by a properly constituted authority. To be moral or "just," the war must be winnable – a state cannot devote the population to a suicide mission with no chance of winning. To meet the requirements of a "just" war, a war cannot result in more evils than it eliminates. After the war is over, only those directly responsible for aggression can be punished. "Revenge" is not a justification for war, nor is "revenge" justified after a victory. Revenge taking is antithetical to Christian values. A "just" war must not be directed at civilians. Finally, the decision to go to war must be taken as a last resort after all efforts to avoid war have been exhausted. Both the cause of the war and the conduct in executing it have to be just.

If these standards had been applied at Nuremberg, all sides would have been guilty of war crimes.

Chapter 22

Germany as Victim

As the Kaiser did not start World War I, Hitler and the Nazis did not start World War II. Moreover, Hitler did everything within his power to avoid a war with Britain, France and the United States. He also made a number of peace initiatives as the war progressed, all of which were either rejected or ignored. Britain and France declared war on Germany, not the other way around. All of Germany's military initiatives in the West, i.e., the invasion of Norway, the invasion of France, the occupation of the Low Countries, etc., were preemptive strikes that were at bottom defensive in nature. The invasion of the Soviet Union was preemptive, as well. Germany also did not start the bombing of civilians, Britain did.

If the question is asked, what did Hitler and the Nazis do to earn their dreadful reputation, the answer will invariably be "the Holocaust." Yet, the Holocaust did not occur (if it occurred at all) until after the war began, and only then as a result of the war. Yet, the Nazis had been characterized as evil monsters long before the war began; but on what basis? Nothing had happened to the Jews up to the time the war began except for certain restrictions placed on them, despite all the false accusations of brutal repression and predictions of extermination constantly spewing out of the Jewish press. What finally happened to the Jews, if it happened at all, was in the nature of a self-fulfilling prophecy, brought on by the very ones doing the prophesying.

There were legitimate reasons for the attitude of the Nazis toward the Jews. Hitler and the Nazis saw Communism as an existential threat, not just to Germany, but to Western Civilization, and they saw the Jews and Communism as one and the same thing. Moreover, conflating Communism with Judaism was not unfounded, in as much as the Communist Party in Germany, before it was outlawed by Hitler, was 78% Jewish. It was also amply clear to the Germans that it was the Jews who had taken control of the Soviet Union in a Communist revolution and they who carried out the Red Terror. It was also clear that the leaders of each and every Communist revolution in Europe, including the 1918 revolution in Germany, was instigated and led by Jews, e.g., Bela Kuhn in Hungary, Karl Liebknecht, Rosa Luxemburg, Kurt Eisner and Eugene Levine, et al, in Germany, and Amadeo Bordiga in Italy. The Spanish Civil War, 1936-1939, was actually caused by at attempted take-over of Spain by Communists, led, as in all the other cases, by Jews with the backing of the Soviet Union.

As if that were not enough, in 1934 immediately after Hitler and the Nazis came to power, World Jewry declared a holy war against Germany and used all its influence and power throughout the world to try to cripple the German economy. This was well before Hitler and the Nazis had the chance to take any kind of action against Germany's Jews. They then pursued a relentless propaganda campaign against Germany and her Nazi leaders, and used their influence over the leaders of Britain and the United States to instigate a war against Germany. The Jews wanted to destroy Germany. This was no idle threat, as the Jews had already succeeded in bringing down the Czarist regime in Russia, after which they took total control of the country. They were now targeting Germany. They organized and funded the Communist International (Comintern), the sole purpose of which was to bring down existing regimes in Europe, including Germany, and replace them with Jewish led Soviet Republics.

World Jewry's attitude toward Germany, as represented in the following statement by the French Jewish professor Alexander Kulisher, was well known by everyone. Kulisher wrote in 1937: *"Germany is the enemy of Judaism and must be pursued with deadly hatred. The goal of Judaism today is: a merciless campaign against all German peoples and the complete destruction of the nation. We demand a complete blockade of trade, the importation of raw materials stopped and retaliation towards every German, woman and child."*

On December 3, 1942, Chaim Weizmann, President of the World Jewish Congress, made the following statement in New York: *"We are not denying and we are not afraid to confess, this war is our war and that it is waged for the liberation of Jewry....stronger than all fronts together is our front, that of Jewry. We are not only giving this war our financial support on which the entire war production is based. We are not only providing our full propaganda power which is the moral energy that keeps this war going. The guarantee of victory is predominantly based on weakening the enemy forces, on destroying them within their own country, within the resistance. **And we are the Trojan horse in the enemy's fortress. Thousands of Jews living in Europe constitute the principal factor in the destruction of our enemy. There, our front is a fact and the most valuable aid for victory."*** (Emphasis added)

It should have been no surprise that the Nazis saw the Jews as Germany's enemy, and the Jews within Germany as a "fifth column," ready and willing to cooperate with Germany's enemies from without.

The Jews in Britain were vigorously behind Churchill's call for war against Germany, and the Jews in America also vigorously supported Roosevelt's determination to go to war with Germany. What else would anyone expect, except that the Nazi regime would take steps to isolate the Jews in Germany in defense of the German state? They put large numbers of them in concentration camps. The United States also locked up the West Coast Japanese in concentration camps after the war with Japan began, with much less justification than Germany had to incarcerate Germany's Jews.

In March 1944, Hitler invaded Hungary to prevent Hungary from switching sides and forming an alliance with the Soviet Union. The combined German and Hungarian armies then began the defense of Hungary against the invasion by the Russian army which was about to begin. The Jewish population in Hungary openly sided with the Soviet Union and constituted a dangerous "fifth column" inside Hungary. There is little doubt once the battle began that they would have done all they could to sabotage the German and Hungarian forces defending Hungary in order to help the Russians. These were desperate times. Rounding up the Jews and shipping them out of Hungary in 1944 was nothing more than self-defense on the part of the Germans and the Hungarians. Exactly where they were sent to and what happened to them afterwards is the subject of debate between proponents of the "official' Holocaust story and proponents of Holocaust revisionism. The former claim they were all exterminated at Auschwitz, while the latter claim they were relocated in the East. In any case, permitting them to remain in Hungary, with the certain knowledge that they would become saboteurs in the coming life and death struggle with the Russian army would have been insane.

When Hitler outlawed the Communist Party in Germany soon after becoming Chancellor, then rounded up the Communists and incarcerated them at Dachau, it turned out that most of these Communists were Jews. These Communists had been involved in revolutionary activities and in attempts to undermine the German state. From the Nazis' point of view, rounding them up and throwing them in jail was only good sense. Yet, Jews around the world hysterically characterized this as an unjustified, unprovoked "persecution" of innocent Jews, only because they were Jews.

Beginning in 1933, Jewish propaganda claimed that the Germans intended to "exterminate" the Jews and they continued to make these unfounded but hysterical claims right up until the war began. After the war got underway, the propaganda then began to claim that the Jews were *actually* being exterminated, though there was no way for them to have known that even if it were true. Both Henry Morganthau, Jr., the Jewish Secretary of the Treasury, as well as his Jewish Communist assistant

Harry Dexter White (Wiese), made this claim. So did Bernard Baruch, the Jewish advisor to Roosevelt. Rumors were rampant throughout the war, the result of Jewish propaganda, that the Nazis were exterminating all the Jews of Europe, though our own State Department scoffed at these reports. As described in a previous chapter, predictions of "extermination" have been a part of Jewish culture for centuries. Yet, when the war ended, sure enough, these same Jewish propagandists claimed that all their super heated speculations had been occurring all along, just as speculated. In the absence of any forensic evidence whatever to support their claim, thousands of Jewish "eye witnesses" described numerous ways in which the Nazis were exterminating the Jews, including steaming them to death, mass electrocutions, throwing them into fire pits, and, of course, the gas chambers.

Holocaust revisionists have done a pretty good job since the war of placing the Holocaust in perspective. There is no doubt that Jews were rounded up in Germany and Europe and sent off to concentration camps, many to "relocation" camps, though many Jews remained in Germany unmolested throughout the war. There is no doubt that these rounded up Jews were used as forced labor in the labor camps, and that conditions there were harsh, not only for the Jews, but for all other detainees in these camps as well. There is no doubt that many Jews died during the war, though certainly nowhere near the 6 million claimed. But there is no evidence whatever that Germany had a plan or a policy to exterminate all of Europe's Jews.

****

Germany made several attempts to negotiate a peace agreement both before the war began and several times during the war, only to be rebuffed at every turn. Even as late as 1944, Heinrich Himmler established a link with Alan Dulles of the OSS (Predecessor to the CIA) through Switzerland to try to negotiate a peaceful end to the war. Dulles, himself, was in favor of trying to end the war in a negotiated settlement, but both Roosevelt and Churchill were obstinate in their demand for unconditional surrender.

Germany, who did not want the war, was trapped and doomed to destruction nevertheless, and there was nothing she could do about it but fight on. The vast majority of the death and destruction in the war was directly attributable to the inhuman Allied demand for unconditional surrender, combined with the plan to implement the genocidal Morganthau Plan immediately following any such unconditional surrender. The demand for unconditional surrender, therefore seems on its face a stupid, counter-productive policy, until one realizes that all the death and destruction which occurred inside Germany was precisely what both Roosevelt and Churchill wanted. They did not want peace with Germany. They wanted to destroy Germany. That is also what International Jewry wanted.

It is estimated that more than 8 million Germans died during the war, but an astonishing 13 million additional Germans died after the war was over; the result of expulsions, mass murder, brutality, exposure and starvation. That would be a total of more than 20 million German deaths as a result of the war. The estimated deaths during the war for the United States and Great Britain were 413,000 and 450,000 respectively. The claim that 6 million Jews died at the hands of the Nazis is patently absurd. Germany was clearly the real victim of the war.

Rape and Slaughter

As the German armies began retreating back into the Reich, unspeakable atrocities were committed against them by all the Allies, who seem to have been seized by a sort of blood lust. All civilized sanctions against killing Germans, both military and civilian, were removed.

Douglas Bazata, in his book, "Target Patton," tells of himself and other "snipers" working for the OSS (forerunner of the CIA). He and the other snipers were assigned to follow along behind the German army as it retreated out of France back into Germany and kill stragglers who had already discarded their arms -- that is, German soldiers, who because of wounds or simple exhaustion, could not keep up. They shot them with sniper rifles from a distance as they struggled along the roads trying to make it back to Germany.

As thousand plane armadas of bombers continued to obliterate German towns right up until the day of surrender, during the last months of the war 1,800 British and American fighter planes were unleashed over Germany with orders to destroy the transportation system of the entire country. All day long, every day, the skies were filled with these fighter planes crisscrossing over the German countryside, strafing anything that moved. They especially targeted trains. They first shot into the steam locomotives, causing them to explode, then circled back around and made strafing runs shooting up the cars, including passenger cars loaded with refugees. They strafed vehicles on the roads, people riding bicycles, or people just walking along the roads. They strafed farmers plowing in their fields, and killed their livestock. They strafed into the windows of houses. They strafed people in the streets. They especially worked over refugee columns on the roads as they fled invading armies. Killing Germans became sport. Germany became a slaughterhouse where anything that moved was fair game. As a result of all of this, the Germans could not feed their people for lack of transport. They could not feed the inmates in the concentration camps. This accounts for the masses of emaciated corpses which so shocked American and British troops who encountered them as they moved into Germany. Typhus epidemics had broken out amongst the starvation weakened inmates.

But the Russians were the worst. When they first entered East Prussia, they raped and slaughtered Germans in their masses. All of East Prussia took to the roads, running away from the advancing Russians, trying to make their way as refugees into the heart of Germany. *"The disaster that befell this area with the entry of the Soviet forces has no parallel in modern European experience. There were considerable sections of it where, to judge by all existing evidence, scarcely a man, woman or child of the indigenous population was left alive after the initial passage of the Soviet forces."* George F. Kennan, Memoirs, 1967

As Russian armies poured into Germany near the end of the war, the Jewish Soviet Propaganda Minister, Ilya Ehrenburg, had millions of leaflets printed up and dropped onto the Russian troops, exhorting them when they entered Germany to: *"Kill the Germans, wherever you*

(L) Ilya Ehrenburg, Stalin's Jewish Propaganda Minister exhorted Russian soldiers to rape German women and to kill women and children.

find them! Every German is our mortal enemy. Have no mercy on women, children, or the aged! Kill every German -- wipe them out!"

In another leaflet drop, Ehrenburg urged the Russian troops to: *"Kill, kill, you brave Red Army soldiers, kill. There is nothing in the Germans that is innocent. Obey the instructions of comrade Stalin and stamp the fascistic beast in its cave. Break with force the racial arrogance of the Germanic women. Take them as your legal loot. Kill, you brave soldiers of the Red Army, kill!"*

And in another leaflet: *"The Germans are not human beings. Henceforth the word German means to us the most terrible curse. From now on the word German will trigger your rifle. We shall not speak any more. We shall not get excited. We shall kill. If you have not killed at least one German a day, you have wasted that day... If you cannot kill your German with a bullet, kill him with your bayonet. If there is calm on your part of the front, if you are waiting for the fighting, kill a German before combat. If you leave a German alive, the German will hang a Russian and rape a Russian woman. If you kill one German, kill another - there is nothing more amusing for us than a heap of German corpses. Do not count days; do not count miles. Count only the number of Germans you have killed. Kill the German - this is your old mother's prayer. Kill the German - this is what your children beseech you to do. Kill the German - this is the cry of your Russian earth. Do not waver. Do not let up. Kill."*

Such leaflets were dropped almost daily onto the Russian army. Spurred on by this kind of racial hatred, it is no wonder that the Red Army committed such horrible atrocities.

"...by eyewitness accounts, loot, pillage, pestilence and rape, wholesale

murder and human suffering from one of the most terrible chapters in human history." Senator Eastland, December, 4th, Congressional Record.

"For three weeks the war had been going on inside Germany, and all of us knew very well that if the girls were German they could be raped and then shot. This was almost a combat distinction." Alexander Solzhenitsyn, as a Russian soldier with the rank of captain.

The following tale of horror was related in a book by Hans Koppe, titled, "In Their Terror All Were Alike," 1995. This tale of horror came from a German-Brazilian citizen Leonora Greier, nee Cavoa, born October 22, 1925 in Sao Paulo, Brazil. She immigrated to Germany before the war. Leonora was employed by the German Women's Labor Service as a typist in a camp in the town of Vilmsee in Neustettin, Germany when the Russian army over ran the area. She wrote:

"On the morning of February 16 [1945] a Russian division occupied the Reich Labour Service camp of Vilmsee in Neustettin. The Commissar, who spoke German well, informed me that the camp was dissolved and that, as we were a uniformed unit, we were to be transported immediately to a collecting camp.

Since 1, being a Brazilian, belonged to a nation on friendly terms with the Allies, he entrusted me with the leadership of the transport which went to Neustettin, into the yard of what used to be an iron foundry. We were some 500 girls from the Women's Reich Labour Service.

The Commissar was very polite to us and assigned us to the foreign workers' barracks of the factory. But the allocated space was too small for all of us, and so I went to speak to the Commissar about it.

He said that it was, after all, only a temporary arrangement, and offered that I could come to the typists' office if it was too crowded for me, which I gladly accepted. He immediately warned me to avoid any further contact with the others, as those were members of an illegal army. My protests that this was not true were cut off with the remark that if I ever said anything like that ever again, I would be shot.

Suddenly I heard loud screams, and immediately two Red Army soldiers brought in five girls. The commissar ordered them to undress. When they refused out of modesty, he ordered me to do it to them, and for all of us to follow him.

We crossed the yard to the former works kitchen, which had been completely cleared out except for a few tables on the window side. It was terribly cold, and the poor girls shivered. In the large, tiled room some Russians were waiting for us, making remarks that must have been very obscene, judging from how everything they said drew gales of laughter.

The Commissar told me to watch and learn how to turn the Master Race into whimpering bits of misery. Now two Poles came in, dressed only in trousers, and the girls cried out at their sight. They quickly grabbed the first of the girls, and bent her backwards over the edge of the table until her joints cracked. I was close to passing out as one of them took his knife and, before the very eyes of the other girls, cut off her right breast. He paused for a moment, then cut off the other side.

I have never-heard anyone scream as desperately as that girl. After this operation he drove his knife into her abdomen several times, which again was accompanied by the cheers of the Russians.

The next girl cried for mercy, but in vain, it even seemed that the gruesome deed was done particularly slowly because she was especially pretty. The other three had collapsed, they cried for their mothers and begged for a quick death, but the same fate awaited them as well.

The last of them was still almost a child, with barely developed breasts. They literally tore the flesh off her ribs until the white bones showed.

Another five girls were brought in. They had been carefully chosen this time. All of them were well-developed and pretty. When they saw the bodies of their predecessors they began to cry and scream. Weakly, they tried desperately to defend themselves, but it did them no good as the Poles grew ever more cruel.

They sliced the body of one of them open lengthwise and poured in a can of machine oil, which they tried to light. A Russian shot one of the other girls in the genitals before they cut off her breasts.

Loud howls of approval began when someone brought a saw from a tool chest. This was used to tear off the breasts of the other girls, which soon caused the floor to be awash in blood. The Russians were in a blood frenzy.

More girls were being brought in continually. I saw these grisly proceedings as through a red haze. Over and over again I heard the terrible screams when the breasts were tortured, and the loud groans at the mutilation of the genitals.

When my knees buckled I was forced onto a chair. The Commissar always made sure that I was watching, and when I had to throw up they even paused in their tortures.

One girl had not undressed completely, she may also have been a little older than the others, who were around seventeen years of age. They soaked her bra with oil and set it on fire, and while she screamed, a thin iron rod was shoved into her vagina until it came out her navel.

In the yard entire groups of girls were clubbed to death after the prettiest of them had been selected for this torture. The air was filled with the death cries of many hundreds of girls. But compared to what happened in here, the beating to death outside was almost humane.

It was a horrible fact that not one of the girls mutilated here ever fainted. Each of them suffered mutilation fully conscious. In their terror all of them were alike in their pleading; it was always the same, the begging for mercy, the high-pitched scream when the breasts were cut and the groans when the genitals were mutilated.

The slaughter was interrupted several times to sweep the blood out of the room and to clear away the bodies. That evening I succumbed to a severe case of nervous fever. I do not remember anything from that point on until I came to in a field hospital.

German troops had temporarily recaptured Neustettin, thus liberating us. As I learned later, some 2,000 girls who had been in RAD, BDM and other camps nearby were murdered in the first three days of Russian occupation."

(signed) Mrs. Leonora Geier, nee Cavoa.

This account was one among many of a similar nature. The exhortations of Ilya Ehrenburg for the Russian troops to rape and murder resulted in such horror as Europe had never seen. The German civilians, particularly the women and girls, were treated as pigs at a slaughter. The following account of what happened in East Prussia when the Russians came in was given by a German soldier after German forces were rushed in to push the Russians back out and to try to protect the civilian population:

"I was an armoured infantryman and had been trained on the most modern German tank of those days, the Panther. Survivors from tank crews were reassembled in the Reserves at Cottbus and kept ready for action.

416

In mid January, 1945, we were transferred to Frankfurt on the Oder River, into a school building. One morning we were issued infantry weapons, guns, bazookas and submachine guns.

The next day we were ordered to march to Neustettin. We traveled the first 60 miles or so by lorry, and after that some 90 miles per day in forced marches.

We were to take over some tanks that were kept ready for us in a forest west of Neustettin. After a march lasting two days and nights, some ten crews reached the forest just before dawn.

Two tanks were immediately readied for action and guarded the approach roads while the other comrades, bone-weary, got a little sleep. By noon all tanks, approximately 20, had been readied.

Our orders were to set up a front-line and to recapture villages and towns from the Russians. My platoon of three tanks attacked a suburb that had a train station with a forecourt. After we destroyed several anti-tank guns the Russians surrendered.

More and more of them emerged from the houses. They were gathered into the forecourt about 200 sat crowded closely together. Then something unexpected happened.

Several German women ran towards the Russians and stabbed at them with cutlery forks and knives. It was our responsibility to protect prisoners, and we could not permit this. But it was not until I fired a submachine gun into the air that the women drew back, and cursed us for presuming to protect these animals. They urged us to go into the houses and take a look at what (the Russians) had done there.

We did so, a few of us at a time, and we were totally devastated. We had never seen anything like it utterly, unbelievably monstrous! Naked, dead women lay in many of the rooms. Swastikas had been cut into their abdomens, in some the intestines bulged out, breasts were cut up, faces beaten to a pulp and swollen puffy.

Others had been tied to the furniture by their hands and feet, and massacred. A broomstick protruded from the vagina of one, a besom from that of another, etc. To me, a young man of 24 years at that time, it was a devastating sight, simply incomprehensible!

Then the women told their story: The mothers had had to witness how their teen and twelve-year-old daughters were raped by some 20 men; the daughters in turn saw their mothers being raped, even their grandmothers.

Women who tried to resist were brutally tortured to death. There was no mercy. Many women were not local; they had come there from other towns, fleeing from the Russians.

They also told us of the fate of the girls from the RAD whose barracks had been captured by the Russians. When the butchery of the girls began, a few of them had been able to crawl underneath the barracks and hide. At night they escaped, and told us what they knew. There were three of them...

The women we liberated were in a state almost impossible to describe. They were over-fatigued and their faces had a confused, vacant look. Some were beyond speaking, ran up and down and moaned the same sentences over and over again.

Having seen the consequences of these bestial atrocities, we were terribly agitated and determined to fight. We knew the war was past winning; but it was our obligation and sacred duty to fight to the last bullet . . ."

This bestiality was the direct result of Stalin's Jewish propagandist Ilya Ehrenburg, who whipped the Russian army into a frenzy of torture, murder, rape and destruction as they advanced into Germany. Wherever Germans lived, similar atrocities became routine.

In Czechoslovakia, atrocities were ghastly as the Germans withdrew. *"Many Germans were hung up by their feet from the big advertising posters in St. Wenceslas Square* [in Prague], *then when the great humanitarian* [Edvard Benes, former Czech President] *approached, their petrol-soaked bodies were set on fire to form living torches."* Louis Marschalko

"Women and children were thrown from the bridge into the river. Germans were shot down in the streets. It is estimated that 2,000 or 3,000 people were killed." F.A Voigt, Berlin correspondent, Manchester Guardian

Those Germans whom they did not kill were forced to abandon all property and leave these lands where their ancestors had lived for a thousand years. "The official Czech register of names of villages reveals that nearly 500 (German) villages no longer appear on the register because they have literally disappeared from the landscape." Munich Report, 1965

"When the French colonial (Negro) troops under his (General Eisenhower's) *command entered the German city of Stuttgart, 'they herded*

German women into the subways and raped some 2,000 of them." "Even a PM reporter, 'reluctantly confirmed the story in its major details.'" Peace Action, July, 1945

After the Germans surrendered on May 5, 1945 the bloodbath began in earnest. Fifteen million Germans were forced to leave their ancestral homes in Eastern Europe, including German East Prussia, parts of Poland, Czechoslovakia, Yugoslavia, Hungary and Romania, headed for Germany, leaving all their property behind. Three million of them died during the trek to Germany as the result of brutal assaults, mass murder, wholesale rape, starvation and exposure.

"God, I hate the Germans..." General Eisenhower wrote in a letter to his wife in September, 1944, and he repeatedly expressed such sentiments to others, and not just about Germany military personnel, but about all Germans. Five and one half million German soldiers were taken prisoner by the Americans under Eisenhower. One month before the end of the war, Eisenhower issued special orders concerning the treatment of German prisoners. The following specific statement was contained within his orders: *"Prison enclosures are to provide no shelter or other comforts."* These German POWs were herded into vast barbed wire enclosures in open fields along the Rhine river without shelter of any kind. He also ordered that they not be given water or food for six days after being herded into these compounds, and thereafter, only starvation rations, even though the Americans had vast stores of food on hand. The prisoners slept on the ground in rain and snow, and were provided no medical care. It is estimated that 1.7 million of these German prisoners died of starvation, gangrene, frostbite, and exposure during the year they were held in American captivity.

Jewish Vengeance

When the Germans were beaten and the fighting stopped in Europe, the Jews flooded into Germany by the thousands to seek their revenge and to obtain their share of the spoils. They immediately began the implementation of the Morganthau Plan, a Jewish vengeance plan to destroy the German economy, subdivide Germany into several smaller states, enslave millions of her citizens, and exterminate as many as 20 million people. Though the Plan was toned down by saner heads, most of it was implemented as Joint Chiefs of Staff Directive (JCS 1067), with brutal consequences for the German people.

Jews flooded into the Nuremburg Trials and used it as a means of exacting vengeance on the German leadership. It was reported that of the 3,000 people who participated in the Trials, 2,400 of them were Jews. Working just behind their gentile front men, the Jews could do whatever they wanted, while the defeated, starving, prostrate Germans were without any means of defending themselves.

The Jewish Brigade

Then there was the Jewish Brigade that not many people know about today, or have ever known about. Formed in Palestine, outfitted in British Army uniforms and riding in American Jeeps, they followed the Allies as they pushed the Germans out of Italy, back into Germany. The officers and senior NCOs of the Jewish Brigade were British Jews, but the ordinary soldiers were Palestinian Jews, a great number of whom were of German origin. The story of the Jewish Brigade is a sordid one which ought to have gotten more publicity. The Brigade was established, not to fight in the war, but to enter into Germany behind the British army to take revenge on the now disarmed and defenseless Germans. After entering defeated Germany, they formed up into what they called "vengeance squads" to track down and kill senior German officers. The Jewish Brigade was technically part of the British Eighth Army, but operated independently, and took their orders from Zionist leaders in Tel Aviv.

Using their British uniforms and British Army credentials they travelled around Germany and Austria hunting down and killing high ranking German officers. The Jewish Brigade had unlimited logistical support from the British Army, could requisition anything they needed, and travelled anywhere in Germany or Austria in an "official" capacity, though they were totally unaccountable to the British Army. All of Germany's official records were now in the hands of the Allies, which the Jewish Brigade had ready access to. Moreover, they knew the German language and could read the German files. After obtaining the home addresses of German officers from these official files, they then drove to their homes in their American jeeps, representing themselves as British officials, and when they found the officers they were looking for, they killed them. By this time, the German Army had capitulated and the officers and enlisted men who were not still detained in POW camps had put down their arms and gone home. They were unarmed and completely defenseless.

According to Morris Beckman, in his book, "The Jewish Brigade": "*These were the first post-war executions of selected top Nazis. There were several dozen revenge squads operating; the highest estimate of executions was 1,500. The exact figure will never be known.*" There were no charges filed against these German officers, no trial, no judge, not even an arrest; they were simply murdered according to the caprice or whim of vengeance seeking Jews. German officers were assumed to be "guilty" by virtue of being German officers. They killed anyone they wanted to kill with total impunity. The Jews called it "vengeance," but, in fact, it was simple murder of defenseless men who may or may not have been guilty of anything except having served in the German Army in defense of their country.

One of these Jewish executioners, Israel Carmi, explains in Beckman's book how they dealt with their selected targets. "*When we arrived at the home of our suspect we would put on [British] Military Police helmets with the white band and police armlets. Then we would enter the home and take the suspect with us, saying that we wanted him for interrogation. Usually they came without a struggle. Once in the car we told the prisoner who we were and why we took him. Some admitted guilt. Others kept silent. We did the job.*" That is, they killed them.

"*We were burning with hatred,*" they said. "*We knew that our people would never forgive us if we did not exploit the opportunity to kill Nazis.*"

Michael Bar-Zohar, an Israeli Jew, wrote a book in 1967 titled "The Avengers," in which he described the many unbelievable atrocities committed by Jews against defenseless Germans, both civilian and former military, immediately after the war. These mass murders were covered up by the American military to prevent the German public from knowing about them. Just one of numerous such events he writes about occurred on April 15, 1946, when a group of East European Jews in Germany (they flooded into Germany at war's end), with the complicity of Jewish American soldiers, poisoned 3,000 loaves of bread which were then delivered to a POW camp holding 36,000 German SS prisoners. The poison turned out to have been too diluted and none of the prisoners died, though thousands became violently ill.

In another passage in his book, Bar-Zohar describes the enthusiastic joy felt by these Jewish soldiers as they were about to enter Germany immediately following the end of hostilities. They fantasized, he says, about what they would do when they got into Germany, about how they intended to kill German civilians and rape German women: *"But now they were going to Germany! The men discussed the news with great excitement. It was too good to be true! Give us just a month there, only a month"* they told each other. *"We'll give them something to remember us by forever. They'll have real reasons for hating us now. We'll have just one pogrom in round numbers, we'll burn down a thousand houses and kill five hundred people and rape one hundred women."* And more than one young Jew was heard to say: *"I must kill a German in cold blood, I must. And I must rape a German girl. That's our war aim, revenge! Not Roosevelt's four freedoms or the greater glory of the British Empire or Stalin's ideology, but vengeance, Jewish vengeance."*

A number of officers in the British army were aware of what was going on, and several tried to stop it, but the British military command refused to act and turned a blind eye to the Jewish Brigade's killing of German officers. *"The Commanders of the Eighth Army knew what was going on but they were sympathetic...to the Brigade...,"* Beckman said.

****

The Germans were brutally treated by all occupying armies after the war, causing the deaths of as many as 13 million Germans after the war was over. Only when the Soviets showed themselves to be a threat to the West did the Allies begin to let up on the Germans. They let up on them only because they now needed their cooperation in the Cold War then shaping up. We then changed our tune about the Germans and began to regard them as an integral part of Western Civilization. Now, suddenly, they were the *good guys*. Had we been wrong about them all along? General Patton thought so. After becoming military governor of Bavaria immediately after the war, Patton completely changed his mind about the Germans and began to realize that we had been fighting the wrong enemy. He was fired from his job as military governor of Bavaria and "kicked upstairs" for refusing to cooperate in Eisenhower's brutal treatment of the defeated Germans. He died soon thereafter under mysterious and suspicious circumstances; many believe, as the result of his recalcitrance.

Chapter 23

Winners and Losers

It has been observed that World War II was a continuation of World War I. While that observation is clearly true, it is not the whole story. World War I was fought to prevent Germany from dominating the continent of Europe, and the Versailles Treaty was then imposed to hold Germany down. When Germany managed to throw off the Versailles fetters and became a great power again, her old antagonists, France and Britain, were determined to have another war. But that was only one element of the Second World War. In the mean time, another predatory force -- International Jewry under the banner of Communism -- had emerged from the wreckage of the First World War to threaten a now prostrate and defenseless Europe. The Jews had always been there as a rival force to Western, Christian Civilization, but they had always been kept in check. Now, they were spreading over *Corpus Europa* like surging bacilli in an ailing body with a weakened immune system.

All of Europe, including Russia, was bankrupt and disorganized as a result of the First World War, and therefore extremely vulnerable to the predations of this new aggressor. Russia was the first to fall into its grip, the result of the 1917 Revolution, which then became its base of operations. Using the economic and military power of Russia which it now controlled, International Jewry, under the banner of Communism, set about to seize control of all of Europe. Their *modus operandi* was to foment revolution amongst the disgruntled masses through a network of Jewish dominated Communist parties (which were organized under the Moscow based "Communist International", or Comintern), and then to coordinate with the Jewish populations in each European country who functioned as "fifth columns." (A "fifth column" is a group who clandestinely undermines the nation from within.)

Germany alone seems to have recognized this new threat to Europe for what it was, and organized itself to oppose it. Germany's old antagonists, Britain and France, eventually initiated a war against Germany (WWII) in pursuit of their same old agenda of holding Germany down, though this aspect of the war became subsidiary to the main struggle. The main struggle was between Germany, as the self-designated defender of Western Christian Civilization, on the one hand, and International Jewry masquerading as Communism, intent upon the conquest of all of Europe, on the other. Germany's Hermann Goering understood the true nature of the war. *"This war is not a Second World War. This is a great racial war. In the final analysis it is about whether the German and Aryan prevails here, or whether the Jew rules the world, and that is what we are fighting for out there."* (Hermann Goering, as quoted in Michael Burleigh's book, "The Third Reich, A New History," 2000)

It is not clear the extent to which President Roosevelt and the Roosevelt administration understood the true nature of the war, and to which of the two aspects of the war it was most devoted. Many in the Roosevelt administration no doubt had been convinced that Germany was a threat to world peace and had to be stopped (nonsense, of course). But what did Roosevelt believe? Roosevelt himself was inclined to socialism and was himself an admirer of Joseph Stalin ("Uncle Joe," as he called him) and of Communist Russia, and he surrounded himself with like-minded men. The Roosevelt administration was infiltrated through and through with Communist Jews who were the devoted agents of Jewish controlled Communist Russia. These men did all in their power to harness American might to the cause of Soviet Russia (and thereby, to the cause of International Jewry). Roosevelt's Jewish Undersecretary of the Treasury Harry Dexter White was a secret Soviet agent, and the majority of Roosevelt's advisory staff were Jews with undisguised Soviet sympathies. Roosevelt's agenda appears to have been to join with the Soviet Union to destroy Germany and then divide control of the Western world between the United States and the Soviet Union. Every decision he made throughout the war indicated that that was his consistent aim.

Through the Lend-Lease program, Roosevelt threw the entire industrial might of the United States behind "Uncle Joe" and the Soviet Union. 20,000 airplanes, 440,000 trucks, and massive quantities of all other kinds of war materiel were funneled into the Soviet Union from the United States. Without this massive support, Russia could not have defeated the Germans.

At the same time that the Soviet Union engaged Germany in a titanic struggle on the ground, both Churchill and Roosevelt, each with a different agenda, worked together to destroy Germany's cities through aerial bombardment. Britain and the United States only entered the ground war at the end when Germany was already essentially beaten.

****

With millions of her people killed and most of her cities destroyed, Germany was the palpable loser of World War II, but the real, long term winners of the war were less obvious, at least, at first. Britain is listed as one of the victors, but for Britain, it was a pyrrhic victory. By forcing Germany into the war, and then doggedly refusing to consider Germany's numerous peace overtures, Churchill accomplished nothing except to bankrupt his country and bring the curtain down on the British Empire.

The two obvious winners of the war were the United States and the Soviet Union. That was clear to everyone. But the other *big* winner, which was perhaps not so obvious, at least not at first, was International Jewry. One could even say that International Jewry was the *primary* winner of the war, though, to make such an assertion violates a very strong taboo today. Jews may only be portrayed as the war's ultimate victims, not as victors. But, in actual fact, the Jews won on all fronts.

After the Soviets entered Eastern Europe at the end of the war, Jews were installed as the ruling elite in nearly every country which fell under the Soviet Union's control. John Gunther, in his book, "Behind the Iron Curtain," Harper, 1949, wrote that *"Poland, Hungary, Romania, and Czechoslovakia all have Jewish Dictators."* The three Jews at the top of the Hungarian government, according to Gunther, were Matyas Rakosi (Rosencranz), Erno Gero (Singer), and Zoltan Vas. In Poland they were the Jews, Minc, Skryeszeqski, Modzelewski, and Berman. In Romania, the Jewish ruler was Anna Pauker. In Czechoslovakia it was Rudolph Slansky. The only non-Jewish dictator behind the Iron Curtain was Tito of Yugoslavia, though his right hand man was the Jew Mosa Pijade. According to Gunther, *"He is Tito's mentor... Whatever ideological structure Tito may have, he got it from the shrewd old man."* Not only were the dictators of these countries Jewish, their administrations were almost entirely Jewish. The key positions were filled by Jews in almost all of the Soviet occupied country. The Jews controlled the Soviet Union, and Jewish elites now controlled nearly all of the countries under Soviet occupation. These ruling Jewish elites were loyal not to the countries they ruled, but to International Jewry, based in the Soviet Union.

The Jews also obtained their long sought after state of Israel as a result of the war, and in the time honored tradition of winners of wars, the International Nation of Israel demanded and received billions of dollars in reparations from the loser, Germany (Germany has paid Israel $75 billion in reparations to date. The reparations demands of the ruinous Treaty of Versailles only required Germany to pay $35 billion.) Today, six and a half decades after the war, Germany is still paying lifetime pensions to half a million so-called "Holocaust survivors" -- that is, to Jews who either lived in German occupied territory during the war, or who were forced to emigrate as a result of the war.

When the war in Europe came to an end, it seemed that the Jews were in control of everything. They controlled the Soviet Union, and virtually controlled Britain and the United States. They were so numerous within the Allied occupying administration in Germany that they dictated all the terms of occupation, including the Morganthau Plan. They were in total control of the Nuremberg Trials. They were even placed in charge of most of the newspapers in occupied Germany.

****

Germany was not only the loser of the war, but also the victim of aggressive war waged against her by Britain, the United States, the Soviet Union, and International Jewry, for reasons which were very different from those publicly declared. Not only did the Jews control the Soviet Union, as has been repeatedly stated herein, but both Roosevelt and Churchill were surrounded by Jews, and their foreign policy decisions were heavily influenced by Jews. International Jewry had as much to do with instigating the war as any other faction, perhaps more, and the Jews were the greatest long term beneficiaries after the war was won. A series of quotes from that time supports this view.

"When the National Socialists and their friends cry or whisper that this [the war] is brought about by Jews, they are perfectly right." - The Jewish magazine Sentinel of Chicago (8 October 1940)

"We managed to drag the United States into the First World War and if they (the US) do what we demand in regards to Palestine and the Jewish armed forces, then we can get the Jews in the USA to drag the United States into this one (the Second World War) too." - Weizmann to Churchill (September 1941)

"Hitler doesn't want war but he will be forced to it, and in fact soon. England has the final say like in 1914." - Zionist Emil Ludwig Cohn

"On the 3rd of June, 1938, the 'American Hebrew' boasted that they had Jews in the foremost positions of influence in Britain, Russia and France, and that these 'three sons of Israel will be sending the Nazi dictator to hell.'" - Joseph Trimble, The American Hebrew.

"The war now proposed is for the purpose of establishing Jewish hegemony throughout the world." - Brigadier General George Van Horn Mosely, The New York Tribune (March 29, 1939)

"The millions of Jews who live in America, England and France, North and South Africa, and, not to forget those in Palestine, are determined to bring

the war of annihilation against Germany to its final end." - Central Blad Voor Israeliten in Nederland (September 13, 1939)

"In losing Germany, Jewry lost a territory from which it exerted power. Therefore it was determined to re-conquer it." - Louis Marschalko, "The World Conquerors" : The Real War Criminals

"The Second World War is being fought for the defense of the fundamentals of Judaism." - Rabbi Felix Mendlesohn, Chicago Sentinel (October 8, 1942)

"We are not denying and are not afraid to confess that this war is our war and that it is waged for the liberation of Jewry... Stronger than all fronts together is our front, that of Jewry. We are not only giving this war our financial support on which the entire war production is based, we are not only providing our full propaganda power which is the moral energy that keeps this war going. The guarantee of victory is predominantly based on weakening the enemy forces, on destroying them in their own country, within the resistance. And we are the Trojan horses in the enemy's fortress. Thousands of Jews living in Europe constitute the principal factor in the destruction of our enemy. There, our front is a fact and the most valuable aid for victory." - Chaim Weizmann, President of the World Jewish Congress, Head of the Jewish Agency and later President of Israel, in a Speech on December 3, 1942, in New York.

"We made a monster, a devil out of Hitler. Therefore we couldn't disavow it after the war. After all, we mobilized the masses against the devil himself. So we were forced to play our part in this diabolic scenario after the war. In no way we could have pointed out to our people that the war only was an economic preventive measure." - US Secretary of State James Baker (1992)

"There can be no doubt: National Socialism was part of a modernization process in German society. It expedited the social changes in Germany. It transferred more to the underprivileged segments of society and brought equality and emancipation to women." - Heinz Hoehne, Gebt mir vier Jahre Zeit [Give me four Years], Ullstein Publishing House, Berlin-Frankfurt 1996, p. 10)

"I see no reason why this war must go on. I am grieved to think of the

sacrifices which it will claim. I would like to avert them." - Adolf Hitler (July, 1940)

"It is untrue that I or anyone else in Germany wanted war in 1939. It was wanted and provoked solely by international statesmen either of Jewish origin or working for Jewish interests. Nor had I ever wished that after the appalling first World War, there would ever be a second against either England or America." - Adolf Hitler (April 1945)

****

Though the Jews emerged as the unequivocal winners of the war, at the same time they managed to establish themselves in the public mind as the war's ultimate victims, entitled to billions of dollars in reparations, while being totally exempt from any criticism for their own violations of civilized standards of behavior and conduct. They were able to do this because they control the news and information media.

For the Jews to continue to characterize themselves today as a threatened minority surrounded by hostile majorities determined to "persecute" them, or even to "exterminate" them (as they claim Iran, and for that matter, the entire Arab world, wants to do), is totally absurd. The Jews are now the most powerful nationality in the world, despite their small numbers. Having won the war, they have abandoned the now defunct Soviet Union (after looting it of its assets), and moved their base of operations to Israel and the United States. Within the past three or four decades, the Jews have risen to elite status in the United States, totally displacing the traditional WASP (White Anglo/ Saxon Protestant) elite who used to run the country. Their infiltration of the highest offices of every American institution, their extreme over-representation in every profession, their control of government, their control of banking and finance, their control of the news and entertainment media, their over-representation in the universities, is even more pervasive in America today than in Weimar Germany. For instance, of the eight Ivey League Universities in America, six have Jewish presidents.

But unlike the WASP elite whom they have displaced, the Jews have become what Professor Kevin McDonald, in his trilogy of books on Jewish culture, calls a "hostile elite." The old WASP elite never lost its sense of *noblesse oblige* towards the ordinary people of America. They were, after all, of the same religion and of the same ethnic origin, and they felt a sense of responsibility for the general welfare of all of their fellow citizens. Our new Jewish elite is different. They feel no identity with ordinary Americans, only disdain, and they concern themselves only with "what is good for Jews."

Not only does this new Jewish elite have no empathy for the traditional European majority in America, they actively work to undermine it. According to E. Michael Jones, in his book, "The Jewish Revolutionary Spirit and Its Impact on World History," 2008, Jews have been behind each and every one of the anti-white, anti-Christian movements in this country, especially since the early 1960s. The NAACP was founded by Jews. The Civil Rights movement was organized and promoted by Jews. So was the Sexual Revolution, the Hippy Movement, the Feminist Movement, the promotion of homosexual rights, same-sex marriage, the Separation-of-Church-and-State movement (an attack on Christianity), and especially the Multicultural movement. It was the Jews who managed to change our immigration law in 1965 which then opened our doors to swarms of non-white, non-Christian immigrants. This new immigration policy bodes to doom the traditional America we knew. It has been projected that the white majority of the United States will be reduced to minority status within two or three decades. This demographic shift will completely change the character of this country, and not for the better. Moreover, the Jews have done precisely the same to Europe, so that the demographics of Europe are being drastically changed also. It is deemed that undermining controlling majorities and promoting multi-culturalism is "good for Jews." Divide and conquer, as it were. While all the different ethnic and religious groups now resident in the United States are squabbling among ourselves, our new Jewish elite uses its power to promote the interests of Israel and International Jewry.

The 5.2 million Jews in the United States, and the 5.8 million Jews in Israel conspire together to manipulate and control the great power and wealth of the United States and direct it to the benefit of International

Jewry and the nation of Israel. American money and technology has been used to build one of the most powerful military forces in the world in tiny Israel. Working through their fellow Jews who control the American government, Israel virtually dictates our foreign policy, especially in the Middle East, and the American Army is being used as a proxy army for the tiny state of Israel, in order to achieve their foreign policy aims. In addition, vast sums of money are continuously siphoned off from the American taxpayers, without their consent, and funneled into Israel. A portion of that money is then sent back to the United States to fund the campaigns of politicians who obediently do their bidding, thereby insuring that the money cycle continues unabated.

By these means, and others, the Jewish AIPAC (The American Israel Public Affairs Committee) totally controls the American government, both the Congress and the Executive branch, and the Jewish dominated news and entertainment industry controls American public opinion. Though Jews claim only to be perpetual victims, under constant threat of persecution and even extermination by their Gentile host populations, they were, in fact, the indisputable winners of World War Two, and they have reaped all the rewards of that victory. They now rule everywhere.

****

The Jewish dominated Soviet Union could not have defeated Germany unassisted, but then one must realize that the war was not *just* a war between Germany and the Soviet Union; it was a war between Germany and International Jewry. The Soviet Union was only a component of that war. Powerful Jews in the United States and Britain pulled both of those countries into the war on the Soviet Union's side. Germany, of course, could not withstand this overwhelming combination of forces arrayed against her and so, Germany was destroyed.

Conventional wisdom still seems unable to comprehend that Germany's destruction was a disaster for the West. Germany has always been an integral component of Western, Christian Civilization; the very heart of the old Holy Roman Empire, which formed the foundation of modern Europe. By allying ourselves with the Soviet Union and International Jewish Communism against Western, Christian Germany, the United States and Britain brought about the virtual suicide of the West. Adolf Hitler, the champion of Western, Christian Civilization and the man most responsible for preventing a complete takeover of Europe by Jewish led Communism during the inter-war period, was driven to suicide, and Europe's great promise under the leadership of Hitler and Germany died with them.

The consequences of the war were immense. Two thousand years of accumulated art, architecture, culture, and science went up in smoke as the heart and soul of Europe was gutted by the war. The European economy was bankrupted. Survivors of the war were starving to death in their millions. The British Empire crumbled. Half of what was left of Europe fell under the control of the Jewish, Communist Soviet Union. A long Cold War between East and West then ensued. As a result of the war, Western Civilization's path was changed from one of limitless possibilities to one of inexorable decline.

At the beginning of the twentieth century, the white race dominated the world. The First World War dealt Western Civilization a deadly blow, though Europe might have recovered from that. But today, some six and a half decades after the devastating Second World War, a war which could easily have been avoided, the white European race faces the danger of eventual extinction. Its birth rate now hovers below the population maintenance level, while hoards of non-white, non-Christian immigrants swarm in from all sides -- both in Europe and the United States -- polluting, diluting, factionalizing, and Balkanizing our once homogeneous populations, to the point that the process now seems irreversible. If "Demographics is destiny," then the destiny of the West is in inexorable decline, while the fortunes of International Jewry are in the ascendency. The so-called "good" war has resulted in a very "bad" end for the West. Even Churchill eventually recognized the great error of Britain and the United States in siding with the Soviet Union against Germany. In a speech long after the war, he said, *"We slaughtered the wrong pig."* The End.

Bibliography

In addition to the numerous books and articles cited within the text, the following list of books, almost all from the author's personal library, were used in writing "The Myth of German Villainy."

Baker, Nicholson, "Human Smoke," 2008

Barnes, Harry Elmer, "The Genesis of the World War," 1929

Barnes, Harry Elmer, "Perpetual War for Perpetual Peace," 1969

Beard, Charles A., "President Roosevelt and the Coming of the War," 1941

Beckman, Morris, "The Jewish Brigade," 2009

Bellock, Hilaire, "The Jews," 1922

Best, Nicholas, "The Greatest Day in History: How, on the Eleventh Hour of the Eleventh Day, of the Eleventh Month, the First World War Finally Came to an End," 2008,

Black, Edwin, "The Transfer Agreement," 1984, about the agreement between Adolf Hitler and the Zionist Jews to help create a Jewish state in Palestine by "transferring" German Jews there.

Blum, Howard, "The Brigade: An Epic Story of Vengeance, Salvation and WWII," 2002, about the Jewish Brigade that entered Germany after surrender.

Britton, Frank L., "Behind Communism," 1952, a history of the Jews in Europe and their founding role in Communism.

Bryant, Sir Arthur, "Unfinished Victory," 1940, a book supporting Nazi Germany.

Bukey, Evan Burr, "Hitler's Austria: Popular Sentiment in the Nazi Era, 1938-1945," 2000

Burleigh, Michael, "The Third Reich, A New History," 2000

Dawson, William Harbutt, "Germany Under the Treaty," 1933

Dilling, Elizabeth, "The Roosevelt Red Record and its Background," 1936

Dreyfus, Paul, in "La Vio de Tanger," May 15, 1939, about Nazi Germany's barter system.

Duffy, Christopher, "Red Storm on the Reich: The Soviet March on Germany, 1945," 1991

Eby, Cecil D., "Comrades and Commissars: The Lincoln Battalion in The Spanish Civil War," 2007.

Evans, Richard J., "Lying About Hitler," 2001

Finkelstein, Norman, "The Holocaust Industry," 2000

Finkelstein, Norman, "Beyond Chutzpah," 2005

Fish, Hamilton, "FDR: The Other Side of the Coin," 1977

Fish, Hamilton, "Tragic Deception," 1983

Fleming, Thomas, "Illusion of Victory," Basic Books, 2003

Flynn, John T., "The Roosevelt Myth," 1948

Friedrich, Jorge, "Der Brand, (The Fire)," 2004, about the bombing of Germany.

Gay, Peter, "Weimar Culture: The Outsider as Insider," 1968

Gilbert, Martin, "Churchill and the Jews," 2007

Gilbert, Martin, "The First World War," 1994

Gooch, John, "Mussolini and His Generals: The Armed Forces and Fascist Foreign Policy, 1922 - 1940," 2007.

Halter, Marek, "The Wind of the Khazars," 1988

Hoggan, David L., "The Forced War," 1961

Hansen, Randall, "Fire and Fury, The Allied Bombing of Germany, 1942-1945," 2008

Howe, Irving, "world of our Fathers," the story of East European Jewish immigration to America, 1976.

Irving, David, "Hitler's War," 1977

Irving, David, "Churchill's War," 1987

Irving, David, "Goering," 1989

Irving, David, "Apocalypse 1945: The Destruction of Dresden," 1963

Jentsch, Mary Hunt, "Trek: An American Woman, Two Small Children, and Survival in World War II Germany," 2008, about the "Trek" out of East Prussia after the Russian invasion near the end of the war.

Johnson, Eric A., "Nazi Terror: The Gestapo, Jews, and Ordinary Germans." 2000

Jones, E. Michael, "The Jewish Revolutionary Spirit, and its Impact on World History," 2008

Kershaw, Ian, "Making Friends with Hitler: Lord Londonderry, the Nazis and the Road to War," 2004, about Londonderry' admiration for Germany and friendship with Hitler.

Kershaw, Ian, "The End: The Defiance and Destruction of Hitler's Germany, 1944-1945," 2011

Kilzer, Louis C., "Churchill's Deception: The Dark Secret that Destroyed Nazi Germany," 1994

Knappe, Siegfried & Ted Brusaw, "Soldat: Reflections of a German Soldier, 1936-1949," 1992

Knight, G.E.O., "In Defense of Germany," 1934

Koestler, Arthur, "The Thirteenth Tribe," 1976, about the Khazar origin of Ashkenazi Jews.

Kramer, Mark (Editor) "The Black Book of Communism: Crimes, Terror, Repression," 1992

Lindbergh, Charles, "Autobiography of Values," 1978

Lindemann, Albert, "Esau's Tears, Modern Anti-Semitism and the Rise of the Jews," 1997

Linge, Heinze, "With Hitler To The End, The Memoirs of Hitler's Valet," 2009

Lowe, Kieth, "Inferno: The Fiery Destruction of Hamburg," 2007

Mandell, Richard D., "The Nazi Olympics," 1971

Marschalko, Louis, "The World Conquerors: The Real War Criminals," 1948

Martin, Ralph G., "Jennie, The Life Of Lady Randolph Churchill: The Romantic Years," 1969

McDonald, Kevin, "A People That Shall Dwell Alone," 1994

McDonald, Kevin, "Separation and it Discontents," 1998

McDonald, Kevin, "The Culture of Critique," 1998, -- a trilogy on Judaism and Jewish Culture.

McDonough, Giles, "After the Reich," 2007

Meyer, Henry Cord, "Five Images of Germany: Half a Century of American Views on German History, 1960.

Mueller, Margarete G., "Lost Years," 2008, a tale of German civilians escaping East Prussia ahead of the Russian army.

Neumann, Franz, "Behemoth: The Structure and Practice of National Socialism, 1933 - 1944," 1944.

Nitsch, Grunter, "Weeds Like Us," 2006, yet another story about a German civilian family escaping East Prussia ahead of the Russians.

Orwell, George, "Homage to Catalonia," 1938

Persico, Joseph E., "Roosevelt's Secret War: FDR and World War II Espionage," 2001

Pine, L.G., "Tales of the British Aristocracy," 1956

Pipes, Richard, "The Russian Revolution," 1990

Preston, Paul, "The Spanish Civil War," 1986

Radzinsky, Edvard, "The Last Czar," 1992

Radzinsky, Evdard, "Stalin," 1998

Raico, Ralph, "Great Wars & Great Leaders," 2010

Rayfield, Donald, "Stalin and his Hangmen," 2004

Reed, Douglas, "Disgrace Abounding," 1939

Rosenberg, Alfred, "Myth of the Twentieth Century," 1935

Service, Robert, "Lenin, A Biography," 2000

Showalter, Dennis E., "Tannenberg: Clash of Empires," 1991

Simpson, Colin, "The Lusitania," 1972

Slezkine, Yuri, "The Jewish Century," 2004.

Solzhenitsyn, Alexander, "The Gulag Archipelago," 1973

Sontag, Raymond J., "A Broken World 1919-1939: The Rise of Modern Europe," 1971

Stinnett, Robert B., "Day of Deceit: The Truth About FDR and Pearl Harbor," 2000

Sutton, Anthony C., "Wall Street and the Bolshevik Revolution," 1974

Tannehill, Evelyne, "Abandoned and Forgotten," 2006, a tale of a nine year old girl orphaned in East Prussia by the war, and left to fend for herself.

Taylor, A.J.P., "The Origins of the Second World War," 1996

Taylor, Frederick, "Dresden," 2004

Ungvary, Krisztian, "The Siege of Budapest: 100 Days in World War II," 2002

Waydenfeld, Stefan, "The Ice Road: An Epic Journey From the Stalinist Labor Camp," 1999

Webster, Nesta, "Germany and England," 1938

Wilton, Robert, "The Last Days of the Romanovs," 1920

Viola, Lynne, "The Unknown Gulag: The Lost World of Stalin's Special Settlements," 2007

About the Author

Benton L. Bradberry served as an officer and aviator in the U.S. Navy from 1955 to 1977, from near the beginning of the Cold War to near its end. His generation was inundated with anti-German propaganda and "Holocaust" lore. Then, in his role as a naval officer and pilot, he was immersed in anti-Communist propaganda and the war psychosis of the Cold War era. He has had a life-long fascination with the history of this period and has read deeply into all aspects of it. He also saw much of Europe during his Navy years and has travelled widely in Europe since. A natural skeptic, he long ago began to doubt that the "propaganda" told the whole story. He has spent years researching "the other side of the story" and has now written a book about it. The author is a graduate of the Naval Post Graduate School in Monterey, California with a degree in Political Science and International Relations.